OUR UNSWERVING LOYALTY

A documentary survey of relations
between the Communist Party of Australia
and Moscow, 1920–1940

OUR UNSWERVING LOYALTY

A documentary survey of relations
between the Communist Party of Australia
and Moscow, 1920–1940

David W. Lovell and Kevin Windle
(editors)

ANU
THE AUSTRALIAN NATIONAL UNIVERSITY

E PRESS

ANU E PRESS

Published by ANU E Press
The Australian National University
Canberra ACT 0200, Australia
Email: anuepress@anu.edu.au
This title is also available online at: http://epress.anu.edu.au/oul_citation.html

---

National Library of Australia
Cataloguing-in-Publication entry

Title:	Our unswerving loyalty : a documentary survey of relations between the Communist Party of Australia and Moscow, 1920-1940 / editor David Lovell, Kevin Windle.
ISBN:	9781921313950 (pbk.)
	9781921313967 (web)
Notes:	Includes index.
	Bibliography.
Subjects:	Communist International.
	Communist Party of Australia.
	Communism--Australia.
	Australia--Politics and government--1901-1945.
	Soviet Union--Relations--Australia.
	Australia--Relations--Soviet Union.

Other Authors/Contributors:
Lovell, David W., 1956-
Windle, Kevin, 1947-

Dewey Number: 335.4230994

Cover design by ANU E Press

Contents

Preface and Acknowledgements

This book brings together 85 documents from the Russian State Archives of Social and Political History (RGASPI), selected and introduced by us from a collection of thousands of documents concerning the relations between the Communist International and the Communist Party of Australia. The entirety of the collection we surveyed is deposited at the Australian Defence Force Academy (ADFA) Library in Canberra, and is available for public consultation. In the first place, we must thank RGASPI's Director, Dr Kirill Anderson, for permitting the Archive to be reproduced, sent to Australia, edited for publication, and made publicly available: the documents add another important dimension to the story of the early Communist Party of Australia. In this process, the preliminary work of Dr Konstantin Samarin and the late Professor Patrick O'Brien was invaluable.

The connection between Drs Anderson and Lovell was facilitated by Chris Mitchell, now Editor-in-Chief of *The Australian* newspaper. Chris Mitchell has been supportive of this project throughout its long journey, and has never made any directions or demands on the material we chose to select, translate and publish.

We must also thank the helpful staff of the Mitchell Library in Sydney, for access to the Comintern Archives held there, allowing us to make a careful comparison with the documents in the Comintern Archive at the ADFA Library (CAAL). We thank the staff of the Public Record Office in London for assistance in trying to track the movements of some of the early communists through the United Kingdom on their way to and from Australia, and for access to files on the CPGB. David Lovell thanks the staff of the Library of Congress in Washington, DC, for assistance in his comparisons of the Comintern files of the CPUSA with the CAAL. Kevin Windle is grateful to the staff of the National Archives of Australia and the Noel Butlin Archive Centre (The Australian National University) for valuable assistance in locating Australian documents pertaining to Russian activists in Australia in 1917–23, and to the staff of RGASPI in Moscow for allowing further access to their documents. Both of us have received financial support and encouragement from our universities which we would like to acknowledge here. In addition, the comments of the anonymous referees proved encouraging and helpful; we thank them for their overall evaluations and their attention to detail.

Some of the material in the introductory essays, and parts of some documents relating to Aleksandr Zuzenko, have been adapted for use in work published on related topics by Lovell and Windle respectively since 2003. We are grateful to the publishers for permission to re use this material: *Australian Slavonic and East European Studies*, publishers of Windle's 2004 '"The Achilles Heel of British Imperialism": A Comintern agent reports on his mission to Australia 1920–22.

An annotated translation', *ASEES*, 18:1–2, pp. 143–76; Crawford House Publishing, publishers of Lovell's 2007 essay 'Strained Relations: Russia, Australia and the Comintern, 1920–40', in A. Massov, J. McNair and T. Poole (eds), *Encounters Under the Southern Cross: Two Centuries of Russian-Australian Relations, 1807-2007*, pp. 163–184; and Quadrant Magazine Co. Inc., publishers of Lovell's 2008 essay '"Unswerving Loyalty": documenting Australian communist relations with Moscow, 1920–40', *Quadrant*, LII:5, pp. 80–86.

Cataloguing the CAAL documents, making the selection presented in this book, and researching the supporting materials, has taken us much longer than we had expected, largely because of the intrusion of other duties (both of us spending much of the period as Heads of our respective Schools). We are particularly grateful to our wives for enduring the book's lengthy gestation with good humour.

David W. Lovell, University of New South Wales

Kevin Windle, The Australian National University

Abbreviations

ACTU	Australian Council of Trades Unions
ALP	Australian Labor Party
ASP	Australian Socialist Party
CAAL	Comintern Archive at ADFA Library, Canberra
CALC	Comintern Archive at the Library of Congress, Washington DC
CAML	Comintern Archive at the Mitchell Library, State Library of NSW
CC	Central Committee
CCC	Central Control Commission
CEC	Central Executive Committee
CI	Communist International, or 'Comintern'
CP	Communist Party
CPA	Communist Party of Australia
CPGB	Communist Party of Great Britain
CPSU	Communist Party of the Soviet Union
CPUSA	Communist Party of the USA
EC	Executive Committee
ECCI	Executive Committee of the Communist International
GPU	Soviet State Security service, variously re-named in later periods, and known by other acronyms: OGPU, NKVD, MVD, and KGB
ICC	International Control Commission
IWW	Industrial Workers of the World: the 'Wobblies'
KGB	see GPU
MM	Minority Movement (sometimes MMM: Militant Minority Movement)
NKVD	People's Commissariat of Internal Affairs (see GPU)
NSW	New South Wales
NZ	New Zealand
OBU	One Big Union
PRO	Public Record Office, London
PPW	*Pan-Pacific Worker*
RILU	Red International of Labour Unions
RCP	Russian Communist Party
RGASPI	Russian State Archive of Social and Political History
RSFSR	Russian Soviet Federated Socialist Republic
RTUI	Red Trade Union International (see RILU)
SLP	Socialist Labour Party
UF	United Front

URCW	Union of Russian Communist Workers
VSP	Socialist Party of Victoria
WIIU	Workers' International Industrial Union
WW	*Workers' Weekly*

Glossary of individuals, organizations and tactics

Individuals, organizations and tactics that appear more than once in the documents, or are the subject of a substantial part of a document, are listed below. Individuals who appear only once are identified wherever possible by a footnote on the relevant page.

Agitprop: Bolshevik jargon for agitation and propaganda; an Agitprop Department was established by the Comintern at its Fourth Congress to advise and supervise the work of its parties in this area.

Anderson, John (1893–1962): philosopher, arrived in Australia from Scotland in 1927 to teach at the University of Sydney. Though a libertarian, he at first sympathized with the CPA and wrote for their publications, but in 1932 he broke with the Party, accusing it of being bureaucratic and afraid of spontaneity; from 1933 to 1936 he supported Trotsky's views but finally could not agree that the USSR remained a 'workers' state', as Trotsky insisted until his death.

Anglo-American Secretariat: organizational unit of the Comintern that supervised Communist parties in the USA, Britain, and the British Dominions (Australia, Canada and New Zealand). Communists in British colonies came under a different Comintern Secretariat. This Secretariat (sometimes 'Bureau') was formed in mid-1922.

Artem: see Sergeev.

Australian Socialist Party: host of the founding conference of the CPA in October 1920. In 1919, the ASP had declared allegiance to the Comintern, but its affiliation was derailed by Petr Simonov. The ASP had focused on Marxist propaganda and opposed participating in the ALP; it had close links with Russian émigrés in Brisbane and with Moscow. The ASP remained an important current within the early Party, but was outmanoeuvred in the struggles over policy and assets that accompanied the attempts to unite the CPA.

Baker, Clarence Wilbur (Carl): founding member of the CPA. Baker was an American by birth, and had been a leading member of the reformist VSP.

Baracchi, Guido (1887–1975): an Australian left-wing intellectual of Italian descent who was close to the CPA, if not always a member, during the period covered by this book. Baracchi was a member of the IWW, was jailed for opposition to conscription in 1918, and attended the CPA's foundation conference in 1920. He made a number of trips to the USSR, but advocated liquidating the CPA in the mid-1920s as a means of breaking out of its isolation; he was consequently expelled in 1925, went to the Soviet Union in the early 1930s with Betty Rowland, rejoined the Party in 1935, and was finally expelled in 1940 over differences with the CPA line on the war. He was subsequently associated with the Australian Trotskyists.

Barker, Tom (1887–1970): British radical and IWW activist in New Zealand and Australia. Barker was editor of the IWW's newspaper, *Direct Action*, and was briefly imprisoned during 1916 on account of charges laid against the IWW. With other IWW members, he was deported from Australia to Chile in 1918. He reached London in 1920. He later spent much time in the USSR, but ended his working life as a town councillor, and at one time Lord Mayor, of St Pancras in London (Fry 1965).

Berzin, Jan Antonovich (1881–1938): secretary of the ECCI in 1919 and later Soviet representative in Britain. He would be executed in the same week as Zuzenko for membership of a 'terrorist organization'.

Billet, J.: see Docker.

Blake, John David (Jack, 1909–2000; pseudonym of Alfred Airey): joined the CPA in 1925, attended the Lenin School in Moscow for two years in the early 1930s, and became a member of the CPA's Central Committee in 1935. He sometimes used the pseudonym 'A. London'. Blake was elected to the Party's National Secretariat in 1951, but was removed in 1954 after being charged with 'factionalism', and thereafter held no paid or leadership position in the Party.

Bolshevik Party: informal name of the majority section of the Russian Social Democratic Labour Party that split at its second congress in July-August 1903 into 'Bolsheviks' and 'Mensheviks'; the Bolsheviks were led by Lenin. The party was later called the Russian Communist Party (Bolshevik), All-Union Communist Party (Bolshevik), and finally the Communist Party of the Soviet Union.

Brookfield, Percy (1878–1921): worker radical; elected as a Labor member for the NSW Legislative Assembly during the First World War, but left the ALP and became an independent socialist parliamentarian representing Broken Hill. He campaigned for the freedom of the 12 IWW members convicted of sedition and arson. Brookfield was killed in March 1921 trying to disarm a crazed gunman.

Bukharin, Nikolai (1888–1938; sometimes 'Bucharin'): prominent Old Bolshevik, and considered as a potential successor to Lenin as leader of the party, Bukharin was president of the Comintern from 1926 to 1929, and leader of the Right Opposition in the late 1920s until he capitulated to Stalin; he was tried and executed in the third Moscow trial of 1938.

Class against Class: a doctrine arising out of the 'Third Period' of capitalist crisis as analysed by the Comintern and adopted as policy in 1928. The doctrine predicted an intensification of the class struggle and directed communists to take the lead in exposing and attacking especially the reformist leaders of the working class in political parties or trades unions, now dubbed 'social fascists'; it was a strategic disaster because the confrontational style it embodied isolated communists from workers during the worst period of the Great Depression.

Considine, Michael Patrick (1885–1959; 'Mick'): a union militant and politician, Considine was President of the Amalgamated Miners' Association during the First World War and in 1917 became the ALP member for the Federal seat of Barrier. Generally supportive of the Russian communist cause, he had taken the unusual step of representing Soviet Russia as 'acting consul' while Simonov was in prison in 1919. He resigned from the ALP in 1920. He stood as a candidate for the 'Industrial Socialist Labor Party' in 1922, but lost the election and later rejoined the ALP in 1926.

Cram, Robert George (b1906): a carpenter who joined the CPA in 1926, Cram returned to his home city of Newcastle as a Party organizer, but resigned from his Party position in 1939 to get paid work.

Denford, Henry Leigh: active in the IWW and the ASP, Denford became financial secretary and editor of the *Workers' Weekly* late in 1923. At one time General Secretary of the CPA, he left the Party and joined the ALP in late 1925.

Dimitrov, Georgi (1882–1949): a Bulgarian Communist who was tried in 1933 for participating in the burning of the German Reichstag. Dimitrov was acquitted and moved to Moscow where he became executive secretary of the Comintern from 1934 to 1943. He was the chief proponent of the Comintern's popular front policy adopted in 1935.

Dixon, Richard (1905–76; 'Dick'; pseudonym of Clifton Reginald Walker, also known as Frank Emery): a communist from Lithgow on the NSW coalfields, Dixon was a member of the CPA's Central Committee from 1929. He underwent party training in Moscow in 1931–33, was afterwards a member of the Party's CC, and became CPA representative to the ECCI in 1937.

Docker, Edward G. (Ted): an early member of the CPA, Docker became a member of the CEC in 1930 and an enthusiastic supporter of the new leadership of Moxon. He attended the International Lenin School in 1935.

Earsman, William Paisley (1884–1965; 'Bill'): a Scottish immigrant to Australia who left Edinburgh in 1910, he was an executive member of the VSP. He moved from Melbourne to Sydney in 1919, and collaborated with Jock Garden. He was a founding member of the CPA and was elected its first secretary. Earsman attended the Third Congress of the Communist International in 1921 and won the confidence of Trotsky while in Moscow; he returned briefly to Australia, but returned to Russia for the Fourth Congress, was refused re-entry into Australia and, after some travels in Europe on Comintern and other business, settled in Scotland.

Everitt, Ray: theoretician of the ASP and editor of its weekly newspaper, *International Socialist*.

Executive Committee of the Communist International (ECCI): the most important directing body within the Comintern, which made binding decisions between Congresses, and to which national communist parties reported.

Freeman, Paul (1884?–1921; sometimes known as 'Miller'): a militant worker whose nationality and birthplace are not known, Freeman was part of the IWW and became an enthusiastic supporter of the Bolshevik Revolution. He was deported from Australia in 1919 and made his way to Moscow. He returned to Australia to organize delegates to the Third Comintern Congress, at which he was an accredited ASP delegate. He was killed with Artem in the crash of an experimental train in Russia in July 1921.

Fried, Eugen (Clément): a member of the Czechoslovak Communist Party since its foundation, Fried was one of its delegates to the Fifth Comintern Congress, and remained in Moscow the following year as a member of the Secretariat's Organizational Bureau. Sent as a Comintern emissary to France from 1931–39, he initiated the phrase 'Popular Front' in 1934, and helped turn the Communist Party of France into a party with substantial membership and influence. The 'Popular Front' was made policy by the Comintern's Seventh Congress in 1935 for all its parties.

Garden, John Smith (1882–1968; 'Jock'): born in Scotland and came to Australia in 1904, Garden was secretary of the NSW Labor Council from 1918, leading a group known as the 'Trades Hall Reds'; he was a founding member of the CPA, became a member of the ECCI at the Fourth Congress of the Comintern in 1922, and from 1923 was a leader of the CPA. He left the Party with his supporters in 1926, but was formally expelled in December that year. He returned to the Party, as a CEC member, but was not re-elected as part of the 'right-wing' deviation in 1929; he was expelled for the last time in 1930.

Gibson, Ralph Siward (1906–1989): having joined the CPA in 1931 after turning down an offer of a university lectureship, Gibson's organizational talents were put to good effect as a full-time Party worker when he was assigned to control the Friends of the Soviet Union.

GPU: acronym for the State Political Department, concerned with state security and espionage; formed from the Cheka in 1922, renamed and known by the acronym OGPU in 1924, it later became the NKVD, the MVD, and finally the KGB.

Higgins, E.M. (Esmonde): an Australian who joined the CPGB in the early 1920s, and the CPA when he returned to Australia in 1924; Higgins was editor of the CPA's newspaper, *Workers' Weekly*, from 1925–29, and was a delegate to the Comintern Congress in 1928. Considered unreliable because of his association with Jack Kavanagh, Higgins was removed from the CPA's Central Committee in 1931, and left the Party in 1934.

Industrial Workers of the World: founded in Chicago in 1905, and reaching Australia in 1907, the IWW was an organization that promoted anarcho-syndicalism, and rejected political action to achieve socialism. IWW members (also known as 'Wobblies') believed that the key task was to build a mass industrial trade union movement that would begin to 'constitute the new society within the body of the old'; despite their apolitical stance, they were major distributors of Marx's ideas. In Australia the IWW was politically persecuted, perhaps because it represented the most serious socialist challenge to the state, especially after its opposition to conscription during the First World War. Banned in 1916, after 12 of its members were tried for treason, the IWW in Australia was effectively finished by 1920. (In 1920 an inquiry was held into the trial, and the imprisoned men were subsequently released.)

Jeffery, Norman: former Wobbly, and a founding member of the CPA, Jeffery was employed as a CPA organizer until 1926; he subsequently worked as a rural organizer of workers and took various positions in the Party organization.

Kavanagh, J.P. (1879–1964; 'Jack'): Irish-born, Canadian communist, and member of the Workers' Party of Canada. Chairman of the CPA from his arrival from Canada in 1925 (and candidate member of ECCI from 1928) until his expulsion in January 1931 for right-wing deviation, after attempting to have Australia exempted from the Comintern's 'social fascist' line towards social democratic parties (in this case, the ALP). He served two years from September 1931 on probation but was never allowed to return to full membership status. Kavanagh supported many of Trotsky's views and was associated with the Australian Trotskyists. He had a reputation as an impressive orator.

Kuusinen, Ottomar W. (1881–1946): a founding member of the Finnish Communist Party who moved to Moscow after the collapse of the Finnish revolution in April 1918, Kuusinen became a bureaucrat in the Comintern.

Laidler, Thomas Percival (1884–1958; 'Percy'): a member of the VSP and impressive orator, Laidler left the Party after 1909 and espoused a syndicalist view similar to the IWW's, a group he supported but apparently did not join. He chaired the inaugural meeting of the CPA's Melbourne branch in 1921, but it soon collapsed. He thereafter continued his activity in the workers' and socialist movements, supporting communism and the Soviet Union, but not rejoining the CPA.

Lenin, V.I. (1870–1924; pseudonym of Vladimir Ilyich Ulyanov): founder of the Bolshevik party, and its preeminent theoretician and leader; Lenin saw the opportunity to take power in Russia in October 1917, and was determined thereafter to retain and extend Bolshevik power, despite his growing concerns about the isolation of Soviet Russia and creeping bureaucratization of the state and ruling party.

Lozovsky, Solomon Abramovich (1878–1952): senior Comintern official, RILU General Secretary, 1921–37, and chief instigator of the Pan-Pacific Trades Union Secretariat. In the late 1930s, he was a member of the CC of the CPSU, and in 1945 was Deputy Chief of the Soviet Information Bureau of the Commissariat of Foreign Affairs. He was shot during Stalin's last anti-semitic campaign.

Martens, Ludwig: a German citizen resident in America, Martens was appointed the first official Soviet government representative to the USA, but gained no official US recognition. Using his business background, he proceeded to arrange contracts with American firms, ignoring the American embargo and non-recognition of the Soviets. He was deported from the USA in January 1921.

Marty, André (1886–1956): a member of the French Communist Party's Politburo from 1931, Marty represented that Party to the ECCI from 1932; he was commander of the International Brigades in Spain, 1936–38, and a member of the ECCI Presidium and Secretariat from 1935–43; he was ousted from the French Party in 1953.

Mason, S. (pseudonym of Stephen Purdy): CPA CC member and the CPA's representative to the ECCI in the 1930s.

Miles, John Bramwell (1888–1969): emigrated from Scotland to Brisbane in 1913, and joined the CPA soon after its foundation; Miles was part of the group that ousted Kavanagh from the Party leadership in the late 1920s. He was secretary of the Party from 1931.

Miller: see Freeman.

Minority Movement: sometimes known as the 'Militant Minority Movement', a communist grouping inside the trades unions to challenge reformist leaderships.

Montefiore, D.B. (Dora, 1851–1934): British communist, well known as a former suffragette, who from January 1921 was an executive member of the CPGB. She visited Australia from late 1922 on a personal matter, and left in October 1923, but was under police surveillance during this time; she represented the CPA at the Comintern's Fourth Congress in mid-1924.

Moore, Herbert (1889–1957; party name of Harry Wicks): an American who took part in the founding conference of the CPUSA in September 1919, Wicks was cleared of spying charges in 1923, and became a delegate to the Sixth Comintern Congress in 1928. He was a North American representative to the Profintern in Moscow in 1928–29 who came to Australia on a Comintern mission in 1930–31 to introduce Bolshevik organizational methods; was expelled from the CPUSA in 1937 on the grounds that he was once (and might still be) a police informer. His FBI file indicates that he was an informer for the Chicago police in 1918, but there is information that he continued as an undercover agent throughout his period as a communist (Macintyre 1998, 171).

Moxon, Herbert: an organizer for the CPA in Queensland in the 1920s, a member of the Party's CC, and a key player in the dramatic change of Party leadership in 1929. Moxon became Party secretary at the Ninth Conference, and proceeded to implement the Third Period line and expel a number of former leaders; he was relieved of his duties by Moore at the end of 1930, and was ultimately expelled early in 1932.

Murphy, John T. (1888–1966): elected to the CC of the CPGB in 1921, Murphy was a member of the ICC in 1924, and became a member of the Presidium of the ECCI in 1926. He was afterwards nominated the Comintern representative on the directorate of the Lenin School, and remained there until late 1929. He broke with communism in 1932.

Naumann, R: member of the Secretariat of the Comintern in the late 1930s.

One Big Union: the objective of the IWW in organizing the working class and overcoming the stultifying effects of capitalism on the mentality of that class. The IWW rejected parliamentarism, but also the craft unionism of the nineteenth century, which it saw as dividing the working class. Instead, it advocated the formation of One Big Union of 'all workers, regardless of sex, creed, or color, [that] will be able to attain the solidarity which alone can abolish wage-slavery and usher in the new society' (cited Burgmann 1995, 50).

One Big Union Propaganda League: formed by 'Wobblies' in 1918 after the IWW was declared an unlawful association in Australia in December 1916.

Pankhurst, Sylvia (1882–1960): the second daughter of the champion of women's suffrage, Emmeline Pankhurst (1858–1928), E. Sylvia Pankhurst was active in the Women's Social and Political Union and in the British Labour Party. She endured prison after being convicted of sedition. She supported the Bolshevik Revolution, writing a sympathetic account of her visit to Soviet Russia (Pankhurst 1921) and later supported Spanish republicans in the Civil War and helped Jewish refugees from Nazi Germany.

Pan-Pacific Trades Union Secretariat: organization established in 1927 and based in Shanghai, coordinating trade unions in countries that bordered the Pacific Ocean. The Australian Council of Trade Unions affiliated to the Pan-Pacific Secretariat, and relations with the Secretariat were conducted by two communists, Jack Ryan and Jock Garden. ACTU affiliation ceased when Ryan was prevented in 1930 by the CPA from putting the case for continued affiliation. The organization was largely inactive after 1932.

Payne, Tom; an anti-conscriptionist during the First World War, Payne was a worker socialist who joined the new CPA and became one of its delegates to the Fourth Congress of the Comintern in December 1922, he stood as a CPA candidate in the NSW state elections of 1925 but was expelled from the Party late in 1925.

He rejoined the CPA in 1932. In 1970 he published his account of meeting Lenin in 1922.

Pepper, John (1886–1937; pseudonym of Joszef Pogány): a Hungarian communist who escaped the collapse of the Hungarian Soviet Republic in 1919 and became a Comintern official; during most of the 1920s he served as Moscow's emissary to the CPUSA. He was attacked at the Sixth Congress by Besso Lominadze, and soon after fell out of favour.

Piatnitsky, Osip (1882–1939): Comintern official, elected to the ECCI in 1924, and headed the Comintern's International Liaison Department (OMS) in the 1920s. He headed the Comintern's Organizational Bureau from about 1927, receiving reports from national communist parties, and was thus a key figure in the Comintern bureaucracy. He fell victim to Stalin's purges, and died in prison in 1939.

Piddington, Albert Bathurst (1862–1945): lawyer and member of the pre-Federation NSW Legislative Assembly (1895–98), Piddington was best known for his contributions to industrial law and his support for a decent basic wage for workers. He was President of the Industrial Relations Commission from 1926–32.

Pollitt, Harry (1890–1960): founding member of the CPGB, member of the ECCI 1924–43, and General Secretary of the CPGB 1929–39 and 1941–56.

Popular Front: a tactic adopted by communists from the mid-1930s to try to resist fascism, it sanctioned alliances between the communist parties and parties representing other ('progressive') classes in popular campaigns, elections and even governments in democratic states. It attempted to use patriotism for the progressive, anti-fascist cause, defended liberal democracy against fascist dictatorship, and succeeded in winning a number of artists and intellectuals to communism, if only for a time. The Popular Front tactic was abandoned with the advent of the Second World War.

Profintern: see RILU.

Prichard, Katharine Susannah (1883–1969): highly regarded Australian novelist, known especially for her 'Goldfields Trilogy', Prichard was a member of the CPA from 1920 and a supporter of the Soviet Union until her death; she married Victoria Cross recipient Captain Hugo Throssell.

Quinton, Jim: formerly a Wobbly, Quinton joined the CPA in its early, divided, phase; he was imprisoned in 1921 in England on his way to the Third Comintern Congress. By the 1930s, Quinton had joined the ALP, but remained an advocate for free speech for communists.

Radek, Karl (1885–1939): one of the Comintern's leading propagandists in Lenin's time, Radek was subsequently a member of the (Trotskyist) Left

Opposition until Trotsky's expulsion from the USSR in 1929. He renounced his oppositionist views and was allowed to rejoin the RCP; he was convicted in the 1937 Moscow purge trial.

Reardon, Arthur: worker-intellectual; secretary of the ASP and founding member of the CPA; Reardon was involved in the early manoeuvres over the direction of the Party, but was effectively left behind by the July 1922 Unity Conference of Australian communists.

Reardon, Marcia: wife of Arthur and a founding member of the CPA; she was known as a forceful speaker and writer in the anti-capitalist cause.

Reed, John (1887–1920): poet, journalist, author and radical activist, Reed was a Harvard-educated American who became an eyewitness to the Bolshevik Revolution (recorded in his *Ten Days that Shook the World* (1919)). He subsequently helped to found the CPUSA, was indicted for treason and escaped to Russia where he died of typhus; he is buried beside the Kremlin wall.

RILU (Red International of Labour Unions; also RTUI; Russian acronym MOPR): an international association of communist-led trade unions, established by the Comintern in July 1920 as a rival to the (reformist) International Federation of Trade Unions; RILU had its founding conference in 1921, but had little activity after 1937, apart from making a short-lived organizational alliance with the reformists in 1945.

Robson, Robert William (1897–?): founding member of the CPGB (later London district organizer 1927–33 and head of the Organisation Department during the 1930s and '40s) who briefly visited Australia in late 1927 on behalf of the Comintern, despite his (British) passport having been declared invalid in 1925 for travel within the British Empire.

Ross, Lloyd (1901–1987): son of veteran socialist, Bob Ross, and brother of fellow communist, Edgar Ross, Lloyd Ross was a Melbourne University History graduate who joined the CPA in the mid-1930s. He was elected in 1935 as NSW secretary of the Australian Railways Union. He was expelled from the CPA in September 1940 for supporting the ('inter-imperialist') war against Hitler.

Ryan, Jack: CPA leader and member of Party's CEC until the Ninth Conference in 1929, as well as Australian organizer of RILU's Pan-Pacific Trades Union Secretariat; he was expelled from the Party in 1930 for 'defying CEC instructions'. Ryan was subsequently a Research Officer of the NSW Trades and Labour Council, and prominent in the Australian trade union movement.

Sergeev, Fedor Andreevich (1883–1921; sometimes Sergeeff or Sergaeff; also 'Artem' and 'Big Tom'): Russian revolutionary who was exiled to Siberia but escaped and travelled to Australia in 1911. Artem established the Russian Workers' Association in Brisbane, as well as the first Russian newspaper in Australia. He returned to Russia in May 1917 and became a member of the

Bolshevik Party's CC. He was killed with Freeman and others in the crash of a propeller-driven locomotive between Tula and Moscow in July 1921.

Sharkey, Lawrence Louis (1898–1967; 'Lance'): leading member of the CPA from 1927 onwards; in the late 1920s he was part of a group that received Comintern support to remove Kavanagh and implement the 'social fascist' line towards the ALP; first visited the USSR as a delegate to the Fifth Comintern Congress in 1924. Sharkey became the chairman of the CC of the CPA from 1931, and a candidate member of the ECCI in 1935. He was jailed in 1949 for sedition.

Simonov, Petr (1883–?; sometimes 'Peter Simonoff'): Russian émigré in Australia at the time of the Bolshevik Revolution. He was jailed in Australia for addressing public meetings in support of the Revolution, but released in July 1919. Simonov was appointed Soviet consul in Australia, but the Australian government would not accept his credentials; he left for Russia in September 1921, but fell from favour in Moscow.

Simpson, John ('Jack'): a CPA leader from 1934 (when he was elected to the Central Committee), Simpson was a New Zealander who had fought in the First World War, including at Gallipoli. He was sent by the Party from Sydney to Perth in June 1940, after the leaders of the Western Australian branch had been arrested, but he was also arrested.

Small Bureau: precursor of the Presidium of the ECCI.

Stalin, Joseph (1878–1953; pseudonym of J.V. Dzhugashvili): early member of the Bolshevik party and eventual leader of the Soviet Union until his death, Stalin used his organizational skills to control the Russian Communist Party and to outmanoeuvre and ultimately destroy rival Bolshevik leaders Trotsky, Bukharin, Zinoviev and Kamenev, and then used the state and intelligence apparatuses to hold the Party and the country in thrall to a virtual reign of terror.

Stewart, Bob (1877–?): founding member of the CPGB in 1921, and the Party's Scottish organizer from 1922, in 1924 he was appointed British representative to ECCI, and was elected to the Comintern's Presidium at the Fifth Congress the same year. He remained a member of the CPGB's Executive Committee until 1936. From the late 1920s, he seems to have been involved in substantial covert activity—in Ireland and Germany, in particular—on behalf of the CPGB and the Comintern. His activities and conversations were monitored closely by MI5, Britain's Security Service, a surveillance undermined by the fact that Stewart knew of it.

Tolmachev, G.F. (1886–1937; sometimes 'Piddubny' or 'Poddubny'): a schoolteacher, journalist and agitator from the Kharkov region. Joined the Socialist Revolutionary Party in 1905. Exiled to Siberia in 1909. Escaped and travelled via Manchuria to Australia, where he lived from 1913 to 1917, mostly in Queensland. Contributed occasionally to the Brisbane newspaper *Rabochaia* *zhizn* (*Worker's Life*). Active in Ukrainian revolutionary politics from his return in 1917. From 1919 to 1926 represented the Ukrainian government and later the CP in Vienna. In Kharkov from 1926 he held posts in the ministry of education and as an editor. He was executed in October 1937 for 'bourgeois nationalism'.

Trotsky, Leon (1879–1940; pseudonym of Lev Bronstein): Russian communist who joined the Bolsheviks shortly before the October Revolution and was instrumental in the Bolshevik coup and in defence of the Soviet state through the organization of the Red Army. Expelled from the RCP in 1927 and finally exiled from the Soviet Union, he spent the following years hounded from one country to another (Turkey, France, Norway and then Mexico) criticizing the Soviet leadership and finally forming a 'Fourth International' of Trotskyist communist parties in September 1938. He was assassinated in Mexico by a Soviet agent.

United Front: tactic advocated by the Comintern from 1921, whereby communist parties should form alliances with ('reformist') working class organizations for particular campaigns, but would remain free to criticize the non-communist leaderships of such organizations. It was hoped in this way to connect with the working class and to raise its class consciousness. When rebuffed, communists advocated the 'united front from below', attempting to bypass reformist leaders.

Walsh, Tom (1871–1943): early leader of the Australian communists, and of the Seamen's Union, Walsh was the husband of Adela Pankhurst, a daughter of Emmeline (and sister of Sylvia) and a longstanding Australian socialist. Both had been members of the VSP, and attended the foundation meeting of the CPA in 1920. Walsh was a member of the 'Sussex Street' party during the period before unity in 1922. Though he left the Communist Party, Walsh attempted nevertheless to escalate a number of union disputes to embarrass Labor Party governments (in Western Australia, for example), and expose them as supporters of capitalism.

Wright, Tom (1902–81): secretary of the CPA 1925–29, Wright at first opposed the Comintern's Third Period line but was persuaded by self-criticism in 1930. He remained a communist and became secretary of the Sheet Metal Workers' Union in 1936, eventually leaving the Party in the early 1970s.

Zinoviev, Grigory (1883–1936; pseudonym of Radomyslsky): Bolshevik leader, and first President of the Comintern. In the mid-1920s he joined with the Trotskyist Opposition in the RCP, but was defeated by Stalin, recanted and continued to enjoy the privileges of leadership, and was ultimately tried and executed in Stalin's purges of 1936–38.

Zuzenko, Aleksandr Mikhailovich (1884–1938; sometimes 'Soosenko', 'Susenko', 'Nargen', 'Mamin' or 'Matulichenko'): Russian revolutionary who arrived in Australia in 1911 and was deported in April 1919 for his political activities, especially his leadership of the Red Flag demonstration of 23 March 1919 in Brisbane. Zuzenko then abandoned his revolutionary anarchism for the iron discipline of Bolshevism; he returned to Australia in July 1922 as an agent of the Comintern, and was deported again in September. He was subsequently a captain of Soviet merchant ships, but was charged in 1938 with espionage and executed as a 'British spy'.

Some key dates in the history of Australian communism to 1943

1916   IWW declared an unlawful association (December)

1917   Bolshevik Revolution (7 November)

1919   formation of the Communist International (March); Red Flag demonstration, Brisbane; Zuzenko deported from Australia (March); other Russian activists deported (September)

1920   CPA founding conference (October, reconvened November and December)

1921   failed CPA unity conference (March); Simonov leaves Australia (September)

1922   ineffectual 'All-Australian Unity Conference' (February); CPA unity conference (July; Zuzenko attends); CPA accepted as the Australian Section of the Comintern (9 August); Zuzenko deported from Australia for the second time (September); Jock Garden elected as candidate member of ECCI (September)

1925   Baracchi advocates liquidation of the CPA, then resigns (December); Jack Kavanagh becomes CPA Secretary at Fifth Conference (December)

1926   ECCI examines 'the Australian question' (April-May)

1927   ECCI examines 'the Australian question' (October)

1928   ECCI examines 'the Australian question' (April); Kavanagh elected as a candidate member of ECCI (September)

1929   Wall Street stock market crash (October), Great Depression ensues; Ninth Annual Conference (December); major change in leadership

1930   Herbert Moore arrives in Australia (April)

1931   CPA Tenth Annual Congress (April); Herbert Moore departs Australia (July)

1933   Adolf Hitler becomes Chancellor of Germany (January)

1935   Lance Sharkey elected as a candidate member of ECCI (August); CPA Eleventh Congress (December)

1937   Anglo-American Secretariat considers 'the Australian question' (July)

1938   CPA Twelfth Congress (November)

1939   German-Soviet Non-aggression Pact (August); Second World War declared (September)

1940   CPA declared illegal (15 June)

1941   German armed forces invade the Soviet Union (22 June)

1942   CPA's legality reinstated (December)

1943   Comintern disbanded (May)

Dates of key Comintern meetings

First Congress   2–6 March 1919 (Moscow)

Second Congress   19 July – 7 August 1920 (Moscow and Petrograd)

Third Congress   22 June – 12 July 1921 (Moscow)

   First Enlarged Plenum of the ECCI   24 February – 4 March 1922

   Second Enlarged Plenum of the ECCI   7 – 11 June 1922

Fourth Congress   5 November – 5 December 1922 (Moscow and Petrograd)

   Third Enlarged Plenum of the ECCI   12 – 23 June 1923

Fifth Congress   17 June – 8 July 1924 (Moscow)

   Fourth Enlarged Plenum of the ECCI   12 – 13 July 1924

   Fifth Enlarged Plenum of the ECCI   21 March – 6 April 1925

   Sixth Enlarged Plenum of the ECCI   17 February – 15 March 1926

   Seventh Enlarged Plenum of the ECCI   22 November – 16 December 1926

   Eighth Plenum of the ECCI   18 – 30 May 1927

   Ninth Plenum of the ECCI   9 – 25 February 1928

Sixth Congress   17 July – 1 September 1928 (Moscow)

   Tenth Plenum of the ECCI   3 – 19 July 1929

   Eleventh Plenum of the ECCI   26 March – 11 April 1931

   Twelfth Plenum of the ECCI   27 August – 15 September 1932

   Thirteenth Plenum of the ECCI   28 November – 12 December 1933

Seventh Congress 25 July – 21 August 1935 (Moscow)

The organization of the Comintern

A thorough knowledge of the Communist International, or Comintern, is not essential to follow the documents in this collection. Nevertheless, it is useful to have a general overview of its key organizational features (ignoring minor modifications over time). In essence, the organization was a strict hierarchy in which Lenin's 'democratic centralism' held sway: the highest bodies had the greatest control and the least accountability to the membership.

The Comintern was composed of **Sections**, which were the various national Communist Parties. Sections were bound by the '21 Conditions' adopted by the Second Comintern Congress, and by all the other decisions of Congresses. The sections were organized in much the same fashion as the Comintern itself.

The **World Congress** was described in Comintern documents as the 'supreme organ' of the organization. It was, however, only convened twice after 1924, and seven times in total, and it never had the character of a chamber for debate. Its sessions were dominated by set-piece speeches, often by leaders of the Russian Communist Party. Congresses were attended by delegates from the sections, in proportion to their size: the RCP always had the largest number of delegates, followed by (mostly European) parties in the second rank, and then by parties such as the CPUSA. Congresses were always held in Russia.

Congress ratified the election of the Executive Committee, **ECCI**, which was the 'leading organ' of the Comintern between Congresses. Directives to Communist Parties made by the ECCI were binding until overturned by Congress. The leaderships of sections were accountable to the ECCI, and had to forward national reports and copies of minutes to it. The ECCI was originally composed of 25 full members and 20 candidate members, but the numbers had doubled by the time of the last Congress in 1935. The ECCI was based in Moscow, and the largest single number of its members was always Russian. It was not, and was not intended to be, 'representative' of the national composition of the Comintern.

The ECCI elected a **Presidium**, an **Organizational Bureau** (from 1923–28), and a **Secretariat**, which handled in their various ways quotidian matters. The ECCI also convened (irregularly) conferences described as 'Enlarged Executives of the Plenum', or simply **Plenums**. These met between Congresses, and were designed to examine particular issues as the need arose. There was a total of 13 Plenums.

The ECCI organized the Comintern's sections into a number of country Secretariats, as a type of intermediary between individual sections and the ECCI itself. These were gradually modified into geographical or cultural groupings, of which the **Anglo-American Secretariat** was one.

The Comintern had a **Cadres Department** which kept information on all members, information which was useful for the periodic campaigns of verification of members and for purges. It also created an **International Control Commission**, which heard appeals from those who had been expelled by the Comintern's parties, and had the power to investigate and pass judgement on Comintern members accused of inappropriate conduct.

Reproducing the documents: some conventions

Most of the documents in the Comintern Archive at the ADFA Library, whatever their original form, come to us as typescripts. Judging by the notations on them, many were the products of a typing pool. Consequently, most of the documents selected for this volume were reproduced from typescripts, though there were some manuscripts. This note explains the conventions we have adopted in reproducing them.

If errors occurred in the documents themselves, for example over the transliteration of names from English to Russian, or errors of grammar or spelling, they have been retained in this volume. Where the authors (or typists, if not the authors) have corrected an error that they themselves have made, we have not reproduced the error or its deletion. Nor have we reproduced the various notations made on the documents when they were deposited in the archive, or reorganized within the archive (these usually consist of a series of numbers at the top of the pages). Many other changes, additions or emphases made to the documents do, however, warrant our attention. To indicate them, we have followed the straightforward conventions used for the 'Annals of Communism' series published by Yale University Press, as follows:

- handwritten comments added to typescripts appear in *italic* type;
- interpolations made by the authors of this book, and illegible or indecipherable words, are enclosed in [square brackets], including deliberate omissions, thus [...];
- <u>single underlining</u> identifies words or phrases underlined on a typewriter;
- <u>double underlining</u> identifies words or phrases underlined by hand.

Each document is introduced by a note that identifies its archival location (*fond-opis-delo*), date (or probable date), its author and a title (sometimes bestowed by us, and sometimes taken from the document itself), the language in which it appears, whether it appears in the archive as a typescript or manuscript, and a brief discussion of its context. There is a more detailed discussion in the 'Notes on the Texts and Translations', below, about the language of the documents.

Where an archive document is cited in introductory and other material simply by providing its three-part archival location figure, that means it was sourced from the Comintern Archive at the ADFA Library. If Comintern archive material has been cited from another location, either at the Mitchell Library or at the Library of Congress, the reference to the archival location figure will be preceded by the acronym CAML or CALC, respectively.

Notes on the texts and translations

Translations comprise a substantial proportion of the documents in this collection. Many of the translations were made for the present edition. Some documents, however, are preserved in the archive in several languages. The notes below attempt to explain our policy in selecting or producing versions for this edition, and the coding accompanying each document.

If we give no indication of the language of a particular document, it is to be understood that that document appears in the archive in English and no other language.

If we indicate that a document is present in more than one language, including English, we have reproduced that English version, whether or not that version is the original. If that version is a translation in which obvious faults distort or obscure the meaning, we have used the other versions to effect small corrections. Where this has not been possible we have resorted to sparing use of [sic].

If a document is our translation, there being no other English version in the archive, we indicate the language from which it is translated. We have thought it prudent to avoid the word 'original', since in certain cases it is clear that the version we are translating is itself a translation. For example, it is known that Peter Simonoff (Petr Simonov) did not write in Polish, but in one case the only available version of a document by him is in that language. We are fairly sure that Paul Freeman, Jock Garden and Bill Earsman did not write in Russian, but when their documents exist in the archive in Russian only we have little choice but to supply a back-translation, however unsatisfactory this procedure may be.

Many small typographical errors have been corrected in the English-language documents, without special note being taken of them. Likewise, punctuation has occasionally been modified for clarity, and inadvertently repeated words deleted. In no case has this affected the meaning of any document. The layout of the documents in this book is not identical to the typescripts and manuscripts, but nothing is thereby lost.

There are inconsistencies of spelling within and between documents. We have not attempted to impose complete uniformity. Odd or awkward formulations, some no doubt introduced by rapid typing, translation or dictation at the time these documents were drafted, have been left as they are.

Treatment of Proper Names

Russian personal names are usually given in modified Library of Congress transliteration. Exceptions are made where the owners of the names used other forms in non-Russian environments (e.g. Rosenberg), and for names widely known in other guises. 'Modified' means that we have ignored the hard and soft signs and written -*sky* rather than -*skii*.

Non-Russian names occurring in Russian documents present their own problems. Some of the typewritten documents are in poor condition and difficult to read, while those in handwriting add a further level of difficulty. Where typewritten and handwritten versions of the same document appear, it is clear that on occasion the typists were baffled by the handwriting. Where the discrepancies are substantial we have indicated these in footnotes. The cause of the typist's difficulty may be the author's insertion in the Russian text of a non-Russian personal name or place-name written in its original form, in Latin script (not transcribed into Russian Cyrillic). The unsuspecting typist, perhaps knowing no English, thus produces 'Gon Velkech' in Cyrillic script for what is clearly 'Tom Barker' in Latin script, and 'Velassy' for [Guido] Baracchi. The latter appears in a Polish document as 'Barecki', and *Brisbane* in the same document becomes 'Gryzben'.

Unfortunately, not all such riddles are so easily solved, and some documents appear in single copies only, whether in typed or handwritten form, so no cross-checking is possible.

Non-Russian names clearly caused difficulties not only for the typists, but also for the authors, who in any case treated names in cavalier fashion. Zuzenko's travels in the cause of world revolution can mostly be traced, but some smaller localities defy positive identification. He tells of being transferred by the British authorities from Brixton Prison to 'Vleit' or 'Vleis' in Scotland for deportation to Petrograd. Since 'Vleit/Vleis' is clearly a port with a prison close at hand, it is likely that Leith is meant.

Even where the Russian transcription of names is accurate, the original English form often cannot be accurately reconstructed. *Maclean, McLean, MacLean* and *Macklin*, for example, will all assume the same Cyrillic form. An Australian whose name occurs in various Cyrillic guises, as *Ganet, Gannett, Khannet* and *Khennett*, appears to be *Hannett*, though we cannot exclude *Hannet*. When the form of a name is derived from a Russian transcription, we have indicated this by [phon.], meaning that we have produced a phonetic reconstruction taking into account known English forms and the laws of probability.

In documents written in English, as in those in Russian, names are casually treated and it is common to find a name either consistently misspelt or spelt in a variety of ways. In some cases the correct form cannot be re-established from the documents themselves, but may be known from other sources (e.g. *Norman Jeffery*, often appearing as *Jeffries* or *Jeffrey*). Names which cannot be verified have been left in the forms given, which may not necessarily be correct.

A note on currency

In the period covered by the documents in this book, the currency used in Australia was the Australian pound, established by the national government in 1910. The Australian pound was at times directly linked to the value of the pound sterling, and at other times unlinked, but its basic divisions were nevertheless the same. There were 12 pennies (d) in a shilling (s), and 20 shillings in a pound (£).

Piecing together the past: the Comintern, the CPA, and the archives

David W. Lovell

The story of the Communist Party of Australia can be, and has been, told in various ways: official, personal, polemical and scholarly. Until now, archival collections that have borne on this story have been relatively inaccessible to the ordinary, interested reader. This book begins to redress that deficiency by making available a selection of documents from a larger collection, now publicly available. The selection focuses on the relationship between the CPA and the Communist International because the activities of the CPA are essentially incomprehensible without understanding the international communist context within which the CPA operated. That context was dominated by the newly-created Soviet state and its decision to authorize and utilize a network of communist parties throughout the world.

The documents in this work suggest three major propositions about the relationship between the CPA and the Comintern. First, that the Comintern was crucial in the formation of the CPA, via its emissaries, instructions and authority. Second, that the Comintern played a major role in directing the policies of the CPA in domestic matters (not to mention in international matters, where the Comintern's decisions were supreme). And third, that the leadership of the CPA was, from 1929 onwards, shaped, trained and authorized by the Comintern. There are two points that the evidence available to us does not sustain, though it does not mean that we should entirely exclude them: that Comintern money played a major role in the life of the CPA during the period we are examining; and that the CPA, under Comintern instruction, maintained an illegal or underground secretariat. Both these latter points have been persuasively argued and documented in the case of the Communist Party of the United States (Klehr, Haynes and Firsov 1995; Klehr, Haynes and Anderson 1998) and the Communist Party of Great Britain. The evidence of the documents we have examined suggests that funding of the CPA from Moscow took place, though its extent is impossible to quantify. It also suggests that there were no illegal operations of the sort encouraged by the Comintern, and engaged in by the CPUSA and to a lesser extent by the CPGB, and by many other communist parties. Australia became a much more interesting target for Soviet intelligence agencies from the middle of the Second World War, around the time of the disbanding of the Comintern in 1943. It is noteworthy, however, that Soviet agents used the CPA and its—by then functioning—network of illegal cells and covert members, but that is another story.

In this essay, I shall explore the origins, functions and development of the Comintern to explain its extraordinary ability to impose its will on its parties, and argue for the importance of archival contributions to deepening our understanding of its history. In the following essay, I shall provide an overview of the main features and turning points in the relationship between the CPA and the Comintern. Taken together, these essays provide a framework within which the documents can be contextualized and evaluated. I hope they will also encourage further work in this area.

The Comintern and the Soviet state

The Communist International, the Third International, or simply the 'Comintern' as it is most commonly known, came into existence in Moscow in 1919. It was established in the wake of the Bolshevik Revolution of 25 October 1917 (Old Style; or 7 November 1917, in the Gregorian calendar, which the new regime soon adopted). The Comintern was the third in a series of groupings of international socialist and workers' parties, the first of which was established in 1864 in London. Karl Marx may have played an important ideological role in the International Working Men's Association, drafting one of its major documents, but it was a collection of workers' groups with diverse and divergent strategies. The Second International, much more firmly in the Marxist tradition, was established in 1889 and was guided at first by the aging survivor of the Marx-Engels partnership, Frederick Engels, and after his death in 1895 by Karl Kautsky, a leader of the German Social Democratic Party (SPD), literary executor of the Marx and Engels manuscripts, and acknowledged 'Pope' of Social Democracy.

In its attempts to knit together socialist parties of the world and to give effect to Marx's declaration of the 1848 *Manifesto of the Communist Party*—'workers of all countries, unite!'—the Second International was a triumph of form over substance. It was a collection of socialists who had, as it turned out, rather diverse ideas about nationalism and their role in dealing with the (increasingly evident) national loyalties of the working class they purported to represent and lead. Furthermore, it was a *collection* of socialists rather than a centralized organization; indeed, it was criticized for being simply a 'mail box'. The Second International, already sullied in the eyes of radical socialists by the inconclusive debate over 'Revisionism' near the turn of the century and a general fuzziness about reform versus insurrection as the method of establishing socialism, was dealt a mortal blow in the same eyes in 1914 after the outbreak of the First World War. The major European socialist parties, especially the German and the French (that had dominated the International), supported their own national governments rather than opposing the 'imperialist war' and adopting an approach of 'revolutionary defeatism' as the radicals advocated.

In response to the perceived betrayal of the interests of the working class, radical socialists met a number of times during the war, notably at Zimmerwald and Kienthal in Switzerland, to establish the foundations of a response that was simultaneously socialist and internationalist. Lenin and Trotsky were part of this group. Lenin railed against the horrendous human cost of the war, and pressed into service the analysis of imperialism by the English liberal J.A. Hobson to declare that capitalism had entered its final stage, and would inevitably generate ever more destructive imperialist wars. Having taken power in war-weary Russia towards the end of 1917, the Bolsheviks eventually withdrew Russian forces from the war and signed the Treaty of Brest-Litovsk in March 1918, surrendering to the Germans half of Russia's industrial capacity and a third of its agricultural land. The treaty signalled an approach that would become much more evident in later years: that the Bolsheviks were prepared to compromise, adjust, or manoeuvre (depending on one's ideological predilections) to stay in power. In the end, the Comintern would also be sacrificed to this imperative.

Lenin and Trotsky, as the most prominent leaders and thinkers of the new regime, were internationalists. They believed that socialism in Russia alone could not survive, and that socialism itself would succeed only as an international phenomenon. Thus, Soviet Russia's best protection lay in exporting revolution to the world, and its best chance for the type of economic development they saw as required for socialism lay in leapfrogging Russia's backward economy with the assistance of advanced (socialist) countries (amongst which they invested their greatest hopes in Germany).

The mood of the times should not be underestimated. After the Bolshevik revolution, there were high hopes among many socialists—however much they knew about the Bolsheviks, and at first that was very little—and especially among the Bolsheviks themselves, that revolution would spread like wildfire. Russia would simply be the harbinger of the world revolution, and would be able to transfer leadership to more economically advanced socialist countries. At first the Bolsheviks seemed to be right, with a communist revolt breaking out in Germany in January 1919 (soon bloodily put down), and a communist government in Hungary in the first half of 1919. By 1920 the Red Army was in Poland, but was repulsed. But from the early 1920s, and especially after Lenin's death at the beginning of 1924, the Bolsheviks set about coming to terms with their condition as a proto-socialist state in a world of capitalist states.

The Bolsheviks took two major approaches to what they saw as their embattled isolation. The first was conventional, and consisted in the development of diplomatic and economic ties with other countries. However, given Bolshevik rhetoric about their mission of world revolution and implacable hostility to all capitalist states, normal relations with such states were understandably rather

3

difficult to establish and slow to deepen. The second, unconventional, approach consisted in the encouragement or development of communist parties in all the countries of the world, organized, and sometimes directed and financed, by Moscow, and also the development of a network of spies in the West to determine where and when the enemy would move against the Soviet Union. Trotsky, who played a major role in the formation and early development of the Comintern, called it the 'General Staff of the World Revolution'.

The American communists, for example, were enlisted in efforts to help lift the trade blockade of Soviet Russia, especially by holding public meetings (CALC, 515–1–36). The Soviet government signed a trade agreement with the British government in March 1921; yet despite the agreement's preamble proclaiming an end to propaganda for the overthrow of capitalism in Britain, the Soviets persisted in it through both the trade mission and the CPGB.

The role of the communist parties in this unconventional approach became increasingly instrumental and expedient, and—it must also be said—increasingly unimportant. From the 1930s onwards espionage became the more important aspect of the unconventional approach, conferences of the Comintern became less frequent, and eventually the Comintern was sacrificed to the Soviet alliance with the allied powers in the Second World War. Communist parties, of course, remained after the war, as did a popular but nebulous sense that they were working in the interests of the Soviet bloc (and, after its fracture, for either Moscow or Peking), but the coordination of their efforts was not as systematic or as overt as before. Furthermore, the Soviet Union had gained a measure of protection by its development of the atomic bomb and its East European buffer zone, and it had a measure of international recognition as a permanent member of the United Nations' Security Council, with the consequent right to veto Council decisions. Diplomatic recognition was no longer a problem, defence was managed by the nuclear stalemate, and spying became a regular industry for both sides in the Cold War.

The fear—perhaps paranoia—induced by capitalist encirclement had another, altogether more terrible, consequence within the Soviet Union. The notion that the world's first socialist state faced imminent attack from capitalism, a theme that permeated Comintern documents from about 1926 onwards, contributed in large part to the Soviet purges of the 1930s, during which millions were imprisoned or killed. New archival evidence makes it clear that despite the great mass of purge victims being ordinary people, and many having fallen victim by reason of the raising of bureaucratic quotas, foreigners and those with foreign forebears were singled out for particularly harsh treatment. Stalin feared that in a war against capitalism these would be the most 'unreliable' elements in Soviet Russia. Those with Polish or German connections, above all, were liquidated, whether they were communists, refugees, or simply those unlucky enough to have been caught up in history (McLoughlin and McDermott 2003). Indeed, many foreign Comintern members residing in the USSR also became victims of the purges.

In 1919, these sad outcomes could not have been predicted. Communists from many parts of the world who happened to be in Moscow, or had run the Allied blockade, were in buoyant mood as the First Congress of the Third International was held. But they represented themselves more than parties or groups, and the organization proper should really be dated from its Second Congress in 1920. It was at the Second Congress that the Comintern began to take definite shape. Because of the numerous requests from various socialist groups to join it and become its national sections, a set of 'Twenty One Conditions' for affiliation to the Comintern was promulgated, and the issue of whether the organization would be a federation of equal parties or a centralized party was settled in favour of the latter.

The Comintern's organizational structure crystallized during the early 1920s, with the Russian delegation dominating the Executive Committee, and the day-to-day control being exercised by the 'Small Bureau', which became the Presidium of the ECCI. This too was dominated by Russians. In 1926 a new supreme body was created: the Political Secretariat of the ECCI, initially with eight members and three candidate members.

The Russians were effectively in charge, both by virtue of having Comintern headquarters based in Moscow, and by being the largest single bloc of votes on the Executive Committee. In the prevailing atmosphere approaching worship of the Bolsheviks and their revolutionary achievements, few thought through the consequences of this Bolshevization, and fewer openly challenged it. For those who did, there was always the possibility of expulsion. Lenin, in his *'Left-Wing' Communism—An infantile disorder*, reinforced the point that the Bolshevik style of organization with its democratic centralist arrangements was the only acceptable form of communist organization. (Trotsky, in 1903, had presciently described democratic centralism as inviting 'substitutionism': 'The party organisation at first substitutes itself for the party as a whole; then the Central Committee substitutes itself for the organisation; and finally a single 'dictator' substitutes himself for the Central Committee …' (cited Deutscher 1970, 90)) As Lenin continued to insist, and as Trotsky eventually agreed, 'absolute centralisation and rigorous discipline in the proletariat are an essential condition of victory over the bourgeoisie' (Lenin 1976, 295). In the period from 1919 to 1923, then, the Russians achieved what McDermott and Agnew (1996, 14) called the 'universalisation of Bolshevism'.

The Comintern and its parties

If there were ever doubts about the centrality of the Comintern, its political and organizational predominance among, its financial subsidies to, and even its role in forming and accrediting the communist parties of the world, they arise both from the formal equality between communists and from the inability of some parties to carry out all of Moscow's directions. Formal equality, as the communists themselves have rightly pointed out in other connections, generally obscures real power relations; and, as much as Moscow demanded, sent emissaries, and hauled leaders of recalcitrant parties before inquiries, parties could not always do what they were told. Moscow made broad decisions—and sometimes even quite detailed decisions—about 'in-country' matters; it took sides in key internal debates and leadership disputes; it was often asked for advice. The Comintern sent an organizer, the American Herbert Moore, to reorganize the Australian party in 1930. But it did the same elsewhere. Bela Kun was sent in March 1921 as an ECCI emissary to Germany, where he provoked an insurrection and brought down disastrous repercussions on the German Communist Party. Otto Braun, having trained at the Frunze Military Academy in Moscow, was sent to China in 1932 as the Comintern's military adviser to the Chinese Communist Party, although the victory of Mao Zedong in 1935 as party leader was not the Comintern's preferred option (Braun 1982). Emissaries from Moscow were a common means of enforcing control (Lazitch 1966). Parties sometimes even asked for such assistance; in a confidential letter Israel Amter, an American communist delegate to the ECCI, wrote to the Presidium of the ECCI, on 30 May 1924: 'I would recommend that the Presidium without delay send to the U.S. one or more good Russian comrades ... both in view of a possible factional struggle in the Party, and in order to stiffen the backbone of the CEC and of the Party ...' (CALC, 515–1–273).

The relative weight between centre and periphery in the Comintern in particular cases is a matter of debate, but while the initial hope may have been for a partnership, the Comintern soon became an instrument of the Soviets. It may be too sharp a contrast, however, to say as Jacobson does that 'What was initiated as the organization of independent parties of revolutionary socialists ended as a manipulated tool of Soviet security interests' (Jacobson 1994, 32). E.H. Carr also supported this view, which relies on a rather too strict separation between the influence of Lenin and of Stalin. Carr argued that:

> The slow process of 'Bolshevization' of foreign communist parties ... reached its logical conclusion with the consolidation of Stalin's dictatorship. By the end of 1929, long and often bitter struggles within the German, French, Polish, Czechoslovak, British and American parties had been ended by firm decisions of Comintern to cast its mantle over one of the contending factions, and by the

expulsion from the party, or removal from the leadership, of those who contested
the decisions. (Carr 1982, 5)

Bolshevization took hold much earlier than Carr allowed; but it was perhaps less
successful than he believed.

With the lull in revolution in the early 1920s, the terms of the Comintern
agreement with its national sections came to be changed. There was much less
hope for an immediate end to the Soviet Union's condition as the only socialist
state. The Third Congress in 1921 declared that 'unconditional support of Soviet
Russia remains ... the cardinal duty of Communists in all countries'. By the
Comintern's Fourth Congress, near the end of 1922, proletarian internationalism
chiefly meant support for the Soviet Union. By the Fifth Congress, after Lenin's
death in 1924, 'socialism in one country' was the key issue. By 1926, the Soviet
leadership was constantly warning about the threat of military attacks from the
capitalist world. In the late 1920s, Soviet diplomat (and former People's
Commissar of Foreign Affairs) Georgi Chicherin bravely, but accurately, told
Stalin that talk about a foreign invasion of the Soviet Union at the time was
'ridiculous' (McDermott and Agnew 1996, 95). But fear of invasion was a theme
in Comintern communications for the next 14 years, after which time the Soviet
Union signed a thoroughly cynical 'nonaggression pact' with Germany, the only
country that was likely to invade it (and, despite the pact, soon did).

The divisions between socialists were many, and not simply national. Lenin
had some success in claiming the mantle of Marx prior to the Bolshevik
Revolution, but even more success after it in the 'battle of the books' with Karl
Kautsky (exemplified by Lenin's *The Proletarian Revolution and the Renegade
Kautsky* (1918)). In the end, Kautsky ceded the field, suggesting that if Lenin
were a Marxist, and if Marxism meant dictatorship of the Bolshevik kind, that
was something he didn't want to be. The grounds for Lenin's claims to be faithful
to Marx in this area are thin (Lovell 1984, 164–81), but historical arguments are
not always won with logic. Lenin's contributions to Marxism were distinguished
by his hierarchical, professional and centralized notion of a revolutionary socialist
party, his insurrectionary methods, and his insistence that the 'dictatorship of
the proletariat' meant the rule of the communist party unrestricted by laws,
even its own. His contributions fully justify the new label 'Marxism-Leninism',
as a distinct theoretical current. Few people, even socialists, had heard of Lenin
and Trotsky outside Europe before the First World War. They were unlikely to
be aware of Lenin's extensive theoretical contributions when he burst onto the
international stage in 1917, and were chiefly struck by the novelty of the creation
of an avowedly socialist regime. Most socialists were amazed, sympathetic and
even overjoyed, though many quickly became wary. Socialist parties throughout
the world had to decide where they stood, and whether they sided with Lenin's
regime and his views on socialism. If they did, the Communist International had

harsh news for them: form a unified communist party, learn Bolshevik lessons, and organize a revolution.

Throughout these introductory essays, and the book itself, I use the term 'Comintern' and 'Moscow' almost interchangeably. This raises the question of whether the line proposed by the Comintern's executive, the ECCI, was formulated or authorized by the leadership of the Russian Communist Party; so I shall address it here. There is some evidence that the relationship between the ECCI and the RCP changed, and that there were sometimes differences between the two, but ultimately nothing that the Comintern proposed as policy, through its Congresses or Executive Plenums, could be endorsed as policy without the sanction of the RCP, and later—especially after Stalin consolidated undisputed power in his own hands in Russia (perhaps around the time of the assassination of Sergei Kirov in 1934)—the Comintern simply echoed Stalin's views. The Russian party became so powerful within the Comintern 'that its delegation often decided among themselves not only which tactics and strategies the Comintern would pursue but who to remove from and appoint to the Central Committees of fraternal parties' (Chase 2001, 18).

The pre-eminence of Moscow was built into the organization of the Comintern. To challenge the Comintern meant, in most cases, to exclude oneself from the Comintern. Those who tried to change the Comintern from within—and only Trotsky and Bukharin ever really had a chance, for only a Bolshevik with outstanding revolutionary credentials could even hope to make an impact—were soon expelled, and their revolutionary credentials denied, as Trotsky himself had been expelled from the CPSU at the end of 1927 and openly slandered thereafter.

Congresses of the Comintern were held annually at first, but then became less frequent. At these congresses, the communist parties had rights to definite numbers of delegates, depending chiefly on their size. The party of the first rank, with the largest number of delegates, was the Russian. The Germans, French and Czechs were in the second rank. The CPUSA—well organized, but relatively ineffective—was entitled to about 20 delegates to Comintern Congresses by the end of the 1920s, which put it in the third rank of communist parties.

The communist parties were expected regularly to send details of their own operations, and of the political situations they faced, to the ECCI. Many parties, including the Australian, did so. The Americans, for example, sent minutes of most of their conventions and Central Committee plenum meetings and kept up a regular flow of correspondence and telegrams. The CPUSA kept in regular touch with Moscow, having a number of leading comrades at any one time in Moscow working for the Comintern, in the Lenin School, and at Comintern Congresses. The main 'line' for each communist party to follow, however, was decided in Moscow, sometimes (depending on the party involved) by members of those parties based in or visiting Moscow before major congresses or meetings of their own parties. In a letter of 29 November 1935 to 'Dear Friends', 'Randolph' let the party know how it stood in Moscow and what the American comrades were being criticized for, but revealed much about the practical side of relations between the Comintern and its parties. In a section subtitled 'Organizational Questions', he wrote:

> The greybeard who manages me has really followed our work very closely. He reads all the material carefully, and we have almost daily meetings on various questions … [H]e pointed out that almost all our 'brati' are increasing their families considerably. Thus, he compared the Frogs [French], who, from March till now, have increased from forty odd thousand to about 75,000. (CALC, 515–1–3737)

The Comintern's role was as a 'general HQ', an arbiter of disputes, a setter of the political (and organizational) 'line' to be followed by member communist parties, a supporter and a punisher. This was a position which was easily and naturally accepted by most communist parties around the world. The disputes in which the Comintern intervened—or was asked to intervene—ranged from relatively trivial questions of personality to major questions of strategy, though trivial matters tended to be invested with a class significance beyond their real import, and strategic questions tended to display the hallmarks of personality clashes. And just as the Comintern could recognize affiliated parties, so it could abolish them: in 1937, the Comintern ordered the dissolution of the Communist Party of Poland, claiming infiltration by fascist agents.

The Comintern often overcame local communist opposition, or simply discounted local opinion, in drafting its decisions: to a large degree it was centrally driven. It may have had the assistance of national party officials to draft decisions for its sections, but they tended to be resident in Moscow for months if not years, and were likely to be detached from local conditions; they would thus have seen matters from the perspective of the centre and its imperatives. Yet the Comintern was not a monolith. Not everything done by the communists can be seen as being directed from Moscow (see Rees and Thorpe 1998). There is no doubt that there were disagreements and conflicts between the Comintern and some of its national sections. There were, for example, serious divisions between the Comintern agents in China and the Chinese Communist leadership more generally (Smith 2000). These would never be entirely resolved. Likewise, there were decisions taken by the Comintern that were not implemented, or only half-heartedly implemented, by some of these sections, taking advantage of ambiguity of expression, or distance in miles, from Moscow. But the Comintern always had the last word. It changed section leaderships, expelled some communist dissenters or made them undergo 'self-criticism' as a means of returning to good standing, and insisted on policies being implemented.

To be a communist meant to be affiliated to an officially recognized communist party; such recognition could only be conferred by the Comintern. The pre-eminence of the Russian party, and the generally recognized primary need for all communists to support the continued existence of the Soviet Union—that too was a condition *sine qua non* of being a communist at the time—meant that the parties of the Comintern could be put to use by the Russians to advance the interests of the Soviet state. Communists would not have put it in these terms, nor probably even thought of it in these terms. For them, supporting the Soviet state was a concomitant duty of support for the (world) working class; there was little sense of nationalism, or national betrayal, in making this connection. Communists supported the international working class, whose bastion was the USSR, and their hostility was directed against their own 'bourgeois' governments, who manipulated the working class daily. In their eyes, this was not a national struggle, but a class struggle. Many Russians, however, and especially the Soviet leadership, came to see it otherwise, and to see the defence of Russia, not the international working class, as the main point. This view culminated in Stalin's appeal to his people to save the Russian motherland (after he recovered from the shock of the German invasion in June 1941), and in the official Soviet view of the conflict of 1941–45 as the 'Great Patriotic War'. There are strong grounds for believing that the Soviet Union survived the German invasion because its own people fought for *Russia*, not for communism or the Soviet state.

Benefits and risks of Comintern affiliation

During the period examined by this book, the CPA was—for most practical purposes—marginal to Australian political and social life. Despite the terrible hardships of the Depression years, especially its worst years from late 1929 to late 1932 when unemployment peaked at 28% (Schedvin 1970, 47), it struggled to gain a membership of more than a couple of thousand dedicated communists and perhaps a few thousand sympathizers. While its leadership remained fairly constant throughout the 1930s, there seems to have been a high membership turnover; such was also the case in the CPUSA, the CPGB and other parties (Borkenau 1962, 367–70), where membership re-subscription campaigns became public relations embarrassments. The CPA, understandably for a small but highly articulate and motivated group, put a particular emphasis on strategic gains, especially on winning leadership positions in trade unions; in that aim it had some success. Union politics, however, are sometimes corrupt, and communists could also play this game. The showcase communist and Ironworkers' Association leader, Ernie Thornton, was eventually dethroned by the legal actions of a former Trotskyist, Laurie Short in the 1940s, after Thornton's methods were finally exposed (Short 1992).

Yet despite my assessment of its marginality, the CPA was also part of a worldwide, organized communist movement centred on, and encouraged by, another state, the USSR, lending it the aura of a serious threat to the established order. The CPA loomed larger in government calculations, and larger in the public imagination than its size and activities warranted, precisely because of its Soviet connections. The communists and the government believed that they were involved in mortal combat. It is easy, in retrospect, to belittle both sides and their conceptions of what they represented. Australian communists were only one influence in the trade union movement, and were far less influential in politics and society. Politically, the charge of communism soon became a potent negative factor, and the Australian Labor Party paid dearly for the association of any type of socialism with communism.

Members of the CPA were well aware that their close relationship with Moscow was interpreted by their political enemies as subservience, and that this could be, as indeed it was, used against them in political debate. In a 1927 article on 'Politics and Publicity', the Sydney-based philosopher and communist sympathizer Professor John Anderson described the daily press version of communism as follows: 'Communism is a criminal conspiracy, conducted under "orders from Moscow"'. The phrase itself was commonplace. The issues it raised were broached directly by communists themselves on a number of occasions, but especially in a report to the CPA conference by a representative who had attended the Comintern's Sixth Congress (see Document 53). Esmonde Higgins here explained the situation in a way that would have seemed perfectly fair to communists, given their understanding of the united struggle they faced and Russia's demonstrated leadership in it, but which allowed a much more cynical interpretation. On balance, the latter interpretation is better founded.

The control exerted by the CPSU over foreign communist parties was something that communists—in Australia and elsewhere—were keen to deny. Lance Sharkey, General Secretary of the Party, in his 1947 pamphlet *Australian communists and Soviet Russia* put the official view: that the CPA had never had relations with the Soviet Government, since the Comintern itself had no relation to the Soviet government. It was a necessary fiction, required to deny that the CPA was the agent of a foreign power. But it had always been a difficult fiction to maintain, given that Soviet diplomats often had Comintern connections, and that CPSU leaders sat on the ECCI.

The tone of the contacts between the Comintern and the CPA, and its other parties, was generally demanding, and suggests a relationship of superiority and command. Even, or perhaps especially, in its secret messages to its sections, the Comintern language is predominantly 'instruct' and 'must', and only occasionally 'propose' or 'request'. We shall see that the Comintern took a direct role in the major change of leadership in the CPA in 1929. But in February 1931, the following coded message was sent to Harry Pollitt of the CPGB in reference to one Comrade Horner: 'consider you sanction expelling him from Party

Secretariat' (PRO HW/17/71). It is doubtful that major leadership changes could be made by the 1930s without consultation with Moscow, and sometimes they were made at Moscow's behest.

Thorpe has examined in the British case the question which logically arises: whether the CPGB was essentially a tool of the Soviet government. Communist parties were deeply linked to Moscow, by virtue of their regular contacts, financial support, and the echoing of Moscow's positions, but they were not simply its servants. Thorpe argues that the truth is somewhere in the middle, and that although 'it would be foolish to argue that the CPGB was autonomous of, and still less independent' from the Comintern, 'it would be equally fallacious to see it simply as a tool of Moscow without a significant life of its own' (Thorpe 2000, 282). Much the same can be said of the CPA.

As with other communist parties, the CPA's connections with the Comintern and its wholehearted support for the Soviet Union were a double-edged sword. In some respects, and earlier rather than later, it gave the party enormous prestige and appeal. It sustained the party with moral, and unquantifiable financial, support. On the whole, however, the connection was a liability: the Party's ideological conformity with Moscow made its policies at times out of touch with the concerns of ordinary workers; and its clear praise for the workers' paradise of the USSR did not ring true to most workers, for the jaundiced accounts of the USSR given in the capitalist press were essentially correct. J.B. Miles' Political Report to the CPA's Eleventh Congress in 1935 is typical of the CPA's approach:

> I want to say a word about the Soviet Union. I have given a lot of attention to developments over there in the past. My study of the position recently reveals astounding progress. I feel enthused, I feel amazed, I feel happy, when I read about the reports to the XVIIth Congress. It is necessary that we give a good deal of time to popularise the achievements of the Soviet Union ... this is part of our work towards destroying capitalism in Australia ... We go before the workers full of confidence that the Soviet Union is a living example which can be followed by the toiling masses in Australia. (CAML 495–94–123)

The success of political ideas is sometimes related to whether they can be 'naturalized'. Jean Jaurès, for example, was highly successful in naturalizing socialism into the republican tradition in France (Lovell 1994). But communism was often seen as a 'Russian' idea; praise of the Soviet Union reinforced the stubbornness of this view. Indeed, there was little attempt to link communism to national traditions until communists had seen the success of fascists in doing so. From the mid-1930s, many communist parties made this an explicit part of their pitch to workers. The ninth Convention of the CPUSA (24–28 June 1936) had as its main slogan 'Communism is the 20th Century Americanism' (CALC 515–1–3964). Richard Dixon similarly declared to the Australian Party's Central Committee that 'We are the real Australians, the inheritors of everything that is good and decent in the history of Australia' (cited Macintyre 1998, 317). The claim was not widely accepted.

However valid the political issues raised by the CPA—and issues related to living standards, restrictive immigration, and the future of Aboriginal Australians were very important indeed—the Party was burdened, and the issues tainted, by the charge that they were simply doing Moscow's bidding. The CPA objected to the 'White Australia' policy championed by the major established parties, and it drew attention to the mistreatment of Aborigines. For the rest, however, its policies for Australian workers were far in advance of what was permitted in the USSR, and foreign communists visiting the USSR (including Australians) sometimes expressed—almost always in private—their disgust at unsafe, dirty and inappropriate working conditions in Soviet factories. Unable to influence Australia's political agenda, the CPA could act neither to extend the revolution to Australia, nor to influence Australian foreign policy in the Soviet Union's favour.

The decline and demise of the Comintern

There is an important sense in which, after about 1927, the Comintern became marginal both because it had ceased to organize world revolution and because it no longer served Soviet foreign policy very effectively. Communist parties may have had some minor successes as another arm of Soviet diplomacy, but the Soviet government, like governments everywhere, soon realized that government-to-government dealings were effectual ways to conduct business, and that popular movements, mass or otherwise, were not. E.H. Carr saw the 1935 Franco-Soviet pact as a turning-point, in that Moscow had begun to rely for its security on traditional means, not its network of foreign parties. Moscow would also learn later to its cost that communists who took power elsewhere were not always under its control, and could even establish alternative centres of gravity for communists around the world.

The particular failures, and the overall failure, of the Comintern must also be noted. The centralized control of communist strategy by Moscow led to some terrible setbacks, as in China in 1927 when the 'united front from above' was short-circuited by Kuomintang expulsion and then massacres of Chinese communists (Pontsov 1999), or in Germany in 1933 when the doctrine of 'social fascism' had communists fighting the German Social Democrats instead of Hitler, or in the Spanish civil war of 1936–39, when the Soviet People's Commissariat for Internal Affairs (NKVD) under the leadership of 'adviser' Aleksandr Orlov, weakened the republican effort by murdering non-communist socialists and anarchists (Beevor 2006, 286–293, 300–306, 478). In addition, the communist parties failed to be seen as a major alternative during one of world capitalism's greatest trials, the Great Depression, which lasted for much of the 1930s in its heartland, the United States. Communist parties in most of the industrialized

13

world remained politically marginal, and their entry into 'popular front' (i.e., anti-fascist) alliances had more to do with defending the Soviet Union than advancing the socialist revolution.

In a crucial respect, the failure of the Comintern and its national sections is not so surprising. Given their connections to the Soviet Union, these sections followed the line of the Soviet Communist Party as it successively repudiated Trotskyism, Zinovievism, and Bukharinism and made Stalin's position as leader virtually impregnable. The Russian style of debate and denunciation was generalized across the communist movement, raising barriers between workers and communists. Good, talented communists were hounded out of the movement for one 'deviation' or another, until national leaderships looked to Moscow before they made any significant move. (A telegram of March 1930 from Australia asks: 'DOES EKKI DENDORSE [sic] PRESENT CEC APPOINTED CONFERENCE ADVISE SIGNED BARRAS LOUGHRAN DOCKER SIMPSON SHARKEY WALKER SHEILEY (sic) ISAACS MOXON' (CAML 495–4–17).) It was harder to kill deviationists outside Russia, but GPU agents seemed to have succeeded in the case of some prominent Trotskyists. All this was described under the euphemism 'iron discipline'. The fortunes of the Soviet Union also involved the image of life in Russia. And though communists worked hard to convey the image of happy, prosperous Russians (and even fooled some non-communist visitors, including the Webbs, with modern-day 'Potemkin villages'), there was enough unadorned truth about Russia to ensure that workers in industrialized countries did not find it an attractive prospect. At a time when the Soviets should have been winning the propaganda war, during the capitalist economic crisis of the 1930s, they were hampered by problems in their own industrialization efforts. As one sympathetic economist, Alec Nove, explained, the year 1933 in the Soviet Union 'was the culmination of the most precipitous peacetime decline in living standards known in recorded history' (Nove 1972, 207), when workers' real earnings represented one-tenth of what they had been in 1926/27. 'Bourgeois propaganda' at the time—hysterical though it often was—probably didn't know the half of it.

One of the systemic problems of the Comintern was its attempt to parcel world development into overarching formulae. The most disastrous of these arose from the Sixth Congress in 1928, which declared the advent of the 'third period of the general crisis of world capitalism'. This included the notion that the 'third period' would 'inevitably give rise to a fresh era of imperialist wars among the imperialist States themselves; wars of the imperialist States against the USSR; wars of national liberation against imperialism; wars of imperialist intervention and gigantic class battles' (Degras 1960, 456). This is a period in which all the antagonisms of capitalism would be accentuated, leading to 'the most severe intensification of the general capitalist crisis' (457). Therefore, the 'main danger' to the communist parties, so the argument went, was the danger of 'Right opportunism', which soon included Trotskyism. The Comintern was used extensively for the campaign against Trotskyism in the international parties, essentially an attempt to root out any opposition to the leadership of the Russian Communist Party. In Russia, that could be achieved by purges, prisons and murder; elsewhere, it had to be done by 'argument' and expulsion.

The disputes within and ultimately the struggle for control over the Russian Communist Party found their echoes and parallels in the Comintern. Opposition was removed from within the Russian party first, and then elsewhere. All of this was done via the language of theoretical debate in which Lenin had earlier specialized, and there was—in hindsight—a bizarre quality to debates about theoretical positions which could mean the difference literally between life and death and which, after being used to defeat one set of opponents, could be discarded for a new position. The text obscured the pretext. Very few outside the inner circles of the ECCI could have known how this game was being played, even if they had inklings or concerns. Those parties remote from Moscow—including the Australians—were in this respect not much worse off than those closer. Delegates to the Sixth and Seventh Comintern Congresses began to understand, and were forced to take sides in, the Russian disputes. Local issues were taken up if they were grist to the larger Comintern mill. The highest virtue of communists was not independence of spirit and critical thought, but loyalty. Stalin made it very clear to the Americans in 1928 that, if they believed they could persist in their view of 'American exceptionalism' in spite of the Comintern, they would find they had no support when they got home (McDermott and Agnew 1996, 90–94).

The Communist International was dissolved by Stalin in 1943, as a concession to the other Allied powers and a gesture of good faith in their unity and mutual non-interference. Its life had been drained away since the Seventh Congress in 1935, when 76 member parties had met; there had been no subsequent congresses, and no major session of the ECCI. The Comintern had become largely redundant in the calculations of Stalin, who had not even attended the 1935 Congress. The Resolution of the Presidium of the ECCI proposing the dissolution of the Comintern of 15 May 1943 declared that the organizational form of the Comintern had 'outlived itself' (Claudin 1975, 40–43). After the Second World War the 'Cominform' was established, but the functions of the Comintern were delegated to the Department of Foreign Policy of the Central Committee of the CPSU. The work of directing the world's communist parties from Moscow went on much as before, though under different official auspices, and soon under very different conditions. The Chinese Communist Party under Mao Zedong took power in 1949, and chafed under Soviet direction until a final rupture between the two powers in 1963. In addition, the 1956 'revelations' about Stalin's errors made the loyalty of many individual communists and some communist parties themselves conditional.

What has added to the Comintern's aura is the importance which one of its founders, Trotsky, accorded it in his (already doomed) struggle for leadership of the Russian Communist Party in the mid-1920s, and his subsequent struggle for moral and organizational leadership of the international communist movement after he was expelled from the USSR in 1929. Trotsky continued the illusion that the Comintern was important, with his incisive analyses of communist failures in China, Germany, and Spain. To believe that had the Comintern followed Trotsky's policies in these events the outcomes would have been fundamentally different seems heroic, though in a strict sense it is unknowable. Trotsky further reinforced the myth of the importance of the international communist movement with his founding of the 'Fourth International' in September 1938.

The conspiracy view of history assumes that there is a plan to be implemented. The Comintern, even on a casual view of its decisions over the 23 years of its existence, had no such 'plan'. Its positions veered wildly from one extreme to another. Even if the formalized periodization of modern history into 'First', 'Second, and 'Third' periods by which it justified some of these swings is accepted—and that seemed absurd even to some communist critics at the time, including Trotsky—we nevertheless need to acknowledge that the Comintern was primarily *reactive* to events, and that much of the time it did not really know what should be done to advance its goal of world revolution. What became a substitute, of course, was the *raison d'état* of the Soviet Union. The Comintern's confusion seems apparent, for example, in some of the letters between Stalin and Comintern Secretary-General Dimitrov in the 1930s, in contradictory views on the proper approach in Spain (Dallin and Firsov 2000, 71–73), in the attempts to recreate the alliance between Chiang Kai-shek and the Chinese Communist Party (106), and in Stalin's generally low regard for the Comintern and its national sections. To see the Comintern as having a logical policy-making process is to mistake its propaganda image for reality. Yet whatever he thought of the value of the Comintern—and there are good reasons for believing he did not think highly of it—Stalin nevertheless wanted it under his control. Dallin and Firsov (2000) show that from the mid-1930s, at least, the Comintern was totally subordinated to Stalin's will.

Archival contributions to the history of communism

History—not the march of 'one damn thing after another', as Churchill is reputed to have said, but the selection, arrangement and construction of a narrative from the apparent confusion of events; history as the creative task in which historians are engaged—can be a highly contentious matter. Even where 'the facts' have been established (sometimes a difficult process in itself, notwithstanding an argument about whether facts may ever be separated from interpretation), historians may disagree over their relative importance, or may choose to highlight some facts over others to propose a particular case.

The history of communism as a whole spans roughly what Eric Hobsbawm (1994) described as the 'short' twentieth century: 1914–1991. It is a particularly contentious history both because communism was a political ideology and movement that took definite stands and divided communities, and because communists were often secretive about their activities and organizations. The cause of this secrecy (whether, for example, it was out of self-defence as the communists sometimes insisted, or for fear of losing support as their critics would argue) need not detain us here. But because communism is, in effect, now dead, some of this secrecy can be lifted. Making available the archives of the Comintern is an important step in this process.

The Comintern was intended by its founders as the world party of socialist revolution. Its sections, the communist parties of many countries around the world, were authorized as 'communist' by the Comintern, and in return for this recognition (the authority it bestowed upon them, and the subsidies from Moscow it usually entailed) they proclaimed their support for, and attempted to implement, the various decisions made by Comintern congresses and by its Executive Committee. The Comintern was both keenly aware of its 'world-historical' role, and highly bureaucratic in its structure and habits. Consequently, it collected and filed extensive records of its own meetings, correspondence with its sections, and records of their meetings (congresses, central committee meetings, central control commission meetings, and sometimes even local branch meetings).

After the Comintern's demise in 1943, its records were stored in an archive that by late 1991 had come to be called the Russian Centre for the Preservation and Study of Documents of Recent History (RTsKhIDNI). The failed Communist Party coup in Moscow in 1991 and the subsequent seizure by the Russian government of the property of the CPSU, including the archive, enabled these records to be put into the public domain. Since 1999 the RTsKhIDNI has become the Russian State Archive of Social and Political History (RGASPI). RGASPI has been cooperating with scholars, libraries and publishing houses around the world in disseminating much of this material, which contains records of many communist parties, and amounts to perhaps 20 million documents. The major products of this initiative so far have included: a number of volumes in a projected multi-volume series entitled 'Annals of Communism' published by Yale University Press; the deposit of the very extensive archive of the Communist Party of the USA in the Library of Congress in Washington, DC, which was opened to the public in 2000; and the current issuing, by RGASPI and the microfilm publisher IDC, of the Comintern archives on nearly 12,000 microfiches.

The Comintern Archive at the ADFA Library (CAAL), on microfilm, is also part of this process of making the Comintern archives more accessible.

During the 1920s and 1930s, Australian communist leaders went to Moscow to attend Comintern conferences and report on the prospects for revolution in Australia. The CPA submitted reports on its conferences and Central Committee meetings to the ECCI and the Anglo-American Secretariat. Local leadership disputes were referred to Moscow, and a great deal of advice and some 'orders' came the other way. On all these matters CAAL has much to tell us. It reminds us, in particular, of the difficulties of communicating over such long distances in the days before faxes, email and jumbo jets. Australians were stationed in Moscow for varying periods of time (often on their way to conferences or at the Lenin School), but because of the length of time away from Australia their usefulness in reporting on party matters, or helping Comintern leaders to resolve antipodean disputes that were put before them—sometimes by telegram—was limited. The Comintern, for its part, sent occasional representatives to Australia and New Zealand, the most significant of whom (Herbert Moore) stayed for over a year to reorganize the CPA.

All the Comintern's archives are organized in a series of collections and stored in folders, with individual designations based on a triple classification of *fond*, *opis*, and *delo*. The separate collections (*fondy*), and sub-collections, or inventories (*opisi*) are numbered. Within the sub-collections are numerous (sometimes hundreds of) *dela*, translated as 'files' or 'folders'. Some *dela* contain only a few pages, others contain several hundred. Many of the documents are in English, with Russian (and other) translations. Many deal with routine matters, or are drafts of documents finally (and sometimes publicly) proclaimed. Some documents are repeated. Some documents are designated 'Secret', 'Most Secret', or 'Confidential', though it is not easy to see in all cases why such a designation was made. The coverage can also be patchy. In general, records in CAAL from the earlier period (especially the 1920s) are fuller than those from the 1930s; towards the end of the 1930s there is not much available. If this is the case in the materials dealing with Australia, it is also the case in materials we have examined in Washington, DC, concerning the Communist Party of the USA. A key difference between the two archives, apart from the massive size of the CPUSA Archive, is that there is little in CAAL from individual branches of the CPA. None of these observations diminishes the fact that CAAL provides a new avenue to explore the early history of the CPA (and not just its relations with Moscow, on which the selections in this work focus), but they do demonstrate the need to draw on diverse types of source materials in studying the complex and multi-dimensional story of the early CPA.

The documents in CAAL encompass and extend the archival material from the Comintern already available at the Mitchell Library in Sydney, brought to

Australia in 1990 by Barbara Curthoys. The additional material in CAAL includes directives from Moscow in 1926–27, materials on the internal situation of the party (which was, at times, unsettled), Comintern resolutions on the 'Australian question', and early correspondence about the formation of the CPA. There is a further 250 pages from the period 1948–52 (postdating the end of the Comintern) on the CPA and youth organizations in Australia. Large though the CAAL collection may be, it does not seem to be complete; some documents, for example, refer to others that cannot be found, or to attachments that are missing.

The CAAL documents supplement existing archival materials on the CPA available in the Normington-Rawling Collection held at the Noel Butlin Archive Centre at The Australian National University, and other collections described elsewhere (Symons, Wells and Macintyre 1994; Symons 2002). The Oral History project stored at the National Library of Australia in Canberra also provides valuable materials for reconstructing the early period of Australian communism from reminiscences of CPA leaders and members. We are sure that as further Comintern documents come to light the story of the CPA will gain even more interest and complexity.

It may be appealing to agitate for 'archival parity', and to insist that we should not use the Soviet archives until all the Western archives for a similar period are available. But all history must be constructed on the evidence available, and the evidence is rarely, if ever, complete. Historical writing is thus intrinsically selective. The essential ingredient is good judgement in the use of available evidence: something that is fundamental to the way we do our work as scholars. We have been selective in this work, but not in order to support some preconceived opinions. Our selections have been representative of the material in the archive that sheds light on the relations between the Comintern and the CPA. Because the CAAL material is more extensive on the earlier period, for example, that is where our emphasis also lies.

Secrecy and misinformation were characteristic of all states during the Cold War, and can be explained in part as a consequence of that period of 'hostilities'. But the secrecy of the communist system was systemic: there was no civil society to act as a countervailing power against the state, to question secrecy. Freedom of information legislation in many Western states has allowed some access to security files; government confrontation with security services has led to the destruction of many files; and the press is intermittently in hot pursuit of security scandals. The veil of secrecy in former communist states is being lifted both more gradually and less systematically, and it still takes considerable courage to reveal some communist secrets. Through the defectors Ken Alibek and Vasili Mitrokhin we have had some interesting glimpses. From the former we have discovered, for example, that despite signing a treaty in 1972 with the United States for banning bioweapons, the Soviets continued a secret and large program of offensive biological warfare (Alibek 1999). From the latter, we have an idea of the extent of Soviet espionage in the West (Andrew and Mitrokhin 1999).

It should also be noted that Western archives provide an interesting perspective on communism during this period, with the Australian Archives providing—in the usual way—access to classified documents after 30 years. Here we learn of police and other surveillance over communists, and actions against them. On the highly secret matters of Cold War intelligence, some Western sources have become available in recent years, even on the World Wide Web. Some of the Venona decrypts which prove Soviet spying against Australia, Britain and the United States in the mid- to late-1940s, were published in 1995 (at www.nsa.gov/docs/venona/). Furthermore, decrypts of Comintern radio traffic to stations in Europe in the 1930s are now available at the Public Record Office in London (in their 'HW 17' series), giving a much better idea of the pattern of the Comintern's relations with its parties. In the United Kingdom, the archives of MI5, the Security Service branch of British state intelligence, are also being released to The National Archives, thus far covering the period up to 1957 (www.mi5.gov.uk/output/Page233.html).

The collapse of communism, and opening of some of its archives, gives us a better chance to see how Soviet communism worked internally (especially its surveillance operations), and how it conducted its foreign relations (directly with foreign governments, through its network of communist parties, and through 'front' organizations). It also gives us a chance to re-evaluate certain issues that have had to be left open until now because of inadequate evidence.

The communists were great bureaucratic collectors; little was discarded. KGB archives even contain those letters and poems—sent but never delivered—from political prisoners to Stalin, protesting their innocence. Much, therefore, can be found out about what happened in these systems from the archives. There was, of course, some attempt in the closing days of the East European communist regimes to destroy files that might incriminate serving state functionaries—especially in the former German Democratic Republic, which had extensive surveillance operations of both its own populations and elsewhere (Funder 2002)—but the scale of the archives was too great. What remains of these archives, and that seems to be the bulk of them, enables us to get a more accurate picture of a system where secrecy was paramount.

Opening the archives has meant a great deal more light being shed on particular parties. The practical difficulties of accessing Comintern documents in Moscow (Taylor 1993) have been reduced by the wider dissemination of parts of the RGASPI collection to various libraries elsewhere. Those documents that concern the CPUSA, lodged in the Library of Congress, have been examined and some published by Harvey Klehr and his colleagues through the 'Annals of Communism' series. Klehr's views about the US communists as 'creatures' of the

Soviet Union are strong but well documented. The opening of the RGASPI archives in particular has led to interesting contributions on the American Communist Party, already noted, on the British Communist Party (Thorpe 2000), on the Chinese Communist Party in the 1920s (Pontsov 1999; Smith 2000), and on the relationship between Dimitrov, last Secretary of the Comintern, and Stalin (Dallin and Firsov 2000). This book adds another part to this mosaic of new information, and its source material on microfilm is now available on open access at the ADFA Library.

Not surprisingly, more information often means more disagreement. When *The Black Book of Communism*, which seeks to document the crimes of communism, was first published in French in 1997, it created a considerable stir in academic circles. Its appearance has been paralleled by further, and still inconclusive, debates between Robert Conquest and others about the number of deaths in the Soviet prison camps (the 'gulag' made known, and notorious, by Alexander Solzhenitsyn). In one respect at least the *Black Book* goes too far: it claims that 'All Communist parties, including the legally constituted ones in democratic countries, possessed a secret military wing that made occasional public appearances' (Courtois 1999, 282, 286). While this may have been true of West European communist parties, we can find no evidence of it in Australia (despite the semi-public presence of threatening right-wing militias, including the New Guard, in the early 1930s, and communist concern at that time about the imminent threat of illegality (495–94–95)).

While we have concentrated on throwing light on the relationship between the Comintern and the CPA in our search of the Comintern archives, our efforts do not exhaust all that may be gleaned from this source. There may be additional theses that suggest themselves in a perusal of all the documents, but we do not believe that our theses can be controverted by appeal to the entire archive. We have tried to be as fair as possible in our selections, and that fairness can be tested by consulting the archives themselves.

Conclusion

Like all Communist Parties, the CPA's history is anchored in developments in the international communist movement, with its campaigns, debates, and splits. A strong international connection defined from the very beginning what was new about the communist movement. Nevertheless, the relationship between the CPA and the Comintern, though vital, was not always an easy or straightforward one, as we shall see in the next essay. The CAAL documents show us that during the mid-1920s, for example, the CPA had a relative autonomy from the Comintern chiefly by virtue of poor communications. They also show that the CPA was poorly organized, small, and perhaps faltering, and the influence of the Comintern may have been decisive in its survival through this period. The CPA looked for and accepted the Comintern's advice, even if it could not always successfully act on it. After 1929, however, there was a change in the relationship, brought about in part by changes in the Comintern's leadership, in the organization of the CPA itself, and by the installation of the Comintern's representative in the Party. The notion that Comintern instructions had to be obeyed became axiomatic.

The link between anti-capitalism and pro-Sovietism at first gave communists a *raison d'être* and a burst of enthusiasm, as they established communist parties throughout the world and bound themselves to the 21 conditions of the Communist International; it sustained many of them throughout their political careers; but it also caused them increasing problems as time wore on. The importance of the link is underlined by the fact that the most important dates for communists were generally those in the international communist calendar. In the West, the link became a political liability, with the fear that a communist victory would mean a Soviet-style (if not Soviet-dominated) regime. Communists were often commanded to support the policies of the Soviet state, irrespective of whether such support was politically appropriate in a given country, and even if it meant espionage. Anti-capitalism became subordinated to pro-Sovietism.

There are some things, however, that the CAAL documents cannot tell us. They are silent on the intensely personal side of the commitment that communists made to the cause of world revolution. We may catch glimpses of it, especially in reports of high membership turnover. But the decision to accept a 'line' from Moscow with which one disagreed, or to be economical with the truth in the interests of solidarity with Moscow, required a level of naïveté or self-deception that is hard to credit in long-term activists. Since the collapse of communism in 1989–91, it has become almost customary for Australian communists to present their membership of the Party as well meaning, and their experience as having a human richness of idealism, yearning and suffering (Inglis 1995; Smith 1985). But this approach tends to obscure the fact that it was their serious intention to make the most far-reaching social and political changes to liberal democracy based on a theory that was flawed, and that they held up as a model a regime that was systematically brutal and inhuman.

It does not much help to insist, as many former communists do, that they not only had good intentions, but were also committed and idealistic. This seems to be a comfort only to them. With regard to Australian communists, Eric Aarons urges us to 'appreciate the depth of their idealism and their commitment to their socialist dream' (Aarons 1993, 3). Bernie Taft asserts that the CPA 'had attracted some of the most idealistic and selfless people in our society' (Taft 1994, 305), while making a sharp distinction between the 'apparatchiks' and the exemplary character 'of tens of thousands of ordinary communists' (Taft 1994, 2). Ric Throssell makes a similar point about the novelist Katharine Susannah Prichard: 'My mother was proud of her dedication to the party but in everything she did she had been self-sacrificing, loving, forgiving, indomitably courageous in her life-long commitment to socialism' (Throssell 1997, 365). Humphrey McQueen (1997, 184) declares that the 'vast majority' of communists in Australia 'were selfless, generous and decent'.

The jury is still out on whether the communist experiment was a historical detour for socialism and, if so, whether socialism has been so compromised that it will never recover. Meanwhile, we are left to ponder over the Party experience. John Sendy, who joined the CPA in 1942, asked: 'How then do good idealistic people become tyrants who will stop at nothing?' (Sendy 1997, 43). We can only wonder at the extent of Moscow's authority that it could turn strong, independently-minded people struggling for human dignity into its creatures: obeying every twist and turn from Moscow; abasing themselves in rituals of self-criticism; denying the plain truth. That experience, akin to a religious faith, is one of the fascinating sub-texts of the Comintern documents.

The CPA and the Comintern: from loyalty to subservience

David W. Lovell

The documentary material presented in this book, some of it previously unavailable, and most of it not widely available, adds a vital dimension to the story of the pre-Second World War CPA. The main lines of this period are well known to scholars who work in this field, but this book is significant because it shows that the Comintern exercised a very important, and at some points a decisive, sway over the CPA. The book's title itself may need some explanation. The Party throughout the period 1920–1940 was 'unswervingly loyal' to the Comintern and the Soviet Union—that was what made it a *communist* party—even if the phrase itself was used first by the CPA leadership only in 1929. At the end of the Ninth Conference in December 1929 at which there had been a major change in leadership supported by the Comintern, the victors telegraphed to the Secretary of the Comintern: 'annual conference greets comintern declares unswerving loyalty new line' (CAML 495–94–53). At the first Plenum of the new Central Committee in June the next year, greetings were sent to the Comintern along with a repeated declaration of 'unswerving loyalty' (495–94–61). Loyalty is a complex matter; it should not be thought that in this context it meant—or always meant—blind obedience. From its origins until the end of 1929, the political line and organizational instructions coming from the Comintern in Moscow were considered and sometimes robustly debated, even if they were rarely challenged directly. After the Ninth Conference, however, there was a major change: the CPA was much more finely attuned to the wishes of the Comintern, and twisted and turned at its behest. The price of dissent was now a humiliating 'self-criticism', or even expulsion. Difficult though it may be for us to appreciate, expulsions were a genuinely feared punishment, even if for the vast majority of those communists outside the Soviet Union the stakes were not life-or-death. After 1929, to be sure, some decisions handed down from above caused consternation and confusion, but there was no sense in which they could any longer be genuinely debated within the Party.

It is not surprising that the CPA's loyalty to communism was at first, and quite readily, expressed as loyalty to the Comintern. But this loyalty turned into a slavish subordination to its decisions: decisions about what communist policy was, and who was and was not a 'communist'. Such decisions were increasingly based on narrow calculations about what was best for the Soviet state, and—since that state was instantly identified with its leadership—what was best for Stalin and whichever group of henchmen was then in his favour. It is a story that would have been difficult, and perhaps impossible, to predict in 1917. The main elements in that story are outlined in this essay.

The emergence of communism in Australia

Communism as an ideology was not entirely 'foreign' to Australia. To a very large extent Australia was an outpost of Europe on the 'great south land', and was undertaking an experiment with European forms of constitutionalism, conservatism, republicanism, and socialism. While claims to local ideological traditions in all these areas of political thought have been made, they are not strong: it is much more a case of 'liberalism in Australia' than 'Australian liberalism', and *mutatis mutandis* for other political ideas. Australia, for example, had a long tradition of socialist groups, but Albert Métin (another of the Europeans who came to see this great experiment in action) described it as a 'socialism without doctrines'. Like similar groups elsewhere, socialists in Australia were characteristically fractious and divided on a number of issues, though the influence of Marxism was much less pronounced than in Europe, and the existence of a Labor Party (with a 'socialist objective') created additional complications. The Labor Party had held government in the states, and at the national level its leader J.C. Watson became the first Labor Prime Minister of any country in the world—briefly—in 1904. Before and during the First World War, the Industrial Workers of the World gained influence and notoriety as the most militant of the anti-capitalist groups, to such an extent that they were banned in 1916 on trumped up charges. The Russian Revolution, erupting in 1917, excited curiosity (and fear) about Russia and Bolshevism. Some Australian socialists, most prominently R.S. Ross of the Victorian Socialist Party (Farrell 1981), resisted the insurrectionary message, insisting that Australia was not Russia. But the image of an apparently successful socialist revolution—or, at the very least, of the successful capture of state power—led many socialists to try to create a communist party and to be associated with the Soviet state.

Given the Anglo-Irish roots of Australia's European population, and the xenophobia of that population (particularly the working class), as demonstrated by the official 'White Australia' immigration policy, communism was widely seen as a 'foreign' phenomenon, particularly a Russian phenomenon. Communism may have been as 'foreign' as most other complex political ideas then in circulation in Australia, but it was unusual for two reasons: first, it was linked very closely with distinctively Russian ideas of organization, ideas that Lenin had derived directly from the *Zemlia i volia* ('Land and freedom' party) of the 1870s (Lovell 1984, 145), the like of which were uncharacteristic not just of Australia but also of the socialist movement in general; second, it introduced a style of political debate which we would now recognize as 'ideological', but whose circularity, impenetrability, and recourse from rational argument to class insult was at once novel, frustrating, and immensely powerful.

It would be misleading to consider the 'foreignness' of Bolshevism as consisting chiefly in its export from Russia by Russians. Yet Russians in Australia did play a role in its early transmission, and they were amongst its earliest enthusiasts in the Russian diaspora around the world. There had been Russians in Australia in moderately large numbers since 1905, many of them located in Queensland (perhaps their first Australian port of call), who had been exiled by Tsarism. Some were socialists, such as Nikolai Ilin, who arrived in Queensland in 1910 (Govor 2001, 87–8). Few were revolutionaries, and even fewer Bolsheviks. Whatever their views, they seem to have been heartened by the overthrow of Tsarism in March 1917, and impressed by the resolution of the Bolsheviks. Many returned home within the first few years after the Revolution. (A despatch from Australia's Governor-General to the Colonial Office in London in February 1921, for example, asks for advice about a group of 700 Russians who wanted to return to Russia but had not the means (PRO, CO 418/205).) It was a similar story with Russian exiles elsewhere in the world.

Some of those Russians who remained in Australia came to public notice in the 'Red Flag' disturbances of March 1919, when a demonstration of workers in Brisbane was attacked by soldiers (Evans 1988). Some of them used their rapidly acquired knowledge of Bolshevism and of Australia to claim special status. Petr Simonov (or 'Peter Simonoff', as his name was often spelt) was proposed by the Bolsheviks as Soviet consul to Australia, but his accreditation was not accepted by the Australian government. Responding to the heightened interest in Russia, Simonov wrote a book intended for Australians about the history of Russia. Practically none of it was about the Revolution as such. He argued that the 'Russian people are naturally inclined towards communism', and cautioned against the destruction of socialism by 'outside force' (Simonoff 1919), a reference to the Allied blockade. Prosecuted for incendiary speeches extolling the Bolshevik way, Simonov ultimately left Australia in 1921. Aleksandr Zuzenko—who will feature in Section 1 of this book—had also been in Australia for some time (since 1911), and acted as an agent of the Comintern in the early period of the CPA's development. He was present, and may have played a key unifying role, at the conference of 15–16 July 1922 which finally united the warring CPA factions. He was deported from Australia in 1919 after the 'Red Flag' riots, and again in September 1922 after fulfilling at least part of his Comintern mission.

The ideological style of communist argumentation adapted itself quite neatly to political debate in general. At first the Australian socialists, although accustomed to vigorous debates, disliked the centralizing and authoritative tone of the communist style. 'Proof by quotation', from the works of Marx, Engels, Lenin, and later Stalin, became the order of the day, which is why Stalin rushed to appropriate Lenin in publishing his *Fundamentals of Leninism* shortly after Lenin's death in 1924. There were few issues about which one could freely debate and learn; rather, there were answers that had to be accepted and applied. The rather too discursive CPA was pulled into line by Herbert Moore in the early 1930s. Sent by Moscow, Moore soon changed the party's 'education' program into a 'training' program. Ideological conformity was encouraged, and dissent met with threats of expulsion. Disputes among the leadership became highly charged, and though seeming to turn on tactical or non-fundamental issues, polarized supporters into what came to be seen as 'class' formations. This was a long way from the mood of the pre- and post-war socialists, and few of them survived in the communist movement through the 1930s. One survivor, Guido Baracchi—an intellectual and thus suspected dilettante and possible class enemy—moved in and out of the party during the 1920s and '30s, until he was finally expelled in 1940.

To become adept at the communist style, Australian communists participated in training provided by the Soviets through the International Lenin School, especially during the 1930s, and were annoyed when they believed they were being left out of invitations to the School (Document 52). Aspiring leaders went to such schools. Not everything went smoothly, however, and the expectations of different cultures did not always mesh with Leninist norms. The Anglo-Americans sometimes had problems with what they described as the 'police methods' of the administration, and some were disappointed with Soviet reality (despite their general understanding of the adverse conditions that the Soviets confronted). But it was the Russians' response to criticism that was particularly telling. Skorobogatykh (nd, 9) relates that one of the Soviet leaders of the English speaking students of the Lenin School declared: 'There are traces in the group of the influence of social-democracy, for example the question "Why?"' From the American Comintern archives comes another interesting example, a letter of 27 May 1936, from 'the collective of Sector 'D'', referring to the expulsion of an American, Karl Meredith, from the Lenin School. It appears that Meredith:

> did not feel fully at home in the USSR ... By a mechanical, typically bourgeois method of comparison of figures, he repeatedly stressed the erroneous conclusion that the standard of living in USSR is lower than in the USA. (CALC 515–1–3968)

The CPA's relationship with Moscow

It is worth dwelling on a number of aspects of the relationship between the CPA and Moscow. During the 'short twentieth century', it was a commonplace of communist politicians to downplay this relationship, and of conservative politicians to emphasize it. We know that it was a major issue in the United States, where the CPUSA insisted that it was a home-grown phenomenon, responding to local needs, against charges—especially through the 1950s—that it was acting at the behest of the Soviets. It is a matter now put beyond doubt by the opening of the Comintern's archives that in large measure the CPUSA was acting as a local advocate for the Soviet state. Indeed, it was one of the most slavish of all the Western communist parties to Moscow's 'line'. The CPGB, which faced similar problems to the CPA—internally, with organizational shortcomings and externally, in trying to win workers away from the established Labour Party—also took its directions from Moscow.

What do the Comintern's archives tell us about the Australian party? We already know that in Australia (as elsewhere), the formation of the Communist Party in 1920 and its internal disputes were arbitrated by the Comintern. It is clear that the Australian party, once it had been recognized by the Comintern, was not just an affiliate, but the 'Australian section' of a world party, and the Congress and Executive of the Comintern had, as Macintyre rightly puts it, 'absolute power over every constituent organisation' (Macintyre 1998, 76). Herbert Moore, the Comintern agent who reorganized the Party—introducing especially the technique of 'self-criticism' as a way of stamping out differences—was later expelled from the CPUSA suspected of being an agent for anti-communist organizations (Macintyre 1998, 171). Whether this was because Moore was a police agent, or had developed political differences, is not clear. The CPA faithfully followed the Soviet line through the excruciating twists of the German-Soviet Nonaggression Pact in 1939, and then its entry into the Second World War. Macintyre writes of its 'bewildered loyalty', and its relative cohesion, in contrast to the mass resignations from the British Communist Party, for example. Webb (1954, 6) explained that during the first few months of the Second World War, 'the Party's efforts to follow the swift and frequent zig-zags of Russian policy made it comical, ineffectual, and mildly seditious'.

'Moscow gold'

How communist parties were funded became an issue in many countries, sometimes precipitated by the indiscretions or bragging of communists themselves. For whom did these parties actually work: for Moscow, or for their own working class? In England, for example, the Home Secretary was often asked in Parliament in the early 1920s about the activities and funding of 'Bolshevist agents', but kept his public pronouncements circumspect and reiterated his view of what the law allowed. In the House of Commons on 13 July 1921 John Baird, the Parliamentary Under-Secretary of State for the Home Office, declared: 'I do not know the total amount of money introduced from abroad to subsidise the Communist agitation. In the present state of the law it is not a criminal offence to introduce foreign money for the purpose of such agitation' (Parliamentary Debates, Commons, vol. 144). Indeed, the British authorities insisted that they would prosecute agitators (and deport aliens) only where they incited violence. Baird had earlier that year given some indication that the British government was watching carefully the activities of the communists—or 'Bolshevists', as they were usually called (probably to stress their 'foreign-ness')—and that the Russian Trade Agreement signed in 1921 was dedicated in part to stopping them. On 20 April 1921, Baird declared:

> My attention is constantly directed to the Bolshevist propaganda in this country. It falls under three heads: the payment of salaries to Communist officials, ranging from £5 to £10 per week, subsidies to the extremist Press, and the free distribution of revolutionary literature. An accurate estimate of the amount spent cannot be given, but in December last a Bolshevist agent stated that it exceeded £23,000 a month ... There is evidence that some, at any rate, of the money came direct from the Moscow Government, but that was before the signing of the Trade Agreement [the preamble of which declared that the propaganda would cease]. (Parliamentary Debates, Commons, vol. 140)

There is no doubt that Moscow funded most, if not all, communist parties to some extent. It is difficult to say in every instance what form this support took (whether in cash or in kind), and how significant it was for the particular party. In the early years of the Comintern, the amounts seem to have been considerable, totalling millions of roubles (McDermott and Agnew 1996, 21–22). In the American case, the support seems to have been substantial and long-term, increasing as a proportion of the party's total budget as it lost members and influence in the 1970s and '80s (Klehr, Haynes and Anderson 1998; Draper 2003b, 202–209). The reaction to this funding also seems to differ according to the case. The British government clearly did not like it, and tried to stop it, but for the American government the sore point was that communist agitation was 'foreign' and thus 'un-American'. This position would ultimately be formalized by the investigations, and aspersions, of the House Un-American Activities Committee (HUAC) in the 1940s and '50s, but it is a theme that pervades American discussions of communism. American communists themselves confirmed the importance of such a critique by insisting—against the truth, as we now know—that American communism was indigenous, self-supporting, and self-directed. That the HUAC was staffed by what the UPI journalist, and later political aide and historian, George Reedy described as 'the worst collection of people that have ever been assembled in the entire history of American politics', does not diminish the fact that American communism was largely a Soviet creature.

CPUSA leader Earl Browder, for example, gave false testimony before the Dies Committee of the US Congress in late 1939. In a confidential letter of 2 October 1939, to the Secretariat of the ECCI, Pat Toohey wrote: 'The Committee sought to prove that the CP is a branch of Moscow, that it is financed by Moscow ... that the CP is an agent of a "foreign principal", i.e. Moscow and the Comintern' (CALC 515–1–4084). The Committee brought in a former CPUSA member, Ben Gitlow—'stool-pigeon and provocateur'—who testified that from 1922–29, the Comintern sent to the CPUSA $US100,000 to $US150,000 yearly and made other claims of subsidies to the *Daily Worker* and other publications. Toohey describes this as 'lies', but though the amounts may be exaggerated, they were not impossible. (In a letter of 10 January 1924, the Executive Secretary of the US party, Ruthenberg, asked Moscow for a subsidy of $64,000 (CALC 515–1–297).) Indeed, the evidence suggests that the CPUSA would have collapsed, or ceased most of its activities—at various points in its history—without Comintern subsidies.

As for Australia, there is little evidence of direct, annual funding of the CPA by Moscow in the documents in CAAL, and it may be that such funding did not happen. There is certainly evidence that money was requested by those who helped to establish the CPA (Document 4), and at the end of one of the documents in this collection (Document 5) occurs the following paragraph (not included in the collection, but relevant here):

> 3. Please reconsider the question of financial support to the Communist daily paper in America. The amount of money appropriated for this purpose—twenty-five thousand dollars—is much too small. (495–94–127)

Sums of money—so-called 'Moscow gold'—were given to the Australian communists. Macintyre suggests that this began in about 1923 (Macintyre 1998, 148), but the CAAL documents indicate that Zuzenko and Freeman planned to bring a substantial amount in 1921–22, though how much they delivered in the end is not clear. The requirements of the Australian communists, not to mention the perceived strategic importance of Australia to the world revolution, were markedly less than the Americans'. There was no daily newspaper to support at first, nor a large organization; for example, the Party's main paper, *The Workers' Weekly*, appeared three times a week in the 1930s, but *The Red Star* in Western Australia was weekly for the period we are examining. There were times when no-one seems to have been a full-time, paid employee of the CPA, and when there was the pay was worse than that of an ordinary worker. As Macintyre (1998, 356) relates, the Party president's pay in 1939 was below the level of the basic wage.

The documents in CAAL do not give us a sense of the scale of 'Moscow gold'. Given our current level of knowledge, however, the scale of funds was probably rather small. The documents tell us that the CPA was constantly in need of money, and it could not properly fund the small number of full-time party workers it had on its staff. The state of our knowledge on this score is summarized by Macintyre (1998, 356–57).

If there is no evidence of regular payments, occasional glimpses are nevertheless given of individual requests. On 29 March 1936, for example, Mason (the CPA's representative to the Comintern) wrote to Comrade Marty that he had been instructed by the Political Bureau to ask the ECCI for a grant of £5000:

'My fare took most of the cash.' He explained that if more students and delegates came to Moscow, more cash would be needed (495–14–302). Australian Military Intelligence agents in the 1930s seemed to believe that the Party received £500 per year from Moscow, and that this was only a small proportion of its operating costs (Cain 1983, 253). It may reasonably be assumed that when Australian communists went to the Soviet Union for congresses or study tours, their in-country expenses were paid by the CPSU.

The question of Moscow funding for the CPA arose once again in the 1949 Royal Commission of inquiry into the Party (in the state of Victoria, which empowered the Royal Commission) and its relations with the Comintern. The Royal Commissioner, Sir Charles Lowe, concluded that the CPA had to comply with all decisions of the Comintern; he cited the importance of the Comintern in unifying the original party in the 1920s, and its 1929 intervention on behalf of Moxon and Sharkey against the rest of the Central Executive Committee (Victoria 1950, 33–36). He surveyed the evidence of the Comintern imposing a range of policies on the CPA (including: on the united front with the ALP; on conscription; and on the League of Nations); and also discussed the communists' reaction to the Second World War, with the CPA at first supporting the war, then opposing it at the direction of the Comintern, and then in 1941 supporting it again. Commissioner Lowe talks of the various ways of 'harmonising the CPA's policy with the Comintern' (Victoria 1950, 37). He noted that large amounts of money had passed through Party accounts, many thousands of pounds that were not sufficiently explained in the evidence. Nevertheless his 21st finding states that 'The funds of the Party come from various local sources and there is no evidence of funds coming from overseas.' This may be considered too benign an account of the true situation, but the evidence at the time would allow the Commissioner to venture safely no further.

The fact that we cannot tell precisely how much money was sent by Moscow to Australia does not mean that the Australians did not try to get as much as possible (Skorobogatykh nd, 6–7), or that the Comintern was not organized to respond to such requests. At the broadest level, the Comintern's International Control Commission spent more than three-quarters of a million US dollars per year, more than half of that subsidizing publications by foreign communist parties. In the period 1928–34 the Comintern spent over seven million US dollars by its own figures (Skorobogatykh nd, 7). There is substantial evidence from decrypts of Comintern radio messages that the Comintern was paying a quarterly subsidy of tens of thousands of Swiss francs to many European communist parties (PRO HW/17/1, HW/17/4).

The debate on whether or not Moscow subsidized communist parties abroad should have ended long ago: the documentary evidence is now overwhelming. Klehr, Haynes and Firsov (1995, 22–25) discuss the evidence in the case of the

CPUSA; Thorpe (2000) puts an end to any doubt about the funds given to the CPGB. The genuine debate is over what this subsidization really meant. It cannot be said that financial support equals automatic control of the parties. What can defensibly be said is that communist parties continued to exist where sometimes they might have failed for want of funds; and that they probably had more influence by virtue of their press and presence than they might otherwise have had.

Moscow's frustration

It seems likely that the Comintern expected its recommendations, advice, instructions and 'demands' to be carried out by its sections, in the spirit of working for one cause: not Soviet success, as such, but the historically imminent victory of the world working class. Its expectations were not always met. The CAAL documents reveal Moscow's almost constant sense of frustration at Communist Party activity in Australia.

In this respect, there are some instructive comparisons to be made between Comintern relations with the CPUSA and the CPA. As with the American party, the Comintern sent to Australia many schoolmasterly 'not good enough' report cards from its headquarters. The American communists were well organized, but relatively small and ineffective; the Australian party was poorly organized, as well as relatively small and ineffective.

Both parties had been formed from amalgamations of previous socialist groups who wanted to be allied to the new revolution in Russia. In both cases, these amalgamations were not easily achieved, and for some years there were personal and other disputes between the members—though rarely programmatic differences, as Moscow kept noting, with annoyance—which made building a united and, more importantly, effective communist party difficult. For example, in a resolution of the ECCI on 8 August 1920, both communist parties in America were told to unite, though the date for completion of this task was extended from 20 September 1920 to 1 January 1921 (CALC 515–1–17). Even as late as 1928, a Comintern 'Resolution on the American Question' declared 'categorically that the resumption of factional struggle within the American Party will be a crime against the Party and the International, and will be met by the expulsion of those responsible from the Party' (CALC 515–1–1227).

Furthermore, both parties had great difficulties making practical headway in winning the workers for communism and becoming a mass party. The task in the United States may have been party building, as in Australia, but the situation was in many respects quite different. The American party, like the American labour movement, was divided between an elite of native born, English speaking workers and a large number of foreign-born, poorly-paid workers whose command of English was not good. How to connect the two was a major challenge. The Americans' first response was to have a type of decentralized and federated party, but this led to problems, and seems never to have been accepted in Moscow. Unity and centralization were the key concepts. Even by the early 1930s these had not been fully achieved. The party had a daily (English) newspaper, the *Daily Worker*, but it also had eight or more foreign-language papers as well as some foreign-language weekly or monthly journals (CALC 515–1–2621).

A major problem for the Comintern was this: how to wean the workers of developed capitalist countries away from existing political allegiances? The general position of the Comintern on existing labour—i.e., social democratic—parties was that their leadership had to be 'exposed' to the working class as unworthy. This was a position designed for Europe, fitted Australia, but did not apply to the United States, since it had no such party. How the American communists could contrive to 'expose' labour leaders was a matter contentious and shifting, and was probably doomed from the start. They even tried to form such a labour party. The problem, in all jurisdictions, was that communists had difficulty in convincing workers they were being betrayed, even when they hysterically denounced social democrats as 'social fascists', and in some ways as worse than the fascists. This position was both dishonest as well as disastrous, especially in Germany, where it divided the working class and helped Adolf Hitler to take power in 1933.

As in many other countries, the radical groups that had merged in Britain to form the CPGB found it difficult to maintain political unity, and to create a Bolshevik style of organization, two issues that were inextricably linked. Syndicalist groups were wary of politics and excoriated the Labour Party; the Socialist Labour Party which had become part of the CPGB opposed its members becoming union officials. In 1922, the Comintern created a Commission of Investigation into the CPGB, which reported in September. It noted that the Party had made no real progress in the two years of its life, and criticized its organization and apparatus. The Report was adopted at the Party's Battersea Congress in October 1922, and organizational centralization and membership growth ensued, but Trotsky—insisting that a revolutionary crisis was rapidly approaching—asked in 1925: 'Will it be possible to organize a Communist Party in England, which shall be strong enough and which shall have sufficiently large masses behind it, to enable it, at the psychological moment, to carry out the necessary practical conclusions of this ever-sharpening crisis?' (Trotsky 1973a, 36).

In the Australian case, the frustration emanating from Moscow was at first about the unity of the Australian party; there seemed no good reason for the continuing disunity. Subsequently the Comintern in general, and various sub-sections of it in particular (such as the Agitprop department) criticized the party's lack of recruits, its inadequate responses to political opportunities, its unprofessional organization, and even its sloppy publications.

The Comintern took a very close interest in the activities of its parties. From the Americans it wanted constantly updated information about the economic and political situation in the USA, and about the state of the party itself. It kept up a stream of critical letters. In a letter of 21 September 1932, for example, 'To the Central Committee of the Communist Party of USA', the Comintern explained that 'in spite of a number of concrete instructions from the ECCI, the question of the line, methods and slogans of the Party in the struggle against war and intervention [against the USSR] has not been presented clearly and concretely by the Party leadership' (CALC 515–1–2604). It directed the Party's attention to 'insufficient activity' with regard to a list of items. This was less the case with Australia, even though the Australians kept insisting that they were important, and that the opportunities for revolution were larger than Moscow assumed. Comintern directives to Australia were less intrusive and less detailed (the Comintern even directed the Americans when to have conferences, though there is no similar evidence in CAAL of such instructions to Australians). There was also less personal contact between Australians and the leaders in Moscow. From the early 1920s, there were always at least a handful of Americans and Britons in the Comintern offices in Moscow, but personal contact with Australians tended to be sporadic until the 1930s and the arrival of Moore and the more regular travel of communists to Moscow. Perhaps all this is merely a reflection of the different views that the Comintern had of the prospects for revolution in different countries, as well as of the difficulties and costs of travel.

In November 1935 an American representative in Moscow gave an insight into how the foreign parties were treated. 'In connection with this [Abyssinian] situation, in a general way, us dignitaries have been called all together and criticised, not naming any specific brethren especially, for our weaknesses at home' (CALC 515–1–3737). The communist parties took their medicine without sugar. Like children of demanding parents, they did not receive much praise. But it was enough for them to be associated with revolutionaries. As the generations moved on, and the Moscow trials 'exposed' the 'rottenness' of even the Old Bolsheviks, more material forms of recognition for foreign communist party leaders became the norm, especially being feted during visits to the Soviet Union.

A CPA 'underground'?

Compared with the United States or the United Kingdom, the very bastions of international capitalism, Australia figured rather low in Moscow's estimation as a likely site for socialist revolution. Some Australians, and some Comintern agents who worked in Australia from 1919 to 1922, heroically attempted to bolster Australia's claims as the Achilles heel of British imperialism. But it was not until the 1940s, a period beyond the limits of our documentary remit, that Australia became significant for Soviet Russia as the 'soft underbelly' of Allied—and later imperialist—intelligence. Though it is outside the scope of this work, Soviet collection of secret (and not so secret) government documents by Walter Clayton and Ian Milner, exposed in part by the Australian Royal Commission of 1954 into Soviet espionage following the defection of the Petrovs, and more openly discussed in the Venona decrypts which had uncovered this espionage, tended not to rely on publicly recognized CPA members. In the period discussed by this book, however, Australia was of interest to Moscow chiefly as a potential site of socialist revolution. The agents, or operatives, whom Moscow deployed in Australia, including Simonov, Zuzenko and Freeman, were not spies in the usual sense. And the intelligence about Australia that the CPA passed on to the Comintern, through its reports and the minutes of its meetings, was publicly available.

It is not surprising that the suspicion of espionage should have fallen on the communists. One important aspect of communist activity in capitalist states, an aspect that was explicitly addressed by the Comintern (and ultimately managed by the Soviet state), was clandestine activity. Communist parties were directed to establish an 'underground' organization as well as a legal one. This was made clear during the earliest years. The third of the twenty-one conditions for affiliation to the Comintern, promulgated in 1920, directed national sections to establish a 'parallel illegal organization':

> In all countries where a state of siege or emergency laws make it impossible for Communists to carry out all their work legally, it is absolutely necessary that legal and illegal activity be combined.

The American Communist Party was continually urged to follow this advice despite its ability to function legally. A document entitled 'Parliamentarism, Soviet Power and the Creation of a Communist Party of America. Thesis of the Executive Committee of the Third International', signed by N. Bukharin and J. Berzin (Winter), for example, included the following: 'We call the attention of the comrades to the necessity of creating illegal underground machinery side by side with the legally functioning apparatus' (CALC 515–1–1). In January 1920, furthermore, in an early letter to the American parties claiming to be communist, Zinoviev as President of the ECCI insisted on the necessity for immediate unification and added that:

> The Executive Committee urges the American Comrades immediately to establish an underground organization, even if it is possible for the party to function legally. This underground organization shall be for the purpose of carrying on direct revolutionary propaganda among the masses, and, in case of violent suppression of the legal Party organization, of carrying on the work. It should be composed of trusted comrades, and kept entirely separate from the legal

Party organization. The fewer people who know about it, the better. (CALC 515–1–17)

The background to these urgings is the prevailing sense that the seizure of power was imminent in the early 1920s. It had long been assumed by Marxists that the capitalist state, under threat, would go on the offensive against legal communist organizations, and thus that the communists had to be prepared to turn to underground work. This had some grounding in Marxist theory, but it resonated particularly with the Russian revolutionists' experience under the Tsars. William Z. Forster, an American communist party leader, was tried for treason in 1922. Such actions bolstered the Russians' insistence on the legal fiction of a complete separation between the Comintern and the Soviet state. In 1933, Soviet diplomat Maxim Litvinov made this distinction publicly in the United States. Thanks to recently available archival material, we can see that the US communists developed their secret apparatus, and that this eventually had a major role to play in espionage, including bringing the atomic secrets to the Soviets.

In the Australian case, and despite the wholesale exhortations to develop an underground apparatus, the CAAL documents give no indication that such an apparatus was ever created. Later in the 1930s, as the prospect of another war loomed, Australian communists took much more seriously the idea that they would have to continue their work 'underground'. But the link between such party preparations and Soviet espionage carried out by Australian communists is not proved, and seems unlikely. (Having a secret apparatus may not be a crime, though spying for a foreign power certainly is.)

The use of communist parties to extend the reach of Soviet espionage was acknowledged by Leon Trotsky, only days before he was assassinated by a Soviet agent. Trotsky wrote: 'As organizations, the GPU and the Comintern are not identical but they are indissoluble. They are subordinated to one another, and moreover it is not the Comintern that gives orders to the GPU but on the contrary, it is the GPU that completely dominates the Comintern' (Trotsky 1973, 370).

One important aspect of opening the archives has been a greater understanding of the extensive surveillance and intelligence-gathering activity of communist states, aimed at their own citizens, Western governments, and Western industry. In postcommunist states, the internal archives were opened, revealing for example the vast scale of Stasi internal surveillance in the former German Democratic Republic. About one in 50 of the adult East German population reported in some way to the Stasi on their friends, colleagues, students, and even families and lovers. Apart from any other consideration, this gives an indication of the suspicion and lack of trust in a society supposedly intended to develop the most complete human solidarity. Timothy Garton Ash (1997), the Oxford historian of Eastern Europe, read the files of his own visits to East Germany partly in order to check their veracity, and to try to understand why people had reported on him. He has observed acutely that—apart from outright errors, which were many and fundamental—even the most innocuous action could seem suspicious to a surveillance officer. Many people in Eastern Europe acted as informants in order to gain privileges, such as travel visas. Markus Wolf was in charge of espionage in the West for East Germany, and claims not to have known about the activities of his internal Stasi colleagues. Koehler (1999) looks at this external role in some depth.

The difficulty with spying is that it creates a self-perpetuating state of mind, which no evidence can dissuade, and this is particularly dangerous for liberal democracies. This may be perfectly illustrated by an Intelligence Branch official's response to Dora Montefiore's apparently uneventful stay in Australia in 1922–23: 'since her arrival she has behaved with decorum ... Outwardly, therefore, she has played her part well just as she has apparently served her Bolshevik Masters well too and she must, therefore, be regarded as dangerous' (cited Cain 1983, 240–41). The more normally people behave, the more suspicious spooks become. The Philby case exemplifies another dilemma of espionage, as Phillip Knightley puts it: the better the information, the less likely is the informant to be believed (Borovik 1994, xiv).

Just as the Comintern archives have revealed the connections between the CPUSA and Soviet espionage in the United States (Klehr, Haynes and Firsov 1995), so the archives brought to England in 1992 by a KGB librarian, Vasili Mitrokhin, and published as *The Mitrokhin Archive* (Andrew and Mitrokhin 1999) have revealed a great deal about Soviet espionage in the West. A number of people—now elderly—have been identified as long-term Soviet spies and agents of influence, adding to the spies already uncovered during the 1950s and '60s: Guy Burgess, Donald Maclean, Kim Philby, Anthony Blunt and John Cairncross. What is perhaps most surprising is the public reaction, which sees this as something of a joke. The 'Bolshevik from Bexleyheath', for example—Melita Norwood, aged at the time of exposure in her late eighties, and unrepentant about passing British nuclear secrets to the Soviets from 1937—was not prosecuted. A newspaper report notes that 'Neighbours describe her as kind and jolly, and say she makes a particularly fine chutney' (Walker 1999, 28). It is her sincerity that is presented, without challenge: 'I thought it was an experiment what they were doing out there—a good experiment and I agreed with it ... I did what I did because I expected them to be attacked again once the war was over ... I thought they should somehow be adequately defended because everyone was against them' (cited Walker 1999, 28).

There was a time when caution was an appropriate response to the charges against Australians of spying for the Soviet Union. As late as 1994, for example, David McKnight declared: 'For many, including the writer, the idea that a left-wing Australian may well have been under the control of Soviet intelligence is a conclusion to be resisted' (McKnight 1994, 92). This was said chiefly in defence of Walter Clayton, but also indirectly in defence of Ian Milner. But the evidence of the archives now seems indisputable. With the release in 1995 of the Venona decrypts of Soviet intelligence traffic from Canberra to Moscow in the 1940s, the role of Clayton—or 'Klod'—is clear. Ball and Horner, on the basis of this evidence, have concluded that 'From 1943–49, a group of about 10 people, all of whom were members of the Communist Party of Australia or close acquaintances of communists, provided information and documentary material to the Soviet State Security Service, commonly known as the KGB' (Ball and Horner 1998, xiv). The Venona decrypts make it clear that there was a significant Soviet espionage effort in Australia during the 1940s and early 1950s. How useful, and how secret, was the material gathered are questions that remain open, as is the issue of Clayton's professionalism as an agent (see Macintyre 1998, 400–401).

The Petrov Royal Commission named both Clayton and Milner as spies, but the evidence for doing so could not be made public at the time, and no-one was charged with espionage. Venona has now definitively exposed Clayton, and the opening of secret Czech archives clears up the case of Ian Milner, about whom there was previously dispute. Milner was a New Zealander who became an Australian academic, secretly joining the Melbourne University branch of the CPA in March 1940; he later joined Australia's Department of External Affairs, then the UN, and in 1950 went to Czechoslovakia and refused to return. Until his death, Milner himself (and his wives, both of whom seem also to have been agents) continued to insist that he was not a spy—much as did Julius Rosenberg and Alger Hiss. But in a major turning point, Phillip Deery in 1997 conceded Milner's espionage. As Deery noted at the time, 'Historians study the past not for comfort but for truths: disclosures about the past usually provide pain more than solace' (Deery 1997, 12).

As long as there was a lack of definitive evidence about communist spying in Australia, much of the discussion in this area centred on espionage as a baseless political charge designed to discredit communists. The political advantage that the Menzies government clearly gained from the Petrov Royal Commission (whether through the electoral victories in 1954 and 1955, the psychological decline of Opposition Leader 'Doc' Evatt, or the split in the Labor Party), and the lack of prosecutions arising from it, have led many including Evatt to conclude—wrongly, as it turns out—that it was a Menzies' plot to defeat Labor at the 1954 election. The authoritative study of Menzies concludes that these notions of conspiracy are indefensible (Martin 1999, 276–85). And Western security organizations—whatever their competence, about which there is legitimate disagreement—were created or bolstered in response to a sustained Soviet effort at espionage against the West.

The Comintern was undoubtedly connected with collecting information for the Soviet intelligence services (Brown and MacDonald 1981). Indeed, the dissolution of the Comintern in 1943 created some difficulties for their intelligence gathering, as the following message from 'Viktor' (Lt Gen P.M. Fitin) in Moscow to his agent in Canberra on 12 September 1943 reveals:

> A change in circumstances—and in particular the dissolution of the BIGHOUSE [i.e., Comintern]—necessitates a change in the method used by the workers of our residencies to keep in touch with the leaders of the local FELLOWCOUNTRYMAN [i.e., Communist] organizations on intelligence matters. (PRO, HW/15/21)

But this is not to say that all communists were spies. There is an important distinction to be made between communists who were loyal to policies (and who joined, and left, communist parties as policies changed—and there were many in that category) and those who were loyal to the party and through it ultimately to the Soviet Union. It was the latter who would respond to the 1930 reminder by the ECCI to Western communist parties that 'legal forms of activity must be combined with systematic illegal work' (cited Klehr, Haynes, Firsov 1995, 71). Walter Clayton, for example, headed the CPA's underground organization in the 1940s. The Venona decrypts reveal his KGB handler describing Clayton's embarrassment at being paid for some information in 1945, Clayton explaining that he passed information for 'duty' (PRO, HW 15/1).

Loyalty to communism and a better future for humanity transferred easily to loyalty to Moscow. Australian (and other) communists believed that in helping Moscow they were not being traitorous: they were doing the best for their country, even as they opposed its present government and social system. In their eyes, perhaps, they were the real loyalists, while the capitalists were loyal only to their own greed and class interests. Moscow took these sentiments and, especially with the domination of the 'socialism in one country' mentality in the Soviet Union, turned communists into a second-tier (and highly expendable) aspect of its foreign relations. The decent motives that turned many people into communists, the wish to improve their own society and confront greed, racism and injustice, were used by Moscow for baser purposes. If communists saw this, they did not recognize it, at least until a major shock threatened their view of the world, a shock such as the Soviet-German Nonaggression Pact, or Khrushchev's 1956 Secret Speech about Stalin's crimes.

Australian, and Australian government, reactions

If an international political movement, with the blessing and apparently under the influence (if not control) of a foreign power, set up business in your country in order to overthrow the political system, it would not be surprising if the existing government was either wary or hostile and kept that movement under surveillance. Communists, as the *Communist Manifesto* proclaimed, disdain to conceal their views; but Bolshevik experience of persecution, imprisonment and exile under the Tsarist secret police, the Okhrana, had recommended a rather different set of rules, all of them designed to take and maintain power. Communists were therefore part of public politics in countries where that was possible, including Australia, and they were always preparing for illegal or 'underground' activity in the event that the state turned on them, as they were convinced it ultimately would.

Surveillance and intelligence agencies were just coming into their own in the first decades of the twentieth century. Surveillance of 'aliens' and 'enemies' began in earnest in the period of the First World War. In Britain, the Special Intelligence Bureau was established in 1909, and in Australia the Commonwealth Investigation Branch was established in 1916. Their chief task was to track enemy agents, and their targets were Germans, Sinn Fein, and soon, socialist agitators. The extensive surveillance organization and activity generated by the war was ready to be turned against internal dissent after it, and the state archives of both Australia and the United Kingdom reveal that informers were part of the communist movement, that mail was intercepted and opened, that headquarters of communist organizations were occasionally raided by police, and that public meetings held by communists were often monitored (eg, PRO, HO 45/25574).

In Australia, the Commonwealth Police force—formed only in late 1917 under the War Precautions Regulations—was tasked with keeping an eye on political subversives. Prior to the First World War, socialists had been imprisoned, and during the war members of the Industrial Workers of the World were tried, imprisoned, and even deported (Turner 1967). There was considerable suspicion of socialists and worker radicals, compounded by the events in Russia in 1917, and deepened by Russian withdrawal from the war. The communists were not going to have an easy time. Nor did they. Those Russians and other foreigners who tried to help them were deported (Evans 1989); their mail was intercepted. The government put other frustrations in the way of the communists, including prohibiting the importation of communist periodical literature, under its censorship powers, and disallowing the mailing of communist newspapers within Australia via the government monopoly mail system. The Bruce-Page government also banned printed material arriving from the USSR.

Political surveillance in Australia was conducted by both Military Intelligence and the Investigation Bureau of the Attorney-General's Department. The government tried to frustrate as well as intimidate the communists. The frustration came from using the office of Censor to identify a number of communist publications that could not be brought into the country: this began in 1921, and by 1927 'a list of 129 papers and journals had been declared to be "prohibited importations"' (Cain 1983, 243) and Australian publications that could not be put through the post. In February 1932 the Post Office declared that six communist papers would not be allowed transmission through the post under Section 30E of the Crimes Act (Cain 1983, 247). One of these papers was the communists' main journal, the *Workers' Weekly*, with a claimed circulation of over 13,000 copies per week in 1931. Subscriptions were understandably affected (and the Western Australian communists as a consequence established their own newspaper). There was, however, an element of bluff involved in this move. The Crimes Act prohibited the transmission of publications of an 'unlawful association', but the CPA had not been found unlawful in any legal proceeding. The CPA, according to Cain, accepted the ban 'rather than challenge it in court and run the risk of being suppressed altogether' (Cain 1983, 248). As it was, the government of Joseph Lyons, under Attorney-General John Latham, pressed the issue. It prosecuted the editor of the *Workers' Weekly* for soliciting funds for an unlawful association, but after being found guilty in a lower court, the conviction was ultimately quashed in the High Court (Macintyre 1998, 214). The High Court's decision was based on a point of law, not on the protection of civil liberties, and the CPA remained nervous about its legality until its situation was definitively clarified on 15 June 1940, when the Party was banned.

With the benefit of hindsight, and given the failure of the CPA to establish any real bases except in leading certain sectors of the industrial trade union movement, we may say that the reaction against the communists was excessive. The Party numbered officially 128 at the end of 1922, 296 in mid-1927, 486 in 1930, 2093 at the end of 1931, 2,873 in 1935, and 4,421 members by the middle of 1939; the vast bulk of its members were unemployed males (Macintyre 1998, 179, 180, 351, 428; Document 49). In the United States, by comparison, there were 10,266 dues-paying members in October 1931, and by March 1932 there were 14,374. In early 1935, a meeting of Central Committee of the CPUSA was told that membership at December 1934 was 31,000, but that the turnover of members was very high (CALC 515–1–3742).

Given the spectre of communism, governments' reactions may be easily understood, but what is less easy for defenders of liberal democracy to justify was the inroads into rights of the freedom to organize and speak, inroads represented by the use of government power to intercept mail and harass communists. It is not enough to say that these were rights that the communists themselves did not respect (though western communists nevertheless expressed outrage when their rights were violated). The British House of Commons was a forum in the early 1920s where these issues were regularly aired, covering matters such as the deportation of aliens, the privacy of the mail, and whether or not advocating communism was illegal. The prohibition of communist organizations in Britain was under active consideration. In December 1925, the Labour Opposition in the Commons moved to censure the government for initiating the prosecution of some members of the CPGB as 'a violation of the traditional British rights of freedom of speech and publication of opinion' (Ramsay MacDonald, Parliamentary Debates, Commons, vol. 188, 1 December 1925). That prosecution had sent 12 men to jail, and followed a police raid of communist headquarters. The Home Secretary, Joynson-Hicks, replied that these men were found guilty of advocating the violent overthrow of the government, and there was additional discussion about the extent to which the Comintern exercised control over the CPGB. Joynson-Hicks invoked 'a conspiracy, with foreign money, with foreign instructions'.

Police and other surveillance of communists may have fed into the latter's sense of their own importance, but it put an emphasis on the secrecy of communications. The CAAL documents do not provide any evidence of ciphered messages in the Australian documents, but it is clear from Australian government files that a cipher was found on Zuzenko when he was arrested in Melbourne in August 1922 (Windle 2004a). Ciphers were extensively used by the American communists. In 1922, for example, there are a number of reports to Moscow from the US party that break into cipher (CALC 515–1–93). Report 8, dated 16 January 1922 includes this: 'Please change the figure system in the heavy code that Gorny is using from the 14321432 combination to the simple system of 21212121 ...'. And it finishes with the sentence 'Expect to report in person when the violets bloom in the spring': a code devised, perhaps, by a devotee of Gilbert and Sullivan. The message was signed 'Carr'. Carr later reported to the Secretariat on 25 January: 'Rush ten thousand [dollars] to be used solely for Damon, Caxton and others release through special arrangements'. This request was sent via cable from America. G. Lewis, in a letter of 2 February, includes ciphered material, but also: 'By the time this letter reaches you our salesman will have reached your territory for the stock holders conference you mentioned' (and so on, in this vein).

Considering that the communist movement was dedicated to the overthrow of the government, the latter's reactions may even be seen as relatively restrained. Australian citizens were uninterested, or mildly hostile to communism, linking it with a foreign power. Membership of the CPA remained small throughout this period, and was mostly concentrated in metropolitan areas, except for a lively base in northern Queensland during the 1930s and 40s (McIlroy 2001). This is not to say that the influence of the CPA was negligible, for it agitated among trade unionized workers (and Australian workers were the most heavily trade unionized in the world, largely on account of the centralized wage fixing system). Communists attempted to gain positions of responsibility in some trade unions, so that they could exert more influence.

The official response of governments within the liberal tradition to the challenge of communism was put by the British Home Secretary a number of times in the House of Commons, but its characteristic theme was as follows: 'I have no power to stop mere propaganda of opinions, however false or harmful, even when the propagandists are in receipt of pay from foreign sources' (Parliamentary Debates, Commons, vol. 151, 7 March 1922). What would be stopped, he made clear, was incitement to violence. But there was nevertheless a great deal of activity to gain information about and to frustrate the communists. The fundamental question was how far one could tolerate those who would show you no tolerance.

The CPA: autonomous or subordinate?

The relationship between the Comintern and its constituent parties is often misunderstood as a simple case of foreign control of a local organization, or as a branch structure. It is certainly true that the amount of local autonomy was limited, that policies and leaders ultimately required the authorization of Moscow. But the idea that Moscow acted as a grand puppeteer should not be too readily accepted. Apart from anything else—and in Australia's case in particular—the difficulties of regular and rapid communication between the Comintern and the CPA made such detailed control impossible. Some of the more jarring conflicts in the relationship may be put down to time lapses. In the notorious case of Moscow's surprise rapprochement with Nazism in 1939 (after years of pillorying Nazism), the local communists were taken unawares, and insisted on calling for the defeat of the Nazis in the war that broke out only a week later. They were soon brought into line by Moscow explaining that the war was an inter-imperialist one in which Nazi Germany and liberal democracies were equally evil. In the relationship between the Comintern and its parties, Moscow ultimately had its way.

CPA leaders and members did not see themselves as puppets of Moscow, but rather as part of, or partners in, the same struggle against capitalism. Communists were citizens of the world. The opposition of capitalist governments to the Soviet Union was seen as an attack on all communists, and opposition to one's government was not difficult to justify or sustain. Where nationalism intruded, as it did in those countries which fought against the Soviet Union, communists were sometimes torn, but at least until the 1950s tended to regard Soviet victory not as Russian domination, but as socialist unity. These illusions would collapse completely by the 1980s, but that was a long time away from the period with which we are concerned.

Communists believed that Russia was not a foreign power but a glimpse of the future, where 'foreignness' would be irrelevant. Perhaps the closest parallel that can be drawn with the communist quest is the Roman Catholic Church, which has a type of self-rule in the various countries in which it operates, but whose head is—in a celebrated phrase from the seventeenth century—a 'foreign prince', and whose emissaries and leaders are appointed in and by the Vatican in Rome. Catholics do not think of themselves as agents of the Vatican, but rather as engaged in a universal struggle for human redemption and against evil.

The parallel between Moscow and the Vatican is not fanciful. In Australia there was until the 1960s a sectarian edge to mainstream parliamentary politics, with the conservatives distrustful of the role of the (in the early period largely Irish) Church. As a result of Cardinal Moran's part in opposing and helping defeat the proposal for conscription put at two referendums during the First World War (October 1916 and December 1917), the Australian government was unhappy about the use of ciphered messages in communications between the Vatican and the Australian outpost of the Church, and complained in 1920 to the Colonial Office (PRO, CO 418/186). The Church saw itself as the implacable foe of communism, in a struggle it waged by means ordinary and extraordinary. Stalin may have underestimated its resources—'how many divisions has the Pope?', he is reputed to have asked in the Second World War—but the Church mobilized in various ways to defeat what it saw as its mortal enemy. In Australia, the Catholic Social Studies Movement (the 'Movement') adopted communist methods to defeat the communists in the trade unions and in the Australian Labor Party, and precipitated the split within that party in 1955. (More recently, Pope John Paul II seems to have played a key role in the collapse of communism in Eastern Europe and the Soviet Union (Bernstein and Politi 1997).) In the absence of communism, Catholicism can perhaps now refocus its opposition to materialistic and individualistic capitalism, begun in the Papal encyclical of *Rerum Novarum* (which opposed socialism, but also stressed the responsibilities of property).

CPA members knew that their party was closely connected with Moscow. One of the conditions of affiliation with the Comintern was that the Soviet Union had to be defended. That was done in official party resolutions, in their newspapers and theoretical journals, and in their discussions and arguments with ordinary workers. The exact nature of the relationship was probably less well known by ordinary members, though it was certainly a fact of life for all CPA leaders. In particular, conference resolutions and general strategic directions had to be approved by Moscow, and many were initiated in Moscow. Nevertheless, CPA members would probably not have baulked at this level of contact, or 'interference', with their party, because of Moscow's enormous reserves of authority.

Defending the Soviet Union became more and more difficult, not just because of the greater amount of critical information being published in the 'bourgeois' press, but because of the sometimes erratic political line emanating from Moscow. It is difficult to know to what extent communists discounted this negative information, but they probably dismissed much of it as lies and propaganda. Dismissal became much more difficult after 1956, when for the first time a Soviet leader admitted that communists had made mistakes. That was a striking change that disturbed many communists around the world.

Khrushchev's testimony given in a secret speech to the Twentieth Congress of the CPSU was damning. Nevertheless Ted Hill, one of the CPA's leaders, at first lied about the authenticity of Khrushchev's speech when it was published in the West, even though he had seen a copy of the original. By the end of 1956, the Party would concede only that Stalin had made 'mistakes' (rather than 'crimes'), public discussion of the matter in its newspaper, *Tribune*, was prohibited, and portraits of Stalin were still displayed prominently in Party offices. The CPA made some grudging criticisms of Stalin during its 1958 conference, but turned them into an attack on the 'revisionists' in the Party—those who wanted a fuller discussion of Khrushchev's report—as enemies of socialism (Blake 1984, 96).

Of all the shocks to have affected the communist movement—dramatic changes of political direction, communist invasions of neighbours, splits between communist states, and even the collapse of communism—1956 was perhaps the greatest. Khrushchev's speech, recalls Georgi Arbatov, 'came like a bolt out of the blue, shaking the Party and our whole society to its roots' (cited Gaddis 1997, 208). Above all, the aura of infallibility surrounding the leadership had been destroyed. That claim had virtually paralysed independent thought in the communist movement. But the logic of admitting fallibility could be devastating. The British communist playwright, Arnold Wesker, reflected on this point in 1956 when explaining his mother's dilemma: 'If she admits that the party has been wrong, that Stalin committed grave offences, then she admits that she has been wrong. All the people she so mistrusted and hated she must now have second thoughts about, and this she cannot do … You can admit the error of an idea but not the conduct of a whole life' (cited Beckett 1995, 140).

In the wake of 1956, however, other arguments emerged to balance the equation. In defending the increasingly evident brutality of communist regimes, many communists began to argue that the First World War and its senseless carnage had changed the whole moral equation of modern life. Humphrey McQueen, for example, took this approach when he insisted that 'the Great War had altered the rules of every game' (McQueen 1997, 174). Any means necessary to stop this slaughter, and end this system of slaughter, were justified. If it was not stopped, it would happen again. The First World War, in other words, had exposed the true nature and tendency of capitalist society, which was murderous. A system bent on murder cannot be argued away; it requires force and even deception. But if this can be used as a justification for the Bolshevik Revolution—and it relies upon a questionable assumption about the systemic causes of the war—it cannot be used as justification for all its consequences.

This outlook is brought to a sharp focus in the widely differing treatment accorded by many analysts to Hitler and Stalin, which forgives Stalin's crimes (but not Hitler's) on the grounds that he led a 'progressive' state. Historian Alan Bullock argues that, leaving aside the Second World War, Stalinist repression killed perhaps double those killed by Nazis, but the difference lay in the Holocaust being a *planned* extermination (Bullock 1992, 1073). Bullock concedes, however, that jointly Hitler and Stalin are responsible for a level of human suffering hitherto unparalleled. Doris Lessing, by contrast, argues that the 'decent, kind people' who joined the Soviet-supporting communist parties of the West in the 1950s and afterwards:

> supported the worst, the most brutal tyranny of our time—with the exception of communist China. Hitler's Germany, which lasted thirteen years, was an infant in terror compared to Stalin's regime ... The first and main fact, the 'mind-set' of those times, was that it was taken for granted capitalism was doomed, was on its way out. Capitalism was responsible for every social ill, war included. Communism was the future for all mankind (Lessing 1997, 52).

Whether communists actually believed the argument from moral equivalence, or used it simply as a political tactic, it points to a choice in outlook between an ethic of responsibility and an ethic of absolute principles, discussed by Max Weber in 1919 (Weber 1994). It is a choice which, in the memoirs of most communists, comes down on the side of absolute principles. In supporting and justifying their activities, communists have looked not to consequences but to intentions. They find succour in their commitment and idealism. This point has been aptly put in a novel which traces the career of the well-connected (and once knighted) British spy, Anthony Blunt. In John Banville's *The Untouchable*, the Blunt character complains: 'What have I done to be so reviled in a nation of traitors who daily betray friends, wives, children, tax inspectors? I think that what they find so shocking is that someone—one of their own, that is—should actually have held to an ideal'. Robert Manne describes McQueen and many other members of the former communist Left as having 'their own moral blind spot concerning their support for totalitarian regimes and what this failure of understanding might mean' (Manne 1997).

The Comintern represented an obvious link between the CPA and Soviet Russia, but that link was not broken when the Comintern was dissolved. Indeed, it was the characteristic of the CPA's politics (and of communists more generally) that defence of the Soviet Union and its political twists and turns was an article of faith. As Otto Braun declared, 'all my life I have considered the touchstone of every Communist, regardless of nationality or situation, to be his posture towards the Soviet Union' (Braun 1982, 264). The CPA was thus hostage to the fortunes of the Soviet Union. When times were good—and they were really good for the CPA only after the Nazis had invaded the Soviet Union in June

1941, and the war had thus also become a defence of the Soviet motherland—then the Party's fortunes were good and membership was high. (Lance Sharkey claimed near the end of the war that membership was 20,000 (Sharkey 1944, 70).) When times were bad, as they were especially during the 1950s and in the Cold War more generally, membership declined. Many committed communists could not reconcile their Party membership with Khrushchev's revelations in 1956, and many moved away (some to form the 'New Left', others to shun politics or become conservatives).

The CPA after the Comintern

Though it is outside the scope of the documents presented in this book, it is worth outlining the story of the Communist Party of Australia after the end of the Comintern in 1943. The CPA survived its declaration of illegality in 1940, was reinstated to legality at the end of 1942, and achieved its highest-ever membership just after the Second World War. Ironically, its success at this time was soon to be its failure, and was linked to the fact that dogged most of its existence: its real and imagined links with the Soviet Union. In 1946, the Soviet Union—as one of the victorious allies, having sustained terrible losses during the war and been a decisive factor in the defeat of Hitler, and with an (apparently) avuncular Stalin at the helm—looked as if it would join the world in an era of post-war stability and peace. But as the Soviet presence in Eastern Europe remained, with the blockade of Berlin in 1948 and rigged communist elections elsewhere over the next couple of years, the mood soured and the Soviet Union became an inscrutable enemy behind Winston Churchill's evocative image of the Iron Curtain, 'from Stettin in the Baltic to Trieste in the Adriatic'. Membership of the CPA dropped, trade union headquarters (with the notable exception of the Federated Ironworkers Association) became communist redoubts, the Australian Security Intelligence Organization was formed by the Chifley Labor government in 1949, and the succeeding Menzies government attempted to outlaw the CPA.

What is particularly relevant for our story, however, is that—of those who were still alive—the generation who joined the CPA in the 1930s were the most dedicated, or stubborn, depending on one's view. That is because of their experience of one of capitalism's greatest human disasters: the Great Depression. It was an experience that none of them forgot (Lovell 2001). Their opposition to capitalism and their 'outsider' status threw them increasingly on their own resources to find not just political colleagues but also a social life and even marital partners. The party was a family, and Herbert Moore used the language of 'family' in his correspondence of the early 1930s (see Document 65). It comes as little surprise, therefore, that in ciphered Comintern and Soviet espionage messages, the Comintern is denoted by the term 'Bighouse'. As a family, however, they could become isolated and inward looking. Arthur Koestler described joining a communist party as akin to a spiritual conversion (Crossman 2001). In the memoirs of Eric Aarons and Bernie Taft—both of whom devoted most of their adult lives to communism and held leadership positions in the CPA—this view is reinforced (Aarons 1993, Taft 1994). Aarons likened the CPA to a church, with its distinctive world outlook; Taft talks of the emotional attachments he had made to the Party. Intellectual conviction is only one part of the communist experience and, if it is primary in the decision to join a communist party, it is soon matched by emotional commitments that are developed to and within the Party. Joining a communist party in the West was a momentous decision. There was no confluence of ideology and self-interest, as in the communist states. As John Murphy explained, 'Once having crossed the threshold and declared party allegiance, communists found it all the harder to step back' (Murphy 1994, 115). Loyalty to, and support of, each other and discipline in cleaving to the party line, therefore, were types of self-defence.

In the face of widespread popular suspicion and government hostility to communists in the West, communists were sustained in their pro-Sovietism not just by their debating strategies, but also by the solidarity of the communist movement itself, as an international family. These genuine and often deeply-felt emotional bonds were an important reason why some remained communists, despite their doubts, for the threat of these bonds ending upon their renouncing pro-Sovietism was a credible deterrent. The charge of 'traitor' was perhaps the most devastating that could be made within the communist movement.

The relationship after the Second World War between the CPA and Moscow—no longer the Comintern, but the CPSU without intermediaries—was much more complex and convoluted. The loyalty that had been at the base of this relationship was sorely challenged. We have less detailed documentary evidence about the relationship for the period after 1943. The subservience certainly continued, but 1956—the year of Khrushchev's 'Secret Speech' and the Soviet invasion of Hungary—represents a major shift. It was the time when in international anti-capitalist circles the 'New Left' began to form, finding its inspiration in Marx's early, 'humanist' writings. The Soviet interpretation of Marxism—'orthodoxy'—came under sustained theoretical challenge from within the Marxist tradition itself.

Prime Minister Menzies' attempts to ban the CPA by legislation and then by Constitutional amendment were unsuccessful, but the fear of communism—in contrast to communism itself—was a factor in Australian political life for many years afterwards. This fear affected the Australian Labor Party, leading in 1955 to a split with hard-line anti-communists who formed the Democratic Labour Party and helped to keep the ALP out of federal government for a further 17 years, and influenced a popular perception of the ALP as akin to, or soft on, communists. That perception was brought to a fitting end by ridicule in the

1983 election campaign, when Labor leader (and soon-to-be Prime Minister) Bob Hawke made a successful joke out of the longstanding 'Reds-under-the-beds' scare. The CPA, having split in 1963 between those who supported Moscow and Peking, and having split again in 1971 between those who supported an independent communist line against Moscow, had a brief resurgence around the Vietnam Moratorium movement in the late 1960s and early 1970s, but ultimately dissolved itself at a conference in March 1991. Following its opposition to the Soviet invasion of Czechoslovakia in 1968, the CPA became one of the most independent of the world's communist parties, and no longer enjoyed the support (political or financial) of Moscow. For many communists, it was not communism that had failed in the changes of 1989–91, as Eastern Europe rejected communism and then the USSR imploded; rather, it was a flawed version of communism, corrupted at various stages, depending on the commentator, by Stalin in the 1920s, Khrushchev in 1956, or Mikhail Gorbachev in 1985.

Though the CPA gained new vitality and members from the student and anti-Vietnam War movements in the late 1960s and early '70s, it keenly sensed its isolation from its preferred audience, the working class. Programmatic documents of the time reveal a sense of crisis and lack of direction. In 1987 the main resolution of the National Congress was 'Socialist Renewal: Where to Now?'. In 1984, the Australian Security Intelligence Organization (ASIO) ceased its surveillance of the CPA. In 1991 the Party dissolved itself. It had finally met the classic conditions of irrelevance: its friends no longer understood what it was trying to say, and its enemies no longer cared.

Conclusion

As the Comintern aged, its relationship with its parties became more demanding. The key turning point came in Australia in 1929, with the change of CPA leadership. The importance of this change is not the merits of the respective positions, but the intervention of Moscow, the Party's compliance, and the subsequent subservience to Moscow. This led ultimately to the zig-zag of policy in late 1939 over the Second World War, and a 'defeatism' that justified the Australian government's decision to declare the Party unlawful in 1940. The CPA paid a heavy price for its slavish obedience to Moscow. The story was similar elsewhere. In the United States, Theodore Draper argued, the communist movement 'was transformed from a new expression of American radicalism to the American appendage of a Russian revolutionary power' (Draper 2003a, xi).

In the formation and early years of the Party, the CAAL documents suggest that the Comintern played a larger role than previously believed. That the Comintern was crucial for the unity of the CPA goes almost without saying: Australian communists would have split into many warring groups, and lost direction, were it not for their desire to be the Australian section of the Comintern. Their relationship was shaped by the deference and respect in which the Comintern was held. The Australians, in general, did not question the authority (or the arguments) of whoever won the inner-party struggles in the RCP. Was it thinkable that a party that had won a revolution and was running a state could be wrong? If Communist Party members (and especially leaders) stood to gain by the relationship with Moscow, it was very little—an occasional trip to Moscow, as well as recognition. Otherwise, it was a matter of hard work, being constantly criticized for not coming up to scratch, and putting yourself in the line of government surveillance. If the ultimate prize was envisaged as taking power and enjoying its fruits, the real reward was simply a life of continuing hardship.

The main lines of the relationship between the Comintern and the CPA have been known for a long time. This collection of documents adds substance to the notion that the loyalty that the CPA paid to the Comintern was transformed into subservience. The CPA drew on a native radical tradition and on working class discontent, but its Bolshevik elements probably did more to alienate it from its Australian audience than to help its cause. Ironically, in Moscow's own calculations, the Comintern itself seems to have become far less important. After Lenin and Trotsky, the Comintern became an instrument of Soviet diplomacy, and an expendable one.

The scope and limits of this book

This book is a documentary survey of the relationship between the Communist International and the Communist Party of Australia from the latter's origins until 1940, when the CPA was declared an illegal organization by the Australian government. It is intended to provide an insight into one very important aspect of the story of the CPA. It is not a history of the CPA. The various campaigns, conferences, personalities, and travails of the CPA during this period can be followed in their details elsewhere (notably in Davidson (1969) and Macintyre (1998)), though there are inevitably echoes of these dimensions here. This work as a whole supplements and extends the story of the CPA by focusing on its international commitments and how they influenced its work and its leadership. The introductory essays have set the larger scene within which these documents can be placed, and have drawn some general conclusions about the nature of the relationship between the CPA and the Comintern. At the head of each of the four documentary sections of the book that follow will be found brief introductions giving a sense of the context, issues, and key themes of the particular period.

The documents selected here tell only one part of a multi-faceted story. Given the limited material from local branch level in Australia, we are witness largely to a conversation between leaders and other 'insiders'. It is, in other words, an unavoidably 'top-down' view of this period in the CPA's history. It tends, therefore, to reflect the high-policy preoccupations of the leadership, and does not give much insight into local campaigns, successes and problems. How an ordinary CPA member would have experienced the Party's relationship with Moscow, from the material available here, can only be guessed at. In important respects, the national leadership was a buffer between the Comintern and the local branches, explaining a new policy line and its local ramifications to members, and parrying questions from the centre about whether or how successfully the new line was being implemented. Yet Party members seem to have been remarkably compliant to changes in the 'line' coming from Moscow; even the reversal in policy over the Nazis signalled by the Molotov-Ribbentrop pact did not see large numbers leaving the Party, as it did in other countries (Macintyre 1998, 386).

This book could not include all the documents in the Comintern Archive at the ADFA Library from which it is drawn. There are simply too many documents, and many of those are mundane or repetitive. Many documents were circulated in all the primary languages of the Comintern: Russian, English, German and French. This collection represents less than 1% of the documents we have examined. How, then, did we choose? The first goal in our process of selection was to identify documents that illuminated the relationship between the

Comintern and the CPA. There are doubtless other documents yet to be uncovered in Moscow that may have a further bearing on the details of this account, but not the general outline. There may be other ways to select the documents, especially to shed light on different aspects of the early CPA; but our interest was in the relations between the Comintern and the CPA, because this was perhaps the most important relationship the early CPA had. Our second goal was that this collection should not include documents that are relatively easily accessible elsewhere, such as those that have previously been published by the CPA itself, for example its major conference resolutions.

The documents are organized into four main sections, on a chronological basis, covering first the early 1920s, then the mid-1920s, then the Great Depression and the bulk of the 1930s, and finally the period approaching the Second World War. These are periods of quite different length, and they do not fully correspond to the periodization usually given in works on the Comintern itself. There are generally five periods identified in most histories of the Comintern: from its origins in 1919 until 1921, when the prospect of imminent revolution spurred on the communists; from 1921 to 1928 when the Comintern adopted the policy of a 'united front' with other working class and socialist forces to deal with the apparent stabilization of capitalism; from 1928 to 1933, the time of the so-called 'third period', when capitalist crisis was once again thought imminent and other socialists became the main enemy ('social fascists'); from 1933 to 1939, after the victory of Nazism in Germany and General Franco in Spain, when communists sought alliances (and even the formation of coalition 'Popular Front' governments) against fascism; and 1939 to 1943, the final period when communist parties were pushed in all directions—first, against the 'imperialist war', then in support of the 'great patriotic war'—to support Soviet foreign policy aims.

The periodization adopted in this book, however, has emerged in the course of selecting and preparing the CAAL documents for publication. It seems to reflect better the dynamic of the relationship than a more traditional account would allow. In brief, the first section, to 1924, covers the period of forging the CPA, a process which involved an important, and perhaps decisive, Comintern contribution. This contribution was expressed as much in the authority and instructions of the Comintern, to which the squabbling groups of Australian communists appealed for recognition, as in the Comintern agents who liaised with them. Having finally united, the Australian communists in the period 1924–28, whence the second selection of documents comes, came close to collapse. They were disunited over policy (especially towards the Australian Labor Party), disorganized, and often disheartened. The Comintern may not have saved the Party during this period, but it seems to have helped stiffen its members' resolve to continue; it was a stern voice in the distance: sometimes supporting, sometimes instructing, and sometimes goading. The third section covers the period from

1929 to 1937, when the Party underwent a major leadership change (in 1929) with the support of Moscow, when it was reorganized by an agent Moscow sent to Australia—indeed, requested by the Australians—for the purpose, and when it began to ape the 'line' from Moscow. This approach culminated in the attitudes reflected in the documents of the fourth section, covering 1938–40, when subservience to Moscow's orders overshadowed every other consideration. Subservience led to Communist support for the Molotov-Ribbentrop Pact, Communist defeatism in the war against Hitler, and consequently to the CPA's outlawing by the Australian government in 1940.

Section 1

Forging a Communist Party for Australia: 1920–1923

The documents in this section cover the period from April 1920 to late 1923, that is, from before the inaugural conference of Australian communists to a time when the CPA had emerged as the Australian section of the Comintern, but was still dealing with issues of unity, and was coming to terms with the realities of being a section of a world revolutionary party. The main theme of this section is organizational unity, because that is what the Australian communists and their Comintern colleagues saw as the chief priority. As the ECCI wrote to the feuding Australian communists in June 1922: 'The existence of two small groups, *amidst a seething current of world shaking events,* engaged almost entirely in airing their petty differences, instead of unitedly plunging into the current and mastering it, is not only a ridiculous and shameful spectacle, but also a crime committed against the working class movement' (see Document 15). The crucial unity meeting finally occurred in July that year.

The CAAL documents reveal that the Comintern played a larger role in forging the CPA than has previously been thought. There were supporters of the Bolshevik Revolution in Australia, and people who wanted to create a party like the Bolsheviks', to be sure, but Petr Simonov, Paul Freeman and Aleksandr Zuzenko helped to bring the at first wary—and later squabbling—currents of former Wobblies, former ASP socialists, and former worker radicals together. Indeed the ASP believed that it (the ASP) was, or ought to be, the Australian communist party, and it somewhat begrudgingly went through the unity process demanded by the Comintern. The ASP's relative organizational strength allied with its reluctance to accept the others explains much of the infighting of the CPA's first 20 months. That a communist party emerged out of this period is due in no small part to the intervention of the Comintern and its agents. The fact that it was not a rebadged ASP owed much to ill luck, as will be seen. We have used this section, in part, to allow the agents for the Comintern to speak for themselves, and we have given substantial space to Aleksandr Zuzenko, whose role in the CPA's formation is only now receiving its due recognition because of the CAAL documents (Windle 2004a, b; Windle 2005c; Windle 2007a).

Communism of the Leninist variety came to general attention only during the First World War, despite Lenin's seminal pamphlet *What is to be Done?* having appeared in 1902. Lenin's Bolshevik Party took control of key centres in Russia in the so-called October Revolution in 1917,[1] and consolidated and extended its control over the remainder of Russia during the years following. Australia had emerged from the First World War having endured more casualties per capita than any other combatant country, yet its young democracy survived while European empires—the Ottoman, Russian, and Austro-Hungarian—crumbled. The war had touched the lives of most Australians deeply, as the monuments to the fallen soldiers that soon sprang up in almost every town and city attested (Inglis 1998). And while Australia emerged as a more united nation than its founding fathers had hoped (especially with the ANZAC myth beginning to nourish an Australian identity), the war had in at least one respect divided the country. Two bitterly fought referendums on the issue of introducing conscription were narrowly lost, intensifying sectarian divisions (Catholic Archbishop Daniel Mannix of Melbourne being a vociferous opponent of conscription) and splitting the Labor Party (with Labor Prime Minister 'Billy' Hughes walking out of his own party in November 1916 and eventually forming the Nationalist Party with the support of the parliamentary opposition). Australia's political party alignment was fundamentally changed, and Australia's armed services would remain a volunteer force until the next war. But the returned soldiers who had served their country and the British Empire were poorly recompensed, and established their own organization, the Returned Soldiers and Sailors and Imperial League of Australia (RSSILA; later to become the Returned and Services League, but under whichever name a potent political lobbying group). The government eventually granted many of them plots of land for farming. The 'soldier settlement scheme' was not a great success; but despite their troubles few ex-soldiers were attracted to communism. Amongst other reasons, the Russian Revolutions of 1917—February and October, in the Old Style calendar—had effectively taken Russia out of the War. Communism, with its Russian connection, was considered both frightening and disloyal. Some returned soldiers attacked those who paraded the prohibited red flag in Brisbane on 23 March 1919, and serious riots ensued; some went on to join the fascist New Guard movement in the 1930s in response to the Great Depression.

As for the Australian working classes, they were no more susceptible to communist propaganda than the soldiers. With its own ('reformist') political party, the ALP, and with restrictive immigration under the 'White Australia Policy', Australian workers enjoyed relatively high standards of living at least until the Great Depression put many out of work and reduced the wages of others. Perhaps the most highly unionized working class in the world, its form was a product of the centralized wage fixing system built under the Arbitration Court and assisted by decisions such as Mr Justice Higgins' 1907 'Harvester'

---

[1] 'So-called' in two respects: first, because it took place according to the modern, Gregorian calendar on November 7; second, because it is arguable whether it was a revolution or a coup.

judgment, which determined a basic wage that would provide a fair standard of living for a (male) worker and his family. Thus the CPA was composed, at least in this foundation period, of existing socialists and radicals of various stripes, some working class and some not; as it grew in later years it never established a mass base among workers, and at times consisted chiefly of unemployed men.

That the Comintern was crucial to the foundation of the CPA is confirmed by these documents: those Australian socialists who gathered at the 'founding conference' on 30 October 1920 would have split into many warring groups, and lost direction, had it not been for their desire to be the Australian section of the Comintern. Their relationship was shaped by respect for and deference to the Comintern, and its leading party, the Russian Communist Party. The Comintern itself would go through a number of different phases, generally reflecting the internecine struggles over leadership of the RCP and thus Soviet Russia. But the Australians, in general, never questioned the arguments of those phases, nor the authority of the winners, except for those attracted to Trotsky's views in the 1930s. Was it thinkable that a party that had won a revolution, and was running a state, could be wrong? In the end, the authority of the Revolution (even for Trotskyists) was always the trump card.

The story of the formation of the CPA is first of all a story of the manoeuvres of the various groups that came together in October 1920 for the founding conference. The level of trust between them, despite their apparent dedication to the same cause, was not particularly high. The details can be found elsewhere (Macintyre 1998, 12–27, 53–75). The basic moves in this game, however, are familiar and predictable. Let us review them briefly. To win, use any favourable opportunity to press home a momentary advantage (say, in numbers at particular meetings); attempt to possess, or at least control, key assets such as premises and printing presses; having won an advantage, claim the moral high ground of dedication to the cause; and attempt further to turn might into right by gaining recognition from a bestower of authority, in this case the Comintern. For the losers, too, the moves are predictable: split or wreck if outnumbered, align oneself to high principle or some notion of legality, and regroup to counter-attack and prevail, whereupon employ the devices of the winners. The game is over when one side loses interest or walks away to create its own game. These moves are in no wise peculiar to communists. Furthermore, it is no criticism to say that Lenin himself was a master of such tactics (especially in connection with the 1903 conference of the RSDLP which produced the split between the fortuitously named 'Bolsheviks', 'majority-ites', and 'Mensheviks', 'minority-ites'), but the early Australian communists would have known little of this.

In connection with the Comintern documents, each phase of the manoeuvres sketched above was reflected in correspondence with, and especially appeals to, the Comintern. The would-be Communists hung on the advice and the promises of the Comintern's agents. And so there were for a time, in effect, two communist parties, usually designated the 'Liverpool Street' and 'Sussex Street' parties because of the location of their premises in Sydney. In these early years, it was a struggle of Reardon and Everitt versus Earsman and Garden. Whatever the real policy differences between them—and there were some—they were overshadowed by the struggle itself. The eventual victory of 'Sussex Street' was to some extent a matter of luck, if the misfortune of opposing delegates before the crucial Comintern congress in 1921 may be described as luck: the jailing of Jim Quinton and the accidental deaths of Artem and Freeman.

The story of the formation of the CPA is also a story of some larger-than-life characters in the Australian socialist movement, especially of Freeman, Zuzenko, and Simonov (Windle 2005). Paul Freeman was deported as an alien, without charge or trial, in January 1919, but crossed the Pacific Ocean four times as US, and then Australian, authorities denied him a landing (Evans 1989, 16). He seems to have come to the attention of authorities for his labour radicalism and for his unknown (but possibly German) origins. He returned from Moscow to Australia to organize delegates to the Third Comintern Congress, at which he was an accredited ASP delegate. He was killed with Artem Sergeev—a Russian Bolshevik with strong Australian connections—in the crash of an experimental train in July 1921. Aleksandr Zuzenko was a Russian revolutionary who arrived in Australia in 1911 but was deported in April 1919 for his political activities, particularly his leadership of the Red Flag demonstration. Back in Russia, Zuzenko abandoned his revolutionary anarchism for Bolshevism; he entreated the Comintern to send him on a mission to Australia, which he argued had enormous revolutionary potential. After a journey lasting more than a year he arrived in Australia in time for the crucial unity meeting of communists in July 1922; he was deported again in September. He never returned to Australia, but became a captain of Soviet merchant ships, and was charged in 1938 with espionage and executed. Petr Simonov was a Russian émigré in Australia at the time of the Bolshevik Revolution. He was jailed in Australia for addressing public meetings in support of the Revolution, but released in July 1919. Simonov's credentials as 'Soviet consul' were not accepted by the Australian government, and he left for Russia in September 1921. Simonov—like the others, as we shall see in this section—advised the Comintern on the situation among Australian communists and despite sponsoring the 'Sussex Street' communists seemed more interested in promoting his own role in the formation of the CPA. However, the influence of his contribution to the Comintern on the matter of the CPA is difficult for us to assess.

Communist publications in Australia during this formative period of the CPA played an important part not just in informing workers about communist aims, but in the organizational game of advantage between the different groups.

Volume 1, Number 1 of the weekly *The Australian Communist* was published in Sydney on 24 December 1920. It began with an article on 'Where We Stand', insisting—rightly—that the notion of the 'dictatorship of the proletariat' separated the communists from the socialist parties that had preceded it. But this same issue contained a vigorous attack on the Australian Socialist Party 'communists', as not desiring unity, even though the conference of communists held at the end of October was (somewhat reluctantly) hosted by the ASP itself. In the meantime, of course, that conference had been reconvened twice and the new executive, unable to gain control of the ASP's journal *International Socialist* at its session of 11 December, published its own paper and commenced hostilities. Nevertheless, getting the message to workers about the changes taking place in Russia was important, and in March 1921, the paper sponsored Professor William Goode's public lectures on Russia. In May 1921, after another failed attempt at unity between communists in March, the paper was renamed simply *The Communist*, and described the Party (inaccurately) as the 'Australian section of the Third International'. The 21 conditions for affiliation to the Comintern, adopted by the Comintern in 1920, were published in the issue of 10 June 1921.

On 24 June 1921, *The Communist* published a 'special unity number', proposing to explain, as it put it in large type, 'Why There are Two Communist Parties in Australia', and laying bare the 'complete correspondence' on the discussions on unity between the ASP and CPA. There followed a blow-by-blow account. In July, the paper noted that the Comintern had also directed the two American communist parties to unite, and later in that month Petr Simonov—'Soviet Russian Consul for Australia'—contributed an article under the heading 'Starving Russia!' which denied press reports of starvation. Thus began a tendency not merely to 'gild the lily' about conditions in Russia, but to lie. Ironically, it was not long before the paper was making desperate demands for aid to starving Russians. These would not be made by Simonov, however, who used the paper to announce that he had closed the Consulate (in August), and booked a passage back to Russia (in September).

From September 1921 to August 1922, when the Comintern formally accepted the affiliation of the CPA, the question of unity among Australian communists was a major theme of *The Communist*. Unity was desirable, it seemed, not simply because of the effectiveness it might bring to their efforts, but especially because the Third Congress of the Comintern 'demanded' it. On 21 October 1921, a front page headline declared: 'Moscow Demands Unity Within Three Months', followed by the text of the resolution. On 20 January 1922, having registered continuing problems in uniting, *The Communist* declared that the other communists (what it called the 'ASP', and what since the end of 1920 is more appropriately described as the 'Liverpool Street Communist Party') had ruled 'the Third International Out of Order' and rejected the demand for unity. To show its bona fides in the discussions between communists, it published further correspondence between the two groups over the unity question (including the letter by Marcia Reardon of 28 December 1921 included here as part of Document 14). Comparisons with children snitching on each other to their parents, or to the classroom teacher, are irresistible.

A conference of communists in February 1922—held by the 'Sussex Street' comrades partly at the behest of Moscow, but chiefly to best the 'Liverpool Street' comrades—established the so-called 'United CPA', and dutifully reported to Moscow. But the game had begun to drift in the direction of 'Sussex Street' as dissent (over a couple of important matters) in the 'Liverpool Street Communist Party' saw the Sydney branch join with the United CPA at the crucial June 1922 meeting attended by Zuzenko. This was the core of the Communist Party of Australia that was formally affiliated to the Comintern in August 1922. But it was not yet over: in December 1922, just as the Comintern was formally welcoming its Australian section at the Fourth Congress in Russia, many of those in the Sydney branch of the (former) 'Liverpool Street' party, whose decision for unity in July had been critical to Comintern recognition, split from the CPA and requested that an ECCI member be sent from Moscow to adjudicate the dispute (Document 23). There were further matters to clarify over the course of 1922 and 1923, many of them related to applying the Comintern's 'united front' policy, as the documents below attest. But while the CPA had by this time virtually seen off the challenge from the former ASP, there were others in Australia who believed that they should be affiliated to the Comintern. In particular, a group of Russian workers in Brisbane contacted the Comintern asking for recognition. They were ultimately advised to join the CPA. The Comintern, once again, was arbiter and ultimate authority in such matters. At this time, and despite small branches in a number of centres and state capitals, the major geographical centre of gravity of the CPA was on Australia's eastern seaboard, with particular strength of numbers only in Sydney and Brisbane. That continued for much of the 1920s, but the Queensland Russians would not become part of the CPA. At the Party's Seventh Annual Conference, Jack Howie reported that for the year 1927 'The C.E. has received only one or two considered reports from Brisbane Group, several complaints about what is taking place in Russia, a failure to recognise the duty of the Community Party ... No contact whatever has been made with Ipswich Group during the year. In 1926 a small Group existed mainly of Russian comrades, and as far as my records show, was broken up, owing to personal differences' (495–94–35).

Late in 1922, as CPA delegates gathered in Russia to attend the Fourth Comintern Congress—and had their celebrated audiences with Lenin and Trotsky (Macintyre 1998, 85–86)—some of the realities of life in a section of the Comintern began to dawn. There were organizational issues to be addressed but, above all, the task of drawing the workers away from the ALP and towards the communist revolution, perhaps the key task confronting Australian communists throughout their entire history, was now located firmly within the framework of Comintern policy. At this stage, 1922, it would be the 'United Front'; later in the 1920s, it would be the 'Third Period', or 'Class against Class', or 'Social Fascism'; and then in the mid-1930s it became the 'Popular Front'. Arguments about the 'exceptionalism' of particular countries may have worked for short periods, but did not go down well in Moscow. We shall have cause to revisit the phases of this policy, but for now it reinforces a key message that emerges from these documents: the centrality of Moscow.

Document 1

RGASPI 495–94–2. 14 April 1920, A.M. Zuzenko: Addresses, for Brisbane, for Sydney. In Russian, manuscript; over-written in Latin script: 'Susenko 14.IV [1920]'. Trans. by KW.

Zuzenko, having been deported from Australia, and landing finally in Russia, contacts the Comintern early in 1920 by way of the following documents. The first fragment seems to indicate Australian contacts to whom communist publications could safely be sent; the note and attached letter attempt to establish Zuzenko's credentials to help create a Communist Party in Australia.

… best via Vladivostok—Japan, San Francisco—Sydney or Brisbane.

Addresses

For Brisbane

1. Mr Norman Freeberg, Sub-editor of 'Worker', Brisbane, Australia. Home address: Mr Norman Freeberg, Laura St, Sth Brisbane, Q-nd, Australia.
2. Mr A. Gorsky, G.P.O. Brisbane, Q-nd, Australia.
3. Mr Alex Robinson, Sub-editor of Daily Standard, Brisbane, Q-nd, Australia.

For Sydney

4. Mr Peter Brookfield,[2] M.P., Parliament House, NSW Sydney, Australia

For Melbourne

5. Mr Considine, M.F.P., Federal Parliament House, Melbourne, Victoria, Australia

9. [3] As soon as I am asked I can send the documents which my wife managed to send from Australia: issues of the newspaper *Knowledge and Unity* in English, proclamations addressed to English [sic] workers, a number of documents concerning my being banned from speaking out in the press and at meetings, the order to deport me from Australia, a number of

---

[2] As given, meaning Percy Brookfield.
[3] Part of the text seems to be missing before this paragraph.

clippings from the English-language press describing our work, and the addresses of some comrades. At present I am the editor of the newspaper *Izvestiia Tiraspolskago Revkoma* [News of the Tiraspol Revolutionary Committee]. If you decide to send me to Australia for liaison with the Third International and to transmit information, I shall be very glad to serve the cause of the Social Revolution once again. The field for ideological work in Australia is very wide and presents opportunities for work such as cannot be found in Europe.

While working in Australia I earned the trust of the working masses. They heeded my words and believed them. The help accorded to my wife, who was left without income (after my arrest) and the deep concern shown for her welfare demonstrate to me that I was well liked there as an efficient [Party] worker. Having been deported under the War Precautions Act, I will be able to go to Brisbane (being a seaman by trade) and quickly begin work again with the aid of the local comrades.

Aleksandr Mikhailov [i.e. Mikhailovich] Zuzenko
Tiraspol Party Committee
Odessa region

14 April 1920,
Moscow

The Organizational Question

Establishing a Communist Party in Australia

1. It is essential to send an experienced communist organizer who is familiar with the workers' milieu and conditions of work in Australia, to organize districts and [Party] cells.
2. The districts and cells of each Australian state should be linked to form a single core, which will form the Central Committee of the Communist Party in Australia.
3. The Central Committee will be the leader of all organizational, agitational, cultural, educational and political work (to the extent that circumstances permit) in Australia.
4. Once it has joined the Third International, the Central Committee will carry out all orders and implement the decisions of the Third International and be accountable to it for its work.
5. From the ranks of the existing League of Communists and from among the Russian workers in Australia, who are mostly Bolsheviks, and from politically aware English workers, we should build cadres of propagandists and organizers, having trained them at courses in propaganda and the plans of the Russian Communist Party.

6. The cadres of propagandists and organizers, when trained for their work, should disperse throughout Australia (through all regions and states) and deepen and extend the communist movement, while reporting on their activities and work to the regions and the regions to the Central Committee.

7. The Australian Communist Party should establish close links with the CP of America, aiding the growth of communism in America by means of literature [i.e. agitprop publications—*Trans.*], since Australia offers opportunities unimaginable in America.

8. Since the proletariat in Australia is already organized into trade unions, it is essential that all Party work be directed towards reorganizing the old unions along industrial lines.

9. Every communist must take it upon himself to be a trade union member and work within the old organizations to promote the idea of rebuilding them on new principles, in order to prepare to take control of production from the very first steps of the revolution.

10. The political work of the Party in Australia is a matter of the broadest propagation of the ideas of anti-parliamentary preparation of the cadres of revolutionary minded workers in order to seize power by revolutionary means.

A.M. Zuzenko
Tiraspol Party Committee

Document 2

RGASPI 495–94–2. 30 April 1920, A.M. Zuzenko: To the Third Communist International, Report on the work of the Union of Russian Workers in Australia. In Russian, manuscript and typescript copies; overwritten by hand: 'to Com. Radek'. Trans. by KW.

In this letter to the Comintern, Zuzenko outlines his own work among émigré Russian workers in Brisbane as a revolutionary journalist and organizer, describes his hazardous journey back to Russia following his deportation, and makes another claim to be returned to Australia on Comintern business. As Zuzenko maintains: 'It is vital that an experienced organizer, familiar with working conditions in Australia, be sent to organize the Australian Communist Party and establish links between Australia and the Third International.'

A version of this document was published in *Kommunisticheskii international*, No. 11, 14 June 1920, signed 'R'.

A.M. Zuzenko
Moscow, 30 April 1920
To The Third Communist International

Report on the Work of the Union of Russian Workers in Australia and the Ideological Work of the League of Communists in Queensland

According to the Tsarist Consul-General d'Abaza, in May 1917 there were up to five thousand people in Australia [sic; i.e. 5,000 Russians]. Of that total, only about four or five hundred were political emigrants. The others were workers and peasants who had come to Australia with the aim of earning a couple of hundred pounds as quickly as possible so as to return home to begin a more comfortable life. The peasants and workers were mostly Siberians from the Ussuri region and settlers from Manchuria. The political emigrants formed groups of Russian workers in Brisbane, Sydney and Melbourne. The number of members of all groups before the 1917 revolution barely reached a total of 100 to 150.

In Brisbane a newspaper was published with the title *Ekho Avstralii* [Australian Echo]. It enjoyed little success and closed about six weeks after being founded. In 1913 the Union of Russian Workers in Brisbane began to publish a paper called *Izvestiia Soiuza Rossiiskikh Rabochikh* [News of the Union of Russian Workers], which appeared until 1916. After representations from the Tsarist government, this paper was closed down at the end of 1916 by decision of the Australian military authorities. A paper with the title *Rabochaia zhizn* [Worker's Life] then began to appear.

None of the afore-named newspapers were popular among the workers, owing to the marked Menshevik tendency of some articles by their correspondents, the unpopular manner of presentation of the articles, which were larded with foreign words, and an excess of battlefield reports. Only after the departure for Russia from Australia of several groups of political emigrants, with fares paid by the Provisional Government, in early 1917, when the Bolsheviks took over the leadership of the Union, did *Rabochaia zhizn* become the voice of the ideas of the Social Revolution and a true workers' paper.

In June 1917 Comrade Petr Simonov was elected Secretary of the Union of Russian Workers in Brisbane and editor of the newspaper. In December 1917, under the War Precautions Act, *Rabochaia zhizn* was closed down. In January 1918, by telegram from Comrade Litvinov in London, Comrade Simonov was appointed Consul General in Australia and surrendered the secretaryship of the Union of Russian Workers in Brisbane to travel to Melbourne, dreaming perhaps of becoming an official of Soviet Russia, who would sit in an office issuing passports to departing Russians ... and nothing more.

In July 1918 the Union of Russian Workers elected me as its secretary. Since 1912 I had been travelling all over Australia, from Port Pirie and Adelaide, to the Far North, organizing IWW groups, collecting aid for the English-language newspaper *Direct Action*, organizing a number of strikes, some of which, like the one in the Mossman sugar-growing district and the shearers' strike in the Townsville area, ended in complete success owing to the application of Russian fighting methods. My ideological work had been mostly among English workers. When elected secretary of the Union I left an organized cane-cutters' strike in northern Australia in full swing—a month later it was broken by the trade unions—and hastened to Brisbane, knowing that with the aid of the established organization of the Union of Russian Workers in Australia much could be done to propagate Bolshevik ideas among English workers.

By this time a rift had occurred in the Union of Russian Workers between the Bolshevik members (mostly workers) and the Mensheviks (intellectuals and profiteering shopkeepers). From my very first steps in this work I succeeded in uniting the Melbourne, Sydney, Brisbane, Ipswich and Port Darwin unions into a federation of unions and groups of Russian workers in Australia. The number of members exceeded five hundred.

While lending material assistance to Comrade Simonov, who had been appointed the Bolshevik consul in Australia, we compelled him to address meetings in Sydney and Melbourne and explain to English workers the great significance of the Russian Social Revolution. Having received permission to publish a Russian-language newspaper *Znanie i edinenie* [Knowledge and Unity], we made it a communist paper which won favour with the Russian workers by its plain presentation, direct manner and truthful articles.[4]

In November Comrade P. Simonov and I were forbidden to play any part at all in propaganda work anywhere in Australia. I was denied the right to edit a newspaper. My wife, née Civa Rosenberg, then became the nominal editor of the paper and secretary of the Union of Russian Workers in Australia. I went on with my work and also insisted that Comrade P. Simonov continue to address meetings of workers, paying no attention to the bans. In early December 1918 the Russian-language *Znanie i edinenie* was closed down by decision of the Australian military authorities. We started publishing it as *Knowledge and Unity* in English and set up three illegal printing shops to print proclamations, while arranging a series of demonstration marches with red placards. A march through the streets of Brisbane to mark the anniversary of the October Revolution was particularly successful. The authorities closed Centennial Hall, which we had rented for the day, but we organized an evening march and meeting, which was very successful, in South Brisbane markets.

---

[4] The last phrase is omitted in the typed copy.

In December 1918 publication began of an illegal Russian paper entitled *Deviatyi val* [The Ninth Wave], of which only four issues appeared. At about this time we set up the Queensland League of Communists, which functioned on an illegal basis. To arrange marches and coordinate ideological work (propaganda and aid to *Knowledge and Unity*) we established a group of organizations: the Industrial Council of Queensland,[5] the Queensland Socialist League, the IWW ('Industrialists') and the Union of Russian Workers in Australia. *Knowledge and Unity* in English, which I edited, enjoyed immense and fully deserved success. It was nothing less than 'mental dynamite',[6] as the delivery boys called it. We received no information or financial support from Russia, so had to rely on our own resources. We managed to obtain John Reed's journal *The Liberator*, smuggled from America, and the newspaper *The Socialist*, the organ of the British Independent Labour Party. Our paper carried the constitution of the RSFSR, speeches by Comrades Lenin and Trotsky, and short articles by [Arthur] Ransome, John Reed, Betsy-Betty and others.[7]

After a successful demonstration on 25 March 1919 with red banners (in protest against the intervention in Russia and the War Precautions Act),[8] we were routed by armed troops. In the clash several people received minor or severe injuries. Three were killed.[9]

On 27 March 1919 I was arrested in Brisbane and compelled to make the journey from Australia to Constantinople in chains. From Brisbane prison I was sent to Sydney prison, then on board ship to Hobart prison (on the island of Tasmania), then the prisons of Colombo (Ceylon), Bombay (India), Suez, Port Tewfik,[10] Cairo, Alexandria (Egypt) and Constantinople (Turkey), whence I was released after three and a half days at the insistence of my wife, who had followed me from Australia. Having departed from Australia a month after me, in late May 1919, she passed on to me some items of news from the month following my deportation. In early May 1919 a conference of trade union workers' representatives had taken place in Melbourne. A plan for 'One Big Union' had been adopted and a decision taken to launch the struggle for a six-hour working day and the nationalization of the means of production. Our paper *Knowledge and Unity*, which I had handed over shortly before my arrest to the Queensland Socialist League, was still appearing and enjoying well deserved success among the workers. Comrade Petr Simonov (the Bolshevik consul in Australia) was

---

[5] Zuzenko may mean the Brisbane Industrial Council.

[6] This phrase given in English, spelt 'dinamite'.

[7] Betsy-Betty: probably a reference to Bessie Beatty, 1886–1947. Beatty was an American journalist who travelled in Russia in 1917 and met Lenin and Trotsky in the Smolny. She was there at the same time as John Reed. Back in the USA in 1918 she wrote a book, *The Red Heart of Russia*, and later in the 1920s visited the USSR. She remained a devoted supporter of the Bolshevik cause.

[8] The actual date was Sunday, 23 March 1919.

[9] Australian documents relating to these events report numerous injuries, but no deaths.

[10] Now more commonly anglicized as Port Taufiq or Bur Taufiq..

arrested and held in Sydney's Long Bay Prison for six months for breaching an injunction not to address public meetings. After my arrest, Russians and Englishmen [i.e. Australians—*Trans.*] had been put on trial for taking part in the demonstrations with red flags on 25 May 1919. Of the Russians, Rezanov, Tolstobrov, Kreslin, Rosenberg and Kliushin were sentenced to six months each. Six prominent English orators and organizers of the IWW at their trial called themselves Australian Bolsheviks and were all sentenced to six months' imprisonment. My wife, who had travelled to Egypt as a free citizen of Australia, was arrested in Suez and sent to the [Gelova?] military prison (for female German colonists) and spent about two months there before being dispatched from Alexandria to Constantinople on the same ship as me.[11]

It is my view, as one who has been at the centre of ideological work in Australia, that we can successfully reply to British intervention in Russia only by Russian Bolshevik intervention in British affairs. British workers pay close attention to events in 'the freest of democracies', Australia, and Bolshevik successes in Australia could have decisive influence on the course of events in England and speed the progress of revolution there. In Australia there are numerous opportunities for ideological work, such as are absent in Europe and America. The broadest material support for *Knowledge and Unity* is essential, if it has not yet withered and still exists, or, if it has died, another paper should be launched.

It is vital that an experienced organizer, familiar with working conditions in Australia, be sent to organize the Australian Communist Party and establish links between Australia and the Third International. It is essential to send literature and provide information to Australia about events in Russia. The shortest route, Siberia – Japan – Australia, can hardly be used at present. The safer route is Arkhangelsk – Norway – San Francisco – Sydney.

If the Third Communist International should need to send me to Australia, I shall be very glad to serve the cause of the Social Revolution in Australia once again. I enclose some documents concerning the ban preventing me from speaking, the warrant for my arrest, my wife's correspondence with the IWW representatives in the New South Wales Parliament, and others. I shall be able to supply several issues of *Knowledge and Unity* in English, some cuttings from the Australian press about my arrest and deportation, and some typical reactions from the capitalist Australian press to our ideological work and reports of the trials of some Australian Bolsheviks, as well as the addresses of some comrades and profiles of them as [Party] workers.

My address:

---

[11] 'Gelova': not positively identified; possibly Yi'allaq.

Aleksandr Zuzenko, Editor of *Izvestiia Tiraspolskago Revkoma* [News of the Tiraspol Revolutionary Committee], Tiraspol, Kherson Region.

Document 3

RGASPI 495–94–2. 15 August 1920, A.M. Zuzenko: memorandum to the Secretary of the ECCI. In Russian, manuscript. Trans. by KW.

Zuzenko's entreaties to the Comintern to return to Australia on its behalf met with success, but he learned that he would be travelling with another deportee from Australia, Paul Freeman. This document is intended to besmirch Freeman's political reputation and ensure that he should not take part in this mission. The substance of Zuzenko's allegations is open to question, but this letter gives an indication of the personal rivalries at play in the early Comintern.

To: Comrade Secretary of the Comintern Executive Committee
From: A. Zuzenko
Delovoi dvor,[12] Room 190, Moscow
Date: 15 August 1920

MEMORANDUM

In early May this year, by a decision of the Comintern Executive Committee, I was instructed to travel to Australia to set up the Communist Party and establish links between the Comintern and the revolutionary element of the Australian proletariat. Having returned to Moscow from Tiraspol, where I had called to wind up my affairs, I learned that Comrade Freeman, whom I had tried to get to know better, was being sent with me so that we could work together in Australia. I knew Comrade Freeman in Australia as a proponent of the ideas of 'Industrialism' (the IWW), who had been arrested in Cloncurry (northern Australia) in January 1919 and deported from the country.

From the earliest days of my personal acquaintance with Comrade Freeman (in Australia we knew each other by repute) I gained the impression that he had a negative attitude to everything that was happening in Russia. In his words, Soviet power meant the oligarchy of a power-hungry few. The dictatorship of the proletariat in Russia was a dictatorship of politicos, ring-leaders of parties who were dishonestly exploiting the revolutionary impulses of the working masses for their own personal ends. The red terror, the persecution of the Mensheviks and anarchists, the struggle against the free market and profiteering all gave him cause to loudly decry 'the dishonest, careerist leaders of the RCP, whom the workers of the world would call to account.' The Comintern, as a 'Russian Muscovite machine for trapping the simple-minded', evoked only sarcastic remarks from him. 'Of all those who have been in Russia,' Comrade

---

[12] Delovoi Dvor (sometimes 'Dielovoy Dvor'): a hotel in central Moscow used by the Comintern to house visiting foreign delegates.

Freeman would say, 'I alone have learned the truth about what is going on there, the vile unvarnished truth!'[13] From cautious questioning it emerged that Comrade Freeman and some of the syndicalists who had come to Russia had dealings with groups of Mensheviks, SRs and anarchists. The Moscow anarchist Pavlov and the SRs supplied him with a mandate and materials to be made public abroad. I did not manage to see what these materials were.

Before the opening of the Second Comintern Congress I gave Comrade K. Radek a brief warning of the suspicious behaviour of Comrade Freeman. In Petrograd, after the celebrations in honour of the Congress, returning to the station with Comrade Freeman, I asked him what impression Petrograd and the Petrograd workers had made on him. He replied maliciously, 'a blind flock led by blind shepherds!' His negative attitude to Soviet Russia did not prevent him declaring to Comrade Radek that he was a communist.

At first I thought that Comrade Freeman wanted to set off to Australia with the aid of the Comintern in order to engage in malicious agitation against the Soviet government, but subsequently I had to discard this supposition. A number of Comrade Freeman's projects, for example, buying a radio-station for Australia (for communication with Soviet Russia) using Comintern funds; immediately razing the 'hideous Kremlin walls' and monstrous cathedrals with that idiotic Tsar-cannon and Tsar-bell in order to build a splendid temple to Freedom; handing over the body of Augusta Aasen, a female delegate who had died, to be turned into soap—all this leads one to suppose that Comrade Freeman is suffering from a mental illness.[14]

On Sunday 8 August, at a gathering to fete the red commanders, Comrade Freeman in his address to the red commanders (quite a fine and cogent speech) stressed that having arrived in Russia as an 'Industrialist' [IWW supporter], he had become a communist under the influence of the Great Revolution. 'You, the vanguard of the world revolution, have made me a communist!' Comrade Freeman exclaimed with great passion. Comrade Bilan, with whom I shared my impressions of Comrade Freeman, added to the knowledge I had acquired of him.[15] According to Comrade Bilan, Comrade Freeman had twice visited P. Krapotkin;[16] more than once the ring-leaders of the SRs called on him in his room at Delovoi Dvor; and

---

[13] Zuzenko's claims about Freeman's attitude to Soviet Russia are hard to square with Freeman's own enthusiastic descriptions of life under the Soviet regime, published in *The International Communist* 28/5/21, 4/6 and 11/6 under the headline 'Red Russia's Growth'.

[14] Augusta Aasen ('Osen' in Russian documents): a Norwegian communist who died shortly after an accident which occurred on 2 August 1920, while she was inspecting the aircraft of the Soviet state's new air force at Khodynka field in Moscow. Her passing was mentioned by Angelika Balabanova during the proceedings of the Congress on 4 August, and mourned by the delegates.

[15] Alexander Bilan, a leading American communist.

[16] As given, meaning Prince Petr Kropotkin, the veteran anarchist revolutionary who in old age returned from exile after the February revolution and died in February 1921. His funeral was the occasion for anarchist demonstrations against the new regime.

on a journey to the Volga Comrade Freeman quarrelled and almost came to blows with Comrade Lozovsky, and so on. Comrade Bilan's view is that Freeman is a sick man and not normal.

Whether Comrade Freeman is sick or whether he is clumsily concealing his hostile attitude to Soviet Russia and its leaders is hard to say, but to send a man like him on a responsible and dangerous mission is risky in the highest degree. I beg you, Comrade Secretary, to bring my statement to the attention of the Comintern Executive Committee so that an enquiry may be conducted.

If the Comintern Executive Committee decides to remove Comrade Freeman from the mission to Australia, I am sure that I shall be able alone to carry out the task entrusted to me. In Brisbane there is the Communist League, which we have set up, a group of communist journalists who have managed the publication of *Knowledge and Unity* and helped to disseminate the ideas of Bolshevism through the workers' press in Queensland and New South Wales. There are firm links in place with the 'Industrialist' organizations (IWW) in Sydney, Brisbane and Melbourne, and with the body called One Big Union, operating independently of the IWW, a fairly strong organization (over 40,000 members) which has broken away from the trade unions. In carrying through our communist programme, we are assured a majority in the Queensland Socialist League and the ASP (Australian Socialist Party), where we shall probably succeed in taking control of the whole party once we have removed the opportunist minority.

In Brisbane and Sydney it will be vital to publish two communist newspapers and arrange the reproduction of pamphlets, the speeches of Comrades Lenin, Trotsky, Zinoviev and Bukharin, as well as fliers and proclamations. Secure and permanent lines of communication must be established between Australia and Soviet Russia. All this can be completed in a period of five or six months. I am convinced that by the time the Third Congress of Comintern is convened a strong cohesive Australian Communist Party, organized along the lines of the RCP will have representation, just as the Australian trade unions will have representation at the International Congress of Trade Unions next February in Moscow.

A. Zuzenko

Document 4

RGASPI 495–94–2. 16 August 1920, P. Freeman and A.M. Zuzenko: to ECCI. First part handwritten in English. Spelling and grammar as given; 'Addendum' handwritten in Russian. Trans. by KW.

This document is an estimate by Freeman and Zuzenko for expenses from the Comintern for their proposed Australian mission. The sum requested is, for the time, extremely high. The 'Addendum', signed by Zuzenko alone, distances him from the first estimate, and attempts to cast Freeman in a poor light as either a profiteer or as profligate.

To the Executive Committee of the Communist International, Moscow
August 16th, 1920
Dielovoy Dvor, Moscow

Comrades,

After careful consideration of Australian Revolutionary Movement needs and great difficulties under which we would be compelled to work, we have decided to submit, for your consideration, the following estimate of aproximate expences. The estimate covers a period of six months.

Personal

A.   (for two men) A journey to Australia and back with possible unforeseen expences etc: £600
B.   (for two men) Full outfit of garments etc: £100
C.   (for two men) Traveling expences in Australia: £100
D.   (for two men) Board, lodging etc. at the rate of £4 per week: £208

Propaganda and Organizing

1.   Communist paper in Sydney: £2000
2.   Communist paper in Brisbane: £2000
3.   Communist paper in Western Australia: £2000
4.   Communist paper in New Zealand: £2000
5.   Communist paper in Melbourne and assistance to *Ross Magazine* (Militant Socialist publication): £2000
6.   Assistance to three IWW and one socialist papers with a view of controling them or at least directing their activities: £4000
7.   Assistance to *Barrier Daily Truth* Union paper in Broken Hill, NSW (Red Petrograd of Australia): £1000
8.   Printing Office for printing Soviet books, pamphlets, speeches of Comrades Lenin, Trotsky, Radek etc: £3000
9.   Possible expences during the formation of Communist Party: £1000
10.   Organization of the underground chanels of comunications from Australia to England and Scandinavia with a view of causing continuous flow of Australian and New Zealand newspapers etc. to the Executive Committee in Moscow: £500
11.   Expences impossible to forsee or account for: £492

Total: £21,000

Considering carrying large sums of money on ourselves inadvisable we urgently request the Executive Committee, if possible, to arrange the matter in such a way as to enable us on arrival in Australia to receive money when needed, from some source outside of it, by cable.

Awaiting your orders and instructions, we are,

Yours in the Cause of Communism,

Paul Freeman, A. Zuzenko

Addendum
Estimate of funds needed for journey to Australia

Newspaper in Brisbane, print-run of 6000 copies at £30 per issue, 25 issues: £750
Newspaper in Sydney, print-run of 6000 copies at £30 per issue, 25 issues: £750
Reproduction of pamphlets and fliers: £1000
Establishment of two illegal printing shops: £700
Personal expenses for return journey and six months' residence there: £300

Total expenses: £3,500

The figure of £3,500 is a maximum amount. Expenditure on newspapers and the reproduction of pamphlets will soon bring a return on investment to cover the organizational expenses (involved in setting up the Communist Party, party congresses and the like) and items not listed in the estimate.

A. Zuzenko

Moscow,

16 August 1920

P.S. Please regard my signature beneath the estimate drawn up by Comrade Freeman as invalid.

A. Zuzenko

Document 5

RGASPI 495–94–127. no date [internal evidence indicates August 1920], letter: To the Small Bureau. Typescript. Excerpt.

Zuzenko seems to have enlisted influential support in his campaign to exclude Freeman from any Comintern-sponsored mission to Australia. In this letter the writer adds weight to the doubts already expressed by Zuzenko about Freeman's abilities.

The copy of the letter at this location is unsigned, but another copy, in Zuzenko's personal file, bears the signature 'John Reed'.

Sunday 22nd

To the Small Bureau –

I. The project of sending Comrade <u>Paul Freeman</u>, member of the Australian IWW to Australia in any capacity representing the Communist International, is, I think, not a good one.

Freeman is an IWW, he is very well known in Australia, and can do a lot of work—until he is arrested, for he has no idea of illegal work at all. He should be allowed perhaps to go to Australia, and some money should be sent there for assisting the IWW but it is my opinion that this money should be sent through the Communists, as we don't know what the attitude of the Australian IWW is.

I think that Freeman is thoroughly sincere, but I believe that his many sufferings have a little unsettled his mind. For this reason I should not like to have him sent with any representative powers.

On the other hand, Comrade Zuzenko, the Russian Comrade who is going, seems to know the Australian movement well, and to be a good Communist and thoroughly trustworthy. He has objections to Freeman which seem to be well-founded. To Comrade Zuzenko I think all instructions and money should be given. In my opinion Comrade Zuzenko received a miserably insufficient amount of money—five hundred pounds—for the work which should immediately be done in Australia. It is a strategic colonial country, with a powerful, fighting mass of workers, who have had some experience of street fighting and are revolutionary in their instincts, with more Socialism perhaps than there is among American workers. And in Australia there is not the division between the Russian immigrants and the Anglo-Saxon workers which exists in America. I believe that even the amount of money asked for by Comrade Zuzenko is too little—although that demanded by Freeman is preposterous.

I wish that the Small Bureau would once more consider the Australian situation, if necessary calling before it Freeman or Zuzenko.

Document 6

RGASPI 495–94–2. 18 August 1920, Simonov: Letter from Australia. In Polish, from an unidentified newspaper. Trans. by KW.

Simonov wrote this letter from Sydney to the Polish Communist Party, which published it. It provides an indication of the range of socialist groups in Australia, and the political complexion of a number of European ethnic groups in Australia, before the founding conference of the CPA. There is no indication of source newspaper; presumably in Poland, judging by the total distortion of Australian and English names. This letter would later be used against him, as he complains in Document 9, below.

Dear Comrades,

I have just received your letter and the journal *wit*, for which I thank you very much. At the same time I am sending you five issues of our official organ, *Soviet Russia* (Sydney), and a book by R. Roll [as given; untraced], a follower of Bernstein, opposed to the communists, and other materials concerning the movement.

It grieves me that we suffer from a general shortage of communist press material. We rely mainly on European press material, which of course is in the spirit of our worthy *trudoviki*, that is, what is known here as the 'Labour Press'.[17]

In the editorial offices of some of these 'Labour papers' there are some bold spirits, who try to push through 'radical' material, but they are isolated cases. There is nothing socialist in it, of course, let alone anything 'radical'. Here in Sydney there is the 'Socialist Labour Party', consisting of female followers of De Leon, who however is only superficially known. In addition, in Melbourne there is the 'Victorian Socialist Party', led by R. Ross, the Plekhanov of Australia but intellectually greatly inferior.

In Sydney there is another socialist party, 'The Australian Socialist Party'. Its core is made up of five or six workers who have some political awareness and try to hold to a communist line as much as possible, openly asserting that they are following in the footsteps of the Third International.

They work hard and do everything they can, but the cause of their unpopularity lies in the fact that they are extremely weak. Their efforts amount to no more than the distribution of European and American revolutionary literature and organizing rallies at which the speakers loudly criticize their opponents. They do not even understand organizational work and one could hardly expect them to understand since they think organizational work is necessary only in countries like Russia. A few individuals are beginning to realize the need for active work, but they are afraid of it, and what is more, it is difficult to get them together. Last year, before I was arrested, I managed to set up some thirty groups in Sydney, each with ten members, but by the time I was released from prison I couldn't find them. My aim was to leave them the means of organization. But of course I couldn't make communists of them in so little time, especially because when I was not there the connecting element was missing, and the nascent organizations folded.

The trouble is that there is nobody here with the intellectual power to influence his milieu. But the workers here are nevertheless sympathetic to the communist movement.

In Melbourne I have managed to find a very promising young man, a former law student. His name is G. Barecki.[18] During the war he took part in the campaign against conscription, for which he received a six-month jail sentence and was expelled from university. He took an interest in the socialist movement and learned Marx off by heart. He and I and another young man have worked together many times. At first they were drawn more to IWW ideas, but after we had had long conversations both of them adopted a communist viewpoint,

---

[17] 'Labour Press': this phrase given in English.
[18] G. Barecki: the writer almost certainly means Guido Baracchi.

and so far they have formed three groups with the aim of having lectures given on economics and sociology, so that when the audience has sufficient preparation it will be possible to form a communist party from them. At the moment *The Proletarian Review* is appearing (on my initiative) as a private paper, with the aim of making it the official organ of the party once the party is formed. Thus far however the Australian Socialist Party, which does splendid agitation work with its official organ *The International Socialist*, may be considered a party close to communism in Australia. The Party secretary is Arthur Reardon and the editor of the paper is Ray Everitt. My journal is printed in their printery. I enjoy very good friendly relations with them and work with them more than with any other organization, even though I am *persona grata* in all the workers' organizations and am in constant contact with the trade unionists. In other words, although there is no communist party in the full sense of the words here, the workers are sympathetic to communism. When it is formed, the communist party will immediately enjoy great influence, thanks to the mood of the broad masses.

The old political machine is breaking down. The capitalist political party (before the war it was called 'Liberal' and during the war 'Nationalist'), thanks to the leadership of William Morris Hughes, an able charlatan and renegade from the workers' movement, has discredited itself even in the eyes of the bourgeoisie. The capitalists themselves would like to break away from the so-called 'Nationalist Party' but cannot do this because, having no other party, they are afraid of ending up under the rule of the Labor Party. But the latter party stands in the same relation to the workers as the Nationalist Party to the capitalists.

Thanks to its squalid, ill-founded and charlatan tactics, the Labor Party has made itself hated by the workers just as much as the party of the bourgeoisie. But they still vote for the candidates of that party, above all because of tradition, but secondly because, except for the Socialist Party, which lacks the strength to stand in elections, there is no more radical party than the Labor Party.

Australians do not understand a refusal to vote. Even while abstaining from voting they still boast that they are 'free Britons', not realizing that 'free Britons' are firmly in the clutches of a group of pitiless killers and their various lackeys, and dregs of society from the Nationalist Party and the Labor Party. But lately that old British political machine, the Australian parliament, has been subjected to criticism by two of its members, Considine and Brookfield. Three years ago Brookfield was expelled from the Labor Party less than three weeks after being elected. But as the Labor Party realized that Brookfield had a huge number of miners on his side, they decided to keep him in the Party. This year he was again expelled just before an election was due, with the intention of depriving him of his seat. But he was elected by a huge majority of 'independent' votes, and a strange situation has arisen in parliament. It turns out that Brookfield stands in the middle, between the Labor Party and the Nationalist Party. It was up to him whether Labor or the Nationalists formed a government. The Nationalist Party offered him £4000 in cash and a position for five years with an annual salary of £700. Brookfield agreed to give his vote to the Nationalists, but not for the money. He demanded only (1) the freeing from prison of twelve IWW members, (2) the introduction of a six-hour working day for miners, and (3) the reinstatement of all railwaymen sacked for the general strike in 1917. But the Nationalists replied that they would not do that. Brookfield then lent his vote to the Labor Party, which has now freed ten of the twelve IWW prisoners. A fortnight ago Considine was summoned to appear before the central committee of the Labor Party for a summary trial, accused of forming a party which would adhere to the Third International, as well as other crimes against the Labor Party.

In conclusion I will say a little about the Russians and Poles. In Brisbane, Sydney and Melbourne there are organizations of workers of all the nationalities in Russia. Brisbane has the strongest of these. The organizations are formed not only from representatives of different ethnic groups but also, to a degree, from different tendencies. There are Bolsheviks, Mensheviks and anarchists (as well as Tolstoyans etc.). Before and during the war, until the time I took over as secretary of the Brisbane organization, the Menshevik tendency was dominant. At that time I was mostly in the country areas, where I organized the Russians into groups, into branches of the Brisbane organization, in whose organ I continued to work.

The revolution came while I was in the mines with Brookfield and Considine. I was secretary of a local branch when we learned that our Brisbane central committee was telegraphing good wishes to Kerensky. Our branch, under my leadership, protested and independently sent good wishes to the Petersburg Soviet of Workers' and Soldiers' Delegates. In April 1917 Brookfield was elected to State Parliament and in May Considine to Federal Parliament, while I was elected secretary of our central committee and editor of our paper *Rabochaia zhizn / Worker's Life*. The anarchists also played their part here, but their anarchism mostly took the form of taking an active part in the work of our organization—and secondly everybody followed and supported the 'Leninists', as we then called the Bolsheviks. Our paper was closed down and I was hauled through the hoops. The Russian Tsarist consul Abaza took a dislike to me, together with the renegade Abramovich, who had claimed on paper to be a revolutionary but in the end sold out to Abaza. They took out citizenship of the Kerensky government, and since I was waging all-out war with the representatives of that government they tried to present me as a German spy. This time I managed to avoid prison or a POW camp by chance, only because they were also accusing a rich Russian Jew of the same crimes as me. He of course hired the very best lawyer and made use of all his business connections, and the lawyer who defended him also defended me. I got out of it, but only to get a year of hard labour later. The court case dragged on for five months, during which time I was appointed the Bolshevik consul. One court imposed a sentence of one year, another made it six months, which was then reduced to four. I spent this period in the most dreadful conditions you can possibly imagine. But thanks to the efforts of Brookfield and Considine I was set free and am back at work.

Here of course there are ethnic groups of Jews, Lithuanians, Estonians and Poles, but none of them are at all active. In fact I was very displeased when a Polish club of workers and bourgeois was formed under the guidance of Pilsudski's representative, the Polish consul, (who of course is English). They are trying to pin everything on me because I wrote that the current Polish government is made up of adventurers. But they will soon realize that I was right. It goes without saying that the more politically aware Poles are members of the Union of Russian Workers.

I think this should give you some idea of the political face of Australia.

I'm not sending much literature, as I haven't got much. Please send some printed material from Europe, I mean mostly English and Russian, as I am weak in other languages. I am not in a position to hire a secretary or assistant as my finances won't permit it.

With my greetings,
P. Simonov

Document 7

RGASPI 495–94–2. 2 November 1920, Simonov: Letter to Tolmachev. In Russian, manuscript and typescript copies. Written at top (in Ukrainian): 'Forward to Com[munist] Inter[national], Russia'. Trans. by KW.

Simonov wrote this letter to the Comintern to explain his activities and the character of the currents within the newly-formed CPA. The letter conveys the importance of Simonov's own contribution, and indicates that the clandestine communist groupings established by Simonov forced the ASP into calling the founding conference. Simonov's groups were able to dominate the proceedings.

Sydney,
2 November, 1920

Dear Comrade Tolmachev,[19]

In order that European communists should be aware of the state of affairs with regard to the communist movement here, I am now in a position to communicate some matters of interest. Of course we do not expect the revolution to take place here soon, but the idea of communism, the idea of social revolution according to the Third International is evidently nonetheless taking firm hold.

---

[19] Also known as Piddubny. (See Document 9.)

It was very difficult to make the workers here understand the true perspective of the Third International. I spent much time trying to nurture the existing socialist organizations here before absolutely losing hope of achieving anything with them.[20] I then began selecting individual worker activists and bringing each of them individually to an understanding of communism. These individual workers began selecting others in their turn, and in this way I managed to form clandestine groups in Sydney and Melbourne. These groups rapidly became more and more active. In Sydney we gained a firm foothold in Trades Hall and even took control of their Labor College. I wrote their manifesto and a programme which was printed on behalf of 'the Communist Party of Australia' by the Central Committee, without of course indicating where this Central Committee was, and concluding by saying that in due course a conference of delegates of all groups established according to our programme would be convened. We issued some other leaflets too, but the main thing is that they have all started to work well in the unions. The active nature of the party has begun to be clearly apparent to all. The Australian Socialist Party was the first to take note. It realized that if our party declared itself openly it would wield great power and other parties would either have to die out or lead a miserable existence. It then called a conference of all leading worker activists and representatives of sections of the socialist parties, both its own and others. Of course, our party, which was not known openly to anybody, proved itself master of the conference. The conference was convened to establish general agreement for co-operation and collaboration between all existing parties and groups, while our party used it to found an openly communist party. Our name, the Communist Party of Australia, was adopted, as was our programme with very insignificant amendments, and our secretary was elected secretary. Of twelve places on the executive, our party won eight (including the secretaryship), the ASP three (one of them only just scraped in), and the twelfth, although not of our party, also adopted its ideas from the very first day that our programme was issued, so he was effectively ours. All our groups are of course joining at once, as are all the left wings of the other socialist and industrial parties and groups. The ASP is completely ceasing to exist and handing over all its assets to the Communist Party. The VSP and the SLP are howling at us for all they are worth but huge numbers of their members are also coming over to us. The secretary is Earsman. His address for the time being is: Mr Earsman, Trades Hall Labor College, Sydney, Australia. But in a week or two the party's organ *The Communist* will start to appear and I will send it to you. You will see its official address. Everitt, the editor of *The International Socialist*, the official organ of the ASP, wants to write something for Europe. He has asked me for an address and I gave him yours as well.

With comradely greetings,

---

[20] 'Absolutely' omitted in typed version.

P. Simonov

Document 8

RGASPI 495–94–7. no date [internal evidence indicates late 1920], W. Thomas: Letter to 'dear comrades'. Manuscript.

This letter appears to have been written early in 1921 by Bill Thomas,[21] recently arrived in Sydney, to his colleagues in Brisbane, whence he hailed. It represents a personal angle on the manoeuvring in the newly-formed CPA, especially over the assets of the ASP, with whom Thomas clearly sympathizes. It casts a jaundiced eye over the activities of Simonov, and it reinforces the view that the early Australian communist movement was both small and rather inward-looking.

Bell Street
Watson's Bay

Dear Comrades,

I arrived in Sydney last Friday and, despite the fact that I promised myself a rest from propaganda, I am at it just as hard as ever. The movement here is in a very complicated condition—I will endeavour to explain it as clearly as possible. Some weeks ago the ASP called a conference for the purposes of forming a Communist Party: the conference did not represent any organisation and some were men with very bad political careers such as Denford, Charlesworth and others. The ASP delegates were out-numbered but thought that there would be some possibility of forming a united body. The just thing the conference members did was to declare themselves the provisional executives of the Party; no re-election to be held until next Easter because "we will be well known to the revolutionary movement by that time". This means that at the present time they are unknown and if a party vote was taken they would not be elected. The ASP offered the printing press and the whole of the party property to the newcomers. This offer they readily accepted and proceeded to elect an editor. Glynn, the IWW prisoner got the job; he is utterly incapable. Then the other jobs were given to other "friends"—in fact it was simply a job catching scheme for a gang of opportunists. The chief schemer is all of this dirty business was Simonoff! He was going to take the credit of forming the Communist Party and then leave for Central Russia via Italy. Last Monday morning I called on Garden and met Simonoff and Glynn. Garden told me the arrangements which had been made and I naturally thought that they had been passed by the executive but when I called at the ASP office I was informed that the executive <u>had not even discussed the</u> matter! You will understand that Garden, Glynn, Simonoff and Co. simply engineered anything they wanted because they had a majority of tools on the

---

[21] Thomas, W.J. (Bill): founding member of the CPA, lecturer on problems of venereal disease and editor of the Brisbane *Communist* in the early 1920s. Thomas became a Party journalist and eventually in the 1930s the national organizer of the Friends of the Soviet Union.

executive. On Monday night the executive met, and spent half the time discussing myself! Simonoff said: "Thomas is in town and I suppose he will apply for membership to the party. I would like to hand these letters to you." He then read the blackmail letter which he sent to the ASP. A Russian named Zanders then moved that "The Communist Party has every confidence in Com. Simonoff and we take no notice of Thomas' childish nonsense." The ASP delegates opposed this and it was withdrawn in favour of this motion: "When Thomas applies for membership he is to be brought before the executive with Simonoff." Which means that Simonoff's executive would condemn me; <u>a bunch of damn scoundrels whom I have been fighting for years</u>, renegades and disappointed Labour politicians, job hunters and hooligans. When the ASP saw how things were going they called a special meeting and withdrew from the whole dirty business. When the Simonoff crowd received a letter to the effect I called on them as though I knew nothing and asked if I could join the new Party, they said "Certainly". I questioned the new secretary and he deliberately lied and told me there were no restrictions or objections to my membership—this was evidently a way of getting my support. Also: the new executive agreed that Simonoff will be allowed to attend all meetings. You will want to know what actions I have taken. I am again a member of the ASP which is now known as the Communist Party of Australia because "they definitely stand by the principles of the Third International and are recognised as the Australian section by Moscow." The ASP has now taken a definite stand against Simonoff and are getting into touch with Martens and Central Russia for his removal. In a matter like this it is impossible to remain neutral. One must take sides. The ASP has agreed to assist me with the sale of *The Communist*. In this matter I am having some trouble as the man I sent there 20 doz has gone over to the enemy and has not yet delivered them to me, however I will do my best with them. The Russian Assoc. in Brisbane sent a letter to the executive of the ASP asking about 12 questions, concerning myself including the £30 business. The answer was NO. If the Assoc. has not read the letter I will send you copies of the letter and answer. Jerry Cahill Secretary of the Trades Hall Council in Brisbane also wrote and asked if there was anything against me in the ASP and he received the same answer as the Assoc. I was almost certain that Simonoff told him something when he was in Brisbane. I want you to ask him for a copy of that letter and tell Com Kusmenkoff to go the Assoc. meeting and expose the lies of Simonoff and his gang. I am enclosing a bill which has been sent to me by *The Standard* the item for £1, should be 16/-[22] <u>don't pay any more!</u> It was Anstey's lecture. At the beginning of the year *The International Socialist* will be called *The International Communist* and the Party is considering publishing a magazine. With regard to Simonoff I want you to send me every scrap of information you can get. He is

---

[22] The symbol '/-' denotes shillings, a unit of money equal to one-twentieth of a pound (£).

running around like a sick child since his plot failed. I have not seen Jaginoff yet but tomorrow night I am going to the Assoc. meeting—Simonoff is sure to be there. Quinton has 10 doz, 5 doz No 1 and 5 doz No 2. It is all in the account book I left you. I have not had time to visit Com. Fine yet. Do not read all of this letter to the meeting, particularly the part where the ASP take a stand against Simonoff because we do not want him to know anything he is like a rat in a trap. I delivered a lecture last night on Bolshevism and the world war. I would be pleased if you would send me anything of interest to which comes through from Russia. Have you had any mail from Japan? In my room you will find some of No 1 magazines addressed ready for posting put No 2 and 3 with them and post; also to Martens. I will conclude as I have a big mail to attend to. For any information I am at your disposal.

W. Thomas

Document 9

RGASPI 495–94–6. 8 April 1921, Simonov: to ECCI concerning an 'All-Australian Socialist Organization'. In Russian, manuscript and typescript copies. Trans. by KW.

Simonov's letter was forwarded to the ECCI in June 1921 by a correspondent in Vienna, whose covering note appears first. The letter is a damning indictment of Paul Freeman, who had been sent by the Comintern to Australia to identify delegates for the next Congress in Russia, but who seems to have upset Simonov's plans by his preference for ASP, or 'Liverpool Street Communist Party', members. The letter traces some of the history of the complicated relations between the two major currents within the early CPA. Freeman had left Australia for the Third Congress on 7 April 1921, the day before this letter was written. At this stage he was using the name 'Miller'.

To the Comintern Executive Committee, Moscow
4 June, 1921
Vienna

Dear Comrades,

I received the enclosed letter from Petr Simonov after the departure of the delegation to the Third Comintern Congress, and it may arrive too late. At the same time I am sending three newspapers of the (new) CPA and one of the CPA (ASP): *The Australian Communist, The Proletarian, Knowledge and Unity* and *The International Communist.*

Petr Simonov, with whom the editor of *Nasha Pravda* is corresponding, has written previously about Miuler,[23] but we thought that Tom Barker (apparently the one who arrived from Australia and was in Argentina) lived in Berlin and

---

[23] 'Miuler' as given, meaning 'Miller'.

was *au courant*. We are now forwarding this letter at the request of the Australian communists. Miuler has another name: Paul Freeman.[24]

With communist greetings,
G. Piddubny[25]
Algerstrasse 69
Vienna VIII

8 April, 1921
To the Third International Executive Committee, Moscow

Dear Comrades,

Many years have passed since I read the immortal Gogol's Government Inspector and saw it staged. Personally I had never previously come across anybody resembling the hero of the play, but suddenly, completely unexpectedly, I have now encountered one, and in utterly new circumstances. On Wednesday evening, 6 April, from 7.30 to 11.30, I had to listen to a Khlestakov of the revolution.[26] This was Comrade Miller, who claims to have been sent here by the Third International from Moscow. Whether they sent him or not, I do not know, but if they did I do not know what for or what he has done. All that he could demonstrate was his Khlestakovism. I am writing this letter and giving his name because his 'mission', to use his own words, is over and he has now spent a full day on a ship working his passage home, and this letter will not be posted until he is clear of the shores of this country and out of all personal danger. He personally thanked me for averting by my actions any danger to him, which was building up owing to the carelessness of others and above all his own. I learned that he was here from at least ten people at once, but not from him personally. And if he thanked me, it was for using all my influence to ensure, as far as possible, that there was absolutely no more talk of him, even though he personally placed me in the most foolish and idiotic position with regard to himself, as you will see from what follows and as will probably be explained to you personally.

The idiotic position is as follows. About three months ago a certain Jim Quinton from Queensland called on me in my office, bringing with him a Russian 'communist comrade', as Quinton introduced him. I had personally never met

---

[24] The typed copy has 'Peter Freeman'; the handwritten copy is correct.

[25] Typist has 'signature illegible'. It is indeed difficult to read, but the writer's name is written clearly, with his address, at top right, in Latin script. He is almost certainly Piddubny (i.e. Tolmachev). (See Document 7.)

[26] Khlestakov is the hero of Nikolai Gogol's famous play *The Government Inspector* (1836), a vain and empty poseur who is mistaken by the people of a provincial town for an important dignitary travelling incognito. Khlestakov relishes the attention and grows in self-importance as the situation develops. Curiously, one of Simonov's associates, W. P. Tuitene (V. Tiutin), described him (Simonov) as a Khlestakov, and as Mr Jingle. (Noel Butlin Archive Centre, James Normington Rawling Collection, 'Simonoff', N57/299)

this Russian 'comrade' before, although I know all the Russians who can be taken as communists (there are not that many, and I have personally visited almost every corner of Australia). Of course all kinds of people come to see me, even government sleuths, who for the past six years have been most concerned about my health and therefore watch my every step, though highly unsuccessfully, or not always successfully. So I received these two 'comrades' from Queensland the same way I receive all strangers. A few days later they came again. In the meantime Quinton had been mingling with some socialists, and I also learned that in Queensland he had long mingled with so called 'rebel circles'.[27] This of course does not mean that he is necessarily a true revolutionary. In those circles it is possible to be a splendid revolutionary comrade and the most unprincipled charlatan and scoundrel. In any case, I took Quinton to be one of those whom one should not put much trust in, but not one to be suspected of anything bad, except that persistent rumours circulate in Brisbane about his lack of caution, or even his lack of scruples. So he and this Russian 'comrade' again came calling, this time about an important matter. The Russian 'comrade' and apparently Quinton himself were going to Europe with the intention of getting into Soviet Russia. The Russian 'comrade' already had a passport and ticket to sail. What they wanted from me was a letter of recommendation for the Russian 'comrade', issued by me, to revolutionary circles in Europe, stating that he was an upstanding and reliable communist and that I personally knew him to be such a one. I asked his name and was shown his passport, in which I read the name of Alfons Frederik Erosh. By this time one of the Russians had warned me that this Russian 'comrade' was Erosh, and this name came back to me in connection with the name 'Alfons', and I knew of Alfons because of a connection with the name of Mendrin, a well-known Tsarist agent provocateur, acting in this capacity as recently as the current revolution. So as to be quite sure, I sent a telegram to the secretary of the Brisbane Union of Russian Communist Workers to ask whether Erosh was Alfons. In reply he said yes, and warned me that he was Mendrin's right-hand man. For this reason, when shown his passport I simply told them that the best thing they could do would be to go and get back the money they'd paid for their fares as this Russian 'comrade' would not get into Russia. I did not let slip that I knew anything about Erosh. Quinton tried to insist and begged me to give him a letter of introduction to help him get into Russia. He tried to shame me with reproaches, saying it was my duty to help a 'communist' comrade. In the end I simply stated flatly that I would not give him any letter at all. I knew that Quinton often visited the printery of the Australian Socialist Party, and later even learned that he lived with the editor of their newspaper. I therefore hastened to call on him there, to see him without the Russian 'comrade' being present. Quinton was there and I asked him at once if

---

[27] This phrase given in English.

he knew the Russian 'comrade' well. He said he did. I asked if he knew that rumours were circulating about this 'comrade'. He said he knew it was being said that he was a police agent provocateur, but this was untrue. Then I suggested that he tell his good friend that, in addition to the name of Peter Simonoff, I was also called Artur Simens. I mentioned this because this was the name I had used to sign many of my articles, including some about the antics of Mendrin and Alfons. The next day Quinton told me that he had found out everything and that his Russian 'comrade' had been deceiving him. His Russian 'comrade' then came to me straight after Quinton and declared that he really was the scoundrel, rogue and miscreant that he was alleged to be, but that he had been inveigled by Mendrin and had now turned over a new leaf and intended to be a good man if I would only give him the opportunity to make his way to Soviet Russia. When I refused to give him anything in response to his repeated promise, he offered me money for a letter of introduction and at this our conversation ended. I immediately wrote a letter to London and Stockholm to warn them that this character was on his way to Europe with the aim of entering Russia. After this Quinton asked me not to take his behaviour as deliberate deception. He had done this solely to help a Russian comrade, little knowing that the Russian was such a scoundrel. But I have just learned from an ASP member, whom you will probably soon see in person (B),[28] that Erosh brought Quinton down from Queensland and maintained him here at his own expense, and either offered to pay or actually paid his fare to Europe and Russia. Comrade Sergeev[29] in Russia can probably confirm that Quinton could not help knowing who Alfons Erosh was. I am not saying this to accuse Quinton of anything. This is not about Quinton, as you will shortly see. Soon after this Quinton applied to join two parties at the same time: the ASP and the Communist Party of Australia. The ASP accepted him and the CP of A did not, on the grounds that he evidently had a poor grasp of party discipline if he believed that he could be a member of two political parties at once. So he became a member of the ASP, or, since this party changed its name, the Australian Communist Party, when it came into existence.

One fine morning this Quinton brought along a new communist comrade to see me, this time not Russian and not from Queensland, but a German from Broken Hill. Quinton at once declared that this time he wasn't bringing an agent provocateur but a true communist. Would you believe him, comrades, the second time round? I don't know. Perhaps you would, but I could not. That this new comrade was from Broken Hill I learned later from others, first from Kilburn, through Comrade Garden. Comrade Kilburn found out from the ASP that Comrade Miller was not from Broken Hill at all, but was a delegate from Moscow!!! I

---

[28] The initial read by the typist as 'B' is almost certainly a Latin 'R', possibly standing for Alf Rees, one of the group of Australians then en route to Moscow.
[29] Fedor Andreevich Sergeev (Artem).

learned from the Melbourne newspapers that a delegate had arrived from Moscow. Soon people who had seen Comrade Miller in person started coming to see me one after another, and of course I knew his every move. All I did was ask every one of them to keep quiet and not spread the word, in order not to compromise his security. For this Comrade Miller thanked me the day before yesterday, saying that by doing this I had assured him that he could meet me openly, but when? The evening before he embarked, when, in his words, he had accomplished his mission, which he did not explain to me but which I learned of from others—and I also learned that he had not accomplished it, as might have been expected—he gave me a lecture which lasted from half past seven till half past eleven. I will not mention the matter of a certain person known to you. I shall write about that later, whenever possible. His lecture consisted of an explanation of the greatness of the ASP. He kept revealing more and more new things about that party. To me the main revelation was that the ASP had five hundred members. This came as news to me and this is why: over the past two and a half years I have visited that party's office and printery almost every day. I have attended many meetings of the central executive as well as general meetings of all its branches which ever existed even earlier than two and a half years ago. Two years ago I sat right through their annual congress. The delegates voted on behalf of 290 members from the whole of Australia. The party then had branches in Broken Hill, Melbourne, Newtown and, I believe, in Newcastle. Today this party has no branches at all except the Sydney one. All the others have died off one by one, just as the whole party has been gradually dying off, from the fairly solid base of an All-Australian Socialist Organization.[30] It has been dying little by little, without any sudden jolts, but particularly fast in the last five years. I have been following it constantly. I saw its Brisbane branch, which had its premises with our Russian Association, die because the centre showed absolutely no sign of doing anything to bind the party together. The centre was dying, and the branches were dying even faster. The IWW was smashed by the police, while the ASP was dying because of its greyness, vacuity and personal squabbles that had absolutely nothing in common with an ideological movement. But the main reason seemed to me a very odd thing. It was the acquisition of a printery. It was odd because acquiring such a valuable asset ought to be a tremendous incentive to energize a party, but this acquisition damped all energy. This party should not be viewed, of course, from the standpoint of the revolutionary movement in Russia. It should be seen more or less as a replica of British socialist organizations, that is, rather like a religious sect, worlds apart from the workers' movement as a whole. If you were to introduce to the British socialist party and to some British religious sect somebody with no understanding of English and no knowledge of the world socialist

---

[30] The ASP aspired to become an 'All-Australian Socialist Organization'; Simonov's point was that it had lost the opportunity.

movement, he would be unlikely to notice any substantial difference between them.

To return to the matter of the printery, before the war a so-called socialist club existed here, made up mainly of Germans. During the war it was closed down and the people in charge of its assets handed over the club's printery and some other assets to the ASP for its use, placing it in the hands of three trustees, of whom two are still alive, with the editor of the party's paper. In this way all power to influence the party fell to the printery and the people controlling it. I do not wish to suggest that these people are abusing their position. They themselves believe that they are doing their very best for the revolutionary movement. They may even be working completely honestly, although there are many who do not believe in their honesty. But all their energies have been directed above all towards retaining control over the printery and thus the party, while they fail to notice that for all other purposes their energies increasingly dissipate and evaporate.

Early last year I was in Melbourne and witnessed the closure of the last branch of the party outside Sydney. Soon after this I moved to Sydney and received some financial support from Comrade Martens and started working with this party. I saw at once that in its membership and its branches, as well as its finances, the party was going bankrupt. It owed about forty pounds to a bookshop (Andrade) and had five or six pounds' worth of books in its store. This apart, it owed one of its members, Everitt, sixty pounds odd for paper and other current expenses. The printery has two printing machines and a sufficient quantity of print. Printing work could have been done, but the printery stood idle. All the work was done by Everitt, who was at once editor, manager, typesetter and printer. (By trade, curiously, he is a cobbler.) He is a good, hard-working fellow, but such a task is far too much for one person. I insisted that they take on a qualified printer, so as to make full use of the facility, but they were afraid they would not be able to afford his wages. I then guaranteed them two pounds a week until the printery paid for itself. I paid them six pounds for three weeks, although the printer showed me that he made ends meet by private work over and above his work for the party. I insisted that they start printing pamphlets and even books of a kind that could easily be sold. In order to provide them with regular assistance I started publishing my official organ on the model of Soviet Russia, put out by Comrade Martens in America. They printed it and the publication and sales brought them at least five pounds a week, while I lost about twenty-five pounds a month on it. They printed this magazine for me for seven months, although a private printer offered to do it for a lower price. I tried everything I could to activate them. At the same time I set up independent groups in Melbourne, Brisbane, Newcastle and Sydney, so as to be able to draw them together later in a unified communist party. The ASP knew that I had formed these groups, and they had no objections. They even had friendly relations with the Melbourne group. The ASP slowly improved its efforts, although these found expression only in purely local activity which had no effect whatever on the movement as a whole. At least they were able to pay off most of their debts and build up quite a respectable stock of literature, etc. But soon Everitt quarrelled with the printer and dismissed him, taking on a girl to help out. As it turned out later, the girl was not needed at all, as her work could be done on a casual basis by unemployed party members. What I could not manage to do was draw them closer to the workers' movement as a whole. They feared the trade unions and 'Trades Hall' like the plague. Instead of winning over the workers and recruiting new members, they only yapped and snarled at everybody, blindly mimicking communist criticism of reactionary European political organizations without understanding it and without knowing where or how to exploit this criticism. More than anything they resembled the lap-dog that yapped at an elephant in old Krylov's fable. The elephant needed to be led in a certain direction, not yapped at pointlessly. Nonetheless the Melbourne, Brisbane, Sydney and Newcastle groups realized that instead of yapping at the elephant it was better to try and lead it, and soon they achieved great success, especially in Sydney, where these groups operated in the strictest secrecy. Their success was so promising that they even ventured to declare themselves a communist party, while still remaining secret. They put out their manifesto and programme, printed in secret, and many other fliers. The manifesto and programme were written by me. I will not boast of their quality, but they met the requirements of the day in splendid fashion. I am enclosing the original, as first printed. Here I must say that these actions were in no way aimed at the ASP. On the contrary, it was my intention to rouse the ASP, to stimulate them to greater activity and show them that much could be done even without a printery and assets, that there was more to the party than its printery and assets.

However, I did not tell them, or course, that I personally ran those groups. My aim was to build a strong party and unite it with the ASP, but the ASP was seriously alarmed by the energetic activity of the new party. They raced round all the printeries to see who had printed the programme and other materials, and where, but without success. Then they hit on other tactics, or rather, on their old tactics. They reprinted the manifesto and programme in their newspaper, indicating that they fully accepted the policy in them, except for some insignificant amendments, but it showed that those who had issued them had apparently taken fright at their own boldness and not given their names or address. They then convened a conference to set up a communist party. They invited sixty people, including those selected from the ranks of their own party, the SLP. Their aim in calling this conference was insincere from the very start, because if those who issued the manifesto and programme had not taken part in the conference the ASP would have declared itself a communist party and thus demonstrated that it was right to call the others cowards undeserving of any attention. And if some of them accepted the invitation and joined them, they counted on remaining in control by controlling the assets and the printery, and being thus able to squeeze out of the party all who did not submit to their absolute control.

The invited communist party members, including those from Melbourne, accepted the invitation and compelled them to accept a correct, broad-based structure for the communist party. The ASP delegates could not reject the proposal by the communist party delegates. A single, unified communist party was formed. Everything went well. The ASP delegates apparently agreed to everything. The party was functioning as a party, using the ASP premises and printery, or Trades Hall. The ASP delegates stated that they themselves and their central executive agreed to everything, but that to ensure full unification they had to conduct a poll of all members and obtain the full agreement of the membership of their party. In the end this was done.

They then set forth the terms under which the ASP would hand over its assets: the printery would not belong to the party but was private property entrusted for the party's use to two individuals, so that nobody other than those two individuals had any control over those assets. This was accepted. The assets of the ASP were turned over to the Communist Party, with the proviso that, if the current members of the ASP found within six months that the Communist Party was not a true communist party, they had the right to reclaim their assets and premises. The other delegates did not accept these terms, not wishing to see the continuance of a party within the party, viz. the ASP within the Communist Party. They preferred to appoint trustees with the right to claim the assets at any time within six months, but without having to give grounds. This was accepted by the ASP. It remained only to attend to the accounts and balance, and agree on the inventories and debits.

On Monday 13 December a meeting was held of the Communist Party's executive, attended by delegates from the ASP executive, and everything apparently passed off with the full agreement of all present. On Tuesday the ASP wrote a letter to Comrade Earsman, the secretary of the Communist Party, declaring that the ASP was withdrawing from the Communist Party and adopting the name of the Communist Party?!!.[31] The executive of the Communist Party comprised twelve people and only three ASP members withdrew. What was the executive to do? They decided to take no notice of the ASP and continue the work of the party. The ASP made haste to dispatch Everitt to Melbourne, where the Communist Party branch was well established on the basis of the workers' groups that I mentioned earlier. The Communist Party secretary also went. All the Melbourne membership, except for two members, remained a branch of the

---

[31] Author's punctuation from handwritten version, not retained by typist.

Communist Party. The Newcastle membership provisionally declared their independence until the schism was fully clarified. They called a conference and invited delegates from groups in the coal-mining centres and representatives of the central executives of the Communist Party and the ASP. Having heard the ASP and Communist Party delegates, they unanimously elected to adhere to the Communist Party, including even the former ASP members, and declared the ASP a breakaway section. The same occurred in Brisbane, Adelaide, Perth and other centres.

As a result there are two communist parties. One of them, as you, comrades, will see from the latest issue of its newspaper, has branches in all major centres and three official organs: the weekly Australian Communist, the organ of the central executive; the fortnightly Knowledge and Unity, the organ of the Brisbane branch; and the monthly Proletarian, the organ of the Melbourne branch. This is the party that controls the Trades Hall Labor College in Sydney, Melbourne and Brisbane, the secretaries of which are members of the Communist Party. This party exerts great influence on the trade unions through its members on the executive of the big unions and the Trades and Labor Council. Its members include the very best Marxists in Australia and the most energetic and boldest party staff. And this, as you will see from the enclosed press samples, is no isolated case, but an example of systematic and determined application.

On the other hand the ASP, or the Communist Party of Australia, as it now styles itself, is restricted to the functions of its Sydney group, whose meetings I have often attended and never seen more than twenty people present. This is the party Comrade Miller wanted me to see through his eyes, as a party with five hundred members and the best revolutionary forces. Of course, I can quite understand Comrade Miller's blindness. From the very first day, thanks to his personal friend Paddy Lamb, he succumbed completely to the control and guardianship of the ASP, and from 7.30 to 11.30 he repeated to me exactly what the ASP had fed him. He did not even notice that whenever something was done for him, it was members of the Communist Party who did it. This even includes his departure from Australia. Five hundred influential communist ASP members could not so much as get him on board a ship. He had to resort to the services of the Communist Party, whom he wanted nothing to do with until he was forced to.

To show that I am not dreaming this up, although the enclosed magazines illustrate quite well what I am saying, I am also attaching some cuttings from the newspaper of the Polish Communist Party, which printed a letter which I wrote nine or ten months ago, when no communist party yet existed and only the first steps had been taken towards creating one.[32] This letter was held up

---

[32] See Document 6, above.

against me by my opponents here. They translated it into English and threatened to publish it in English. But they soon realized that it could only serve them as an instrument of provocation, not as an accusation against me in front of the revolutionaries. For this reason the threat remained no more than a threat. They went to Baracchi,[33] whom I have mentioned, and he confirmed that the letter was genuine, that is, that it fully accorded with the facts.

You will probably also soon receive the opinion of Professor Goode about the parties here,[34] and I fear his opinion will not concur with that of Comrade Miller. I do not mean to suggest that the Communist Party of Australia is exactly as I would like to see it. I am writing this only because Comrade Miller painted such a fantastic picture of the ASP for me that I had to either laugh or keep silent. I chose the latter.

He wanted me to express my opinion of his view of the parties here, my opinion after he had taken me severely to task for not collaborating with the ASP against the Communist Party, express my opinion when he felt it necessary to conduct even this last conversation in the presence of ASP members in the ASP printery, my opinion after he had, in his words, accomplished his mission and was set to embark the next morning. What his mission was, I do not know, except that he played the part of Khlestakov to perfection. The Australian trade union delegates had been elected before he appeared, according to a letter from Tom Barker in Berlin,[35] and Comrade Miller had seen none of the people whom he should have seen by that time. The delegates representing the three biggest centres of workers' organizations will have something to say about this. He explained the fact that he had not met me openly earlier by saying that after his arrival in Australia he had received such an impression of me that he doubted whether he should trust me. But he was perfectly well aware all the time that I was fully informed about his every movement and he knew that everybody he had seen outside the ASP immediately relayed to me not only this fact, but also everything he said. So if I was a person not to be trusted, in view of his dangerous situation, I was perfectly placed to betray him without even having set eyes on him. Yet as it turned out he learned that I had actually helped secure his position, even though he had behaved towards me entirely in the manner of Khlestakov.

He insisted that the ASP had been recognized by the Third International. Perhaps it has. I know that it was represented at the first congress, when the Third International was formed. I even know how it was represented, because the mandate for Comrade Sergeev was sent on behalf of the ASP by me to the address of his sister or relative (Sergeeva's hardware shop). And this was not

---

[33] i.e. Guido Baracchi, misread by typist as 'Velassy'.
[34] i.e. Professor William T. Goode.
[35] Clearly Tom Barker in the handwritten version; misread by typist as 'Gon Velkech' (in Cyrillic).

even done on the initiative of the Central Committee of the party, but by the Brisbane branch together with me (this branch no longer exists, of course).

I knew then that such representation was very important for the formation of the Third International. I also know that if Comrade Sergeev were here he would act exactly as I have acted towards the ASP and the Communist Party, because although I argued a lot with Comrade Sergeev about Comrade Cook (the Social Patriot), I was in full agreement with him about everything else. I will go so far as to say that if the Third International officially declares that only the ASP is recognized as a communist party in Australia I shall hold to my view of the two parties, if they continue to work in the way they work now. This is because it is plain to me that the ASP is simply a religious sect, while the Communist Party is a living, vibrant revolutionary body. My view is of them as they are now. What they may become in the future, I cannot tell. I am not a prophet.

With comradely greetings,
Petr Simonov

Post Scriptum: As I have not yet posted this letter today (9 April), I have read and am enclosing a newspaper dispatch from London which shows clearly that the matter of sending delegates was being discussed here long before the arrival of Comrade Miller. By his tactless behaviour he has done only harm here, as the journey of the other delegates came close to being sabotaged, as you can see from the other cutting. This interview was given by Comrade Garden (a member of the Communist Party), because in Melbourne the people whom Comrade Miller saw operated openly, not having properly seen through him, and discussed the matter of sending delegates openly, even debating the matter of subsidies for the fare, while the delegates, as you see, embarked as working members of the ship's complement.

After the Melbourne incident, which was reported in the Melbourne papers, the local press attacked Garden and Bazova. Badelei did something fairly silly,[36] forcing Garden to give the enclosed interview the next day,[37] since the names of the two who had departed were known, of course, but up to this point nobody had paid any attention to them. If Comrade Miller's mission was to ensure that delegates were sent from here, he would have done much better to remain in Europe and write a letter, like Comrade Tom Barker and Comrade Ziuzenko [sic; for Zuzenko], who sent me the manifesto in Russian. It was immediately translated, as you can see from the enclosed, and printed.

---

[36] 'Bazova', 'Badelei'—as read by the typist. In handwriting these appear to be the same name, in one case partly latinized, and most likely [Jack] Beasley, a known associate of Garden's. The miners' leader and Labor member of parliament J.M. Baddeley cannot, however, be excluded.
[37] 'Enclosed interview' not traced.

You can see that we here have not been idle. But it has not been easy to prod the local unions into action, of course. From all the enclosed material you will see clearly that, to my great chagrin, Comrade Miller, as I said earlier, has merely acted out a Khlestakov role. I am not blaming him. He was not familiar with the workers' movement in Australia in the way that he thought he was, as until he was deported he spent some time in the wilds of Queensland and then was arrested and transported to and fro between Australia and Canada. He was held on a steamer here, and then deported. All his popularity derived from the argument about his deportation. Many of those who protested energetically against it had never known him or had the slightest idea about him. Many took him to be a wealthy mine-owner, not a worker, so the well-to-do among the Irish Catholics assisted in the propaganda against his deportation.

P.S.

Document 10

RGASPI 495–94–128. no date [1920 or early 1921], Paul Freeman: A Glimpse into the Working Class Movement in Australia. Manuscript and typescript versions. The typescript is inaccurate at several points.

This document seems to be a report to the Comintern, but may well have been intended for publication (infelicities of style notwithstanding). It reinforces two themes important to radical workers at this time: the importance of the recent World War in demonstrating the bankruptcy of the capitalist system; and the inability of politics and politicians to change the capitalist system for the better.

A Glimpse into the Working Class Movement in Australia

To understand the correct Industrial as well as Parliamentary positions in Australia it is necessary to somewhat review both from the time 'The International Pirate Crew' inaugurated 'The Human Slaughter House of Europe', where many millions of men, women and children with all the pomp peculiar to the capitalist society were sacrificed on the altar of greedy God Mammon.

It is well to remember that in Australia [the] Labor Party under the leadership of Andrew Fisher was in full possession of the Federal and State Parliament for many years prior to the declaration of war in 1914 and continued in power under the leadership of William Morris Hughes long after the war was declared.[38]

---

[38] At the beginning of the First World War, the ALP won back government at the federal level and formed governments in most of the state parliaments in Australia. Andrew Fisher was the moderate Labor leader at federal level, who was replaced in October 1915, when William Morris ('Billy') Hughes became prime minister. Early in 1917, Hughes and a minority of members of the Parliamentary Labor Party made a pact with conservative Members of Parliament and formed a new party, the Nationalists. In May 1917, the Nationalists won the federal election. By the end of the war, conservative governments had been elected in most jurisdictions in Australia, some of them supported by Hughes' state counterparts who had followed him out of the Labor Party. Hughes' prime ministership survived his change of

Working men and women being in vast majority in the Labor Party and knowing that they nominated and elected every member of Parliament believed that the Cabinet consisting wholly of members of [the] Labor Party would try and settle every industrial dispute in their favor. A vast majority of them also believed that the Labor Party, while in power, that is in the possession of Parliament would eventually legislate out of existence the abominable 'Wage Slavery'. Of course politicians and would-be politicians had done all in their power to mentally chloroform the wage slaves into believing in the exclusive power of Parliamentary Action.

Just prior to the declaration of war in 1914 in Australia unemployment was so great that it would not be an exaggeration to say that scores of thousands of young, healthy, vigorous men and many women were all over the country, looking for an opportunity to sell their 'Labour Power'. In spite of the wage slaves' anxiety to be exploited, capitalists instead of employing numerous out of work toilers, took advantage of the large army of unemployed and actively engaged in reducing their already more than meagre standard of living.

Immense majority of workers were organised in Craft Unions and with the exception of the 'Industrial Workers of the World' who knew better, believed in the efficacy of the Parliamentary Action and the ability of Parliament to adjust all the industrial disputes favorably to the wage slaves and to eventually bring in the millennium. But, not being organised industrially, hopelessly split into small or fairly large loosely amalgamated craft unions bound up by their contracts for a certain number of years expiring on widely different dates, workers found themselves absolutely helpless against the onslaughts of the internationally organised capitalists, backed up by the very parliaments that the workers looked upon as the bulwarks of their own strength.

The wages slaves in general excepting the IWW and a small but very militant group called 'the Australian Socialist Party' did not recognise the economic fact that the parliamentary action was merely a reflex of the industrial action, that is direct action taken principally at the point of production of the commodities and their distribution. They did not recognise the fact that Parliaments reflected only those who control the direction of production and distribution of the good things of life. Since the Australian capitalists had the fate of Industries in the hollow of their hands their clumsily acting, wasteful blundering putrid and ruthlessly pitiless Parliament reflected anything but the workers' desires.

The war broke out and the Labor Party being in power immediately declared themselves of the side of the International Pirate Crew, ready to do their bidding, ready and even anxious to force into the European Slaughter House the great

---

political party, and the fact that his referendum to introduce conscription for the armed forces was twice defeated.

starving armies of unemployed, armies which were already beginning to threaten the very existence of capitalism. At the outbreak of the war the prime minister and leader of the Labor Party Andrew Fisher said that he would give (for slaughter of course) the last man in Australia and would spend the last shilling. True, the capitalists in Australia spared no effort in trying to force the last workingman into their armies, but as to spending the last shilling—well they simply gathered the last shillings workmen and women possessed for the capitalist's benefit. They called it a good business.

Recruiting was conducted in all its brutal hideousness and was helped by the master class throughout the country who refused to give employment to able bodied men.

The IWW seeing the favorable conditions redoubled their propaganda in Industries and steadily gained in strength. As time went on influence of the IWW propaganda was felt throughout the country which expressed itself in Direct Action indulged in by the working man almost everywhere. Wage slaves in Australia had good tutors and were slowly learning their lesson—for in general they have commenced to show an unmistakable desire to organise on better lines than heretofore. Then the anti-conscription campaign came which offered so favorable a field for the IWW propaganda that the IWW took a part in it and by successfully conducting a vigorous Industrial revolutionary propaganda impressed its popularity and influence to an extent so great that the master class genuinely alarmed started a systematic campaign against it. Thanking the IWW for infusing much militancy[39] into the action of the wage slaves the Anti-conscription campaign was successful. William Morris Hughes the prime minister announced his intention of attacking the IWW with a ferocity of the Bengal tiger. He started by causing the arrest of the 12 IWW men on false charges and a specially appointed judge sentenced them to from 5 to 15 years' imprisonment with hard labour. Shortly after wholesale arrest of the IWW men the IWW organisation was declared illegal. Finding that the IWW men when arrested and tried were doing a very telling industrial propaganda through the capitalistic courts, the government changed their tactics and started to secretly deport without an open trial or even a shadow of an enquiry all the IWW men they considered dangerous. Thus over 200 working men of all nationalities were secretly deported. It would do no harm for the working class to remember and to draw a lesson from the fact that although Australia is an English colony, [the] Australian government did not hesitate to deport Englishmen, Scotsmen, Irishmen and even Australians when it suited their purpose. [The] Great majority of them instead of being deported to the places of their birth were deported to South America and dumped there.

---

[39] The typist incorrectly put 'military' at this point; the handwritten original has 'militancy'.

Persecution and oppression forced the IWW men to scatter all over the country, give up the open methods and resort to purely underground tactics. As a matter of fact, the period of persecution of the IWW marked the sure awakening of the class consciousness in Australian Unions which manifested itself in many interesting ways. It also marked very important changes within the Parliamentary Labor Party which in Parliament and out of it was compelled to reflect the purely industrial activities and aspirations of the workers.

[The] Labor Party on account of the big groups of workers of different shades of opinion taking very militant stand right in Industries even way back in 1915 brought about a split in its ranks and consequently new elections. Reactionary section of the Labor Party and so-called Liberal (Tory Party) in order to defeat the section of the Labor Party which reflected more or less militant section of the working class combined, called themselves the 'Nationalist' or 'Win the war Party' and by most unscrupulous means carried the elections with William Morris Hughes remaining Prime Minister of the Commonwealth.

The Nationalist or Win the War (for the international capitalists against the World Proletariat) Party was purely a military party. Shortly after the elections, when the sinister significance of the War Party activities commenced dawning upon the workers' minds and the oppression became almost unbearable, Win the War Party became thoroughly disliked and discredited by the great majority of the working class. Win the War Party clung to the reigns [sic] of government with bulldog's pertinacity [sic] for over a year after the supposed conclusion of the World's War. In the end, even the master class, seeing the inability of their flunkeys in Parliament to cope with the advancing militancy of the Union men were getting uneasy and were talking of the necessity of the change of Government. That of course coming from the capitalistic press foreshadowed an early general election.

In [a] great many cases complete disregard of the craft union official mandates, deliberate breaking of the contracts, men striking on their own initiative and talking about the advisability of organising on purely industrial lines prove beyond doubt the great influence of the IWW men's propaganda accomplished under the cloak of craft unionism. IWW tactics were adopted and used with varying success almost everywhere. Capitalist press howled against the IWW and the Government continued to persecute them. If a man was arrested and the IWW card was found upon him, he was sentenced to six months' imprisonment with hard labour without the option of a fine. However the spirit of IWW-ism so permeated the craft union organisations that some of the aspiring politicians have deliberately and shamelessly taken the IWW preamble in almost its entirety [and] added to it the clause recognising the Parliamentary Action and started organising what they pleased to term 'The One Big Union'. All that was done with a view of preventing the possibility of the working class developing a healthy desire of acting on their own initiative instead of depending on so-called labour leaders which would have prevented the mental prostitutes betraying the workers while trying hard to safeguard the capitalist's right to exploit the toiler by successfully running, for a princely remuneration, their administrative machine called Parliament.

At the time of the writer's deportation from Australia to Germany October 10th 1919 it became apparent that the new psychology of the wage slaves forced the politicians in general to very much review their opinions and change their parliamentary attitude—for the reason that diverse opinions entertained by different electorates of the same party ranged politicians in the party into definite groups; the groups having opposite opinions rendered the formation of generally acceptable policy not only very difficult but almost impossible. The psychology of the wage slaves in general became so changed that at the Interstate Conference of the Labor Party at 1919 in order to get the workers' support politicians and would-be politicians passed most sweeping resolutions promising slaves practically everything under the sun. During the sitting differences of opinion became so great that the so-called extreme section withdrew and held their own conference where they however have eventually decided to do everything possible to prevent a split. Of course it is easy to understand that the only way for the Labor Party to again get into power was to avoid a split. Withdrawal of the extremist section brought about a great danger of the second split in the ranks of the Labor Party. The executive of the Labor Party consisting of the conservative section demanded the expulsion of some of the extreme members of the party but were not supported by their electors in their demands.

The Win the War Party at that time appeared to be quite helpless as to what course to take and impatiently awaited the return of the Prime Minister William Morris Hughes from England who, as their leader, was expected to formulate a sufficiently palatable new policy for the people to carry the party through. On his arrival in Australia, Hughes, hoping to gain the support of about 400,000 returned soldiers, promised them all sorts of impossible things, thundered against the agitators and threatened to hang them and [the] profiteer[s] and that in spite of the fact that Hughes himself is a heavy shareholder in some of the rich companies. He draws big profits from Dalgety and Co. alone. After [a] great deal of bombast and hot air, he without announcing his policy intimated that the election in all probability would take place on Dec 13th 1919. Politics! Oh! Dirty, rotten politics!

It is true that some politicians honestly believe that they could and have sincere intention to do, if in power, everything possible to take the yoke off the workers' necks. What an impossible dream. What a delusion. Politicians have got to run the Parliament for the master class with the express purpose of keeping the yoke firmly fastened upon the workers' necks—for they themselves draw their fat salaries from the surplus value extracted from the very life's blood of the working class. As a rule, [a] politician is an animal which very, very often disregards his own views and opinions for the sake of adopting the shade of opinion entertained by his electorate at the time of elections, but as soon as he ensures his seat in Parliament for a number of years and finds himself in a different atmosphere and environment—the atmosphere and environment of parasitism—he immediately hears his master's voice and performs the tricks of a well-trained docile dog. Truly [the] politician is a human chameleon.

My personal experience and a long careful study of the capitalistic parliamentary activities prove conclusively the fact that [the] capitalist is a man who would do everything for the working man but to get off his back and his [sic] politician is a man who would do everything but to help the working man to throw the capitalist off his back. Also that the only hope for the working class of gaining the 'Industrial Freedom' is to organise industries on purely revolutionary Industrial lines for by virtue of their economic position in society as a whole that is their natural tower of strength.

I am
Yours for the Proletarian World Revolution
Paul Freeman.

Document 11

RGASPI 495–94–128. no date [internal evidence indicates April-May 1921], unsigned, but believed to be by Paul Freeman: The Birth of the Communist Movement in Australia. Present only in a Russian version, typescript. Document apparently incomplete. Trans. by KW.

Freeman sailed from Australia (Sydney) on 7 April 1921. This letter indicates that the Australian delegates to the Third Comintern Congress (to be held in June) had departed for Moscow. Quinton's arrest in Britain is not mentioned, so presumably it had not yet occurred. Freeman and Artem were killed in an accident in Russia on 24 July 1921. Freeman's close relations with Jim Quinton and Paddy Lamb are mentioned in Simonov's letter, Document 9, above. The letter is significant because it shows that Freeman, like Zuzenko and others who attempted to engage the attention of the Comintern in Australian affairs at this time, believed that revolution in Australia was imminent.

The Birth of the Communist Movement in Australia

1. Australia as a Colony

The unusually rapid growth of the revolutionary movement in Australia in the last few years, like the political and economic situation as a whole in that country, has received very poor coverage in the Russian and foreign press alike. The remoteness of Australia, and above all its complete isolation from the outside world, most strictly maintained thanks to the British government's complete control over all Australia's contacts with other countries, have all created a screen over events in Australia, events which have frequently caused the British imperialists to tremble in fear for their power over this colony. Before proceeding to a survey of the stage which has now begun in the working class's struggle in Australia, it is necessary to provide a cursory overview of the objective conditions in which the Australian proletariat was and is now compelled to enter the lists with its exploiters.

The conditions of the struggle in Australia are different from those in England or the United States, although Australia is often considered to be America in miniature. Both politically and economically, Australia is a true vassal of Britain, a colony in the strictest sense of the word. The 'autonomy' of the colonies, on which the capitalist press is so fond of expatiating, exists for Australia, as for the other British colonies, only on paper. In reality, not a single law can be enacted by the local or federal parliaments without the blessing of the governors appointed from London. In this way the political life of each of the six states, as well as the federal government, is dictated. These British bureaucrats, who occupy the highest administrative positions in the land, not only exercise their prerogatives, they effectively dictate the entire political line of the government of 'autonomous' Australia.

The burden of economic dependence on the British capitalists, although in more concealed form, weighs even more significantly upon Australia. Although Australia's financial and industrial capital, now highly concentrated, appears on the markets as Australian capital, even the official figures demonstrate the signal fact that approximately 75% of Australia's industrial and financial capital is of British origin. A fairly substantial proportion belongs to French financiers, and during the war the participation of American capital in the industrial life of the country began to appear and then increased. The place of truly Australian capital in the development of industry and in Australia's current trade turnover is absolutely insignificant. If we add to this the fact that all the most important industries in Australia and all tonnage, like all shipbuilding, is exclusively in the hands of British capitalists, who as a result totally control all Australia's foreign trade, the full extent of dependence and of exploitation of Australia's working class by the predatory British imperialists will be apparent.

The power of British capital over the Australian proletariat manifested itself not only in the vast profits received, but also in direct support for British imperialist plans. When heated debates were still in full swing in the British press about the desirability or otherwise of large battle cruisers for future imperialist wars, the news that the British government had decided to build four huge cruisers, each with twelve 21-inch guns, to help Britain maintain its naval supremacy, sped round the world. This put an end to all arguments about disarmament.

Tottering British capital, despite the blows it had received from its own rebellious proletariat, recognizing that it stood on shaky foundations, nevertheless decided not to fall behind its younger and fitter competitors—America and Japan —and resolved to continue its frenzied maritime programme. But the economic contradictions which had become so acute in Britain after the world war, and which threatened the very existence of British capitalism, compelled it to seek direct assistance from its colonial 'children'. In Australia a capitalist press fully subservient to the dictates of the London bankers was unleashed, along with all other propaganda media, to persuade the broad masses that Australia needed to have a great navy of its very own. Nothing was said, however, about the fact that the very organization of the navy handed all control over its operations to the British government, leaving in the hands of the federal government only the mechanisms for training the required personnel.

The present campaign for a 'close alliance' of all parts of the British Empire is being waged with the same aim, of seizing influence in Australia's political life. An attempt is being made to bribe the Australian masses and those of other British possessions by granting places to representatives of these countries in the British cabinet, thus creating the illusion that Australia is playing a part in deciding the destiny of the whole British empire, while in reality an Australian representative in the British government would be no more than a conduit for absolute control over his country, a reliable instrument for even greater enslavement of the Australian proletariat. However, as the leftist press has shown, the working masses have not risen to this bait and have come out openly against these new machinations of cunning British imperialism.

2. The Economic Situation and the Workers' Movement

The end of the world war meant terrible unemployment for Australia, as it did for all the capitalist countries. In Australia, as a colonial country, though one with highly developed industry, the crisis assumed more acute form. The government did not possess large economic resources, as in western Europe or Japan, to offer assistance to industries that were in dire straits or by various measures artificially cushion the blows of a painful crisis. The consequences of terrible material disaster soon had an effect on the psychology of the Australian working class, which in an extraordinarily short time became so revolutionary as to be unrecognizable. In all major centres unemployment committees were formed to see to the takeover of public and municipal buildings to provide refuge for hungry and homeless workers cast adrift by the cruel hand of capitalism. Such was the pitch of fury of the unemployed against their enslavers that an utterly reactionary Australian government never once dared oppose the actions of the unemployed, who in broad daylight violated the sacred bourgeois principles of the sanctity of private property. The government was even forced to begin regular distribution of rations to the unemployed, in order to avert open insurgency in major industrial centres.

The most recent crisis, as well as previous defeats in the struggle against capital, has shown the Australian workers, who had been organized on a narrow workshop basis, how utterly wrong the structure of their labour organizations had been and impelled them onto the path of a broad industrial association. The previously dominant, and still existing workers' unions, organized on the same lines as the American Federation of Labor, although not quite so reactionary, were not capable of leading the Australian working class in a united struggle against its exploiters, and reality itself demonstrated that such conservative organizations of workers were not viable. The lessons of defeat in strikes have dictated the need for industrial workers' organizations to defend their interests, and the very first propaganda by the American Industrial Workers of the World, who arrived in Australia in 1910, produced brilliant results. They were the element that brought ferment into the conservative labour unions and did much to bring about their collapse. However, the Industrial Workers of the World, for all the services they undoubtedly rendered to the workers' movement in Australia, in rousing it from the hibernation its reactionary leaders had kept it in, remained unable to bind the workers tightly together in even one major industry, owing to an absence of organizing skills. They attained the summit of their influence in 1916, when they began to implement a plan for the tight-knit organization of industrial unions, but this same period was a difficult time for them as all their organizations were disbanded by a reactionary Australian government and they were driven underground. It was precisely the ruthless repressive measures against the Industrial Workers of the World that served as the spur for more fruitful work by them, as the tactics—rejected outright by the Industrial Workers of the World—of penetrating the conservative labour unions in order to destroy them, had to be accepted, like it or not, in recent years of harsh reaction rampant in Australia, when membership of any such conservative union was often a necessary precondition to receiving a wage. It is understandable that the presence of more revolutionary elements, which had entered every labour organization from a few major centres in which they had been concentrated, very soon made itself felt and did much to prepare the ground for the inculcation of communist ideas in the masses.

3. The Communist Movement

The Communist Party was formed from the Australian Socialist Party, which had existed in the country for more than twenty years. After the Second Congress of the Third International the Australian Socialist Party, in accordance with the resolution of Congress, changed its name to the Communist Party and immediately joined the Third International. Almost the entire membership of the former Socialist Party remained in the Communist Party. The most progressive and politically aware members of the IWW also joined the Communist Party. Thus the membership of the Australian Communist Party consists exclusively of good Marxists and of experienced older fighters, who have given proof of their loyalty to the ideas of communism in determined struggle with the reactionary Australian government. The members of the party are almost exclusively workers, and the leaders of the movement have made admission fairly difficult for new members in order to protect the young party against an influx of wavering elements and *agents provocateurs*, whom the Australian government tries in vain to plant in all Communist Party organizations.

The extraordinary unanimity and singleness of purpose of the members of the Australian Communist Party stood out with particular clarity in the political struggle which the communists were obliged to wage with certain right-wing groupings, although these called themselves 'revolutionary'. Under the leadership of Ross and [George?], these Australian Mensheviks, being a small splinter group of the right wing of the former Australian Socialist Party, resorted to various means to try to shatter the young and growing Communist Party, going so far as to have no qualms about accepting funding from the capitalists to print anti-communist brochures. The firm theoretical foundation on which the Australian Communist Party rests enabled it to crush these right-wing groups without difficulty and to completely divide and effectively terminate the existence of the IWW group, which had been about to launch a determined campaign against the communists.

Besides fighting these insignificant and fast-melting forces of the 'socialists', the Australian Communist Party also has to wage a struggle against the old reactionary leaders of the labour unions, who still control almost all the apparatus of these unions in spite of repeated rifts and the tendency of the Australian proletariat towards freeing itself once and for all from the woeful leadership of these indirect agents of capitalism. The communists in Australia are pursuing tactics of general penetration into all labour unions and gaining influence through them over the toiling masses so as to totally refashion the unions along new industrial lines. This work is made considerably easier by the shortsightedness of the old, conservative labour leaders, who take no account of the necessity for minimal change, at least, to allay growing dissatisfaction.

A more serious and bitter foe of the Australian communists in their ideological and practical work is the extremely reactionary government, which deploys all measures used by the former Russian tsarist regime to try and crush the communist movement in Australia. The capitalist government maintains strict surveillance of all arrivals and departures, and despite all protests by the broad masses has established clandestine censorship. The most outstanding leaders of the communist movement are subjected to arrest without trial or investigation, with deportation to other countries following prolonged detention. Australia's damp, cramped dungeons have been the cause of [*word illegible*] of more than one staunch fighter for communism. Word of arrest and exile to other countries, as of frequent hunger strikes declared by imprisoned communists, rarely reaches the pages of the capitalist press but reaches the masses mainly through the labour unions and protest meetings organized by the communists and broadly attended by the toiling masses. These persecutions have tempered the fighters for communism in Australia and made bold, selfless revolutionaries of them.

In their struggle the Australian communists have recently been receiving broader and broader support from the working masses. Many workers' organizations are, in practice, led by communists [and are? – *words lost on torn corner of page*] thoroughly revolutionary in their nature. The silver and lead miners of Broken Hill are particularly close to communism. The unshakeable determination [with which?] they waged their eighteen-month strike, ending in complete victory for them at the end of last year, has become known to the whole world of labour. These miners not only waged an economic struggle against their oppressors, but also organized their own Red Guard, which experienced several armed clashes with the capitalist hirelings. In this region, which the Australian comrades call 'the Petrograd of Australia', where anyone who speaks out openly against Soviet rule in Russia or against the Bolsheviks risks being beaten to death by an indignant crowd of workers, a truly revolutionary workers' self-perception is being forged. Courses in communism operate, and there are even communist schools for children.

Demobilized soldiers who have experienced the trenches in Europe and know all the horrors of the imperialist war from their own bitter experience constitute the most receptive element for the dissemination of the ideas of communism. They number up to 300,000 and have their own organization, led, however, by officers. But the fact that ex-soldiers are clearly sympathetic to communism has received frequent confirmation in their reluctance to take part on the side of the capitalists in armed clashes between the police and the unemployed, and by their outright refusal to guard a military hospital in Sydney when the workers held demonstrations to demand the release of a well-known communist prisoner held there,[40] as well as by many other demonstrations of their solidarity with the revolutionary part of the Australian proletariat.

In its tactics the Australian Communist Party recognizes the necessity for Soviet rule as a historically inevitable form of dictatorship by the proletariat and wages its struggle on this fundamental principle, taking account of all factors of the Australian way of life and the psychology of the masses. Australia's

---

[40] This most likely refers to Freeman himself and the demonstrations provoked by the attempts to deport him to the USA in 1919. After the failure of two such attempts (the US authorities would not accept him), he went on hunger strike and was held on shore from June 1919. He was eventually deported (successfully) on 10 October 1919, to Germany.

communists clearly realize that the overthrow of capitalism in their country will come about against the bitterest opposition of the bourgeoisie, which is actively preparing to resist the pressure of the revolutionary proletariat, making good use of the lessons of the revolution in Russia and Germany. Given all the repressive measures being taken by the government against the Australian communists, the party will have to function partly on a legal basis and partly on an illegal one. The latter is essential in view of the fact that at every moment the Australian communists must expect new persecution, and the method of organization adopted has shown itself in practice the most expedient. Work is also proceeding through the factory workshop committees, which are at present a revolutionary element in Australian working life.

At the forthcoming Third Congress in Moscow, the Australian Communist Party will be represented by four comrades: Paul F., Patrick L., James K., and Reed [sic], A.[41] Australian labour unions have sent ten delegates from various unions to the International Congress of Red Trade Unions [RILU]. Lack of time precluded calling a conference of all the country's trade unions in order to elect delegates, and in any case this would not have been successful as the government would have taken all steps to prevent the delegates leaving the country. All the delegates departing for Moscow would have had to leave [illegally?...] [*Document breaks off here*].

Document 12

RGASPI 495-94-6. 8 April 1921, Correspondence between C.W. Baker and Miller and A.S. Reardon concerning unity of the Communist party. Typescript.

This set of letters and drafts, from April 1921, represent a part of the manoeuvres between the 'Sussex Street' communist party and the 'Liverpool Street' communist party to join together on a mutually acceptable basis. They indicate not just the hostility and formality that characterized the relations, but also that Miller (i.e. Paul Freeman) as representative of the Comintern was attempting to urge unity and that 'Sussex Street' (Rawson Chambers) was showing Miller himself—by writing directly to him—how compliant they were attempting to be.

110 Rawson Chambers
Rawson Place
5.4.21

Comrades

The Executive of the Communist Party of Australia, after the report and advice of the General Secretary W.P. Earsman, decided to agree to meet your executive on the question of Communist Unity.

---

[41] Names as given in Cyrillic script: i.e. Paul Freeman, Patrick Lamb, James Quinton and Alfred Rees. See Macintyre, *The Reds*, p. 59 ff.

Yours for Communism
(signed) C.W. Baker

Comrade Miller advised altering this to read as [below].

110 Rawson Chambers
Rawson Place
Sydney

A.S. Reardon
General Secretary
Communist Party of Australia
(Late ASP) 115 Goulburn Street
Sydney

Dear Comrade

The Executive of the Communist Party of Australia after the report and advice of the General Secretary, decided to act on the suggestion of Comrade Miller, and agree to comply with the request to meet your Executive on the question of Communist Unity.

Yours for Communism
(signed) C.W. Baker Acting General Secretary

Letter to Com. Miller
110 Rawson Chambers
Rawson Place

Dear Comrade

This party having complied with the request re Unity Conference, informed Comrade Everitt to that effect, and that we were prepared to meet his executive on Wednesday evening.

We were informed by Comrade Everitt that no answer could be given until the matter had been placed before his Executive on Thursday. He agreed to inform us of the decision of his Executive on Friday morning.

Therefore we suggest that we meet his executive on Saturday evening.

Yours for Communism
(signed) C.W. Baker
Acting General Secretary

Letter from 115 Goulburn Street
April 8th 1921
Mr C.W. Baker

Dear Comrade

Your undated letter referring to suggestions of Comrade Miller on the subject of Unity, to hand. Having placed same before our executive I am instructed to reply as follows:-

In anything that transpired between Comrade Miller and your General Secretary, Comrade Miller was in no wise acting officially for our party, nor was he acting at our request, as we have observed no development that would induce us to retract from the position we took up in December last, in fact the case is rather to the contrary.

The essential points of the basis for unity suggested by Comrade Miller were—the recognition of our Party as the Communist Party of Australia: your organisation to be granted a minority representation of three of our Executive, and our Executive representatives to have the right to review your membership for twelve months and if necessary expel those who could by no means be considered as Communists.

As however, we have noticed no attempt on the part of your Party to purge itself on its non-Communist elements, we are of the opinion that a meeting with your executive would at present, be futile and a waste of time.

We understand from Comrade Miller that he made it quite clear to your General Secretary that he was acting on his own initiative, and that he made it still clearer that in organizing against the Australian Section of the Third International, your Party was doing counter-revolutionary work.

When your organisation shall have proved itself to be honest and sincere, and worthy of the claim to be a Communist group we shall be glad to discuss with you the question of Unity.

Until that time, we extend to all individuals who accept the principles laid down by the Third International and who are prepared to work for the realisation of Communism, a hearty invitation to the ranks of our Party.

Yours for the Proletarian Dictatorship
(signed) A.S. Reardon
Hon. Gen. Sec.

Document 13

RGASPI 495–94–7. 1 July 1921, Union of Russian Communist Workers: Minutes of the Unity Conference, Trade Hall Brisbane. Present in English (type) and Russian versions (print).

This document is an account of the attempt to fuse three communist organisations in the Brisbane area in June 1921: the Union of Russian Communist Workers, the Ipswich Communist Party, and the Brisbane Communist Party. It demonstrates not just the diversity within Brisbane, but the importance of Russian communists in that area. In many countries diverse groups either claimed, or tried to unite to claim, the status of a 'communist party'; in Australia the Russian communists in Queensland were ultimately rebuffed in their attempts to unite with others, but continued their revolutionary work in relative isolation until the mid-1920s.

Minutes of the Unity Conference Trade Hall Brisbane

The First Session of the Conference was held on June 12, 1921. The following were elected as delegates to the conference: from Ipswich Communist Party Organisation—comrades Lubimov and Kilimov, from the Brisbane Communist Party Organisation—comrades Hochstand, Lefand and Pikunov: from the Union of Russian Communist Workers, Brisbane—comrades Galchenko, Shakhnovsky, Khrutsky and Gorsky. Comrade Shakhnovsky was elected chairman and comrades Lubimov and Pikunov secretaries. Members of the organisations in question were presented at the Sessions in a consultative capacity.

As laid down by the conference rules, the reporters were delegates of the Ipswich Communist Party Organisation. In their opening speeches they pointed out the necessity and importance for Russian workers of the establishment of one general organisation in Australia. Without presenting a definite plan, they proposed on behalf of their organisation the following conditions for unification.

CONDITIONS: No. 1. To reorganise all the existing organisations and to establish a central organisation. 2) To establish a centre of the fused organisation by means of a conference or a referendum. 3) They agreed to recognise as the centre organisation—the organisation of longest standing and with a preponderating number of members. 4) The statutes to be elaborated and adopted jointly. 5) After fusion to submit the lists of members of the fused organisations to joint investigation. Comrades expressing sympathy for Soviet Russia and for ideas of Communism to be considered members of the fused organisations. Those who can be proved to be an uncommunistic and undesirable element to be considered as having left the Party. 6) To audit the funds and property of all fused organisations. 7) In the interests of the development of organisational capacities, to elaborate plans and methods for future self-determination. 8) Immediately on the organisation of the centre to take in hand the liquidation of conflicts in the existing branches and to begin work among the unorganised. 9) Comrades who, in accord with point 5, will be left outside the organisation and will not alter their attitude to the organisation's aims and tasks previous to the adoptions of the statutes, must not be received as members either in the centre or in the branches, 10) The branches of the fused organisations refusing to adhere to the fused organisation to be declared reactionary—not with us—but against us! 11) To guard common funds and property and to prosecute offenders of the past as well as in future. 12) To proclaim adherence to the Third International.

After the Ipswich delegates, the delegates of the Union of Russian Communist Workers addressed the conference. They pointed out that a party constitution would lead to isolation from the wide masses of Russian workers among whom there is a great awakening and desire to take part in the organisation, but who nevertheless cannot abide by party rules and regulations in view of their lack of political and economic knowledge and revolutionary experience. They welcomed the idea of fusion, but as before insisted on the impossibility of adopting a party constitution. In this respect they referred to their own resolution adopted between the first and the second (the present) conferences and published in their paper on April 26, 1921. They brought it forward as a basis for fusion which was adopted. This resolution is as follows:

RESOLUTION: Re question of fusion of the groups of Russian workers in Australia on a Communist Party basis as proposed by the Ipswich Communist Party Organisation, the Union of Russian Communist Workers, while expressing its views on the wrong attitude taken up by other groups and on the way in which this question has been brought forward, has come to the following deductions and conclusions:

On principle the URCW considers it opportune, in view of dissensions, to reconsider the question of fusion on the basis of communist policy. The experience of the First Conference on this question has shown us the following state of things.

The existing Australian organisations of Russian workers are out of touch with the real conditions of the Russian revolution and also with the conditions of the local labour movement in view of the special character of their aims. Their exceptional position and their lack of experience compel them to be guided in both cases only by ordinary communist aspirations, and not by definite conditions and tasks such as confront the Russian proletariat. Therefore, the idea of the fusion of groups of Russian workers here in Australia on the basis of the program of the Russian Communist Party is fallacious and politically unsound. Apart from the special character of the aims of Russian workers in Australia, such a serious political step would also be impossible because it is not the Russian Communist Party which will be the guide of the Australian proletarian movement, but the Australian Communist Party, not to mention the fact that such a step would be tantamount to establishing here a Soviet Government and the dictatorship of the proletariat. Their national position, their isolation from the Russian revolution and their lack of contact with local life forbid them to consider such a step.

The Union of Russian Communist Workers is of the opinion that a neutral non-party organisation among the wide un-organised masses of sympathisers with communism and the communist party and control of their aims and tasks is the only acceptable organisational basis for fusion. If other groups agree with the above mentioned view point, the question of fusion can be decided without convening the conference, for such a form of organisation already exists—the URCW. Since 1918 this organisation has been, on the basis of the declaration re attitude to the November revolution, such a neutral non-party organisation animated by communist ideas. The Russian workers in Australia, in view of the peculiarity of their position, are in favour of such neutral organisation between communist party and dictatorship of the proletariat. The URCW is of the opinion that such a politico-organisational base with preponderating communist influences will enable us to prepare ourselves for work in any capacity for the Soviet power. The claim of other groups to uniformity of aims will be a significant guarantee for the tendency of the organisation. Therefore to meet the desire for common organisation, the URCW, while refusing to take part in the conference, offers to all those in favour of the communist policy of unification its organisational structure as a field for unification, and opens its ranks for membership.

NOTE TO THE RESOLUTION. In the interval between the First and the Second Conferences the Brisbane Branch of the Australian Communist Party received an instruction from the CEC of the Party to make an attempt to link up into one organisation the Russian workers of Brisbane. In the URCW it was resolved to entrust the Brisbane Branch of the Australian Communist Party with this work. But the decision contained the reservation that in the event of the conference being convened without Brisbane Branch of the ACP the URCW will participate in it directly.[42]

The next speakers were the delegates of the Brisbane Communist Party Organisation who also welcome the idea of fusion. Having expressed their viewpoint, they proposed, as a basis for the realisation of this idea, to establish one non-party workers organisation with a communist nucleus, the latter to exercise its influence in the activity and development of the members of the future unified organisation. Their reason for the establishment of such a non-party organisation was—the diversity of elements among the Russian workers in Australia as far as their general development and their political convictions are concerned. They argued that for this reason the appellation "Communist" was not suitable.

After prolonged discussion it was decided to adjourn the Session of the Conference to the following Sunday, June 26. Before closing the Session, the following resolution was carried: "The present Session of the Conference having taken cognisance of all the proposals (bases) for fusion, is leaving the question open in view of the contradictory nature of these proposals, until the latter will have been independently discussed at the next meetings of each organisation."

---

[42] Manuscript obliterated at the bottom of this page. Last line reconstructed from the Russian version.

The Second Session of the Conference took place on Sunday June 26. After a brief exchange of opinion it was proposed to deal immediately with the elucidation of one or other of the proposed bases for the fusion of the existing organisations.

First to be discussed were: "the conditions of agreement adopted by the URCW for fusion into one organisation"—as an addendum to the adopted resolution. These conditions are as follows: being convinced that the existence of separate homogenous organisations is conducive to splitting up the forces of the Russian workers in Australia, thus frustrating the plans for the establishment of one united working class organisation, (which militates against the aims and tasks of communism) the URCW, being the largest workers' organisation professing communist ideas, proposes through its delegates to the conference to the other organisations to amalgamate with it into one big whole. In the event of the above conditions being recognised as correct by the respective organisations, it is proposed to all the three organisations to either place before the conference (before the final decision) through the delegates the following conditions and principles, or to adopt the contents of the resolution given below as a final decision: 1) The URCW, in the interests of union based on communist ideas and the demands of the Third (communist) International, considers that all reasons for splits are a thing of the past and must not stand in the way of amalgamation and common systematic work based on self education, on the principles of the November Revolution and of International Communism, as well as on a class conscious attitude towards the organisation, which will guarantee proletarian solidarity. With this object in view and as a further guarantee for the achievement of the above mentioned aims, the URCW offers to everyone an opportunity to point out and prove the undesirability of any one member of the organisation and of his continued stay within the organisation. 2) The Ipswich and Brisance communist Party organisations to cease to exist as such in the interests of the establishment of one united organisation imbued with the aims and ideas of the Communist Party. All existing property such as: libraries, inventory and cash, as well as all[43] uncompleted ventures in connection with printing, finding financial and other means etc. are to be handed over to the administration of the URCW. As an amalgamated organisation, all the Executive organs of the Union [are] to be re-elected immediately after the fusion of the above mentioned organisations. 3). To ensure mutual conference [sic][44] all the interested parties to render an unbiased account (before final fusion) through their delegates to the conference of their political activity during the period of group dissensions. To prevent similar misunderstandings and unnecessary disputes in future everything com[ing] to light in this fashion [is] to be considered

---

[43] The following lines struck through by hand: 'illegal ventures such as secret printing works and underground channels for financing the movement etc., to be handed'.
[44] 'confidence'.

as done away with and settled for ever. 4) In the interests of solidarity and comradeship all questions re membership obligations, general relations, elaboration of methods, procuring financial means, questions of self-education and political self-determination, and also opposition to the will of the majority—to be subject to strict public criticism which is to be conducted on general organisational and not on personal grounds. Only such impersonal criticism to be tolerated in the event of any frictions.

The basis (organisational regulations) and the conditions of the URCW were adopted.

After the closing speeches a declaration of the Brisbane Communist Party Organisation was read. Its contents are as follows:

Having taken cognisance of the letter of the Ipswich Party Organisation containing an invitation to send delegates to the Conference for the fusion of the Russian proletariat in Australia, we arrive at the following conclusion:

1) In view of national peculiarities, our organisation, apart from participation in the revolutionary movement among Australian workers in general, must concentrate on the propagation of communist ideas among Russian workers and on familiarising them with the practical application of these ideas in Soviet Russia. 2) The existence here of various organisations of Russian workers (regardless of the reasons for their establishment) is splitting their already weak forces ideally as well as materially.[45] It has a bad effect on their educational activities and consequently impedes the development of their class consciousness.

Basing itself on the above mentioned considerations, the Brisbane Communist Party Organisation welcomes the initiative of the Ipswich Communist Party Organisation and sent three delegates to the conference held on June 12th, 1921 in the Brisbane Trade Hall. On behalf of our organisation the delegates placed before the Conference the following organisational basis for the fusion of the three organisations: 1) formation from the existing organisations of one non-party workers' organisation with branches throughout Australia, capable of receiving in their ranks the class conscious as well as the non-class conscious elements of Russian workers in Australia. 2) Formation of a communist (Party) nucleus within the organisation, the latter to endeavour to conduct the activity of the entire organisation according to communist principles. The delegates of the URCW proposed as a basis the resolution adopted at their general meeting and published in their paper on April 26, 1921 (See minutes of the First Session of the Conference).

Our delegates pointed out that the present title of the union—URCW was not applicable to their basis for the following reasons.

---

[45] meaning 'undermining their morale': Russ. *kak v dukhovnom tak i materialnom otnosheniiakh*.

In the first instance, the Russian workers in Australia consist of class conscious as well as more backward elements, the former holding different political opinions. This being so, the organisation cannot very well bear the title "communist". Secondly, every organisation assuming the title "communist" cannot consider itself non-party and must therefore bear full party responsibility. If it is does not do so, such an organisation is only likely to discredit communism.

The delegates of the URCW declared that their organisation will certainly not give up its title.

At the general meeting of our organisation held on June 12, it was decided after a prolonged discussion that: 1) The objections of our delegation to the conference to the title "communist" were correct. 2) Owing to our separate existence we could not, with the best intentions, carry out our tasks as defined in paragraph 1 of our declaration. 3) The existence of different organisations among Russian workers in Australia creates unfriendly relations between them, thus paralysing every kind of fruitful activity.

In the interests of the tasks which our organisation set itself, it resolved to deviate from its basic principles and to agree to the conditions of the URCW for the sake of fusion. It trusts the joint work will eradicate the existing mutual distrust and that it will assist in the training of steadfast and class conscious communists among the Russian workers in Australia.

The delegation of the Ipswich Community Party Organisation, while fully endorsing the conditions of the URCW and welcoming the declaration of the Brisbane Communist Party Organisation and the accomplished fusion, voiced in their speeches the principle—"Unity is Strength!".

After a general expression of satisfaction it was resolved to convene the first meeting of the amalgamated organisations on Sunday June 3rd at 10 a.m. with the object of re-electing all the Executive organs of the Union and of rendering account. The concluding remarks of the chairman, welcoming the just accomplished fusion, were greeted with loud applause. Thus ended the conference.

Chairman: comrade Shakhnovsky, Secretaries: comrades Pikunov and Lubimov. Delegates: comrades Galchenko, Khrutsky, Gorsky, Kilimov, Hochstand and Lefand.

NOTE: To prevent wrong interpretations in the sense of assuming that the said organisation occupies a neutral position in view of its vague political ideology, we assert that such a conclusion would be incorrect. Basing itself on the principles and demands of the communist platform the said organisation occupies a position in conformity with the existing standard of development of its members, but has nothing in common with political opportunism which misleads the masses by its slogan "Keep outside Parties". Such is not the desire of this organisation. The neutral position between the organised sympathisers with communism and the Communist Party is an outcome of the peculiar national position of the Russian workers and also of the fact that the establishment of a Communist Party is a political act which cannot be undertaken by persons who are only guided by their sympathies with Communism and not by fundamental politico-economic knowledge of the tenets of the Party.

The Russian working masses here want to be organised, but in view of their educational level and prevailing conditions, we find that by forming ourselves into a communist party we would expose the organisation to two extremes: "Leftism" and Isolation from the masses. Russian workers in Australia who are anxious to take part in the revolutionary work without endeavouring to adapt their organisations to the conditions of the local movement, are involuntarily adapting them to the conditions prevailing in revolutionary Russia, and thus create mental conclusion [sic].[46] The movement of the Russian worker here is on narrow national lines. It does not spring from general ideas, but has been called forth and dominated by the Russian revolution and its ideas. Nevertheless they are already beyond being told: "Be communists", for they say themselves that: "We want to, but show us how to do it". But to endeavour to establish a Communist Party without sufficient politico-educational courses within the masses who stand in need of knowledge and not of education would not be rational, for by organising a certain number of workers into a Party we should alienate the masses who are not on the same level of development and class consciousness as the said party. To subject our organisational methods and means to party regulations would be tantamount to erecting a barrier between these methods and the masses. In Soviet Russia this barrier has a raison d'être, as the party there is the executor of proletarian dictatorship. Moreover there was civil war and other revolutionary conditions in Soviet Russia which do not exist here. But in spite of their false position here, the Russian workers' great desire is to organise themselves in order to prepare themselves for service in Soviet Russia. But, as already stated, they cannot take upon themselves the responsibilities of a communist party. Under these circumstances, what shall be our organisational basis here? We are of the opinion that it should be that of a semi-educational, semi-political organisation.

Such, and no other, are the considerations which have induced our organised [sic][47] to adopt its neutral position. Nevertheless, the URCW is aware that its organisational basis is, in principle, far from perfect, and as before our organisation will pursue the aim of raising the standard of development of its members to communist party level. In connection with this immediate question

---

[46] 'confusion'.
[47] 'organisation'.

occupying the attention of the Union is the question of the formation of a Russian Section of the Australian Communist Party. But this is a question of the future.

In conclusion and to sum up the work of the conference, it should be stated that, as far as this was possible a number of misunderstandings disuniting the Russian workers in Australia have been cleared up. The fusion of the three organisations has been accomplished, which gives wider possibilities for further work. It is essential that such a good beginning should not be allowed to drop in localities where there are Russian workers capable of organising themselves. To them we say: comrades, many appeals have been addressed to you to join the common work, but hitherto prejudices and dissensions were stronger than the principles of solidarity. At the present juncture we should like to set an example to every class conscious worker. In enjoining you to educate yourselves and others and thus become class conscious participators in the constructive work of Soviet Russia, we want to set an example by this Conference whose motives are free of any personal bias.

UNION OF RUSSIAN COMMUNIST WORKERS, BRISBANE
July 1, 1921

Document 14

RGASPI 495–94–6. 29 September 1921, Jim Quinton: on the Economic, Political and General Plan of Australia from a Communist viewpoint. Manuscript.

Jim Quinton was an accredited delegate from the 'Liverpool Street' Communist Party who was arrested in England on his way to the Third Comintern Congress and imprisoned. This letter contains a draft of the report that Quinton had intended to present to the Congress. The report is optimistic about prospects for the growth of the communist movement in Australia, does not mention the divisions between the Australian communist organizations, and is notable for linking communism into Australian (settler) traditions.

29.7.21
Foreign Information Dept
Comintern, Moscow

Comrades,

The enclosed is intended as a brief and rough summary of the Economic, Political, and general PLAN of Australia, from a Communist viewpoint.

I have to express regret, that when I was taken from a ship in Hull, England, and imprisoned for 3 months for illegal travelling, a much more complete and infinitely better draft, was lost, together with my Communist Party credentials. These were endorsed by our much lamented late Comrade Paul Freeman. My credentials from the Federated Seamans' Union of Australia, were brought to Moscow, by Paul Freeman.

The enclosed names and addresses are perfectly reliable for use by your Dept.

It was intended by the Communist Party in Australia that your Dept should be asked to consider our situation and give us any necessary advice.

Unfortunately for the movement, Australia is largely isolated at present. This difficulty stands to be quickly remedied in the near future. Already Australian Imperialism has established its economic and political emissaries in China. With the rapid development of the latter Country by Capitalist Agencies and the permeation of the Pacific by World Imperialism, Australia will become a greater factor for Communism, than at present seems likely by the casual observer.

Internally Australia presents one great difficulty to the Communist movement. Although two thirds of her small population of something more than five million people are centred in Cities and Industrial Centers, these arteries of the population are removed one from the other to great distances. As a Communist and Industrial Labour Organiser who has travelled over great distances in Australia, I can truthfully state that the worker is rapidly advancing in class consciousness. Australia's brief industrial and political history is a constant repetition of this fact. From 1854 when the Ballarat Gold Diggers, Victoria, fought with arms, the Crown government military at the Eureka stockade, until the quite recent movement in Townsville when the meat workers during their strike rushed to Arms against the Armed Police of the Queensland Labour Party Government. We then have the recent inspiring example of an 18 months strike by the metalliferous miners of Broken Hill. These miners are protected in Australia by the well known [labour] volunteer army, which developed out of War Coercion. These miners faced starvation, and by solidarity finally won their industrial fight and overturned the Nationalist Government. Two members of Parliament representing Broken Hill gladly attempt to claim the title of Communist. The one big obstacle, as I have stated, is the great distance between the main centres of population, which precludes effective working and cohesion, on a national social basis. This matter in particular your Dept is asked to consider, and give advice. I wish to point out now, that the sugar and meat workers of Queensland in particular are worthy of careful consideration.

These workers are mainly cosmopolitan, having come from all parts of the world. They include Russian, Italian, Greek, English, American and other nationalities including natives from our neighbouring islands.

Quite recently when doing Communist Party organising work in the sugar industry of Queensland, in one district alone "Babinda", it would have been possible for me to have collected 500 names of men who had expressed their desire to join the Communist Party. Such wholesale recruiting the Party Executive rejected. Your Dept is requested to give practical advice for such a situation.

It would be impossible to recount all such details of our movement in a report of this kind, so that, together with the rough diagram I am hoping that your Department will get the gist of our situation.

I am now at your disposal to get the advice of which we are in need, and to act according to instructions from you.

We wish to suggest that our own situation in a country like Australia, makes as a practical possibility, guerrilla military organisation.

Apart from this Communist Party report, it is necessary that I shall forward to Australia the latest situation of the Red Trade Union International, for attention by the Australian Executive of the Federated Seamans' Union of Australia.

Thanking you in anticipation of your expedition in this matter.

Yours fraternally
Jim Quinton
Delegate
Communist Party of Australia and Federated Seaman's Union of Australia.

Document 15

RGASPI 495–94–6. no date [but internal evidence indicates late February 1922]. Report to the Comintern on the Unity Conference of 18 February 1922 and the correspondence preceding it. Typescript.

After its unexpected good fortune and success at the Third Comintern Congress in 1921, the 'Sussex Street' communist party pressed home its advantage in an exchange of letters with the 'Liverpool Street' communist party, inviting the latter to a Unity Conference as the Comintern had requested. The Liverpool Street comrades did not attend, and 'Sussex Street' declared itself the 'United CPA'. It submitted the correspondence to the Comintern within the report below to prove its virtue; as it argued, the Liverpool Street party 'shows utter contempt for your decisions re Unity'. This document gives ample proof of the manoeuvres engaged in by the parties, and especially of the tedious legalism employed by both in an attempt to gain the moral high ground and, more importantly, Moscow's endorsement.

THE UNITED COMMUNIST PARTY OF AUSTRALIA

Headquarters
Communist Hall
Sussex Street
SYDNEY
New South Wales, Australia

The Executive Committee,
The Third (Communist) International

Dear Comrades,

I have been instructed by the Central Executive of the United Communist Party of Australia in which is merged the Communist Party of Australia (whose representative and General Secretary attended the Third Congress of the Third International in June 1921, and who also represented the Party in discussion with the Small Bureau of the Third International on the question of Communist Unity in Australia), to submit to you for your earnest and immediate consideration the following statement of the Unity discussions and proceedings which have taken place in Australia since the Decisions of the Small Bureau were received in Australia. At this stage of the statement, I desire you to note that in all references to the other Party concerned in the Unity Discussions it will be called throughout this statement by its original name the Australian Socialist Party. The reason for this is to make it easier to distinguish one from the other.

The official instructions of the Small Bureau were received in Australia in the early part of December 1921. They were published immediately in the Communist Party's Press "The Communist" issue Vol 1. No ...[48] but nothing to this date has appeared in the Australian Socialist Party's Press. On receiving Instructions of the Small Bureau the Communist Party of Australia immediately sent to the Australian Socialist Party the following letter.

Communist Party of Australia
28 Station House
Dec. 13th 1921

A.S. Reardon
Gen. Sec.
Communist Party of Australia.

Dear Comrade,

I am instructed by my executive to inform you that the report of our delegate to the Third Congress of the Communist International, Comrade Earsman, has been endorsed.

My Executive is willing to carry out the demands of the World Congress on Unity, and proposes that the two councils of action, as called for in demands, meet as soon as possible. The Council of Action elected by my executive consists of Comrades Garden, Denford, and myself.

Please inform me soon as possible as to the decision of your executive on this matter.

Yours for Communist Unity,
C.W. Baker
Acting General Secretary

The Australian Socialist Party replied with the following letter:

The Communist Party of Australia
115 Goulburn St, Sydney
Dec. 21st, 1921

---

[48] A word or number is missing here.

Mr C.W. Baker

In reply to yours of the 13th inst. I have now to inform you that our Central Executive has already appealed against the decisions of the Small Bureau of the Comintern.

The appeal is based upon the fact that we were duly affiliated as the Australian Section of the Third International and that the action of the Small Bureau therefore in suspending said affiliation on the question of unity was out of order.

Further, we refuse to recognise a decision arrived at upon the representation of an opportunist who was not a member of the Communist movement in the person of W. Smith of Melbourne who was credentialed in Moscow by W.P. Earsman, and of the said W.P. Earsman who stands bracketed with Smith on account of such despicable anti-communist conduct.

You will understand therefore, that no delegate will be appointed to meet your representatives.

On behalf of the Central Executive
(signed) A.S. Reardon. Hon. Gen. Secretary

On receiving that reply the Communist Party replied with the following letter:

> Communist Party of Australia
> 28 Station House
> Dec. 27th 1921

Mr A.S. Reardon
Hon. Gen. Secretary
Communist Party of Australia.
(late ASP)

Dear Comrade,

Yours of the 21st of December to hand. I am directed by my CE to state that they have noted the contents, but at the same time desire to draw your attention to several points which should be brought under your notice.

First, you state that you have appealed against the decision of the Small Bureau of the Comintern because your party was already affiliated to that body. In reply to this we think the time has arrived when some evidence of this statement should be furnished to this party and to the workers as a whole. While the delegates of this party were in Moscow they made full inquiries about your party and whether it was affiliated, and they were informed that your party was not and never had been affiliated to the Third International.

The next statement which requires your attention is that Comrade Smith was not a member of the "Communist movement". We do not know what this means unless you desire to say that he was not a member of your party, which is correct, but Comrade Smith is a member of this party. Because of this fact our General Secretary, W.P. Earsman, had full power from his Executive to act as he did in issuing credentials to Comrade Smith. The Executive has endorsed Comrade Earsman's actions.

In conclusion we desire to point out the fact that the conditions of unity drawn up in Moscow were unanimously agreed to by the Australian delegates, and signed by both delegates from your organisation in conjunction with ours. The fact that your executive has rejected these demands for unity, as they have rejected all previous proposals, is a clear demonstration that it is your party that is "anti-communist", and in continuing the disruption of the Communist movement it is your actions which are "despicable".

Yours for Communist Party

W.P. Earsman, General Secretary

Our comments to you on the letter received from the Australian Socialist Party are as follows:-

1. We hold the opinion in keeping with the discipline demanded by the Third International that both Parties were bound by that discipline to accept the decisions of the Small Bureau on Unity in Australia. Therefore we hold that no appeal to sidetrack or delay in settlement of the question can be tolerated by the Third International if Unity is to be achieved and the Communist movement in Australia put upon a sound foundation, and if discipline of the Third International is to mean something more than words.

2. Comrade W.H. Smith, General Secretary of the Australian Railways Union was a member of the Party when he left Australia for Moscow. Prior to his departure the Central Executive had not received any word from his Branch to the contrary and therefore the Party's credentialed Delegate and General Secretary, Comrade W.P. Earsman, acted within his rights in issuing credentials to Comrade W.H. Smith whom he knew to be a member when he left Australia.

3. Even if on that Point Comrade Earsman exceeded his rights he could have still used the full number of votes allotted to him as the official delegate from the Communist Party of Australia and the decision of the Small Bureau would not have been altered in any way.

4. The United Communist Party of Australia holds that the Australian Socialist Party never was affiliated as a Socialist Party or as a Communist Party to the Third International and was therefore never recognised as its Australian section. Therefore we claim that the appeal of the Australian Socialist Party against the decision of the Small Bureau on such grounds is but to say the least pure camouflage and hypocrisy.

Since receiving the letter of reply from the Australian Socialist Party both Parties have held their Annual Conferences between the dates of December 26th and December 31st 1921. It was unanimously agreed by the Communist Party's Conference on December 27th to make a further attempt to solve the Unity Question by approaching by Delegation the Australian Socialist Party's Conference. With [this] end in view the Communist Party's Conference dispatched by messenger to the Socialist Party's Conference the following letter:-

Communist Party of Australia,
28 Station House, Sydney.
Dec. 27th, 1921.

Chairman,
Annual Conference of The Communist Party of Australia,
Late (ASP)

Comrade,

I have been directed by the annual Conference of the above party to request your Annual Conference to receive a delegation of three delegates from our Conference to place proposals before you on the question of the unity of the two parties.

Please inform bearers whether and when your Conference will be ready to receive our delegates.

Yours in Communism,
W.P. Earsman,
General Secretary.

The Socialist Party's Conference replied with the following letter:-

Communist Party of Australia,
115 Goulburn St.,
Sydney. Dec. 27. 1921.

Chairman
Annual Conference,
CP of A
Station House.

Comrade,

In answer to your request for the reception for three delegates I have been instructed to inform you that without deviating from our communication of last week, we are prepared to receive your delegation at 3 P.M. today.

Yours for Communism,
Marcia Reardon, Acting General Secretary.

As a result of that reply three delegates from the Communist Party's Conference attended its conference and were allowed two hours to outline the case for Unity.

The delegates placed before the Socialist Party's Conference definite proposals unanimously agreed to by the Communist Party's Conference as a Basis for Unity. The proposals were as follows:-

1. That the membership of both parties be taken over into full membership of the United Party.
2. That each party have equal representation on the Executive of the United Party.
3. That a Provisional Acting General Secretary be elected by the Executive.
4. That each party have equal representation on the Management Committee which shall have control over press and literature.
5. That if there should be any dispute over the printing press at 115 Goulburn Street, it shall be controlled by those who are present trustees of it, as a private concern.

These proposals were made not as rigid conditions but as a basis for discussion.

At the termination of the discussion at the Socialist Party's Conference the Delegates of the Communist Party invited the Conference to elect three delegates to attend the Communist Party's Conference and place their position before the full conference of delegates.

The Socialist Party's Conference refused to give a decision in the presence of the Communist Party's Delegates and on the following day, the Communist Party's Conference was forced to write and ask for a reply to the invitation issued of its delegates and to the proposals of Unity submitted by the Party.

The letter sent by the Communist Party is as follows:-

> Communist Party of Australia
> 28 Station House.
> 28th December, 1921.

Chairman,
Conference,
CP of A (ASP)

Comrade,

Failing to receive a reply from your party by 3 p.m. today to the concrete proposals for Communist Unity set forth by the delegates from this party which addressed your conference yesterday, I am directed to inform you that the conference of my party will consider the absence of any reply as a further and final refusal of the proposals advanced by this party for unity on the basis of the recommendations of the Small Bureau of the Third International.

Yours for Communist Unity,

W.P. Earsman.

General Secretary

The Socialist Party's Conference replied to same as follows:-

Communist Party of Australia,
115 Goulburn Street,
Sydney, Dec. 28th, 1921.

Chairman,
Conference,
CP of A,
(Station House.)

Comrade,

In reply to your communication to hand. I have been instructed to inform you that Conference has decided no good purpose will be served by sending delegates to address your Conference, also that it has endorsed the attitude of the CE on the unity question, and the reply sent to your General Secretary, last week.

A lengthy statement containing full reasons for this decision will be drawn up and forwarded to you.

Yours for Communism,

Marcia Reardon.

Acting General Secretary.

The above letter was received just on the close of the Communist Party's Conference and on January 4, 1922. Five days after both Conferences had ended, the Communist Party received from the Socialist Party the following letter:-

Communist Party of Australia
115 Goulburn St.,
Sydney. Jan 4, 1922.

Mr W.P. Earsman
General Secretary, CP of A,
(Station House.)

As you are already aware, Conference has endorsed the policy of the CE re unity, and the reply sent to your acting General Secretary on December 21st, 1921. I was instructed to supply the following reasons for this decision:

After hearing your delegates, Conference was more than ever convinced that the attitude taken up by this Executive was correct. Replies to questions admitted the existence of undesirables in your party, also that no attempt had been made to deal with same. Charges of blabbing, treachery, and opportunism were not denied. Two of your delegates were convicted as they stood of contradictory and lying statements.

Our party was urged to unite in order to assist in expelling an admittedly base element, and finally threatened re our standing in Moscow if we refused. Conference instructed me to state that at all times this party, as the ASP and now as the CP of A, has never failed to deal with any individual within its ranks who has violated principles or party discipline. They leave you to do your own cleaning up in this respect.

If your rank and file is not prepared to take action against individuals which through its delegates it admits are corrupt, then their claim to be a Communist falls to the ground.

The CP of A is acting on principle and in an endeavour to build up a clean solid party in Australia, therefore, threats as to what action Moscow might be induced to take on our questioning its behests would have no effect beyond confirming our previous opinion of your party as being non Communist.

Re your communication of 27/12/21, in it you state that your delegates were officially informed in Russia that our party was not affiliated to the Third International. Against this we have the word of our three delegates, Lamb, Rees, and the late Paul Freeman, who were all definite on the point that our party was affiliated with, and recognised by the Third International.

Also in a pamphlet entitled *The Third International* written by Boris Souvarine, we are listed as the only party in Australia recognised by that body. This evidence we are assured would stand against the statement of such men as Earsman and Smith; the former is included among those whom your rank and file, as represented by your delegates, acknowledge to be totally unworthy of a place in the Communist movement, and the latter who was repudiated by the Branch to which he claimed membership. Regarding this W. Smith you claim in your letter that he was a member of your party.

I am instructed to a call your attention to the fact, that at our Conference Comrade Maruschak admitted that he was not, and added to this we have the written statement of the late Secretary of your Melbourne Branch which reads:

> … With regard to your second request, no delegate left Australia for Moscow or anywhere else from Melbourne Branch. Will Smith, Secretary of the Australian Railways Union, went to Russia as a result of a visit to Melbourne of the delegate of the R.T.U.I. He was invited to the first Conference in Melbourne called by your representatives, Baker and Baracchi, but did not attend, sending a message

approving of the formation of a Communist Party of Australia, but like a lot more he never paid any subscriptions, and like a lot more was eager to get a trip to Russia.

If he has represented himself as a delegate from Melbourne of the Communist Party, it is in keeping with the actions of a trades union opportunist. He went to Russia, strange as it may seem, as a representative of the Second International yellow crowd of the Trades Hall Council ...

Signed Charles H. France.

The above Comrade was fully conversant with the Melbourne Branch's books since its inception.

We have likewise an admission from Mr. Earsman at our Conference that he (Earsman) was aware before he left Australia that Smith was practically convicted of blabbing to the press regarding Freeman's visit to Australia.

If under these circumstances Mr. Earsman admittedly credentialed Smith, and Executive endorsed his action as stated in your letter; we say definitely and unhesitatingly that it brands every member upon it as traitors to the Third International and to the Communist movement of the world.

The conditions re unity were NOT unanimously agreed to by our delegates but were drawn up by the Small Bureau of the Comintern after Comrade Lamb had put in his minority report.

In conclusion I am instructed to state that so far as we are concerned, the Communists of AUSTRALIA are UNITED, unfortunately we have no power to prevent individuals from calling themselves what they please; but actions speak louder than words, and while the rank and file of your party endorses by its silence the actions of its officials which members admit are against the best interest of the Communist movement, they must not only forfeit all claim to the title of Communists, but definitely range themselves on the side of the counter-revolutionaries. It is for them to manifest their worthiness by action—not by continued adherence to those whom they condemn.

On behalf of the Communist Party of Australia.
Marcia Reardon,
Acting General Secretary.

After making these attempts to get a reasonable solution to the question of Unity, and being turned down and insulted in every way, the Conference of the Communist Party instructed the Central Executive of the Party—before sending the results to you—to make another effort to obtain Unity by calling an All Communist Conference of unattached Communist Groups, Communist Groups in Trade Unions, Branches of the Communist Party and, any other organisation that in any way claimed to stand by the principles of the Third International.

The purpose of the Conference to be the forming of a United Communist Party in keeping with the 21 points of the Third International.

The Central Executive of the Communist Party issued the call for that Conference and invited all the organisations mentioned.

The letters of invitation and the reply of the Communist Party to the Socialist Party's letter of January 4, 1922, were as follows:-

> Communist Party of Australia,
> 28 Station House,
> January 30, 1922.

Mrs A.S. Reardon,
Secretary. CP of A (ASP)

Dear Comrade,

I have been directed by my General Executive to inform your organisation that we are calling an All-Australian Congress of all revolutionary parties and groups in the Commonwealth, with the object of bringing about a united revolutionary party in this country.

You are therefore invited to send three delegates from your Central Executive, two from your Sydney Branch, and one each from your other Branches.

The basis of unity will be the principles and tactics laid down by the Third, Communist International, and the Red Trade Union International.

It is unnecessary for me to point out the necessity for a united front at the present time and we trust you fully realise the importance of the situation and that you will accept the invitation.

Yours for Communist Unity,
W.P. Earsman.
Hon. General Secretary.

> Communist Party of Australia,
> 28 Station House,
> February 9th 1922.

Mr A.S. Reardon,
Gen. Secretary CP of A (ASP)

Dear Comrade,

I have been directed by my Executive to reply to your letter of the 4th of January. The reason for the delay has been the necessity for us to make full inquiries into your statements. They have now directed me to say that they entirely repudiate your statements.

With reference to the letter you have received from Comrade France of the Melbourne Branch, I have received a communication from that Branch and they deny that France was ever instructed to write to your party on the matter of Smith. Further they also deny having ever stated to you that Smith was not a member of this party. This being so we are now quite satisfied that there is nothing left but to hope that time will show you the errors of your ways and that you will send delegates to the Unity Conference of February 18th.

Yours for Communist Unity,

W.P. Earsman,
General Secretary.

To the invitation of the Communist Party, the Socialist Party replies as follows:-

Communist Party of Australia,
115 Goulburn Street,
Sydney. February 11th, 1922.

Mr W.P. Earsman,

Yours of the 30th ult., and of the 9th instant., to hand. In the matter of the first one I have to inform you that our Executive is really not interested in what you may be doing on February the 18th—or any other particular date.

The second letter will be presented to the Central Executive on the occasion of its next meeting, when I feel sure, the delegates will be all duly impressed.

A.S. Reardon.
Hon. General Secretary

I might here say as a comment on the Socialist Party's reply that it should prove conclusively their insincerity to Communist Unity and their total lack of respect for the decision of your Small Bureau. In fact it shows utter contempt for your decisions re Unity.

However the Conference was held without them and met in Sydney, the principal City of Australia, on Saturday, February 18th 1922.

The minutes of the Conference are as follows:-

Comrade Denford, General Secretary, declared the Conference open. The following delegates were present: C.W. Baker, E.R. Voight (C.E.); Denford and Jeffery (Sydney Branch); Rawstrong and Sinclair (Newcastle); Wolstenholm (Engineers); King (Saddlers Union); Blanc (Painters); Ryrie (Baking Trades); Buchingham and Foley (Communist Group, and Russian Association, Nth Queensland); Arbuthnot (OBU Propaganda League[49]); and Comrade Howie

---

[49] A successor to the IWW.

Australian representative of the RTUI in Australia. (The delegates from the unions were from Communist groups within their union).

Preliminary business: Comrade Sinclair elected to the chair. Com. Jeffery to minute Secretary.

Correspondence: The General Secretary read letters from the following organisations; ASP, the WIIU (Melbourne and Adelaide), the Industrial Union Propaganda Group, Russian Association, Melbourne. All the letters excepting the one from the ASP (which, of course was nasty) expressed a willingness to stand behind any United Communist Party, but that owing to financial reasons it was impossible to send a delegate to Sydney. (Correspondence received).

After some discussion in which the delegates stated their position in relation to Communist unity, it was moved that "The Agenda paper drawn up by the CE of the CP of A be adopted for the Conference". Carried.

Moved "that the General Secretary outline the efforts made by the CP of A since its formation for unity". Agreed.

Comrade Denford then briefly outlined the negotiations which had taken place between the two parties since the split in December 1920. In the discussion which followed Comrade Howie in reply to Comrade Blanc explained the negotiations for unity which took place in Moscow. Comrade Howie said that as he was not a member of either party he saw both sides and was satisfied that the party was the only party prepared to act on the demands of the Communist International. He stated that he had interviewed the ASP since his return but had failed to get them to agree to unity. He had called a conference of delegates from this party and the Industrial Union Propaganda League and that conference had arrived at a working basis for the two organisations proving again that this party was prepared to work for unity. He was satisfied that unity between the two parties was impossible and recommended all delegates to support the party in its efforts to form a United Communist Party of Australia. (Report of General Secretary, received).

Moved by Comrade Baker and seconded by Comrade Voight.

"That realising the impossibility of uniting the two existing Communist Parties owing to one of them refusing to act upon the instructions of the Communist International, and further realising the immediate necessity of a United Communist Party to inspire and direct the revolutionary activities of the working class in Australia, the delegates assembled in this All-Australian Unity Conference now constitute themselves and the Communist groups which they represent the United Communist Party of Australia, and thus comply as far as possible with the demands of the Third World Congress of the Communist International on Communist Unity in Australia, and that each delegate pledge themselves to create a definite Branch of the United Party in their respective districts, and strive to get all Communist groups under their influence to link up with the United Communist Party of Australia as the only revolutionary party worthy of support." AGREED.

Constitution: "Moved that the Constitution of the CP of A to be adopted subject to ratification of delegates present." Agreed.

Amendments: To Section E. clause 12; "A special unemployed stamp be affixed to the dues card of all unemployed and sick members." To Section G. clause 20; "That branches be empowered to issue leaflets for propaganda when necessary provided a copy is sent to the CE." Constitution adopted as amended.

Election of officers: Moved "That the number of the CE be seven including the General Secretary." Agreed.

Officers elected: General Secretary, H.L. Denford; Trustee, J.S. Garden; Editor, C.W. Baker; N. Jeffery, H. Ross, W. Wolstenholm and D. Healy.

Program: Outline of Communist Theory adopted with amendment to clause 7 by the insertion of clause 14 from "Program of Action" on workers control.

Moved: "That agreement reached between the CP and the IUPL be ratified by the United Party." Agreed.

Moved: "That matter of Industrial Unionism be referred to the CE and that branch secretaries contribute towards a party statement of the question of Industrial Unionism". Agreed.

Moved: "That assets and liabilities of the CP of A be taken over by the new party." Agreed.

Moved: "That the proposal of issuing a propaganda ticket for non-party members at 10/- be referred to Comrade Howie." Agreed.

Moved: "That all correspondence on the matter of unity between the ASP and CP of A together with a statement of the position of the Communist Community in Australia, with the minutes of this conference be forwarded to the Small Bureau of the Communist International with the request that affiliation be granted to this party as the only party prepared to act on official instructions of the Communist International." Agreed.

Moved: "That the Conference now adjourn." Agreed.

The Conference assembled at 2.30 P.M. on Saturday, February 18th in the Communist Party Hall, Sussex Street, Sydney, and adjourned, Sunday, February 19th.

(Signed.) E. Sinclair, Chairman of Conference.

N. Jeffery, Minute Secretary of Conference.

H.L. Denford, General Secretary, United Communist Party of Australia.

You can see by the minutes of the conference that the Conference though not large was representative enough to give birth to the United Communist Party of Australia.

The decisions of that Conference have now been endorsed by the organisations represented and the United Communist Party formed, and in its name and for the advancement of the cause of Communism in this country, I appeal to you to grant us affiliation and full recognition as the Australian Section. It must be apparent to you that your endorsement at this juncture will materially help us to build a strong Communist Party and end once and for all the ridiculous Unity proceedings which I assure you are dragging the name of a Communist Party down to the level as low as it can possibly go, and further making it a buttress [sic] of the jokes of all Counter-Revolutionary elements in this country.

The United Communist Party's claim, comrades, for affiliation and full recognition as the Australian Section is based upon the very fundamentals of the Communist International, upon its world discipline and its tactics for winning the working class of Australia for Communism and it can be summed up as follows:-

1. The Communist Party of Australia previous to merging with the United Communist Party of Australia made every effort that was possible to achieve Unity with the Australian Socialist Party; whilst on the other hand the Australian Socialist Party proved by the correspondence contained in this statement, have done all that was possible to prevent it [sic].

    The Communist Party was fooled, humiliated, and sabotaged by the Australian Socialist Party to a degree unheard of in any Unity proceedings. Yet, the Communist Party have let the lies and slander to go by without notice for the purpose of keeping the question of Unity in the forefront and when after being turned down have again and again made other attempts to achieve Unity in spite of the insults hurled at the Party.

2. Because the United Communist Party is the only party in Australia trying to carry out the 21 points of the Third International and using intelligently the tactics of the Communist International in winning the Trade Union movement for Communism.

3. Because with full recognition from the Third International the United Communist Party is the only party capable of organising the mass of the workers within the Trade Union movement to follow the lead of a Communist Party. Without that recognition of course no party can win the Trade Union movement over to Communism.

The above statement (No 3) can be backed up by resolutions taken from a statement issued by the Sydney Labor Council carried by a two to one majority at its meeting of Thursday, March 16th, 1922.

The statement was framed and carried through Council by the Delegates who are members of the United Communist Party. The resolutions are as follows:-

1. This Council declares that, as a part of the Red Trade Union International, it stands for united action with all revolutionary organisations and the Communist Party of the country in all defensive and offensive activities against the capitalist class. As no Communist Party is now recognised in Australia owing to the existence of two Communist Parties, this Council withholds its recognition until one party or another is recognised by the Communist International.

2. This Council, while fighting in the every-day struggle for an improvement in the standard of living for the working class, realises that it is impossible to obtain economic security for the workers under Capitalism. Therefore this Council attempts to direct this every-day struggle of the workers into a struggle for the abolition of Capitalism and the establishment of a working class political State. Such a struggle can only be adequately organised and carried through in the interest of the workers as a whole, when the Trade Unions will act in perfect unity with the revolutionary political party of the working class.

To further clinch our argument for full recognition I give the following outline of our activities within the Trade Union Movement and the important positions occupied by our members.

At the All-Australian Trade Union Conference held in Melbourne in the month of June 1921 our members formed 15% of the Conference. The Conference represented about 500,000 Trade Unionists. The next Conference which will be held in the same place on June 26th 1922, we expect to have at least 30% of the voting strength and we hope with such a bloc to determine the decisions of that Conference.

On the Sydney Labor Council, the largest Industrial Council in the Southern Hemisphere, we have 30 members sitting as delegates of affiliated Unions, and on its Executive we have a majority, including the President and Secretary.

The decisions of the Sydney Labor Council have a great influence of the Trade Union movement of Australia, and in times of trouble, political and industrial, the Trade Union movement approaches the Council for its advice and recommendations. And during the last six months the Communist elements have always maintained a majority vote on all Council meetings. The Council meets weekly, and consists of delegates representing 94 Trade Unions with an aggregate membership of 138,000 members.

Within the Trade Unions we have Communist Groups whose principal members occupy prominent official positions, such as Presidents, Secretaries, and Executive Officers.

On the Newcastle Industrial Council, whose headquarters are at Newcastle, New South Wales, the second largest city in the State and the largest steel producing and coal mining centre in Australia, we have a group of members as delegates from affiliated Unions and its Secretary is a member of the Party.

The Newcastle Industrial Council represents about 30,000 Trade Unionists. In Brisbane, the capital city in the state of Queensland we have a group of members on the Industrial Council of Trade Unions and the Secretary is a member of the Party. The Industrial Council of Brisbane represents about 50,000 Trade Unionists.

In Melbourne, capital city of the state of Victoria, and Adelaide, capital city of the state of South Australia, we have members of the Party representing Trade Unions on the Labor Councils. On these two Councils none of our members occupy official positions but they receive a fairly good support from a minority of delegates. And on other Councils throughout Australia, members of the Party sit as delegates of their Union.

The Party itself has branches in all of the capital cities of Australia and two in other large centres, with members at large scattered all over Australia.

Our influence on the main Council, the Sydney Labor Council can best be judged by the following:-

The Party members moved and carried through the Council, in all stages, motions for the endorsement of the Program of Action of the Red Trade Union International, and the Council's affiliation to that body. These motions were opposed by other elements who claim to be revolutionary but in each case they were carried by overwhelming majorities.

The above statement of our Trade Union activities gives a brief outline of the Party's work and we challenge contradiction from any person or groups in Australia or elsewhere.

In conclusion, Comrades, we appeal to you to end the Unity question in this country. Our task to win the working class is made no lighter by a continuation of the question. Our enemies outside the revolutionary movement are strongly entrenched in most of the Trade Unions and on the political field, a Labor Party, a purely reform party, and hostile to all revolutionary tendencies of the working class, leads the great mass of the working class. To win over that mass unity of the Communist movement is the first move that must be made. The revolutionary movement of the working class in the past, in Australia, never developed any further than mere groups and sects, whose ideas were narrow and dogmatic and as a result never had any influence with the working class. Today as in all countries a revolutionary ideology is fast appearing in the great mass of the working class and perhaps in the midst of some great industrial crisis a revolutionary working class will look for guidance and a lead from the Communist movement of this country, and if, when that time comes, it is still discussing its own Unity and tearing itself asunder with dissensions, the working class will be betrayed and failure stamped upon the Communist movement.

To you Comrades, we look for the solution. If you are not prepared to grant the United Communist Party affiliation and recognition as the Australian Section, we suggest that you settle the Unity Question and send to Australia immediately, a representative armed with the authority of the Third International to call the parties together and from that meeting form a United Communist Party. We suggest that the delegate to carry full power to grant affiliation and full recognition to the party formed.

In the event of you accepting this method to settle Unity Question I am instructed to say that the United Communist Party is prepared to accept without question the decision of your delegate and to carry out his instructions to the letter.

Please accept the fraternal greetings of Comrades here and convey to the rank and file of the Russian Communist movement, the appreciation of our members for their splendid example of Communist solidarity against the armed forces of our common enemies.

I remain,
Yours for the Communist
World Revolution

Document 16

RGASPI 495-94-12. April 1922, Jock Garden: unity conference held. Typescript.

The 'Sussex Street' Communist Party, since 18 February 1922 calling itself the 'United CPA', sent this telegram to the ECCI to make absolutely certain that it knew that the February unity conference had been held and that 'Reardon's party' (the former ASP, and now the 'Liverpool Street' Communist Party) had not co-operated with the Comintern's instructions.

Telegram, 19 April 1922 (or 10 or 18 April?)

unity conference held reardons party repudiated cominterns

instructions all other groups united = garden

Document 17

RGASPI 495–94–8. June 1922, Presidium ECCI: Dear comrades. Typescript.

In June 1922, before the crucial unity meeting of Australian communists in July attended by Zuzenko and perhaps prompted by this letter, the ECCI used the letter below to express its continued exasperation at the continuing disunity. The letter ends with the threat that if unity is not achieved the Comintern reserves the right to make a decision about who will be its Australian section.

Moscow, June ....[50]

To the Communist Party of Australia Goulbourn St.
and to the Communist Party Australia Station House.

Dear Comrades,

It is now nine months since the Executive Committee of the Comintern called upon the Communist Parties to unite, but so far unity has not yet been achieved.

The Presidium of the E.C. cannot but express its extreme disapproval at the failure of the Australian comrades to sink their minor differences and unite the Communist forces in Australia. Since both Parties have accepted the conditions of affiliation laid down by the II. Congress of the Comintern, there can obviously be no differences of principle that keeps them divided. We must assume therefore that the lack of unity is due entirely to personal differences, or to minor disagreements in the estimation of local conditions.

The objective conditions in Australia to-day: the capitalist offensive, unemployment, and the steady deterioration of the standard of living of the working class—are such as to incline the mass of workers towards communism. All the evidence goes to show that the masses of the Australian workers are abandoning their former outlook, and that there is already an increasing mass of opinion in the working class in favour of our point of view. It is only the absence of a united, organised and compact Communist Party that prevents this opinion from being shaped into a definite communist mass movement, destined to decide the political and economic future of Australia.

Those who for any reason do anything to prevent unity, and so prevent the consummation of this purpose, bear a heavy responsibility not only before the Communist International, to which they claim affiliation, but also before the mass of the working class.

The existence of two small groups, *amidst a seething current of world shaking events*, engaged almost entirely in airing their petty differences, instead of unitedly plunging into the current and mastering it, is not only a ridiculous and

---

[50] No day given.

shameful spectacle, but also a crime committed against the working class movement.

Experience has shown that immediate numerical weakness is no bar to the Communist Party commanding an influence in the labour movement, and the support of the labour masses. It is disunity in the ranks of the communists that kills the effectiveness of the Party and dooms the labour movement, ripe for a communist lead, to suffer defeat and demoralisation at the hands of capitalist class.

The quality of a Communist Party is not determined by the select character of its members and the glibness with which each of them can repeat the shibboleths of Marxian doctrine, but is determined by the extent to which it can rally the broad masses around itself in conducting the revolutionary class struggle.

The Presidium of the Executive of the Comintern is of the opinion therefore that the continued disunity and isolation from the broad mass movement of the Communist Parties in Australia must not be tolerated, and imperatively calls upon those who are loyal to communism and to the labour movement immediately to take steps to bring about unity in the communist ranks.

There appears to be some misapprehension as to the status of the Parties in Australia in relation to the Comintern which seems to give further grounds for *dis*unity. The Presidium therefore declares that no Party in Australia has been affiliated to the Comintern. In the first place the Comintern does not accept affiliation from countries where more than one Communist Party exists, until all possibilities of bringing about unity have been exhausted. It is precisely for this reason that the question of accepting the affiliation of an Australian Party was postponed, pending the achievement of unity. Secondly, the attendance of representatives of Parties at meetings of the Executive of the Comintern does not imply the recognition of the respective Party as an affiliated body. The EC of the Comintern permits representatives of Parties, pending their affiliation to the Comintern, to attend its meetings in order that it may become acquainted with the position of, and the point of view in the respective countries, and in order that the representatives may become acquainted with the world situation and obtain a closer knowledge of the workings of the General Staff of the international revolutionary movement. The EC of the Comintern has not cancelled the affiliation of any Australian Party because no Australian Party has been affiliated.

The international working class movement at the present moment is faced with a combined and concerted offensive of the international capitalist class. In countries which hitherto, have been considered the strongest from the point of view of labour organisation, the workers are staggering under the heavy blows showered upon them by the enemy; and due entirely to the treachery of the opportunist leaders of the labour movement there is a *grave* danger of the army of the working class becoming demoralised.

In order to save the situation the Comintern issued the slogan of "The United Labour Front". This was not meant to be a mere political catch-word, but a practical measure to stop the retreat and rally the world labour forces for a counter-offensive. In its desire to achieve this the Comintern was prepared to come to an understanding with the IInd and the 2 1/2 Internationals. True to their character, the latter have sabotaged the United Front, and now the onus of bringing it about is thrown entirely upon the Communist International.

The Comintern therefore issues a rallying cry to all loyal communists to take up their positions in the fight. But before the communists can rally the ranks of the hardest pressed workers, they must themselves be united. They must throw themselves into the thick of the fight and not wrap themselves in the mantle of political purity and stand on the fringe of the fray.

In this respect the Presidium commends the fine example of our comrades in England who, under similar circumstances as now prevail in the Australian movement, loyally responded to the call of the Comintern, dropped their differences and formed a United Communist Party, with splendid results for the movement in England and for International Communism.

The present situation is so serious that those who can find nothing better to do than engage in barren doctrinaire controversy, and petty squabbles over personal dignity, must be regarded as traitors to the movement.

The Presidium of the Comintern therefore declares that no representative of Australian Communist Parties will be admitted to the forthcoming Fourth Congress of the Comintern in November, unless they are the representatives of a United Communist Party.

The Presidium, reaffirming the decision of the Small Bureau of August 20th, 1921, resolves that:

1. In view of the fact that there is no difference in principle, program or tactics, excepting differences arising out of local trouble, the Presidium calls for immediate unity between the two Australian Parties before September the 1st. 1922, this unity to take place at a general conference representing both Parties.
2. That a Committee of Action be set up composed of three delegates from each organisation, whose work shall be to prepare the agenda for the Unity Conference.
3. That the basis for representation at the Conference be one delegate for every 50 members of the Party.
4. All representation at Moscow to be suspended until unity is achieved and one United Communist Party for Australia is formed.

The Presidium hopes that the Australian Communist Parties will loyally respond to this appeal for unity at this critical juncture in the world labour movement. The Comintern reserves for itself the right, in the event of unity not being achieved, after investigating all the circumstances, to fix the responsibility for the failure, and those responsible will forfeit all right of recognition by the Communist International.

With fraternal greetings,

Document 18

RGASPI 495–94–13. 21 July 1922, Zuzenko: letter addressed to wife and daughter but intended for the ECCI. In Russian, manuscript and typescript. Trans. by KW.

After a trip from Russia that lasted more than a year and took him through England, the United States and Canada, Zuzenko arrived in Australia in July 1922 and took part in unity discussions between the communist groups on 15–16 July. This letter puts Zuzenko's own view of his role in what seemed—after such a lengthy division—to be a triumph. Zuzenko is somewhat contemptuous of the Anglo-Saxon approach to discipline as inferior to the Russian, and he is already sceptical of the value of the (former) 'Liverpool Street' comrades, especially Reardon and Everitt.

21 July 1922
Sydney

My dear wife and daughter Ksiuncha![51]

My loving greetings. I arrived safely. I had to do by myself the things that kept holding me up, but as you see I have overcome all obstacles quite successfully.[52] My comrades were overjoyed. Everybody knows me, if not personally (as many do), then by repute. A conference was in preparation to unite the two groups. The conference began rather drily. The adversaries came together after a good deal of bickering. In a two-hour conversation I tried to explain to them what proletarian discipline in the class struggle means (party discipline is something new to Anglo-Saxons). I gave them a full account of my activities throughout the period and my report was accepted unanimously. Everything that was left over I passed to the secretary. At the conclusion of my report, on behalf of the Executive Committee I demanded unification. A resolution on unification was passed unanimously. The atmosphere became more relaxed and the subsequent proceedings were conducted not between ideological foes, but between comrades. The same day (Saturday 15 July) at 2.00 p.m. I spoke at a meeting of the Everitt and Reardon group.[53] A time was set for me to give my report the following day, 16 July, Sunday, at 2.00 p.m. I talked to them until

---

[51] Salutation not given in typed copy. 'Ksiuncha' is an affectionate form of 'Ksenia'.
[52] Note a discrepancy between the handwritten and typed texts. The typist misreads Russ. *prepony* (obstacles) as *pritony* (dens [of vice]).
[53] Zuzenko has 'Everet' and 'Riordan' (in Cyrillic transcription).

five p.m. They keep stalling. They give no justification for operating separately because they have none. They are surprised that there is any other work to be done besides studying Marxism and they are opposed to reaching out to the masses. Reardon's view is, 'We are not obliged to follow Soviet Russia. We have different conditions here and the course of events will be different from that in Soviet Russia.' He does not indicate the kind of course of events he expects to see.

In view of rumours about my supposed anarchism, rumours that I have given all the funds to the anarchists (the sources of all these lies are in America), and also because I did not show them any letterhead paper with Ilich's signature and wax seal,[54] although they do not consider me legally competent, they nevertheless promise to give me in writing, in black and white, all the facts which prevent them from uniting. In the end I spelled out for them that they had only two courses open to them: they could either recognize Uncle Komin's twenty-one conditions and the resolutions of the congresses as binding for all and join the ranks of the organization,[55] or they could plainly state their refusal and remain the same little group of 'sectarian Marxist grasshoppers' as they were before and which abound in Canada. Their obtuseness and unconcealed careerism infuriated me. 'Shame on you! In Soviet Russia the path to Soc.[ial] Revolution is being strewn with mountains of bodies; hundreds of thousands of glorious valiant fighters are perishing with honour at their glorious posts for the great ideals of social restructuring, for communism. There they are making world history, while you here are feeding the gloating bourgeois press with your grubby little intrigues.' But how can you shame such low-grade politicos with mere words? They promised to give me all the material, and I've been waiting for a week now. A conference of both parties has elected me as delegate to the Fourth Congress of the Comintern and a permanent member of the Executive Committee. I have energetically set about putting the newspaper *The Communist* in order, while acquiring my own workers' press. Twelve people have returned here from Russia and are heaping on it all the muck they can. (Why do they let this scum out?) I have been giving lectures and have managed to clear away some of the fog that shrouds events in Soviet Russia. I have launched a fund-raising campaign to pay for agitation and propaganda, which is going quite well. I'm being sent to Melbourne in a few days. I shall also be doing some work in Brisbane, and then at the end of August or the beginning of September I'll be starting back. My view is this: the party has brought together the best and most revolutionary part of the proletarian elite. The bond with the grass roots remains weak as yet. I have proposed working tirelessly to set up party cells and direct the best forces in short order for campaign work and to

---

[54] 'Ilich's signature': signature of Vladimir Ilich Lenin.
[55] Uncle Komin: jocular name for the Comintern.

establish firm links with the grass roots. The paper [i.e. presumably *The Communist*] is sometimes dry and thin in content. It is essential to enlarge it and give it wider appeal. Work is only just beginning but it is already clear that it will be one of the purest organizations in the Anglo-Saxon countries. It is now free from the dirt of America and I hope it will remain so in the future. Ask for moral support to be provided for me. The success of the whole enterprise depends on it. I shall return not as the accused, but as the accuser of the vile-minded brethren who live by falsehoods alone. No decisions should be taken before I have reported. They are flinging mud from New York in advance, so as to appear pure white, but they will not succeed.

The Reardon/Everitt group, which is no more than about twenty strong, ought to be asked to withdraw. No good will come of them. Reardon has openly started campaigning against the red Labor Council in Sydney and is joining forces with the conservatives in his work.

Do write.

My address is: Mr A. Nargen, 432/5 Rawson Chambers, Sydney, NSW, Australia.[56]

Document 19

RGASPI 495–94–12. 21 July 1922, Jock Garden: July unity conference held. Typescript (but there is a manuscript German translation of its contents on the telegram itself).

The United CPA lets the Comintern know in this telegram that the unity conference of 15–16 July has taken place with a successful outcome, and that Zuzenko is in Sydney ('nargin here'). Garden goes on to ask whether the Comintern wants the CPA to call a unity conference of 'all communist sections in Australia during September', as it had previously ordered—Garden here says 'requested'—in a cable from Kuusinen on 15 July 1922 (RGASPI 495–94–8).

Telegram, 21 July 1922

forward moscow nargin here unity conference held fifteenth july
majority reardon party unite twentyone member
including reardon refuse united party going well should we call
another conference september now as requested = garden

Document 20

RGASPI 495–94–11. no date [late July or early August 1922], Earsman: to ECCI. Typescript.

---

[56] Only the handwritten copy bears the author's name (alias) and address, written in the margin. Rawson Chambers were the CPA premises.

> Earsman reports here to ECCI on the progress towards unity between the Australian communist groups in the first half of 1922. Continuing, at the Comintern's behest, to pursue unity, the 'Sussex Street' Communist Party (after the one-sided 'unity' meeting of 18 February 1922 calling itself the 'United CPA') has made a breakthrough in the July meeting. It consequently calls here on the Comintern to recognise the CPA as its Australian section. The ECCI did so on 9 August.

AUSTRALIAN UNITY QUESTION

The Executive of the Committee of Comintern.

Dear Comrades,

In this report I wish only to supplement the report you have already received. After the Conference held on February 18th, 1922, my Executive decided to carry the question of Unity to the membership of the Australian Socialist Party. Our members were instructed to get into close contact with as many of the members of the other organisation as possible, and urge [them] to take up the Unity question.

From this [time] on, a few events hastened our activities which were the means of bringing Unity to the fore again. The first of these was the opposing by comrade Reardon, General Secretary of the Socialist Party, by instruction of his Executive, the affiliation of the Sydney Labor Council to the RILU. The second was the tactics adopted by the Executive of the Socialist Party on the Famine Relief Committee, in which they charged the Labor Council of not assisting the Famine Committee to the fullest extent. This when the Secretary of this Council was also Secretary to the Famine Committee. It was the influence of the Labor Council that secured the vital aid of the Federal, Queensland and New South Wales Governments. The result of this was that Reardon was expelled from the Council of NSW.

At the end of March the activity of our members amongst the membership of the Socialist Party bore fruit, in the fact that the members of the Socialist Party demanded a special conference of their party. The Conference was held and agreed to the Unity conditions of the Comintern. They also removed Reardon as General Secretary and elected another comrade who had been acting in conjunction with myself. The conference also called for the resignation of Everitt, the Managing Editor of their press. The reply of Everitt was, that he took out a "Bill of Sale" over the property, thereby preventing the party from taking full posession. The amount he claimed was £500 which was reduced to £111. On behalf of my Party I agreed, should it be necessary to pay this price to get rid of Everitt, that we would make ourselves responsible for half of the amount.

The Council of Action composed of the two parties then held unofficial meetings because the Reardon faction refused to accept the decision of their conference until it was ratified by their membership.

At this time my Executive were of the opinion that I should leave and place the whole position before you.

Since then you have received cable advice of the result of the conference I have spoken of, which was on July 15th.[57] This we claim is further evidence of the impossibility of an unanimous decision on the question of unity with the Socialist Party.

Therefore, on behalf of my Party and in the interests of the International Movement and the working class of Australia, we demand that our application for affiliation as the Australian Section of the Comintern should be accepted immediately.

Appended is a report of the party's activities since my return to Australia and up to the time I left.

W.P. Earsman.

Document 21

RGASPI 495–94–8. 12 August 1922, Secretariat ECCI: to Cde Garden. Typescript.

In this letter the Comintern finally gives the United CPA what it has worked and lobbied for: recognition as the Australian section of the Communist International.

To the United Communist Party of Australia, for Comrade Garden.

Dear Comrade!

We received your letter of April 18 and well as a more considerable assortment of your correspondence with Reardon's group, and your telegramme which reported the Conference of the middle of July and the going over of a majority of the Reardon group. Furthermore, Comrade Earsman has arrived. The Presidium took up the Australian question once more on August 9, on the ground of these letters, telegrammes and reports and has formed the following decision:

> After the report of Comrade Rakosi it is decided that only the United Communist Party will be recognised as a section of the CI in Australia.

> A new unification-conference is no longer necessary.

We have sent you this decision by telegraph on August 10.

We request you to acknowledge the receipt, and we request you further to send the necessary credentials for Comrade Earsman, in case you wish to entrust him as the delegate of your Party, at the IVth Congress. You have the right to send two delegates to the IVth World Congress.

---

[57] See Document 19, above.

We would be very glad, if you would send us the plan of your prospective activity in all spheres of the movement and a description of the organisation of your Party.

With Communist greetings,
Secretariat of the ECCI

Document 22

RGASPI 495–95–9. 26 August 1922, Soviet chargé d'affaires in Sweden: to Ipswich communist party. In Russian, typescript. Trans. by KW.

At the same time as the Australian communists were working for unity and Comintern recognition, there remained a number of Russian communists in Australia who wished to return to Russia to assist in building socialism. This letter is a response to a request by such a group of Russian communists in Ipswich, Queensland, to establish a co-operative enterprise in Russia. It is neither encouraging nor discouraging, but rather seeks further information. By the mid-1920s, the Comintern indicated to its parties that it would accept communists from elsewhere (Russian or not) to live in the USSR only under exceptional circumstances (CALC 515–1–770), and by the mid-1930s, with war threatening and fear in Soviet Russia growing, immigrants to the Soviet Union were under intense suspicion. In a March 1936 'strictly confidential' report to the Comintern, I. Mingulin estimated that there were more than 10,000 political refugees from the USA in the Soviet Union, and added: 'There are suspicious people among political refugees from the USA' (CALC 515–1–3965).

RSFSR Chargé d'Affaires in Sweden
Svravägen 31, Stockholm
26 August, 1922

No. 02816
To: The Council [Soviet] of the Ipswich Communist Party, Ipswich

Dear Comrade,

I have just received your letter of 5th July. Before replying to your enquiries, I must seek further responses from you to the following questions:

1. What kind of co-operative [*artel*] have you in mind: an agricultural or land-tilling co-operative, a co-operative to rent and set up a metal-working or dress-making workshop, or other?
2. What is the approximate number of individuals wishing to travel? What are their qualifications, age, nationality (citizenship), areas of specialization, marital status, etc.?
3. Does the planned co-operative possess any assets, in the form of its own equipment, accumulated capital, etc.?
4. To which region would the co-operative like to travel and does it wish to set up an independent workshop or independent agricultural co-operative,

or does it wish to take up the rent or a concession on some existing factory or estate, etc.?

5. Do the members plan to travel as a single co-operative or as several co-operatives or separate groups?

Upon receipt of your reply to these questions and other information, I shall be able to obtain detailed information from the commissariats in question, so as to provide you with all the details you require.

With communist greetings,
Kertints [58]

Document 23

RGASPI 495–94–128. December 1922, Earsman: report: Australia: Past and Present. Typescript.

This document is Bill Earsman's report to the Fourth Comintern Congress on Australia, the CPA, and the CPA's prospects. While it emphasizes the CPA's influence in the trade unions, it is quite unlike Jock Garden's extravagant (but well-received) claims to the same Congress that the CPA could 'direct just close on 400,000 workers'. Both Earsman in this report and Garden in his speech declared—contrary to the facts—that One Big Union had been created in Australia.

AUSTRALIA
PAST AND PRESENT

The island continent in the past has attained some fame because of its political adventures in social legislation. That was in the days when the political world was being disturbed by the awakening working class forces; when they were struggling to a full consciousness of their method and that they had left childhood days behind.

This social legislation was recognised everywhere as something beyond all previous conceptions of political measures, and those experiences gave fresh hope to the social reformers and new life to many of the so-called working class leaders. Capitalists themselves began to take cheer and believe that they could well afford to accept the social legislation without giving up any of their power or their wealth. In fact, they saw this social reformation was going to be of great value to them in assisting them to hide the real truth from those who they were exploiting. It was "gilding the pill" of capitalism. We have now arrived at the stage when the poisonous effect of this pill is being felt, and social revulsions are taking place.

For the past twenty years Australia has enjoyed the reputation of being the land of political experiments, but it is over now. The dream of a happy contented

---

[58] Not fully legible.

race of people under capitalism has faded away, and once more we have the people brought face to face with reality and the seriousness of their position.

Again we have experienced the benefit of a Labour Party holding the reins of government; a party which was supposed to represent the workers. A working class party which was supposed to hold everything belonging to their class as holy. Once more the stern reality has forced itself upon the workers of Australia that the Labour Party is not a class party, but a petty bourgeois party. This has only been found after many years' experience, and perhaps it is as well to know what that experience is.

The Labour Party of Australia was organised in 1890 after very bitter industrial strikes, in which the power of the State was used against the workers. After those defeats the workers turned their attention to Parliament, and through their trade unions established the Labour Party. Ten years passed and they found themselves with the reins of the State machinery in their hands. Many times since, they have held those same State reins, till today they find them of little use; that is, the reins do not guide the "State horse". It has taken twenty years to realise, that though the Labour Party held the reins they did not manipulate them.

The roads which have been traversed by the "State coach" with the Labour Party as the drivers, have been named, nationalisation of industry, old age pensions, maternity bonus, compensation for accidents in industry, development of Australian industries, basic wage act under which no person shall be paid, the legalising of the eight-hour day, arbitration courts for settlement of all industrial disputes; these, along with other minor laws, complete the journey which the Labour Party set out on twenty years ago. Each and every one of those roads have been followed to the end, and today the Labour Party and also many of the workers see that they have reached a "dead end". In other words, the workers are beginning to realise that they have gone along the wrong road, and that all those roads within capitalism lead to a "dead end", that the only way out of their misery is by blowing up one of those dead ends. The Labour Party with all their social reforms stand today helplessly surrounded with misery and unemployment with no solution to their problem in their program.

Since the war this has become very clear, and in 1921 we find evidence of it. On every hand the working class were suffering unemployment of previous unknown dimensions, factories closing each day with no outlook of any betterment. The workers' demands for bread becoming louder and more insistent, and the only reply from the capitalists is less wages and a longer working week. The Labour Party were forced to act. So in this year they called an All-Australian Congress of Trade Unions.

This was the first attempt in the history of the country to bring about an organised effort to deal with the economic and political situation from the working class standpoint. The first work of this Congress, was, after examination, to decide that the trade unions must be reorganised on an industrial basis if they were going to be effective in meeting the capitalist offensive. So they agreed to the formation of One Industrial Union for all workers.

Turning to the political organisations we find a similar state of things, and this Congress also decided that the Labour Party program must in future be changed. The Congress examined the political program and decided to draft another one. This has been done and now the objective of the Australian Labour Party is the Socialisation of Industry with workers' control. How this has to be achieved is the burning question. The revolutionaries have no doubt on the subject, but the petty bourgeois politicians insist that only "peaceful" means can be employed. For the time being these people have had a victory, but it won't be for long.

Again this year 1922, the All-Australian Trade Union Congress met and again endorsed the resolutions of the previous year, and further demanded putting into practice the United Front by insisting that the Labour Party accept the affiliation of all revolutionary working class parties, including the Communist Party, with the right of freedom to organise and carry out propaganda work. This will mean the strengthening of the whole working class position and also that of the Communist Party.

The Trade Unions.

As I have already said the trade unions have made great progress in the fact that they recognised their weaknesses, and are taking steps to remedy those weaknesses. This has mainly been in the form of organisation. The organising of the One Big Union has become an accomplished fact. This was carried out in February of this year by the joining together of the agricultural workers (150,000), coal-miners (35,000), railwaymen (48,000), dockers (8,000). The unions in the building industry have agreed to form one union and they too will form a department in the One Big Union. The metal trade unions are doing likewise, and are voting on the formation of organising one union in that industry. So by the end of this year we expect that more than 60% of the organised workers will be in an industrial union. This will be a great achievement, particularly when we remember that 70% of the workers are organised, the total being 700,000.

The Capitalist Offensive.

This was commenced in 1920, and is still being carried on. There was little difference in the capitalist tactics from those carried out in other countries. They opened their offensive by closing of factories and the working of half time. This was followed by a wide newspaper campaign, that the workers must accept less wages and return to the forty-eight hour week in place of forty-four hours. The unions said no and prepared for the fight by binding themselves together to resist any attempt at lowering the standard of living. A big fight looked inevitable, when suddenly the Prime Minister of the Commonwealth called an Economic Conference composed of workers' and employers' representatives. At first the unions refused to have anything to do with this Conference because they said, "We refuse to discuss the lowering of wages or the working of more hours, and this Conference is only a trick to compromise us." The Communist Party had discussed the whole situation, and had issued instructions to all members that they must struggle for the unions going to the conference. In a few days this was accomplished and the workers decided to send representatives. There were 16 delegates on each side, with the Prime Minister in the chair. The conference lasted 10 days, when the employers broke it up by refusing to go any further. Whether the workers had a victory or not can be best seen from the opinion of "The Round Table" of June 1922.

> None the less, the employers made a distinct error in tactics which, under different leadership, might have been avoided. They did not exhaust the possibilities of the situation. The workers had discussed the practical proposals of the *employers*, but the employers acted as if the workers had put forward no immediately practical proposals. Quite possibly discussion might have resulted in no agreement, but to refrain from it on the ground that the workers were BOLSHEVIKS merely gave opportunity to the workers for effective propaganda, of which they have not been slow to avail themselves.

Thus it will be seen that the workers of Australia have benefited from the experience of their comrades in other countries. So far the capitalists have not been successful in obtaining their objectives of less "wages and more hours". At the present moment the attack is concentrated on the coal miners and reports point to a general strike in the near future.

The Communist Party.

The Party was formed in October 1920 by the Socialist Party, who later broke away from it. Their reasons were chiefly because they saw in the formation of a mass party that they would be swallowed up, and all traces of their former existence would be obliterated. In spite of this the Party grew slowly and is now established in every State of the Commonwealth. The year 1921 was taken up chiefly in internal struggles and the exposing of the Socialist Party. This year the Party has had success in the fact that a large majority of the members of the Socialist Party seceded and joined the CP.

The work of the Party has been directed chiefly in the trade unions where they have obtained very great influence. This influence is seen in all struggles of the workers and particularly was this so in the recent economic Conference.

In fact the Prime Minister openly declared that the workers' delegates were entirely in the hands of the CP and that he knew every one of us.

Again in the struggle *on behalf of* the unemployed we were chiefly *the* directing force, and many of our members found themselves in jail. The Party headquarters was the headquarters for the unemployed, where they held their meetings, and had always the assistance of party members or anything else we had at our disposal.

At our indoor meetings we can always rely on large numbers of the workers being present and giving us support in our work. In fact the Party headquarters is a real workers' rendezvous. Today in all questions the trade unions turn to the CP for a lead and as each day goes by the influence of the party increases.

In the trade union work it was mainly the influence of the Party members who carried the affiliation of the Sydney Labour Council to the Red Labour Union International. This, in spite of the opposition of the social reformers and the socialists. This body represents 500,000 trade unionists, and has affiliated to it a majority of the trade unions. It is the real leader of the trade unions of the whole country. The Party influence is great here, having no less that 40 delegates with the official positions under control.

The future is very promising. The Party along with the trade unions realise the acuteness of the capitalist struggle in the Far East, and this is of great importance to Australia. Australia stands at the southern end of the Pacific, Japan at the northern end, America and several groups of islands in between. The Far East is Australia's future market and with her "White Australia Policy" makes her economically and politically very interested in the Far East.

At the last All-Australian Trade Union Congress the workers' representatives decided, that it was imperative a closer relationship should be established between all workers' organisations in all countries in the Pacific. Towards the end they agreed to call a Pan-Pacific Congress to be held in 1925. Thus it will be seen that the workers of Australia are preparing for the future. This gives the Communist Party the opportunity to take the leadership of the masses. With the active support of the Communist International the future of the Communist Party is a bright one, and in the coming struggles will attain that leadership necessary for the social revolution.

W.P. EARSMAN

Document 24

RGASPI 495–94–12. 7 December 1922, S. Stettler: Letter to ECCI. Typescript.

While the Fourth Comintern Congress was in session, the Sydney branch of the CPA met on 4 December 1922, criticized the Central Executive of the Party, and declared itself the Communist Party of Australia, Australian section of the Third International. Many of the members of this group were former ASP members, who had united with the CPA in July 1922. This letter requests recognition from Moscow, declares that some delegates to the Comintern Congress are now a 'breakaway' group who should not be paid, and requests an ECCI member to come to Australia to adjudicate. Moscow, however, had made its decision; it effectively stood by the Garden-Earsman party (see Document 29, below).

December 7th. 1922.

To/ The Secretary,
Executive Committee,
Communist International,
MOSCOW.

Dear Comrade,

Following on my Cable to you, this letter is an explanation of actually what has taken place as regards the split within the Party.

Let me first of all point out that the Party is run on the lines of the old Socialist Parties, also that the Party is very very weak. The majority of the members are not conversant with the [Twenty One] Theses, nor are they with the Rules and Constitution of the Party. In fact the members on the Central Committee of the Party cannot discuss the Theses with you. The membership of the Party for the whole of Australia is only in the vicinity of 500, out of which the majority are members of Sydney Branch. The personnel of the Central Committee is made up of Sydney Branch members.

I am enclosing copy of the Rules and Constitution of the Party, copy of the Leader published in the Paper, and copy of a letter sent by me and endorsed by the Branch, to any member outside the Branch that we could get in touch with.

You will perceive the perfidy of those on the Central Committee in Resolutions F. and G. should Sydney Branch want to appeal to Conference. You will further note the deliberate misquoting of the Theses.

Sydney Branch, realising the absolute necessity for a well disciplined and organised Party, set about to organise groups and nuclei on the lines laid down by the Third Congress of the Communist International, for the different activities of the Branch. At a SPECIAL MEETING of the Branch called for the purpose of bringing about discipline, it was decided that members must attend their Branch meetings, and that should a Comrade miss three consecutive meetings his name be struck off the books; a roll book was procured and members were required to sign at each meeting night; members must pay their dues; an organising committee was elected to start organising the groups etc. It was at this meeting that opposition came from members of the Central Executive on practically all these motions. Re the roll book they started moving amendments that we get a roll book for Sunday night lectures and resolutions just as stupid. On the election of the organising Committee, members of the Central Executive refused nomination and sabotaged it to the best of their ability.

It is the same comrades who talk about enforcing discipline on the rank and file of the Party, while they themselves divorce themselves from the daily work of the Party.

The ASP section before uniting got rid of those officials who were cogs as it were in the further progress of Communism, and most of us were determined to carry out the instructions of the Communist International in helping the rank and file of the United Communist Party in ridding them of the opportunists and Centrists who were officials of the Party. This would have been accomplished at Conference, but the Provisional Central Executive has saved us the trouble; they have broken away from the Party by the methods illustrated in the leader to the paper, and the letter I forwarded to branches.

At a Special Meeting held on Monday December 4th. 1922. Sydney Branch declared itself the Communist Party of Australia, (The Australian Section of the Communist International) and herewith apply for recognition. We have started good and have already started a group in the Breakaway section that is doing good work in exposing the CE members to the rank and file that have followed them.

The Party in the past has only accepted a Communist Programme on paper, their actions have been the actions of Centrists, both in the Party and the Trades and Labor Council. With regard to the Trades and Labor Council, members of the Party have been supporting and formulating go slow policies, scientific strikes, sectional strikes, etc., and the Central Executive of the Party have not only endorsed their actions but have through the official organ of the Party declared them the Policy of the Party.

Comrade Howie signed the resolutions re the expulsion of the Branch as published in the *Leader*, when he was not present at the meeting. He was approached by me to take the chair at Branch meetings, and he replied that he could not as it would not be the thing the acting Secretary of the Trades and Labor Council acting as Chairman of the Communist Party. Com. Voight (director of the Labor Research Bureau) had to lecture in the hall when the trouble began, but refused at the last minute and gave as an excuse "Fancy the Director of the Labor Research Bureau lecturing from the Communist platform when this trouble is on."

This is the brand of Communists that is at the present time supporting the CE members in the breakaway Party.

These individuals are going round boasting words to this effect: "anyway we are going to get the money from Russia and so on." It was on this account that I forwarded the Cable as follows to you:— "Stop payment draft Denford

Australia Denford Baker Howie forming Breakaway Party Explanation following Signed- Stettler, 395 Sussex Street, Sydney." We stopped the letter addressed to Denford advising him of money.

At the time we thought it strange that these individuals should walk out as they did, and start to form another branch.

If the Communist International decides that we readmit them into the Party or that we unite with them again so as to propagate the Communist position and the discussion of the theses, this party is prepared to do so but we would suggest that a member of the Executive Committee be sent out to make enquiries, before acting in regards to the Press etc. We do so actuated by the best of reasons, and in the best interests of Communism. Long live the Communist International.

With fraternal greetings from the Comrades in Australia.
Stettler

We have carried out the instructions of the Comintern as issued to Com. P. Lamb re unity in Australia & hereby apply for affiliation - Stettler

---

Document 25

RGASPI 495–94–11. December 1922, Jock Garden and Bill Earsman: The Communist Party of Australia [and the United Front]. Present only in the Russian version, typescript. Trans. by KW.

This document seems to be a contribution to the lengthy debate at the Fourth Comintern Congress in November-December 1922 on the 'united front' policy. It is an account of the formation of the CPA by Australian delegates to the Fourth Congress. In particular, it attempts to explain the various currents that formed the CPA, and why the Comintern's 'united front' policy was not well received by all of them. It is interesting, in part, because its two authors (who incidentally detested each other) had divergent views on the application of the 'united front' tactic in Australia, Garden wishing to re-enter the Labor Party (which the tactic seemed to sanction), while Earsman was sceptical. Like many grand formulae, the 'united front' gave rise to a range of practical applications around the world. The final point in the document, about 'a serious breach of discipline', seems to refer to the split in the Sydney branch of the CPA which occurred in early December 1922 (see Document 24), and about which Garden and Earsman would have only recently heard.

[Added in handwriting, in Russian: To Presidium, Comrades Kuusinen, Wallenius, Kaliarov [i.e. V. Kolarov] [word illegible] Kuusinen. [Word illegible] resolution. 22/XII/22, (possibly 22/XI/1922).]

The Communist Party of Australia

The party was formed in 1920 from earlier syndicalist elements and from other elements expelled from the Labor Party on account of their revolutionary nature.

In order to understand the full significance of this, it is necessary to pay close attention to the development of the workers' movement.

The workers' movement arose in 1890 after determined strikes spread throughout the country and the government used armed force against the workers. Following these strikes the working class decided to use the trade unions to form its own class's political party, which would seize state power from the employers through the ballot box and use this power in the interests of the working class. This should be done by the nationalization of industry, and in this way the working class would also be liberated. How nationalization would be conducted—by compensation or confiscation—was a matter that at first no thought was given to.

The Labor Party soon acquired influence and support among the workers, and also among many small farmers. In 1904 the Labor Party came to power and the workers thought their time had come. The Labor Party began by implementing its nationalization plan and carried it through within a matter of years, paying compensation to the capitalists. Since that time, Labor has held office in all states except Victoria, and also, several times since 1904, at the federal level.

Gradually, however, the workers came to realize that something was wrong, and in 1912 a strong syndicalist movement arose and gained great influence among the workers. It continued until 1917, when a general strike broke out as a spontaneous uprising by the masses against exploitation in the name of patriotism by the employer class. For eight weeks the workers stayed out and their leaders, try as they might, did not know what to do except return to work for improved conditions. These leaders were Labor Party members and ambitious members of parliament. The strike ended with the workers returning to their factories on the terms offered by the employers.

From this conflict the syndicalists arrived at the conclusion that the trade unions should be turned into industrial unions. A determined campaign began within the unions and the Labor Party. Many leading functions in the trade unions passed into the hands of the proponents of the industrial principle. In 1919 they gained control of the union movement and also tried to take over the Labor Party. At the 1919 Labor Party congress, the adherents of the industrial principle (the Industrialists) waged a determined struggle aimed at changing the party programme, but were defeated, owing to a majority (albeit a tiny one) on the side of their opponents. As a result of this defeat, the Industrialists quit the congress and set about organizing another political party. The Labor Party, for its part, was forced to expel them, and launched a forceful campaign against the industrial unions. The new party soon folded, leaving many union leaders outside the political movement.

Since 1916 there has also been an Australian Socialist Party in existence, and before that a Socialist Labour Party had arisen. But neither of these were based on mass support, and enjoyed no influence, being insignificant sects of orthodox Marxists, dedicated primarily to putting forward candidates to run for parliament against Labor and taking no part in the workers' struggle in the factories, mines and farms.

Thus we had in Australia in 1920 a certain number of trade union leaders bent on political action, and many syndicalists who realized how very feeble their movement was compared with the Russian revolution. For this reason, in late 1920 an attempt was made to found a communist party. The attempt was only partly successful, as it failed to attract the socialists and some other groups. Success was achieved only in July of this year.

This explains why we see in the present Communist Party of Australia one faction expelled from the Labor Party and another consisting of erstwhile parliamentary socialists, and yet a third with strong syndicalist tendencies. Until recently there were no particular theoretical differences between these factions and they all worked harmoniously in a single direction, but the policy of the United Front led to some differences. All members of the party recognized the need for a united front against the capitalist onslaught and (in my opinion), in the political area, if the Labor Party was prepared to carry it through. According to reports, the Labor Party has not turned down the CP request to join, but is conducting a wavering policy, ignoring the whole matter. This led to deep dissatisfaction with the Labor Party among the communists. Then federal elections were held, leading to a crisis in the party. Two schools of thought arose, one of which felt it essential to support Labor, whatever the Labor Party's attitude to the CP request for admission, and the other refusing to support Labor until Labor agreed to consider CP admission and denying its members the right to back Labor. Another faction, regardless of all this, carried on its work and perhaps with this aim set up a provisional party. We believe that following the federal elections this breach will be healed.

In spite of this, at present there exists a serious breach of discipline which demands stern resolution.

GARDEN
EARSMAN

Document 26

RGASPI 495–94–8. December 1922, ECCI: to United CPA. Typescript.

The Fourth Comintern Congress was the first at which Australia appeared as an official section, the CPA, recognition having been given three months earlier, on 9 August 1922. After the Congress, the ECCI wrote to the CPA advising it especially on application of the 'united front' policy which had been reaffirmed by Congress: 'a consistent and determined but not too rigid application'. It meant, however, that Australian communists had to join and work within the ALP. The Comintern also had some astringent advice for the CPA, pointing out the weakness of its press, and declaring: 'Your Party is still weak, your experience of the class struggle as a Party is still inadequate, your preparedness for taking the lead in the future intensified class fights is still deficient'. By following the lead of the experienced Bolsheviks, it implied, the CPA would be able to overcome these weaknesses.

To the United Communist Party of Australia

Comrades,

The Fourth Congress of the Comintern has concluded its work. The present letter is written to you for the purpose of imparting to you some of the decisions of the Fourth Congress which contain concrete proposals for the practical carrying out of the Congress decisions in Australia.

You have accepted the 21 conditions which form the basis of the present and future tactics of the Communist International, as well as the theses and resolutions of the Third World Congress, primarily those which relate to our organisation and our tactics, and you have presumably studied them carefully. As you know, the pivotal point of these theses was substantially contained in the slogan: "To the masses"! The Fourth Congress has again endorsed the correctness of this demand.

The capitalist offensive is carried on today in all countries with the open blessings of the opportunists, of the reformists, of the social-patriots of the 2 and 2 1/2 Internationals, or at best, under the hypocritical protests of the latter, such as the making of pacifist reform motions in Parliament which carefully respect the privileges of the exploiting class and which are intended to hoodwink the proletariat to the real cause of its terrible situation. Turn your glance to England, to France, to Germany, to Italy—everywhere you behold the same picture: reduction of wages, extension of the working day, lock-outs, and brutal suppression of every attempt of the masses at self-action, of every comprehensive new movement of the proletarian masses in the economic as well as the political domain. A period of economic and moral decline continues the infernal work of the five years of butchery.

This can only be met by a Workers' United Front. It requires above all a consistent and determined but not too rigid application of the tactics of the United Front.

In this respect there is a tremendous task before you, our Australian comrades. The Australian Communist Party must now concentrate all its energy and all its ability to win a decisive majority in the trade unions; in every industrial center it should not only take the lead in the larger and smaller economic fights, but it should also really lead the masses in all their political movements as well as in the struggle to raise their cultural standard. During the capitalist offensive the Communist Party as the most revolutionary and best disciplined party must lead the entire proletariat in the struggle, with revolutionary slogans that will be understood by every worker. No matter whether the struggle be for small or great demands, the party must be a leader. Every single strike that is won, every victory in the struggle for daily interests, even if very slight, already signifies the winning of a strong position against the bourgeoisie, and what is even more important, it signifies a strengthening of the influence of the Communist Party among the masses. The younger Communist Parties of the Communist International frequently showed the tendency of isolating themselves from the mass of the proletariat, of applying the principles of Marxism in doctrinaire and sectarian fashion, merely as a means of preserving the purity of their principles. This hampers the development of the Communist Party, which means also hampering the fight of the working class for freedom, and at the present moment it hampers particularly the successful defence against the capitalist offensive. It is for this reason that we draw your special attention to the necessity of expanding and intensifying the Communist activity within the trade unions, in every state, by means of firmly disciplined communist nuclei that should gather round them the the larger masses of sympathising workers. The trade unions are the organisations that offer the best prospects for the practical application of the slogan: "To the masses"! The trade unions provide the best opportunity for communists to show how far they are really connected with the masses, how they feel for the masses, and their ability to overcome the treachery of the reformist trade union leaders.

It must always be remembered that the Communist Party is not a party only of watchwords and slogans, but a real fighting proletarian party, always leading the class struggle. We must never tolerate such a situation in which the workers look upon the party as an accepted fact, but do not feel the need of entering it. Our tactics should be the tactics of struggle, and not the repetition of the same ideas, marking time on the same spot.

It is for this very purpose of strengthening the Communist Party and of accelerating its growth, that the Executive of the Comintern has been recommending tactics of the United Front for more than a year.

In countries like Great Britain and Australia, owing to the existence of a peculiar type of political mass organisation known as the Labour Party, this tactic has a specific form of application.

The Australian Labour Party is even more outspokenly a trade union party than its British counterpart, with an equally petty bourgeois, reformist set of leaders.

Nevertheless, the masses in their bulk continue to cling to the Labour Party. Does this mean to say that if the working masses are to be won for Communism, we should work within this mass party? The Communist International answers this question in the affirmative. The joining of the Labour Party opens wide perspectives for the development of the Communist Party, and provides a possibility for Communist sympathisers in the Labour Party to find practical application for their revolutionary desires. It further gives the Communist Party the possibility to unmask the opportunist leaders of the Labour Party before the masses of their followers in the best and most direct way, demonstrating to the rank and file of the Labour Party, that such leaders will never fight for the serious demands of the proletariat. On the other hand the masses will at the same time have the opportunity to convince themselves that the Communist Party is not only the forward-driving element of the class struggle, but that it is also the only Party that takes a hand in all the fights of the masses, shares unreservedly all their sufferings and misery. Only in this manner it will be possible to win the confidence of the workers, to isolate the opportunist leaders and to separate them from the masses. We have reason no longer to content ourselves with unmasking the treacherous nature and role of the leaders of the Labour Party merely by propaganda, while otherwise letting them have their free play. We should rather fight within the Labour Party and capture it by waging the fight against the social-traitors in the mass party which has been monopolised by them.

Nevertheless we deem it necessary to warn you against the illusion of assuming that a victory over the reformists and opportunists within the Labour Party would make the class struggle any milder, that the mere possession of a majority of the masses in the Labour Party would give you something like "democratic government", a gradual transition to the proletarian rule by the sole application of democratic measures of compulsion against the bourgeoisie. Such a view would be dangerous opportunism. On the contrary, you must be perfectly aware of the fact, and leave no doubt in the minds of the wide masses of the proletariat, that the winning of the majority in the Labour Party will tremendously increase the struggle against the bourgeoisie, accentuating the class antagonism and compelling capitalism to resort to the most savage measures of violence. Such is the logic of all revolutionary class struggles. He who fears the consequences of this logic should cease to call himself a Marxian, a revolutionary and a Communist. The bourgeoisie will become increasingly restless, provocatory, brutal, and ruthless in the precise measure that its reformist agents, the leaders of the Labour Party, will lose that influence over the masses. This is a fact of which you should never lose sight. The winning of the majority of the workers by the Communists does not mean any softening of the intensity of the class struggles, but its aggravation; no slackening of the revolutionary propaganda, but rather the increasing consciousness of the proletarian masses that the bourgeoisie will not shrink from civil war in the defence of its rights.

Emphasise this fact day by day in your big and little actions, in your victories as well as in your defeats and your joining the Labour Party and the consequent stubborn adherence to the United Front tactics will in no way contain the menace of damping your revolutionary watchwords, in a word, of converting you into opportunists.

The EC of the CI therefore deliberately advises the Australian Communist Party to join the State Labour Party as well as the Federal Labour Party, carrying out the resolution of the Australian Trade Union Congress in June 1921 and 1922 on the Unity Question.

We emphasise: the application of the United Front tactics as already emphasised by the Comintern on numerous occasions, does not deprive the Communist Party of its freedom of agitation, propaganda and criticism in all situations and at all times, nor does it impair the organisational independence and the subordination of Communist Party members and organisations to the discipline of their Party under all circumstances; on the contrary, these things are rather emphasised thereby. Wherever we find ourselves as Communists, in carrying out the decisions of the Communist International, we observe the strictest Party discipline and the most complete devotion to the Communist International.

It should be your aim to bring together all the militant elements within and without the Australian Labour Party and to convince them that the working class of Australia needs above all the unity of all the class conscious elements under the banner of the Communist Party.

But should the Labour Party leaders refuse to admit us into their organisation, this is no reason for abandoning the "United Front". It only means that our efforts will have to be redoubled to maintain the "United Front". It must never be said that the Communists divided the workers. That must be left to the leaders of the Labour Party. Our duty as Communists and the party of the working class is to bring our class to victory. This can only be done by pointing the way and working with the masses and showing them that we are the real leaders and that our place is inside the workers' organisations. Again, should the Labour Party leaders refuse to admit you, it is no reason for falling down before these leaders, asking for mercy. We have to carry on the fight as Communists, among the rank and file of the Party, and ultimately they will demand our admittance.

The policy of the bourgeois Labour government was always reactionary in substance. It hindered the workers in the carrying out of their real class struggle against the bourgeoisie. It tied the hands of the exploited masses, and made them the worshippers of the authority of the Capitalist State. As against this, it is the duty of a Communist Party to remove all the influences that hinder the development of the revolutionary forces of the working class, and are obstacles to the class struggle. For this reason the Communist Party must take the initiative in all the mass movements of the workers, and try again to secure the leadership of the various labour organisations, and mobilise them for the fight against the capitalist class. If the Communist Party should find it necessary in this connection, in order to increase the resisting power of the working class, to unite temporarily in joint activity with other labour organisations, by forming a bloc or a workers' coalition government, not a liberal Labour government but a real militant workers' government composed of representatives of the working class, the Communist Party should not shrink from such a task. The intensification of the class struggle against the bourgeoisie, which is bound to follow the formation of such workers' government, will enable the Communist Party to fight for the realisation of the real dictatorship of the proletariat from this intermediary stage.

The United Front tactic is not a peace treaty. It is merely a manoeuvre in the proletarian class struggle. It is not an end in itself, but a tool for the acceleration of the revolutionising process of the masses. The struggle against the leaders of the Right Wing of the Australian Labour Party must be pursued with all emphasis both within and without, constantly and persistently, exposing their policy, which consists of binding the workers hand and foot and delivering them to the bourgeoisie. At all elections the Communists must retain the right of participating in the pre-selection ballot. It is by joining the Labour Party that this will be made possible.

Now a few words about your press. Much as we congratulate the Australian Communist Party for its activity and work accomplished in the trade unions, particularly in New South Wales, we must point out to you on the other hand, that your press leaves a good deal to be desired. It is high time that you should become clearly aware that the whole [activity] of the Communist Party does not consist of the enlisting of adherents, but also of really taking part in the class struggle. It is not enough to show up cleverly the backwardness of the masses, but it is rather necessary to change their class consciousness. The masses cannot be convinced merely by leaflets and cleverly-written articles. The first thing needful is live activity and example by deed. Through your press you should take part in the daily struggles of the workers. Your press should be the mirror not only of the life of the Party, but of the entire proletariat and of all the exploited and oppressed. A proletarian newspaper must play the role of a popular tribune. It is this feature that is lacked by your press. We have no doubt that you will remedy this defect. To make your press more lively your should do your utmost to get the masses of the workers to contribute to your paper by sending letters and descriptive articles of their daily life, and at the same time shaping your papers so that their contents should speak not only to the mind but also to the heart of the workers.

Your Party is still weak, your experience of the class struggle as a Party is still inadequate, your preparedness for taking the lead in the future intensified class fights is still deficient. You should not hide your light under a bushel, but take all the measures to increase your organisation, also numerically, above all in the great organisation of workers, the trade unions, where you ought to make particular efforts to strike deep roots. This requires the untiring self-sacrificing and uninterrupted activity of every member of the Party without exception. The Australian proletariat is still trammelled by the petty-bourgeois democratic illusions. To help them shake these illusions it requires not only vigorous educational activity, but also patient and judicious treatment of the backward elements. Finally, the Communist Party must never forget that the calm periods of the class struggle are merely the calms before the storms, that these moments of respite must be utilised to prepare the *working*-class for the future struggles whether defensive or offensive. If this should be neglected, you are in danger of surprise-attack and provocation on the part of the bourgeoisie, of premature struggles with their inevitable defeats.

By following the advice you get from experience of many years' fighting of the advanced proletariat of all countries you will overcome the capitalist offensive which menaces you with slow destruction, profound misery and brutal disfranchisement, and triumphantly march to the final victory.

Long live the United Front of the workers of Australia!
Long live the Communist Party of Australia!

For the Executive Committee of the Communist International.
Dec. 1922

Document 27

RGASPI 495–94–18. 28 February 1923, Zuzenko: letter/report: to ECCI. In Russian, typescript. Excerpts. (For a complete translation of this long report with details of Zuzenko's activities in the USA and Canada, see Windle 2004b.) Trans. by KW.

Zuzenko reports here on his long mission on behalf of the Comintern to Australia, over the period 1920–22. Zuzenko fears that the Comintern may have forgotten his service, and prepares the ground for further missions to the Anglo-Saxons. Separating this document from the next in CAAL (Zuzenko's memo of 18 March 1923, which appears as Document 28, below), a page bears the manuscript words, in Russian, 'To Wallenius, for the Secretariat. What are we to do about Comrade Zuzenko?'

To the Executive Committee of the Third Communist International from Aleksandr Mikhailovich Zuzenko, Comintern official.

Foreword

In the summer of last year, 1922, I learned to my astonishment from a letter from my wife that nobody in the Comintern Executive Committee remembers me, knows me or thinks they sent me on any assignment at all. In view of this

I consider it my duty to supply the Comintern Executive Committee, at the beginning of my report, with a brief reminder of my existence.

I became a party worker in 1904. In mid-1905 I was discharged as unreliable from the training vessel 'Velikaia Kniaginia Kseniia Aleksandrovna' [Grand Duchess Kseniia Aleksandrovna] and expelled from the Magnushof Maritime Training College. In autumn 1905 I joined the combat organization of the Socialist Revolutionary Party. For organizing a political strike I was expelled from the Riga Maritime Training College in early 1906. I took part in a number of terrorist acts in Riga and in southern Russia. I experienced Tsarist prisons twice—in Riga in early 1906 and in Nikolaev in 1908.

I fled Russia to avoid an investigation and trial in 1911. By my work I assisted in the organization of the Union of Russia Seamen Abroad (in Antwerp, Belgium). Having lost faith in the Socialist Revolutionary Party I broke with it and worked in Australia as an organizer of IWW ('Industrialist') groups and as a proponent of anarchic communism. While working in Australia as a sugar-cane cutter, I organized and conducted a number of strikes in the sugar industry and the industry's first general strike to do away with contract labour.

After the departure from Australia of Comrade Artem Sergeev and others, I acted as secretary of the Union of Russian Workers in Australia, edited the paper *Znanie i edinenie* [Knowledge and Unity] in Russian and founded and edited *Knowledge and Unity* in English. Three times the Australian authorities ordered me to cease my campaigning and organizational work. I continued. *Znanie i edinenie* was closed down. I set about publishing an illegal newspaper, *Deviatyi val* [The Ninth Wave].[59]

For general propaganda work I drew together the more revolutionary element of the socialists and 'Industrialists', arranging revolutionary demonstrations by the unemployed and by revolutionary groups of soldiers. A revolutionary demonstration on 25 March 1919 led to a clash with the police and the temporary success of the demonstrators, but then to the rout of the Union of Russian Workers in Australia and the arrest of its most active members.[60] On 27 March 1919 I was arrested and at the end of April the same year deported from Australia. It was the intention of the Australian authorities to deliver me into the torture chambers of the 'true Russian authorities', that is, of Denikin.[61] Having passed

---

[59] *Znanie i edinenie* was closed down in December 1918. The English-language version began to appear at the end of December 1918 and continued long after Zuzenko's deportation in April. *Deviatyi val*, on the other hand, lasted for only four issues, December 1918 to February 1919.

[60] '25 March 1919': date as given. All Australian archive and press sources give Sunday 23 March as the date of the red flag procession in Brisbane. Street clashes occurred over the following few days.

[61] General Anton Ivanovich Denikin, commander of the anti-Bolshevik Volunteer Army in southern Russia in 1918–20, which was finally expelled by the Bolshevik forces in February 1920. 'Torture chambers' is a free translation of a word for which English has no exact equivalent –*rasprava*, denoting extremes of torture, commonly ending in death, usually without legal sanction. Zuzenko later told of

through several prisons, in October 1919, thanks to the insistence of my sick wife, who was also deported from Australia,[62] I was released under police supervision from a Turkish prison in Constantinople, and at the end of that month made my way to Odessa, where I remained until the Red forces arrived.

While working In Tiraspol (Odessa region) as editor of *Izvestiia tiraspolskago revkoma* [News of the Tiraspol Revolutionary Committee], I joined the Ukrainian Bolshevik Communist Party. In March 1920, as a delegate from Tiraspol, I was sent to the Third All-Russian Congress of Trade Unions in Moscow. Comrades Artem Sergeev and Berzin (the Comintern Secretary) sent me to Petrograd to report to the Small Bureau of the Comintern on the situation in Australia. In May 1920, by a decision of the Large Bureau, I was taken into the employment of the Comintern and directed to Australia to form a Communist Party of Australia.

Aleksandr Zuzenko, alias A. Nargen

Memorandum

In early May 1920, by a decision of the Large Bureau of the Comintern, I was taken into the employment of the Comintern and directed to Australia to form a Communist Party of Australia. I was ordered to go to Tiraspol (Odessa region), hand over the editorship of the newspaper to my deputy, and to be in Moscow with my family by the opening of the Second Congress of the Comintern.

At the Second Congress of the Comintern I represented the communist group of Queensland, Australia, without voting rights. In mid-October I left Soviet Russia by way of Murmansk and Vardö, in Norway, having received £150 sterling for travel expenses and £500 for agitation and propaganda in Australia. I had to leave behind in Murmansk a suitcase full of selected literature for Australia, on the advice of Comrade Vasten.[63] Travelling light, with no luggage, with a seaman's documents in the name of Alexander Holmst [phon.], I set off, accepting the assurances of comrades that I would receive all that I needed in Norway and England. In Christiania [Oslo] Comrade Latimer [phon.] (also known as Jurgis) and in England the Communist Party would supply all necessary documents and render comradely assistance. In Vaida-guba I was just two hours too late to

---

being under sentence of death during this period, but it is clear that no Australian or British court passed such a sentence, and he escaped the clutches of Denikin.

[62] Zuzenko's wife Cecilia (née Rosenberg) was not, in fact, deported, but left Australia voluntarily to follow her husband back to Russia in May 1919. Her father, Michael Rosenberg, was deported in September.

[63] Aleksandr Petrovich Vasten was for a period in charge of Soviet intelligence in the Murmansk area, where Sylvia Pankhurst met him during her visit to Russia in 1920 (Pankhurst 1921). He was later thought to have visited Britain on Soviet ships. PRO KV 3/15 (SF 450–0302–2/ Vol. 2) Appendix H.

catch the group of French comrades, and the storm which sank them held us prisoner for about a week in the fishing settlement of Zemlianoi.[64]

In Vardö I had my first opportunity to experience the 'brilliant' international liaison arrangements that we had heard so much about in Moscow. A certain Bodin [phon.], a louche-looking eighteen-year old with the air of a criminal, was working there. He was engaged in secret work, but the 'secrets' were known to the entire population of Vardö, including the police.

I reached Christiania without incident. (Before my arrival they had been arresting every delegate who passed through.) I had to spend ten aimless days in Christiania before, with the aid of some strong language, managing to see the other 'Comintern boy', the forty-year-old Latimer (otherwise Jurgis), the organizer of the Comintern's international liaison. The storage he had set up for communist literature was stunning in its childishness. Comrade Latimer had established this in the middle of Christiania, in the building which housed the Folkets Hus or cultural centre, permanently ringed by police. Here in broad daylight bundles of literature were delivered and packets of books carried out, before the eyes of the police and their informers. The dispatch of every pound in weight of literature cost almost ten English shillings. It was plain to me that disaster awaited the product of Latimer's endeavours. I shared my concerns with him and received the reply that that was his business. With this I hastened to agree. I read of the seizure of the Comintern store, the arrest of Comrade Kurre-Grep [phon.] and Latimer's flight from Norway when I was in Liverpool, and the news came as no surprise. Latimer refused to give me any help at all, so with the help of Kurre-Grep I set off for Bergen, and from there stowed away to Newcastle-upon-Tyne and on to London. The suitcase of literature that I left behind in Murmansk with Comrade Vasten is probably still there, even though they promised to deliver it to Christiania before I got there.

In England

In London I successfully made contact with Jack Tanner,[65] the editor of *Solidarity*, but he was unable to render any assistance as he had no links at all

---

[64] 'Too late to catch the French comrades.' Accounts of this episode differ, and the dates vary. According to Victor Serge (1963, 112), Serge's friend Sasha Tubin and three French socialists making for Vardö in a fishing smack perished in a storm, in 'August or September 1920'. A warning had been sent by a party of British delegates, including William Gallacher, Sylvia Pankhurst and John Clarke, who had struggled through the storm to Vardö by the same route only days earlier, but the warning came too late (Gallacher 1966, 155 ff). *Bolshaia Sovetskaia Entsiklopediia*, however, (under Lefebvre) dates the disaster as occurring on 1 October, and Zuzenko's list of expenses (National Archives of Australia: A6122/40 111, Summary of Communism, p. 151) also indicates the beginning of October, rather than the mid-October date he gives in this report. The French casualties were Raymond Lefebvre, François (Jules) Lepetit (Louis Berthö), and Jean (Marcel) Vergeat. Sasha Tubin, also from France, was acting as their interpreter (see also Broué 1997, 183).

[65] Jack Tanner: active member of the shop stewards' movement. With Gallacher he attended the 1920 Comintern congress. He was later suspected by British security of industrial espionage on behalf of the Soviet Union. PRO KV 3/15 (SF 450–0302–2/ Vol. 2); KV4/124.

with the seamen's union. He did not know the address of a shop that sold false passports, and for some reason he regarded Tom Barker, the IWW 'industrialist' whom I knew from Australia, as untrustworthy so refused to put me in touch with him. On learning that I was carrying about £100 destined for Australia, Comrade Tanner spent hours trying to persuade me to leave the money with him.[66] He would send it to me in Australia, he said, as it might be confiscated if I was arrested, and so on. But, knowing the financial situation of *Solidarity*, I declined these comradely favours.

Armed with a letter from Comrade Tanner to the Braddock brothers, I set off for Liverpool to take up the place arranged for me as a sailor on a steamer sailing for Australia. The comrades Jack and Wilfred Braddock introduced me to a sailor called Jack White, (a thief with a series of convictions), and through him to some representatives of the seamen's union. I was to pay two representatives £10 each for their time, and the same to the Braddock brothers and other comrades who had arranged my departure.[67]

Owing to the incompetence of those who had undertaken to help me, I was arrested while signing my contract on the ship, for presenting a British unemployment registration card instead of the card issued to foreigners. After questioning me at length at the Aliens' Office, they seized my documents but released me, accepting my assurances that I would be in Southampton the next day and would obtain a passport from my consul, that is, the American consul [sic]. With my papers I lost any opportunity to join the crew of a ship. I could not obtain false papers because the British were unfamiliar with methods of clandestine work. The Communist Party of Great Britain at that time turned out to be the same as it very likely is now, not a united, centralized party of communists, but scattered and uncoordinated communizing crowds. There were crowds following Maclean, Sylvia Pankhurst and Gallacher; there was Jack Tanner's crowd and John Clarke's crowd, grouped around *The Worker*—a total of about a thousand people.[68] In a city like Liverpool, the communist cell numbered just over fifty. Having lost hope of obtaining documents, I decided to make my way to America and count on Russian comrades there to help me manufacture the necessary papers.

In mid-December 1920, on board the steamer 'Baltic', I was arrested again, and released only after a three-hour interrogation, saved this time by the rosary

---

[66] 'About £100': as given, although Zuzenko has stated above that he was carrying £500 for agitation and propaganda in Australia.

[67] Jack Braddock (1893–1963): well known activist of the IWW and early communist movement, later a prominent Labour politician and leader of Liverpool City Council 1955–63. He and his fiancée Elizabeth Bamber took care of Zuzenko during part of his time in Liverpool in 1920–21. Both left the CP in the early 1920s, and Bamber, as Bessie Braddock, achieved fame as the long-serving Labour member for Liverpool Exchange (Braddock 1963.)

[68] John Maclean (1879–1923): prominent Scottish socialist at this period.

I had in my pocket and my exaggerated good manners. In Liverpool raids had started to catch Irishmen, so I had to decamp to Stoke-on-Trent and stay there until the middle of January 1921. Helped by a stoker, I made my way to Saint John, New Brunswick, as a stowaway on the steamer 'The Queen of Ireland', posing as a stoker by night and a passenger by day throughout the ten-day crossing.

In Canada

I found a place in the Salvation Army hostel in Saint John and made the acquaintance of Carland [phon.], a fugitive Sinn Feiner from Ireland and persuaded him to cross the American border with me. I would provide financial help to pay his way to Boston, while he undertook to use the Irish route to get me across the border in the guise of a fellow Sinn Fein fighter. Helped by Irish priests, we crossed the border between Saint Stephen in Canada and Calais in the United States. I had to leave my things in Saint Stephen with a tailor named Higgins. We were given an autumn coat and felt hat each, so as to look like Americans, and crossed the border bridge by night. Then we travelled about twenty-five miles by car before taking a train to Boston. We arrived safely in New York, where I immediately tried to contact the American Communist Party through the Soviet bureau.

In America

I arrived in New York in late January 1921. After a week of daily visits to the office of Isaac Hourwich,[69] I was fortunate enough to see Comrade Cherny,[70] a member of the Executive Committee of the Communist Party, and ask him for the favour I needed. I asked him to help me get some papers forged and advise me—at least—on how I might proceed from there. I gave Comrade Cherny a photograph of myself to show to Alexander Bilan or any other delegates to the Second Comintern Congress, so that they could recognize me. He promised to see me again in one week, for which I was grateful.

On the appointed day there was nobody there to see me, and only after seven weeks of continually pestering Isaac Hourwich did I receive a reply, through Hourwich, which said, 'Zuzenko is staying with Korneev the sailor in his flat, so let Karneev help him.'[71] I was not amused by the wisdom of this advice. I was in no mood for it. I had left Russia in poor health. After those stormy times in Brisbane, after a voyage in chains round the world through the prisons of Australia, Tasmania, Ceylon, India, Egypt and Turkey, after a hunger strike and scurvy in Bombay and all the charms of the condemned cell, after the inferno

---

[69] Hourwich: this is the spelling used by the Hourwich family in the USA. A closer transcription of the Russian form is 'Gurvich'.
[70] Cherny: possibly Chernago, Chernogo or Czerny.
[71] Korneev/Karneev: Zuzenko uses both spellings. It has not been possible to determine which is correct.

of the underground during Denikin's rule and sometimes over-demanding work in the Soviet Ukraine, it is not surprising that my nerves were in shreds. 'Pray tell the authors of this wise advice, Jesus Christ's sky-pilots,[72] that I am not begging but demanding,' I said to Hourwich, 'that one of them comes down from the Olympian heights of the party to my level.' I wrote a memo demanding a meeting, as was my right under Paragraph 11 of the Comintern Statute concerning party discipline.

A week later I had a meeting with Alexander Bilan, who explained that all that time each of two American communist parties had been trying to pass me into the care of the other. As a consequence of the meeting with Bilan, I was sent a letter of introduction to William Costley, the organizer of the united Communist Party in San Francisco.

I spent more than ten weeks in New York altogether. [...]

As I was expecting a reply to a letter sent to the Comintern in Moscow (encoded and sent to Artur Iuzenius, at Tombtabagatten [phon.] 24, Stockholm, Sweden), I asked William Costley to enquire of the Executive Committee of the American Communist Party whether there was any mail for me from Moscow. I also asked him to pass on the fact that I was leaving for Australia on 25 April. A reply came three days before my planned departure, in the form of a telegram saying, 'If Nargen is an Australian he is now undeserving of any trust at all. Do not give him anything,' signed 'ARDEN'.[73] On receiving this cable, Comrade Costley flatly refused to give me any help at all. 'How do I know?' he asked. 'You might be an *agent provocateur* for all I know.'

I did not succeed in departing on 25 April. On 1 May 1921 a seamen's strike began and for several months any possibility of proceeding to my destination was removed. At the end of June, over two months after the cable virtually accusing me of being a provocateur, I met William Costley, who said that he had just received a letter from New York advising him to help me leave America. He proposed that I embark as a strike-breaker and jump ship on arrival, but refused to render any assistance. [...]

For the first few months after the strike it was absolutely impossible to find work on any ship bound for Australia. With the aid of Comrades Edric B. Smith and M. J. [G.?] Smith and some other comrades from the Auckland section of the Society for Technical Aid to Soviet Russia, I tried several times to leave America, without success. The most important thing I lacked in order to sign

---

[72] '*Etim aeroplanam Iisusa Khrista*', more literally 'Jesus Christ's aeroplanes', a figure of speech of a kind regularly found in Zuzenko's prose.
[73] Zuzenko cites this telegram in Russian but it was most probably sent to Costley in English. When Zuzenko was arrested in Melbourne in August 1922, among the material found on him was a telegram in English which read: 'If Nargen is Australian then now unreliable give nothing Arden.' NAA A6122/40 111 p. 147.

on as a crew member was identity papers, and I had no opportunity to acquire any.

In October 1921, on the advice of some comrades, I enlisted Comrade William Sheehan, from Seattle, an influential seaman and IWW 'Industrialist', who could use his contacts to help me embark for Australia. Comrade Sheehan tried until mid-December and found me a job as a galley hand on an Australian ship, but the port authorities refused to let me sail without a passport. Frustrated by this failure, Comrade Sheehan departed for Chicago, leaving me to find my own way out of the situation. [...]

In order to avoid arrest I had to cross to Victoria, B.C., for a while, and thence on the steamship 'Niagara' I sailed for New Zealand, so as to be able to slip into Australia unnoticed on a local tramp steamer rather than an immigrant ship. I left Canada in early May 1922 and in early June arrived in Auckland, where I stayed for one month and obtained the right to permanent residence in New Zealand and a police registration card. I then set off for Sydney, where I disembarked without hindrance at the beginning of July 1922.[74]

The American Communist Party, or rather some of its minions, had put about every conceivable vile story concerning me and sent these on to Australia. For example, much was written about my not wanting to go to jail in Australia again, about my cowardice, and about my going over to the anarchist camp. But none of these fabrications were believed. That I was not a coward was known. The silly fable about my anarchism was also rejected, since my article 'A Reply to Emma Goldman', published in *The British Columbia Federationist* and the American *Worker* and signed Aleksandr Nargen, had been received and read in Australia.[75] The extraordinarily energetic little tale-mongers from America had also written of my rabid anti-semitism, little knowing that I was married to a 'semite' and had a 'semi-semite' daughter.

In Australia

While I was travelling, a Communist Party had been formed in Australia and already a schism had developed over the question of who should lead it: members of the former Australian Socialist Party or members of the trade union movement. The two groups had managed to antagonize each other since the split, and by the time Comrade Freeman arrived there was a deep rift separating them. The

---

[74] His date of arrival in Sydney was 11 July 1922.

[75] Emma Goldman (1869–1940): an exponent of radical feminist politics and anti-capitalist thought. Born in Lithuania, she spent most of her adult life in the USA, but was deported to Russia in 1920. She left Russia in late 1921 and wrote of her deep disillusionment with the revolution. The article referred to here was published in *The Worker* (New York), 15/7/1922, under the headline 'Russian Worker Delivers a Smashing reply to Emma Goldman's Lying and Misleading Articles'. The byline is 'Nargin' (without first name). (Zuzenko used the forms 'Nargin' and 'Nargen' interchangeably.) 'Silly fable': in fact Zuzenko had been a committed anarchist for many years, but had renounced his anarchism some time after the October revolution.

late Comrade Freeman only had dealings with the socialist group.[76] During his short stay he had done nothing to foster the unification of the warring sides, and he had departed leaving a deeper division than before.

Shortly before my arrival the comrades grouped round the trade union movement had appropriated all the Communist Party's furniture at night and placed it on their own premises. They had also seized all their books. The Socialist Party (or rather Reardon, Everitt and Co.,[77] without the knowledge of the others) had responded by selling the party's printing equipment and type. My arrival, as an organizing comrade from Moscow, impelled them to re-examine the matters which had led to the rift. (In a quarrel the origins of the dispute are usually forgotten with time.) I had to listen to both sides, tell both of them that they were in the wrong and demand that a conference be called to unite them.

A report on the conference was sent from Sydney by me to the Executive Committee, in coded form.[78] I sent it as soon as the results of the proceedings became clear. The sides reunited on the basis of equal representation on the Communist Party's Executive Committee. As long as the Communist Party of Australia has existed it has not committed any tactical errors, if we discount the split. Its only organizational weakness was that it was not tightly interwoven with the masses. I informed the comrades of the details of the structure of the Russian Communist Party, and it was decided to devote more attention to the establishment of cells in the trade union membership.

During my stay in Sydney I gave twelve lectures about Soviet Russia and succeeded in dispelling the prejudice against Soviet Russia that was forming in the Russian community in Australia under the influence of anti-Soviet agitation by a group of Russians who had returned from Soviet Russia not long before I arrived.

After Reardon, Everitt and Co. had sold the party's printing equipment, printing of the newspaper *The Communist*, of pamphlets, appeals and the like had to be contracted out to private firms, which is very expensive. The lectures I gave in Sydney and Melbourne were for the benefit of the fund for agitation and propaganda. They yielded about £60. This laid the foundations of an agitation and propaganda fund. I handed over to the party's Executive Committee the £110 I had brought from Moscow (all that I had not expended on the journey). To the addresses of the North Queensland comrades I sent subscription notices, which by my reckoning should yield at least another £60 for the party's funds. All these contributions reinforced the party's financial position, but no more

---

[76] i.e. the Australian Socialist Party.

[77] Zuzenko has 'Riordan' and 'Everet'.

[78] The conference was held on 15 July 1922. The 'report in coded form' is presumably the letter dated 21 July 1922, dealing exclusively with Australian CP matters. CAAL, 495–94–13, p. 31ff. See Document 18, above.

than that. There is much that we cannot do. It will take years to raise the funds to acquire typesetting and printing machinery, and time waits for no man.

Our request is that the Comintern assist us with the acquisition of this equipment. In another report, dealing exclusively with the situation in Australia,[79] I will try to give a clearer account of the need for such expenditure by the Comintern for the good of the communist movement in all the Anglo-Saxon countries, because the course of history is preparing a place for Australia as the first among the Anglo-Saxon countries to have a workers' government (I mean, one on the Soviet model).

In Sydney I laid the foundations for a Society for Technical Aid to Soviet Russia in Australia, and in early August the party sent me to Melbourne to set up a Melbourne Communist Party branch. While the party was divided, the Melbourne branch had come apart at the seams and ceased to exist. I managed to establish a Russian group, to which I intended to link some English cells. In Melbourne I delivered a few lectures, but one evening, while on my way to my next lecture, I was arrested by the police and detained in Melbourne's central prison. I was arrested on 9 August 1922 and on 17 August I was tried for returning to Australia while being a prohibited immigrant.[80] There were photographs of me in all Australian ports, along with my fingerprints. The police were able to prove only that I was the person deported from Australia for organizing the Brisbane riots in March 1919. I insisted that my real name was Toni Tollagsen Tjorn, a Norwegian by birth and that my passport, issued by the Norwegian Consul General in Montreal through the consul in Vancouver, was my genuine passport. If the Australian authorities sought to deport me, they should send me to Norway.

There was little the authorities could do with me without calling forth a hue-and-cry against themselves. The Australian Seamen's Union, led by Tom Walsh, took up my case.[81] The leaders of the Labor Party, the proletarian member of Federal Parliament Considine, and others, set about causing a stir. Two solicitors took on my defence. I was sentenced to three months in prison and deportation, but my comrades would not accept my serving out the prison sentence. I was released on bail and my comrades secured a promise from the authorities that if I paid my own fare the authorities in Britain would not impose their penal hospitality on me. The newly re-established Melbourne branch of the Communist Party raised about £65, paid my fare to London and gave me about £20 for personal expenses. The fare to London came to £48. I did not want

---

[79] Presumably a reference to the document which follows this one—Document 28—at CAAL, 495 94 18, pp. 18–27, Zuzenko's report to the ECCI, 18/3/23.
[80] Zuzenko writes 'emigrant', meaning 'immigrant'.
[81] Walsh and his wife, Adela Pankhurst Walsh, were close friends of Zuzenko at this time. A short time later both defected from the cause and were reviled as traitors to the working class.

this collection for myself, preferring to be deported at the Australian government's expense. I offered to put the money into the party's propaganda fund, but the comrades insisted.

I had no time to visit Brisbane or the North Queensland towns to which people kept inviting me.

Before I left Australia I wrote a series of articles in Russian for the Russian community, explaining everything that was happening in Russia. I published these in the form of a booklet of twenty printer's sheets. In Melbourne a bureau of the Society for Technical Aid to Soviet Russia was set up.

On the steamship 'Hobson's Bay', accompanied by Comrades Jock Garden and Tom Payne, two other delegates of the Communist Party of Australia, I departed Australia's inhospitable shores on 7 September 1922. In Fremantle Comrade Tom Payne was detained and his passport seized by the customs authorities. I insisted that he continue his journey to Moscow, heedless of all prohibitions, to show the rulers of Australia that we would take no notice of their caprices. In Colombo police officers arrested Comrade Payne on board the ship and brought him to my cabin to collect his things. A few minutes later he vanished from my cabin without trace. They searched the ship for two hours, to no avail.[82] By this time the ship's company were fully informed about the mission of communism. Every evening I led discussions with the deck hands and stokers.

A famous Church of England preacher in Australia, Canon Watson, during an argument with me about the nationalization of women in Soviet Russia, challenged me to a debate on the theme 'Religion in the Light of Science and Philosophy'. Not being confident that with my foreign accent I could hold my own against the Holy Father [sic], I suggested to Comrade Garden that he should speak instead of me, but Comrade Garden refused.[83] The Holy Father turned out to be not so strong as I expected. In a debate that lasted about four hours he was unable to overcome a single one of my arguments. The audience of several hundred passengers and over a hundred crew members were on my side, which shows a significant shift in Anglo-Saxon thinking. In 1915 or 1916 the same audience would have tossed me over the side. The debate went better than I had expected. Passengers clustered about in knots until two in the morning, discussing the matters we had raised. When we sailed from Australia, a large crowd packed the dockside in Melbourne, singing revolutionary songs. I

---

[82] Tom Payne: see the tape-recorded interview with Payne conducted on 17 May 1976 by Ann Turner and Andrew Reeves and held in the National Library of Australia, (NLA ORAL TRC 700).

[83] The irony of this request, of which Zuzenko seems to have been fully aware, is that Garden had been a preacher, and could slip into or out of preaching mode as the occasion took him, even after he became a communist.

delivered a farewell speech from the deck of the ship. We sailed to the strains of *The Internationale*.

Looking back over the events on the 'Hobson's Bay', the revolutionary send-off from Melbourne, the mysterious disappearance of Comrade Tom Payne, and our debate, I did not expect to be warmly welcomed in London. I was not mistaken. In London they were waiting for me. I was arrested on board the ship by two Scotland Yard men and flung into Brixton Prison.

In all the prisons I have been in, I have struggled with the prison authorities from the very first day. Knowing that subsequently many of my comrades-in-arms would find themselves in just such conditions, I made it my business to struggle against the brutal, intolerable British prison regime, which destroys not so much a person's body as his spirit, bringing him down to the level of an object: number so-and-so, cell so-and-so. In His Majesty's Brixton Prison I had to wage a prolonged struggle day by day to win one concession after another. I had to fight for the right not to wash the floors, the right to exercise where I felt like it (not round the yard like all the others), the right to smoke in my cell, not to attend parade, not to doff my cap to prison officers, etc. My last demand was to be informed immediately of the progress of my case. I demanded that my case be handed over to Scotland Yard to implement the deportation order, and demanded a change of diet. When the authorities refused to meet my demands, at the end of November I declared a hunger strike. All this time I was being held without trial or investigation. They did not observe so much as a semblance of legality. According to English law, nobody can be detained for more than twenty-four hours without being sentenced by a judge.[84]

On the third day of my hunger strike I was transferred to hospital, and on the fifth they started feeding me by force. They choked me twice a day 'to save my life' (as a doctor put it) for eight days, and then informed me that my case had been transferred from the Home Office to Scotland Yard. I asked that both my demands be met, or else I would continue my hunger strike to the same conclusion as MacSwiney, who had been held in the same isolation cell.[85] The authorities gave in. As a result of the hunger strike I was twice summoned to Scotland Yard and questioned about my work in Australia. To the end I maintained that my name was Toni Tollagsen Tjorn, that I was a Norwegian and that I nothing to do with the Third International, being an anarchist by conviction. I had worked, I said, only on technical assistance to Soviet Russia, setting up farming collectives.[86]

---

[84] Zuzenko displays an imperfect understanding of English law.

[85] Terence MacSwiney, Lord Mayor of Cork, starved to death on hunger strike in October 1920. His death provoked large demonstrations in London and elsewhere.

[86] Zuzenko was interrogated on 19 and 20 December 1922 by Captain Guy Liddell and Captain H.M. Miller. For a transcript of the interrogation see Windle 2005c.

I was prepared to be deported to Norway or Latvia, or anywhere else, if only to avoid telling the enemy I was Russian and an emissary of the Comintern, so as not to give them the chance to speak of the bad faith of Soviet Russia, which was sending forth its propaganda agents in spite of undertakings not to do this. The conservative newspaper *The Times* printed a dispatch late last November, reporting a speech by the Australian Minister for Defence, [George Foster] Pearce, in which he said that a Russian Bolshevik agent had recently been deported from Australia.

In spite of all Scotland Yard's ploys aimed at obtaining any information at all against Soviet Russia, they had to replace my Norwegian passport with an alien's travel document in the name of Toni Tollagsen Tjorn, — 'nationality unknown' — departing for Russia. From prison I wrote several letters to the Soviet mission in England, asking them to forward my things to my wife. I did not want the [British] sleuths rummaging through my things, which contained all issues of *Knowledge and Unity*, the Brisbane paper I had founded, two Australian statistical yearbooks and all published Australian books on agriculture. I wrote several letters to George Lansbury, the editor of the *Daily Herald*, and to Sylvia Pankhurst. (They are known to be opponents of the Comintern.) During my interrogation sessions at Scotland Yard, I was told several times that the actions of my friends, especially Sylvia Pankhurst, were terrible, that it was wrong to behave as they did, and that such behaviour was impermissible in any civilized society, and so on. I asked them several times how that 'poor defenceless lady' could possibly do them any harm, and received the evasive answer that such actions could have adverse effects upon my fate. From the hints and insinuations of the chief of police I deduced that in connection with my imprisonment the Scotland Yard sleuths wanted to charge Sylvia Pankhurst with poisoning the head of Scotland Yard by sending him some poisoned chocolate. With a comrade who was being released I sent a letter to the Soviet representative in London, asking him to warn Sylvia Pankhurst. In the latter part of January this year I was transported to Newcastle, then Leith prisons and delivered to the SS Irtysh, which was sailing from Leith in Scotland to Petrograd, where it arrived on 31 January this year.[87]

If the comrades on the Comintern Executive Committee feel that any parts of my general report on my work over almost two and a half years spent abroad seem imprecise, I will give a more detailed account in person. I will report on the state of affairs in Australia in a separate memorandum. I will try in a report to the ECCI to set forth my reflections on ways in which agitation and propaganda work might be conducted more successfully in the Anglo-Saxon countries. Edric B. Smith, an American communist engineer, former member of the American

---

[87] The Scottish prison and port is named by Zuzenko variously as 'Vleit' and 'Vleis' (in Cyrillic). It seems certain that he is referring to Leith.

Communist Party and now a member of the Russian Communist Party, will be spending two weeks in Moscow. His address will be: Gruzinsky pereulok 4/Staraia ploshchad 10, Apt. 40. He will be able to supply a clearer picture of the moral temper of the leadership of the American Communist Party.

In concluding my report, I would like to remind the ECCI that the Communist Party of Australia has empowered me to represent it at the ECCI until the Fifth Congress of the Comintern, and to represent it at the Fifth Congress if no other decision has been taken on the matter by that time. A person who has forged close ties with the revolutionary movement in Australia and knows what is going on there can have most success in establishing firm links, following the course of organizational work in the young party, reporting its achievements to the ECCI and sending news of the progress of organizational work. I beg the ECCI to recognize the validity of the mandate entrusted to me by the Communist Party of Australia and place the conduct of matters relating to the Australian communist movement in my care. I request that the ECCI accept my assurances that I am insisting on my right to continue working for the Comintern not for the sake of my career, but for the good of the revolutionary movement in Australia, which I regard as the Achilles heel of British imperialism. Working in Soviet Russia, by applying every effort perhaps I shall be able to assist the revolutionary forces of Australia in binding together. And when the period of organizational work comes to an end, the highest honour for me will be to be in Australia as the standard-bearer of the socialist revolution.

I realize that by my report I shall make many new enemies; I realize that such reports do not make 'careers', but my duty as a revolutionary commands me to call things by their proper names, to call a spade a spade.

With communist greetings,
Aleksandr Mikhailov[ich] Zuzenko (A. Nargen)
Official of the Communist International
Moscow, 28 February, 1923

[Lines below appended in handwriting]

I delivered a report similar to this one at the Unification Conference of the Australian Communist Party. My report was adopted and the resolution carried on this matter was communicated to the ECCI in July 1922. This conference entrusted to me the leadership of the Australian delegation to the Fourth Congress of the Comintern. Before I left Australia I was instructed by the party to work on the ECCI as the representative of the Australian Communist Party.

Aleksandr Zuzenko, alias Nargen.[88]

---

[88] A newspaper clipping—'A Soviet Agent Sentenced in City Court to be Deported'—follows in CAAL.

Document 28

RGASPI 495–94–18. 16 March 1923, Zuzenko: report: On the situation of the Communist Movement in Australia. In Russian and German, typescript. Trans. by KW.

Zuzenko used this memorandum to the ECCI to continue his campaign for Comintern employment in Australia. It emphasizes his knowledge of the Australian labour movement. Zuzenko stresses the opportunities for communism in Australia, pointing to the broad sympathy among workers for the CPA, but arguing even more strikingly (after the style of Lenin, in fact) that 'Australia is British imperialism's weakest and most vulnerable point'. He makes an appeal for Comintern aid in financing a proletarian printing works in Australia.

To the Executive Committee of the Third Communist International
by Aleksandr Mikhailov [Mikhailovich] Zuzenko, Comintern official.

Memorandum
On the Situation of the Communist Movement in Australia

The great Russian Revolution with its incredibly great achievements has resounded in every corner of the globe with an upsurge of revolutionary spirit in the proletarian masses and made all socialist organizations, including the IWW (Industrialists) in the Anglo-Saxon countries, confront the need to review their attitude to the proletarian revolution. In Australia, in early 1918, the Queensland Socialist League, under pressure from the rank-and-file majority, drafted a new programme in the spirit of the decisions of the Zimmerwald and Kienthal conferences. In other states, for example New South Wales and Victoria, there has also been a noticeable shift away from the thorny path of socialist petty bourgeois thinking, which the socialist movement had followed until about 1915-16, to the left, towards the path of revolutionary Marxism.

The fierce struggle against the introduction in Australia of compulsory conscription, which mobilized all revolutionary forces in the country to resist rampant chauvinism – successfully, we may add – stirred into life the stagnant swamp of socialist gradualism, while the Russian Revolution forced every socialist to face the question: was he fighting for what was being fought for in distant Soviet Russia, and if so what was the extent of his contribution?

In late September 1918 agreement was reached between representatives of the trade union movement, the Queensland Socialist League and the Industrialists, —with a view to strengthening the rising revolutionary mood of the masses—to embark on coordinated action to organize demonstrations by the unemployed—revolutionary demonstrations with red flags—and take up the struggle for free speech. A demonstration on the evening of 7 November 1918 and a mass meeting in South Brisbane markets, broken up by the police and troops, united all the revolutionary forces of Queensland around the red banner.

The movement felt a need for a revolutionary newspaper of its own. A paper entitled *Znanie i edinenie* (*Knowledge and Unity* in English) was founded, with funds from the Union of Russian Workers, and the socialists and Industrialists took an equal part in its distribution. New venues for street meetings were wrung from the police and bands of soldiers organized by the military authorities, and security teams were formed for meetings. Up to the end of March 1919 a series of very successful demonstrations and mass meetings was held and a mass of unemployed workers deployed for propaganda purposes. On 25 March 1919 a demonstration with red flags culminated in a clash with the police,[89] the rout of the police detachments and mounted troopers, and the temporary triumph of the workers, a triumph which the leaders of the movement were unable to exploit. For the first time in the history of Australia the sacred and untouchable figure of the policeman appeared before the proletariat as 'touchable'. The magic wand in his hands was no more than a truncheon, and the street was the best school for revolutionaries. 'Queensland's Black Friday', when several hundred workers and women were beaten by the police during a demonstration on 27 February 1912, was justly avenged. The next day, gangs of soldiers organized by the military authorities began attacking the area where the Union of Russian Workers and the Industrialists had their premises. Battles between patriots and police left some dead and wounded. The Brisbane events, dubbed by the press 'a Russian Bolshevik revolution', were echoed in Townsville (North Queensland) in battles with the police and exchanges of fire with troops, and trouble in Port Darwin (Northern Territory) and Perth (Western Australia). The most compromised comrades—those involved in organizing the movement—were arrested and sentenced to six months in prison. Twelve Russians were deported to Siberia after serving their sentences, and the secretary of the Union of Russian Workers was deported, with his wife, to Constantinople.[90] The accused exploited the legal processes for propaganda purposes, to propound their programme. Both the socialists and the IWW 'Industrialists' called themselves Bolsheviks. Those comrades who remained at liberty carried on working harmoniously to prepare the ground for the establishment of a communist party of Australia.

In these turbulent conditions a communist movement was born in the northern states of Australia. In the southern states the preparatory phase was calmer, with the exception of a determined attempt by a large crowd of workers at the Sydney docks to free Paul Freeman, who had declared a hunger strike. In New South Wales, after the failed general strike in August 1917, all the revolutionary forces of that state turned to the trade union movement, with the aim of seizing control of it, exploiting the working masses' bitterness against their old leaders, who had betrayed the strike.

---

[89] The date of this event was actually Sunday, 23 March, 1919.
[90] i.e. Zuzenko himself and wife Civa (Tsiva, Cecilia).

Organized on the basis of communist groups in Queensland and New South Wales and the left wing of the Socialist Party of Australia, the Communist Party of Australia assumed the leading role in the workers' movement in the two most industrialized states of Australia, Queensland and New South Wales. After unification in July 1922 the membership of the party was just over five hundred, but the influence of this small party among the proletarian masses was immense. Measured by the power concentrated in its hands, the Communist Party of Australia is the strongest and most influential of all communist parties in the Anglo-Saxon countries. The trade union movement of the entire state of Queensland, over 50,000 workers organized in trade unions, is in the hands of the Communist Party of Australia. All officials—all chairmen and secretaries of the unions—are communists. In New South Wales 120 unions are united in the NSW Labour Council. The membership of these unions exceeds 147,000. Of the fourteen-man executive committee of the Labour Council in the state of New South Wales, twelve are communists, including the secretary and the chairman. In Newcastle, the centre of Australian heavy industry, all members of the executive committee of the Labour Council are members of the Communist Party of Australia. Though weak in numbers of actual members, the Communist Party of Australia is strong in having great numbers of sympathizers, who obediently carry out the orders of the party's centre—great numbers of proletarians in the industrial states of Australia. Thus there are approximately 300,000 organized workers under the direct leadership of the Communist Party. In the states of Victoria and Western Australia the Labour Councils undertake no serious action without consulting the Red Labour Councils of Sydney and Brisbane. Those seeking counsel know full well that through the Sydney and Brisbane Labour Councils they are hearing the voice of the Communist Party of Australia, of leaders experienced in the class struggle, who, in the harsh years of economic crisis have managed to stand firm and not yield so much as an inch to the attacking forces of capitalism, and have not only organized the defence of their class against attempts by the bourgeoisie to reduce workers' pay and extend their working day, but have even counter-attacked and achieved a position that nobody in the world can boast of (except for Soviet Russia). The disparaging tone in which some comrades here in Moscow speak of Australia is comical in the extreme.

'By their deeds shall ye know them,' … The cowed and crushed seamen's unions of Britain, America and Canada … Wages have been reduced to a minimum below which they can fall no further. There is no sign of an eight-hour working day. Abetted by its venal accomplices, such as Havelock Wilson (in England) and Andrew Furuseth (in America), the bourgeoisie is dictating terms to sailors and implementing its 'American plan'—the open shop (the hiring of non-union labour).[91] And a similar 'plan' is being adopted by the capitalists in all other countries of the world. Since 1919 Australian seamen have achieved a great deal. Their pay is about £18 a month; their board is better than it was in 1919 and crews' living quarters have been revamped on all vessels, in accordance with directives from the Seamen's Union. After three months at sea a sailor is entitled to a fortnight's leave etc. The position of Australian sailors is better than it has ever been. The bourgeoisie is afraid to touch 'Tom Walsh's wild red hordes,' having experienced to its cost all the delights of superbly organized resistance. Led by the splendid communist fighter Tom Walsh and having resolved to fight to the last, the sailors cut all links between Tasmania and the mainland for months, bringing ruin to thousands of Tasmanian farmers and threatening to bring industry throughout the country to a standstill. In July and August 1922 an alliance of manufacturers and employers decided to reduce workers' pay at their enterprises by 15% in order to increase productivity. In this way they tried to provoke the workers to strike, hoping to stifle them by their organized power. They even succeeded in forcing some workers to come out on strike. Bearing in mind the fact that in July the number of unemployed had reached 100,000, the Communist Party of Australia decided to retire from an unequal struggle. The NSW and Queensland Labour Councils compelled the striking workers to return to work on the employers' terms. In *The Communist*, and even the bourgeois press, in the articles of Comrades Garden and Howie, so much was said about the need for the workers to respond to lower pay with lower productivity—this form of sabotage was so eagerly promoted—that the nervous bourgeoisie started calling on the workers to turn their backs on the Bolsheviks' 'fiendish, reptilian, treacherous' methods and return to the 'honest' old methods of striking. In proposing sabotage in place of open warfare, the Communist Party was mindful of the psychology of the bourgeoisie. Even if a worker worked himself to exhaustion, the day after sabotage was declared the employer would think that the worker was working more lazily than usual. And indeed, within a few days the employers' attempts to cut pay were abandoned. One after another they began to renounce the venture.

From last September to the present, the situation of the Australian worker may have deteriorated, but it cannot sink to the craven level of the British or American worker. Certain particular traits of the Australian character, the product of the specific conditions of the Australian economy, will never allow the Australian worker to descend to the depths of slavish servility reached by the British worker, disillusioned in everything, whether employed or unemployed.

---

[91] Havelock Wilson (1858–1929): president of the (UK) National Sailors' and Firemens' Union and Liberal member of Parliament; Andrew Furuseth (1854–1938): long-serving leading member of the International Seamen's Union.

Australia should not be spoken of in dismissive tones. Of all the countries drawn into the last murderous war of 1914–18, Australia alone was successful in ensuring the collapse of the imperialist plan to enact a law on compulsory military conscription. That same Australia that 'voluntarily' (under the knout of hunger) supplied Britain with over 300,000 men rejected compulsory conscription by an overwhelming majority in a referendum. Only in Australia were there the stout hearts to wage the struggle against military dictatorship.

Australia, for all that its population is insignificant, is a very important factor in the evolution of legislation and the workers' movement of Britain and all her other colonies alike. And history is undoubtedly preparing for Australia a role in the future as a vitally important factor in the revolution both in Britain herself and in her colonies, since in the field of legislation and social reform Britain is accustomed to imitating what has been implemented and tested in practice for decades in Australia. In 1902 the women of Australia received the right to vote. All women over the age of 21 are entitled to vote. Only two decades later was a law passed in Britain, in maimed and mutilated form, under which the entire active part of the female population (all women under 30) was exempted from voting rights, and this after a prolonged and determined struggle by the suffragettes. In 1901, faced with the rising power of organized labour, the ruling class in Australia had to enact laws on arbitration, under which conflicts between workers' unions and employers would be resolved by industrial arbitration courts (pouring oil on troubled waters). In 1910 the Australian Labor Party proved itself the strongest political force in the land, winning 42 seats in Parliament against the Liberals' 33. On the eve of war the Labor Party gained power not only in Federal Parliament, but also in five of the six Australian states (the exception was Victoria). While in Britain a Labour seizure of power is still a daydream at the limit of people's wildest hopes, Australia has already shown that the future belongs not to the appeasers, not to the gradualists, but to the new and growing revolutionary power. In the twelve years of 'Labor' rule in Queensland, two or three state sugar mills have been built, a few small government fish shops have been opened in a few Queensland towns, and with this their much-vaunted programme of nationalization of industry has come to an end. It is becoming clear to the workers that this is as far as the appeasers will go. In the sphere of social reform, there have been some amendments to the laws regulating working hours and pay, workers' compensation, pensions, insurance etc., but this is all that the heralds of socialism through social legislation have given and can give.

Faith in the Australian Labor Party as a leader is waning in the working masses of Australia, along with faith in the power of the unions. The new leader, the Communist Party of Australia, is one of the purest ideological parties in the Anglo-Saxon countries, and fully deserves the deep respect in which the fighters for communism are held among the proletariat. In the upper echelons of the party are concentrated the best revolutionary forces in the country, tried and tested in the class struggle, and this alone explains the strange fact that a numerically small party has in its grasp all the major workers' associations: the trade unions and the labour councils of Australia's most highly industrialized states. As long as it has existed (leaving aside the schism), the Communist Party has not made a single serious mistake in its work. Every decision of the ECCI and of the congresses is implemented.

One of the weakest aspects of the organization is the fact that cohesion with the working masses led by the Communist Party is insufficient. Due attention has not been paid to the formation of cells within the trade unions. The immense amount of work that all active party members have had to do in the recent turbulent years to resist the thrust of organized capital has claimed all their time. This is why, in spite of huge masses of sympathizers, the party remains numerically insignificant. And this is the reason for the restricted funding base of the Communist Party of Australia.

Not long before my departure from Australia work began on achieving coalescence with the masses; intensive work is in hand to set up cells; a plan has been adopted to transfer party forces from one district to another to arrange successful public meetings. According to this plan one hundred or more comrades will gather at an agreed venue, start an open-air meeting, keep order at it, protect the speakers from thugs, help them by asking questions, and hand out literature and so forth.

Since coming into existence the Communist Party of Australia has done much to popularize the ideas of the Russian Revolution by publishing pamphlets with the works of Comrades Lenin, Zinoviev, Trotsky, Kamenev, Bukharin's *ABC of Communism*, etc. Before I was arrested the last time I handed over to Comrade Garden 35 pamphlets (one copy each of those reprinted in Australia) and asked him to convey them to the Comintern library. The party newspaper *The Communist*, published in Sydney, is one of the most successful papers in the Anglo-Saxon countries. By its work the Communist Party of Australia has measured up to its calling. Much has been achieved, but all past work is as nothing compared to the grave trial of political maturity which awaits it in the near future. I refer to seizing control of the proletarian movement called One Big Union. The party will be able to accomplish this only with the aid of the Comintern.

The idea of One Big Union, that is, a union in which workers are organized not by trade but by their branch of industry (a similar form of organization to that in Soviet Russia) was brought to Australia by American 'Industrialists' (the IWW) in 1911-1912 and in a relatively short span of time became deeply rooted among the working masses. In 1916, at the height of its success, the Industrialists could claim about 75,000 members and sympathizers. The Great Russian

Revolution compelled the IWW to review its attitude to matters of the dictatorship of the proletariat, the political struggle, and parliamentarianism. The review of the IWW programme led to rifts and a separation of strata in the organization. The movement's best forces joined ranks with the Communist Party while the remainder were scattered. The remnants of a once strong organization survived in the International Industrial Workers' Union,[92] which has no strength whatever (it is more like little groups of propagandists than an industrial force), and in Western Australia one or two old-style IWW groups are living out their time.

The lessons of Soviet Russia's Socialist Revolution, and the class struggle itself in recent years have thrown into sharp relief the discrepancy between the Industrialists' theory and the practice of class warfare. They have had to come to a clear understanding of this and accept the inevitability of the revolution, and that of the dictatorship of the proletariat and political struggle. The question of parliamentarism was under discussion much earlier. Comrades Percy Brookfield and Considine were elected to Parliament with Industrialist support at a time when the IWW was still flourishing.

The great service of the IWW to the proletarian movement in the Anglo-Saxon countries lay in their acerbic and truthful criticism of the trade unions, the meretricious old leadership and its conservatism, and their severe, pitiless criticism of the parliamentary fetish. Being proletarians themselves, they called on the workers to overthrow capitalism in the name of an Industrial Republic, and to wage a revolutionary class struggle. They did much to reorganize the proletarian forces. Their plan for One Big Union uniting the workers by their branches of industry is beginning to take firm hold in Australian life. In this movement for One Big Union the errors of the Industrialists who summoned the workers from the trade unions to build industrial unions were taken into account and corrected (the mountain did not come to Mohammed). The builders of One Big Union were those who entered the old trade unions to reorganize them.

In early January of this year, 1923, One Big Union began to function. It brings together the following organizations: the Railwaymen's Union, with 50,000 members; the Miners' Federation, with 45,000 members; the Waterside Workers' Federation, with 32,000 members; the abattoir workers, with 30,000 members; the Australian Building Construction Employees and Builders Labourers Federation, with 40,000 workers; and the Australian Workers' Union, with 120,000 members.[93] This makes a total of 317,000 in One Big Union. According to the statistics for 1921, Australia had 771 trade unions with 627,685 members, which means that over 50% of the country's organized workers have joined One Big Union. Before I left Australia, seventeen separate unions in the building

---

[92] It is not clear from the Russian title exactly which body is meant.
[93] Not all of these organizations can be positively identified from Zuzenko's Russian translations.

industry decided to amalgamate, forming the Building and Construction Section of One Big Union. In the very near future we may expect to see all the scattered groups of industrial workers drawn into the mighty movement of One Big Union.

The urgent task of the Communist Party of Australia in days soon to come is to seize control of One Big Union so as to become master of the situation in the country. This will be very easy if the Comintern pays serious attention to what is happening in Australia and renders assistance in the form of advice and directives, and by sending two or three comrades from the Communist Party of Great Britain (there is a need for speakers and propagandists) and typesetting and printing equipment. The great advantage of the Communist Party of Australia over those of other Anglo-Saxon countries is that former 'Industrialist' proletarians comprise the bulk of the party. The Communist Party is a purely proletarian organization, and this is the secret of its popularity among the working masses and its success in gaining control of a large part of the workers' movement. This is its virtue, its strength, and at the same time its weakness. The party has no major intellectual forces capable of properly organizing political education, lectures or work on newspapers—the party is too proletarian for that.

The Communist Party's publishing affairs have so far looked as follows: about 35 pamphlets containing the speeches of Comrades Lenin, Trotsky, Zinoviev, Kamenev and others were sent for printing to Andrade's Bookshop, 201 Bourke St., Melbourne. The party undertook to assist in the dissemination of literature. In September last year, 1922, the proprietor of the company, an old anarchist, refused under police pressure to print any more revolutionary literature. Through talks with the communist manager of the company, Comrade Laidler, I established that it is possible for us to acquire the company's warehouse and bookshop in Sydney, if the Party obtains the equipment to manage its own publishing affairs. The typesetting and printing equipment will serve as a guarantee that the former proprietors will be reimbursed in regular instalments for the cost of shop. Agitation and propaganda work can be placed on a sound footing only when the Communist Party acquires typesetting and printing equipment, when publishing does not depend on the whim of casual contractors who waver and quail at the first whiff of the police, when it is no longer necessary to pay private printers 30 pounds per month for each issue of *The Communist*. We had to cease publication of our fortnightly magazines solely because the bloodsuckers of private publishing were draining all the Communist Party's funds. If we had our own well-equipped printing shop, it would be possible to publish a daily paper, pamphlets, a fortnightly magazine, fliers, appeals and occasional papers, and take on work from the Labour Councils, printing their reports, appeals etc. A proletarian printing shop would consolidate the Communist Party's material position in perpetuity and give it the kind of strength in election campaigns that it lacks at present.

In requesting that the ECCI assist the Communist Party of Australia by supplying typesetting and printing equipment, I realize that I am contradicting myself. 'If the party is unable to find the funding to sustain itself, it is incapable of anything and might as well stop taking up valuable space.' That is my own view. When I started publishing *Knowledge and Unity* I had £30 in the editorial coffers to publish the paper in Russian and English. The paper began to recoup the investment only after three months. Nothing is impossible. If the Communist Party of Australia is viable and vital, it will collect all the funding it needs and create favourable conditions for its own success, but it will take years for it to do all this using its own resources. The Russian community in Australia and the groups of foreigners who have aided the revolutionary movement by their generous donations are now worn down more than other communities by unemployment ('Australia for the Australians'), and little can be expected of them. Nor will the Anglo-Saxon workers' usual contributions of a few pence go far.

There is no time to lose. The best conditions exist now and only now for consolidating our influence in the proletarian masses who recognize the need to restructure their ranks. Once it has gained control of One Big Union, the Communist Party of Australia will be able to present a 'united front' (without entering into any agreements with the hired clique of gradualists) against the brazen bourgeoisie. Equipment purchased in Germany may be sent to the Communist Party of Australia not as a gift, but on condition that the cost is paid off in an agreed period. I am convinced that the Communist Party will make such a strong recovery that it will soon be able to repay the cost of the equipment. There is no point in sending financial aid as other uses may be found for money.

In my opinion (and in 12 years of work one can learn a few things about a country), Australia is British imperialism's weakest and most vulnerable point. Even an appeaser's organization like the Australian Labor Party, seeking to grow in the esteem of the voters, is promising to struggle against the imperial federation and for absolute national autonomy. The Communist Party of Australia has a broad field of work before it, and, judging by what it has done in the time that it has existed, we may hope that it will cope well with its tasks.

I endeavoured to extort some criticism of the party leaders (members of the executive committee) from those who 'for reasons of principle' have not joined the party, but even those bitter critics who 'could see more clearly from the outside' could not give any valid grounds to justify their inaction. The most serious accusation is that some executive committee members are an unknown quantity to the socialists, although well known to the trade union movement and the industrialists. Comrade Garden was accused of only recently having been a freemason and a Baptist priest. (Comrade Garden is Secretary of the New South Wales Trade Union Council.) Comrade Baker was a soldier in the imperialist war (until the end of last year he was editor of *The Communist*). The ones who work hardest are the ones upon whom all kinds of inactive mediocrities vent the most spleen. This may be taken as a general rule in all squabbles. Both Comrade Garden and Comrade Baker have done much for the Communist Party of Australia in the past. When I was in prison I wrote in letters addressed to my wife warning the ECCI not to place too much trust in Comrade Garden and not to pass to him anything for the Communist movement in Australia. These letters were handed over to Comrade Piatnitsky. The circumstances which induced me to send these warnings were as follows: Comrade Garden and Comrade Tom Payne were passengers on the steamship Hobson's Bay, on which I was being sent to London. A freemason party of thirty-five people was travelling on the same ship. I am of the view that the comedy which was acted out later was prepared in advance by the masons. Comrade Garden was invited by them to a private meeting, at which he was asked to work for the Second International and campaign for cooperation between capital and labour. He was 'unanimously' elected chairman of the Sports Commission, and a delegate to the fourth Congress then had to open and close the ship's concerts with singing of 'God Save the King'. He promised me that he would make use of the masons and their play-acting for purposes of agitation, but instead let himself be fully used for their black propaganda. In Port Said he listened for hours while Egyptian soothsayers and palmists read his fortune, and he gave them written testimonies to their clairvoyance and accurate vision. All these matters are trifles, of course. While he was on board ship he simply forgot that he was a communist and enjoyed himself. He is an Anglo-Saxon, a product of masses to whom revolutionary traditions and revolutionary ethics are alien. Only the stern struggle which is in store for the Anglo-Saxon countries in the near future will produce the fighting type and make plain the rigorous discipline of the Russian revolutionaries. Comrade Garden has done much to promote the success of the CP of Australia, and I would not wish to have exclusive importance attached to what I am saying about him. As secretary of the NSW Trade Union Council he has great influence among the working masses, and only the appeasers will draw satisfaction from the exposure of his failings. However, I felt that I should not conceal what took place on board the steamship.

While engaged in organizational work in Australia, in parallel with my party work I set about establishing an Australian Society for Technical Aid to Soviet Russia. A Provisional Bureau of the Society for Technical Aid to Soviet Russia was founded in Melbourne, and in all the major cites of Australia the toiling masses of Russian emigrants eagerly began to set up groups and agricultural communes. A few days ago letters from Australia told of meetings of a group of New South Wales miners who intend to make their way to Soviet Russia with their equipment and tools, to work in the Donbass coal pits. In Cairns, North Queensland, an agricultural commune of 40 families has been set up. In

Melbourne and Sydney the Society for Technical Aid to Soviet Russia is forming communes of metal-workers.[94]

This spring and summer all these groups and communes plan to set out from Australia to help consolidate the position of industry in Soviet Russia, reinforce the mainstay of the Comintern and support the practical propagation of communism by their work. The members of all these communal associations are members of the Communist Party of Australia. All organizational work is in the hands of the Communist Party's Russian section. The political reliability of the membership of the communes may be vouched for.

The VSNKh [Supreme Council for the National Economy] has a special department which is responsible for immigration matters (or rather, re-immigration).[95] This department very quickly shows new arrivals that 'an uninvited guest is worse than a Tartar'.[96] People become disillusioned, dispirited and lose heart, and are soon dragged down by the routine of dreary day-to-day Russian life, along with all the experience they have acquired abroad. The 'California' commune, which I organized while in America, and the 'America' commune, consisting of groups from Seattle and Vancouver, are at present operating in the south of Soviet Russia. In spring last year when members of these communes came to Moscow they forcefully expressed their feelings about A. Mamin, who had assured them in America that Soviet Russia needed their work and that the Soviet government would do everything to assist them. Having spent all their money on machinery and agricultural equipment, they spent many difficult minutes [sic] seeking the funds to pay the customs duty on imported machinery, grain etc., and for the fare to their place of work. It must be expected that Matulichenko or Zuzenko will not have an easy time when the communes from Australia arrive this spring or summer.[97] The Provisional Bureau of the Society for Technical Aid to Soviet Russia has charged me with applying to the Soviet government for unhindered passage for the communes into the territory of Soviet Russia, and with applying for land for them and other preparatory matters of similar nature.

As long as the ECCI fails to pay due attention to this most important aspect of propaganda for communism, and as long it does not use its influence to change the existing bureaucratic attitude to this matter, the returning communes whose enthusiasm has evaporated and whose faith in the importance of their work has been shaken will be a burden to Soviet Russia, rather than being of value to it.

---

[94] See 495–95–8 (Document 22), which contains a letter of 26 August 1922 from an RSFSR representative in Stockholm to the Ipswich comrades, seeking clarification about what sort of *artel* they wanted to establish in Russia and whether they had any capital.

[95] Zuzenko writes 'emmigration' and 'reemmigration', apparently meaning '(re-)immigration'.

[96] Russian adage with no English equivalent.

[97] Mamin and Matulichenko were two of Zuzenko's many aliases.

The purpose of this report is not merely to present a picture of the communist movement in Australia, but also to make the ECCI aware that, thanks to the particular features of the Australian proletarian movement, opportunities exist there which so far do not exist in the other Anglo-Saxon countries. Based on the broad masses of organized labour, the Communist Party of Australia, though weak in numbers of actual members, is strong in having a huge number (for Australia) of sympathizers of the communist movement. Aid is needed. Not financial aid, which has a corrupting effect on the staff of communist parties, but machinery to equip the first proletarian printing shop in Australia. Equipment purchased in Germany will be inexpensive. The Communist Party of Australia will probably see to the freight charges, as well as the customs duty. Comintern aid will show the Australian comrades that special attention is being paid to Australia, that their work is appreciated, that they have an important and responsible mission, and this will boost their strength and give them renewed energy and confidence in their own strength.

The seizure of the proletarian One Big Union movement by the communists (if it happens) will lend the Communist Party of Australia the strength and weight which until now the Labor Party has undeservedly enjoyed, and in the longer term I am deeply convinced that the first of all the Anglo-Saxon countries to declare itself a true Workers' Republic will be AUSTRALIA.

Aleksandr M. Zuzenko
P.S. I have started a report on measures which can promote the success of the communist movement in the Anglo-Saxon countries.[98]
Moscow, 16 March, 1923

Document 29

RGASPI 495–94–15. 4 April 1923, Presidium ECCI: letter: to CC of CPA. Typescript.

With recognition comes responsibilities. This letter is the first of many that would be sent in coming years from the ECCI to the CPA complaining about a lack of timely information. In this case, the information concerns the split of the Sydney group from the Party in December 1922 (see Document 24, above).

April 4, 1923
To the Central Committee
of the CP of Australia

Dear comrades,

In *The Communist* for January 5—the only number for 1923 received by us—we have read the decision of the CP convention about the split between the Sydney Branch and the former CEC of the Party. But we have received no

---

[98] This report has not been located in the CAAL collection, or in our researches in RGASPI in Moscow.

information direct from you and especially on the expulsions it would have been important for us to have information in due time.

We are now in receipt of information about the split only from the side of the disruptionist Stettler, and he has i.a.[99] asked for recognition of his "party". In a letter, dated December 7 1922 he writes the following:

> At a special meeting held on Monday December 4 1922 Sydney Branch declared itself the Communist Party of Australia /The Australian Section of the Communist International/ and herewith apply for recognition. We have started good and have already started a group in the Breakaway section that is doing good work in exposing the CE members to the rank and file that have followed them.

Because of this we today sent the following cables:

> Denford—Comintern can under no circumstances tolerate two communist parties stop urge you positively to win oppositional Sydney Branch back to party stop send information about split and present situation stop Presidium.

> Stettler—Comintern cannot recognise or tolerate defiance of party central committee or convention decisions stop Request you positively in interest of Australian Working class to unite with old party stop first then you according to statutes of CI have right to appeal to ECCI in all questions when treated wrongly stop Presidium.

We ask you—if not done when you receive this letter—at your earliest convenience to send us a complete report about the split, its origin and its development, and also about the situation in the party. Please notify us about the actions of the expelled former members of the party: Healy, Devlin and Stettler.

We trust that you already have received our letter asking for regular information to be sent to the ECCI.

Yours for communism
THE PRESIDIUM OF THE ECCI

Document 30

RGASPI 495–94–128. 1923 [possibly May or June], Earsman: Report: Report on Australia. Typescript.

Earsman did not return to Australia after the Fourth Comintern Congress at the end of 1922, but stayed and worked for the Comintern in Europe in the following year. In the meantime, he had been told by the Australian authorities in Britain that he would not be allowed to re-enter Australia. This document shows that the Comintern used Earsman's knowledge to interpret information received from Australia, especially about the progress

---

[99] inter alia

of the 'united front' policy. The CPA changed the name of its newspaper—a decision with which Earsman here disagrees—to assist in implementing the 'united front'. Because of this report, the ECCI sent the CPA a 'please explain' request (Kuusinen to CPA, 27 August 1923, CAAL 495–94–15).

REPORT ON AUSTRALIA

The latest news to hand by reports show that the CP is beginning to make some headway. At the Labor Party Conference of New South Wales the CP application for affiliation was accepted. It was by a very narrow majority, on the casting vote of the chairman. Nevertheless it was secured and along with it 3 members of the Party have been elected to the Labor Party executive as representatives of unions. There are also between 8 or 9 sympathisers out of an Executive of thirty (30). For the All-Australian Executive two delegates were elected, one being [a] member of the party.

In the elections of the Labor Party Executive, 15 were direct members of unions and so also is the President and the two vice-presidents. This shows clearly the effect of communist work among the trade unions.

It would be well and helpful to the party if the Secretariat gave a few minutes' consideration to the question of the Australian Party at this time. It must always be remembered that the Party is small and has no great influence outside of New South Wales and now that they have secured affiliation with the Labor Party a little advice would be most helpful. The struggle for working class leadership now begins and there are many pitfalls for so young and so small a party. A letter to the party at this time should be sent.

Along with the report of the Labor Party Conference I have received information that the name of the party organ *The Communist* is going to be changed to the *The Workers Weekly*. This in my opinion is a mistake. There is no justification at this moment for it when the Party has an opportunity to make good and when it seems that the party membership is increasing. It looks as if it is the case of simply following the British CP.

Speaking of conditions generally in Australia the economic conditions are much the same as they have been for the past 2 1/2 years with a good number of unemployed. In spite of this the workers have maintained their conditions and have not yet been forced to accept a lower standard, though there have been many strikes.

W.P. EARSMAN

Document 31

RGASPI 494–94–21. 12 August 1923, Ipswich Branch of the Communist Party: letter to Comrade Bukharin. In Russian and English; typescript.

Despite the years of work on organizational unity among Australian communists, in 1923 there still remained an outpost of Russian communist workers in Brisbane who insisted on their Bolshevik credentials, and maintained hostilities with the CPA (described here as the 'Australian Communist Party', ACP). In this letter to one of the foremost theoreticians of communism, the 'Ipswich Branch of the Communist Party' appeals to Bukharin to urge unity among communists in Australia on Bolshevik grounds. It is doubtful whether the Ipswich communists were familiar with the Comintern debate over the application of the 'united front' in Australia, as the differences of principle with the CPA they cite over the ALP seem to stem from CPA implementation of Comintern policy.

12/8/23. Ipswich

Dear Comrade Bukharin,

We, the members of the Ipswich Branch of the Communist Party[100] send you comradely revolutionary greetings.

We are convinced that you, who have done so much to popularize communist ideas, are steadfastly continuing the work of awakening the class consciousness of the masses. As theorists, we had occasion to make one of the manuals published by you in our endeavours to spread political education from a communist viewpoint. We trust that the fact of our making use in our studies of such publications as your *ABC of Communism*, *Theory of Historical Materialism*, *Marxist Sociology*, and *Program of the Communist Party (Bolshevik)* is sufficient to show you that we the Ipswich Branch of the Communist Party of[101] *Australia* understand the nature and aims of the Communist (Bolshevik) Party and the history of the social revolution. Moreover, we have been working on this field since 1920. You must be of course fully aware of the difficulties confronting our Branch which has to carry on its work in the teeth of the opposition of bureaucratic trade-unionism, the adherents of the Yellow International[102] doing their utmost to eliminate from the political platform the adherents of the Third International, looking upon the latter as their worse enemy. Depending on their numerical superiority, they endeavoured to discredit us by calling us "Bolsheviks" and adherents of the Red International. But we stuck to our guns—opposition and hostility to the bourgeoisie, and carried on in addition to general propaganda among the Australian working class, as strenuous agitation

---

[100] 'of Great Britain' has been struck out, by hand, and 'Australia' which was written by hand in its place has also been struck out.
[101] 'Great Britain' has been struck out, by hand.
[102] i.e., the Second International of social-democratic or 'reformist' workers' parties.

among Russian workers, inculcating into them communist ideas and bringing before them the aims and ideals of the workers of the RSFSR.

As there are many Russian organisations in Australia which, by their titles, claim to be communistic, (the Union of Russian Communist Workers in Brisbane, a similar group in Sydney and the group of Russian communists in Melbourne) so the Ipswich communist party nucleus (Bolshevik) made several attempts to convene a conference with the object of bringing about fusion among these various groups. But all our efforts were in vain. 1921 was a very bad year for us. In 1922 we again convened a fusion conference, but our efforts were frustrated by the appeals which come from abroad in connection with the Russian famine. As the collections on behalf of the famine-stricken districts of Russia continued throughout 1921, 1922 and 1923, none of the above-mentioned communist groups participated in the conference, except Brisbane. Hence, the scrappy nature of the minutes of the conference. As we knew with what kind of people we had to deal, we exercised great caution in connection with the Russian famine. As we were not at all anxious to become actors in Krylov's fable "The Hermit and the Bear" (the bear, having made friends with the hermit, watches over the latter's sleep chasing away the flies from his face. In attempting to kill a troublesome fly, the bear kills his friend—the hermit). Living in an imperialist-democratic State, which is an enemy of the Soviet Government, we never trusted the bourgeoisie, nor the latter's good intentions in connection with famine relief. Therefore, all the conference work came to naught. As we suffer complete defeat and were attacked on all sides by the communists of many shades who attended the conference, we insist [on] depriving those who do not submit to Party discipline of the name of communists. But this only led to closer union between the opportunist communists, which manifested itself by the refusal on the part of the Union of Russian Communists of Brisbane and Ipswich to read at their meeting the political letter received by us from Comrade Herman Bykov[103] of the Far Eastern Bureau of the CC of the RCP. And these people call themselves communists.

Dear Comrade Bukharin, it is stated in the 6th edition of the book on political literacy published by Kovalenko that there is not a single State without a Communisty Party (page 59). In 1921, 51 communist parties in various countries were adherents of the Communist Party. We have here the Australian Communist Party, which is an outcome of the former Socialist Party. Having been made aware of our knowledge of communism and of our belief in communist ideals, we trust that you will assist us by letting us know if the Australian Communist Party was included in the 51 Parties, adherents of the Comintern, in 1921, and

---

[103] Bykov, also known as Rezanov, was active in the community of Russian radicals in Brisbane in 1917–19. With Zuzenko, he took a leading role in the Red Flag procession of 23 March 1919, and was subsequently deported from Australia.

also if our Party is recognised as a full-fledged member of the Third International. We want to be quite sure about this, for we consider that as a Communist Party nucleus our place is in the Third International. In our endeavours to ascertain this, and in order to give them an idea of our work, we trusted them with our minutes book for which we hold an official receipt. We were anxious to know why we received no answer and why the books were never returned. But now we know why: because we enforced party discipline and expelled from our ranks adventurers and friends of Breshkovskaia,[104] which facts were mentioned in the minutes. At present these gentry are in the ACP Brisbane Section. Neither could we admit into our nucleus persons who were not only without any political education, but were even illiterate. It is said in the *ABC of Communism* that political illiteracy cannot be tolerated in the Communist Party. They all entered the ACP. All this shows you what kind of political organisation the Brisbane Section of the ACP is.[105] Understanding the meaning of internationalism, we are also strict with persons who have become British subjects after 1918 without showing any good reason for it, for being a British subject implies allegiance to king and crown. Is this admissible for revolutionaries and communists? All such people joined the ACP.

Having explained our position, we beg of you, Comrade Bukharin, not to allow our request to remain a voice in the wilderness. Common sense and our own feelings tell us that our place is in communist ranks. Do make it possible for us to be with you, for if you do not we as young revolutionaries and communists will be compelled to cede the political arena to the yellow trade unionists. In that case we shall be left without a Party. To show you how earnest we are in our work, we lay before you the following request: in 1922, at the time of the 4th International Congress there were delegations from 62 countries. If at the 5th International Congress there will be a delegation from the Australian CP, we beg of you to demand from it the documents of our Ipswich Communist Party Organisation of Bolsheviks, and to let us know if we are to continue the work planned by us together with Paul Grey Clark in 1920, or if we are to dissolve. For work in the ACP is impossible, for it is with the Third International when it is to its advantage, and passes resolutions in favour of collaboration with the Labour Party when this suits it better. The enclosed newspaper cutting will show you that this is a fact. The Labour Party is the Second International, which betrays the workers. If we join the Labour Party, we must submit to party discipline. When it suits them they will use their power to compel us to support the Labour Party, but we are not willing to support the Amsterdamers in the person of Ramsay MacDonald, which is admissible in the ACP. If your

---

[104] Ekaterina Breshko-Breshkovskaia was a Socialist-Revolutionary activist who became known as 'the grandmother of the Russian Revolution'.
[105] The next line has been cut off the microfilm image of the page. It has here been reconstructed from the Russian version.

constitution allows it we beg of you to assist us or to let us know whom we have to approach for a visa for free entry in to the RSFSR, in order that we may shake hands with you in a truly comradely fashion. If you are acquainted with comrade Paul Grey Clark, please give him, as well as comrade Herman Bykov-Rezanov, our communist greetings.

With Communist Greetings
Executive Committee of the CP Org.
Chairman: V. Tupikov
Treasurer: V. Kugatov
Secretary: Kochetigov-Lubimoff.[106]

Document 32

RGASPI 495–94–17. 1 November 1923, R. Stewart: letter: to The Secretariat (Australia). Present in a German version only, typescript. Trans. by KW.

This letter is a response by the Comintern to requests by Russian communists in Brisbane and Ipswich to affiliate with the Comintern. It was sent to Australians (whether in Moscow or Australia is not clear) and urges them to attempt to win over to the CPA the genuine communists from among these Russians.

Moscow, 1.11.23
The Secretariat (Australia),

Dear Comrades,

The enclosed documents were sent to Comrade Bukharin by a branch of the Union of Russian Workers.

They relate to attempts made in Brisbane in 1921 to set up a unified organization, and to internal differences between two branches of the organization in Ipswich and Brisbane.

I have studied these documents carefully and am of the opinion that the people and organizations concerned are Russians living in Australia and only loosely linked with one another, some of them communists, but mostly non-communists. At their unification conference, unity of the various parts could not be achieved as a result of ideological, political and personal differences.

I propose that the Communist Party of Australia be advised that they should attempt to win over those elements which would make good party members. The authors of the enclosed documents should be told that the CPA is the only organization in Australia that can be recognized by the Comintern.[107]

R. Stewart

---

[106] The signatures appear only in the Russian manuscript version. Lubimoff (Liubimov) signs in Latin script with this spelling. 'Lubimoff' is a pseudonym of Kochetigov.
[107] This last paragraph is sidelined by hand and marked in English, in handwriting: 'Attended to'.

Document 33

RGASPI 495–94–15. November-December 1923, ECCI: letter: to CPA. Typescript.

The Comintern's official reply to the 'Ipswich Branch of the Communist Party' was sent late in 1923 (the letter itself indicates '5 December', but it was attached to a covering latter dated '27 November'). It was included in the following communication to the (affiliated) CPA, with the advice to recruit as many of the Russian communists as possible. CAAL also includes a 'suggested letter' to the Ipswich communists, though it is not clear whether this or the shorter version was sent to them, nor whether the 'suggested letter' was copied to the CPA. The 'suggested letter' remains interesting, however, in hinting at the Comintern's 'united front' policy with regard to the ALP. It was a policy to which a brief letter could not possibly do justice, and was unlikely to have been sent on those grounds alone.

27th November, 1923
To the CP Australia.

Dear Comrades,

We are in receipt of a number of communications from an organisation at Ipswich. These include an address to the Russian Proletariat, Minutes of a Unity Conference held at Brisbane on June 12th and continued later in June, also copies of letters passing between Union of Communist Workers and the Ipswich CP organisation.

From these communications we learn that considerable friction prevails amongst these sections, which our Australian Party should be able to allay and probably, in consequence, recruit any amongst these comrades who would make good members of our Australian Party.

We enclose you copies of the communications and our reply, and ask you to give them attention and convey your observations to us as speedily as possible.

With Communist Greetings,
ECCI

December 5th
TO THE COMMUNIST PARTY ORGANISATION
(BOLSHEVIK)
IPSWICH, AUSTRALIA

Dear Comrades,

We have received your report addressed to comrade Bukharin and have examined the whole matter. We request you to approach the Australian Communist Party which is the only Australian Section recognised by the Communist International. The latter has been informed on this question.

With Communist greetings,

The Secretariat of the ECCI

Suggested letter to the Communist Party Organisation (Bolshevik), Ipswich, Australia.[108]

Dear Comrades,

Your communications have reached us through Comrade Bucharin and have been carefully examined. We regret that Unity Conference of which you enclose Minutes had not completely satisfactory results. Your enquiry as to whether the Communist Party Australia is one of the sections of the Communist International admits of but one answer. Yes. The Communist International recognises only one Party in any country. The policy of the CPA in seeking affiliation to the Labour Party Australia is not because of love for the Labour Party but in keeping with the necessity of the Party to seek to become a party of the masses. That the policy is a right one is being proved by experience, particularly in Great Britain where the CP influence is exposing the reactionary character of the Labour leaders without isolating the party from the workers and their daily struggles. We strongly advise you to get into touch with the CPA as only in loyal cooperation within a definitely constituted section of the CI can your efforts be of real value and the cause of the Australian workers be successful.

For the United Front of the Australian working class and their leadership by the CPA.

With Communist Greetings.
ECCI

---

[108] The body of this letter has a diagonal line drawn across it, indicating either that it was a draft or was superseded by a final version which has not been located in CAAL.

Section 2

Wilderness years: 1924–1928

The documents in this section cover the period from early in 1924 to the end of 1928, that is, from before the Fifth Congress of the Comintern until just after the Sixth. The Sixth Congress marked Stalin's victory within the RCP over Bukharin (though the latter remained—briefly—President of the Comintern), and its principal doctrinal outcome was to declare that the world had entered the 'Third Period', characterized by increasing capitalist crises, imperialist wars, and threats against the Soviet Union. The policy outcomes of the Sixth Congress were highly significant, but they would take another year to impact fully upon Australia, and their momentous effects will be charted in the next section. But for the years which this section covers the reality was that the relative stabilization of capitalism in Australia, according to the communist formula, continued. The Comintern's 'united front' tactic of making an alliance with the ALP produced both confusion and dissension within the Party, and in important respects deflected it from developing. One of the Party's founding members, Guido Baracchi, urged it to dissolve itself in 1925; upon resigning in December that year, Baracchi complimented the communists, but felt 'that the Party itself, as an organisation, is such a tragic farce that I cannot bear to be associated with it a moment longer' (495–94–26). In 1926 it lost the services of Jock Garden to the ALP and Trades Hall. Baracchi and Garden were formally expelled at the Sixth Conference in December 1926, though Baracchi's political journey was complicated and he would take his final leave of the Party only in 1940, and Garden was dogged into the 1930s by claims that he was Moscow's agent inside the ALP (Ellis nd). In sum, in the mid-1920s, the Party was very weak. Furthermore, the Comintern's interest in the CPA was desultory. The Party had worked hard to meet the Comintern's insistence on a united Communist Party; now disappointment crept in and the future began to look bleak. This was reflected in defections from the ranks, such as the two mentioned above, and in the bitterness of in-fighting, particularly over an appropriate orientation toward the ALP. The two main themes of the documents in this section are organizational weakness, and the CPA's preoccupation with the Labor Party.

The organizational side of the CPA came under Comintern scrutiny from the moment the Party was recognized as a national section. The expression 'could do better', which tends to blight every school child's report card at some stage, was almost a refrain in correspondence from the Comintern on organizational matters. In 1924, the ECCI complained that:

We have no up-to date knowledge of the condition of the Party, or whether its membership and influence is increasing or decreasing. We receive no indication as to whether the policy being operated by the Party is correct, and whether it produced results. So long as this silence on your part is maintained, we can never hope to build an effective section of the Communist Party in Australia. (Document 35)

In August 1927 the Organizational Department of ECCI wrote to the CPA to say that mail was not getting through; it asked the Australians to improve their communications, and then criticized them for defective organizational work (495–94–33).

The Australian comrades were defensive, and sometimes even defeatist, in reply. The flavour of this period may be ascertained from some correspondence from Carl Baker in Newcastle, NSW, to the Secretary of the Executive Committee of the International Red Aid organization (created by the Comintern for particular campaigns), which was collecting funds for the defence of strikers around the world. In a letter of 25 March 1926, Baker wrote:

Let me make one or two matters clear. The CP in this country has been on the decline for several years. The party today is smaller than ever before and its activities are more restricted. Its membership is insignificant, its organisation in the trade unions has practically ceased to exist, its paper has but a small circulation and the Executive of the Party today, while made up of existing communist material, has no prestige whatever in the labor movement, and is not taken seriously by any labor organisation.

As an organization, Baker argued, the Party is confined to Sydney; there are a handful in Brisbane and some without direction in northern Queensland. 'To sum up—the CP of A at the present time has ceased to be a serious factor in the Australian Labor Movement and is moving rapidly towards dissolution' (CAML 539–3–232). It came as no surprise when Baker left the Party in 1926, expressing sentiments similar to those of Baracchi. Baker, in any case, was one of the 'unreliable' middle-class communists (he was an optometrist), but in September of the same year, the much more reliable Hector Ross wrote to the same Executive Committee giving other reasons why they still could not fulfil the latter's requests: 'The general condition of the workers is very favorable when compared with that of workers in other countries.' They have a shorter working week, and Labor state governments; it is hard to interest them in the 'White Terror' in Europe (CAML 539–3–232).

The organizational picture painted by Baker may have been dismissed as coming from a class enemy, but it was essentially confirmed by reports given a couple of years later to the April 1928 meeting of the Political Secretariat of the ECCI, which considered matters related to the Australian party (see Documents

47, 48 and 49). Robson, an English communist who had attended the December 1927 conference of the CPA on behalf of the Comintern, reported that 'Politically and organisationally the Party was and remains extremely weak and inexperienced'.

That the CPA was weak did not mean that it was inactive, but rather that its activities lacked steady direction and brought no appreciable gains. In an attempt to respond to the 'united front' policy, communists joined and strove to influence the Labor Party, until the ALP expelled them or absorbed them. It meant attempting to gain positions in trade unions, until officialdom itself became attractive to leading communists. Jock Garden's translation to secretary of the New South Wales Labor Council in 1926 was more than a key factor in his expulsion in December that year; it also led to the CPA's increased focus on influencing rank and file unionists. Jack Kavanagh, who owed his position as an organizer for the NSW Labor Council to Garden, led the ideological charge against him (see Document 41), and soon became a highly influential leader in the trade union movement. (Despite his leadership profile, he himself would be humiliated and expelled by the Party in January 1931 for right-wing deviation, after attempting to have Australia exempted from the Comintern's 'social fascist' line towards the ALP. The CPA, even when it painstakingly built its reputation among the workers, seemed to be expert at destroying its own gains.) In addition, there were frequent—perhaps too frequent—demands from the Comintern and its international front organizations to mount a campaign, or raise money, in this or that cause: 'Hands off China'; against the conviction for murder of the anarchists Sacco and Vanzetti in the United States;[1] and for the International Defence Committee in aid of Colorado miners (as Moxon and Robson reported, among other things, in 1928; see Document 49).

The difficulties of communication are another important theme of the documents in this section. They added to the sense of isolation that communists in Australia felt, and given the reliance of communists on authoritative advice from the centre, it added to their sense of strategic drift. While Earsman and Garden had attended the Fourth Comintern Congress in 1922, there were no Australians at the Fifth Congress in mid-1924, Australia being represented by Dora Montefiore. Hector Ross was in Moscow for the ECCI meeting of April-May 1926. Tom Wright, secretary of the Party since 1924, spent August to October of 1927 in Moscow, discussing Party matters with the ECCI leaders. Chief among these matters were strengthening the Party's work in the trade unions, opposing the 'White Australia' policy, and relations with the ALP. The result was the 'October Resolution', the main thrust of which was to support communist

---

[1] Nicola Sacco (1891–1927) and Bartolomeo Vanzetti (1888–1927) were Italian immigrants to the United States, and anarchists, who were convicted of murder and—after substantial domestic and international protest—executed.

propaganda in Australia, and to attempt to transform the Labor Party into a genuine workers' (i.e. communist) party (see Document 45). Herbert Moxon went to Moscow for a similar meeting in April 1928 (along with the English communist Robson, returning from Australia, and Norman Jeffery and Jack Ryan). Esmonde Higgins was the CPA's delegate to the Sixth Comintern Congress in July-September 1928, but arrived in the midst of its six weeks of sessions. His report on the Congress is Document 53.

While personal contacts were intermittent, mail—as has already been noted—took months to arrive, if it ever did. The Australian secretary noted that one letter from the Agitprop department of the Comintern in 1926 had taken seven months to reach Sydney (Document 42). At the end of 1927, Jack Howie reported to the Party's Seventh Congress that 'Our contact with Headquarters has failed [during the past year] and we are practically isolated from the Communist Parties of other countries of the world' (495–94–35). This may have been due largely to the series of measures taken by the Australian and British governments to confront what they saw as a serious communist threat. In 1921, Australian Customs regulations were expanded to prohibit a wider range of undesirable material from entering Australia; and in 1926 the Crimes Act was amended to broaden the range of activities considered a threat to good order. Meanwhile, the British government had acted to stop the transfer of money from Moscow to Australia through British banks.

The Executive Committee of the Comintern concentrated its attention on 'the Australian question' three times during this period: the first time at a Plenum in April-May 1926; the second in October 1927; and the third at a meeting of the Political Secretariat in April 1928. At the 1926 meeting, Hector Ross travelled to Moscow to present a report (Document 37), and the subsequent 'Resolution on the Australian Question' (Document 40) was adopted at the CPA's Sixth Conference in December that year. Wright went in 1927, and in 1928 Moxon, Jeffery and Ryan (with the Comintern's view put by R.W. Robson). Standard Comintern procedure was followed in each case: seek information from a national section, draft a document that uses this information but reflects Comintern priorities, and expect, allow or require the particular section to adopt it. The quality of such resolutions depended heavily on the clarity, quick-wittedness and forcefulness of the national section's representative(s). Only in the 1928 case was there a change of routine and, once again, policy towards the ALP was at the root of it. Moxon's criticisms of the CPA were driven by his desire to change the Party's policy on the Labor Party by outflanking the ALP rather than building a revolutionary alternative within it. At different periods, Moxon could be described by a variety of communist formulae; let us simply say here that he was a man of the 'Third Period' *avant la lettre* (and while he would initially do well by the Comintern's subsequent change in policy later in 1928, like most communist leaders, he would not survive as leader through the 'Third Period').

Moxon ultimately got his way, at least in the case of Queensland, where his Party support base lay, but Jeffery and Ryan dissented in their report to the ECCI. It would be a taste of the turmoil to come in 1929 in the Australian Party, explored below in Section Three.

The resolutions that were often the product of these trips were part of the prevailing Comintern 'style', which moulded facts, hopes, prediction and guesswork into authoritative sounding position papers, based increasingly on the arbitrary 'periodization' of post-First World War history (reaching its formulaic height in the 'Third Period'). The difficulties with this style are clear from the Australians' confusion about how, as good communists, to deal with the ALP. The fact which communists had to confront in many countries, but particularly in Australia, throughout their existence was that the industrial working class was frustratingly loyal to what the communists saw as 'reformist' parties which could not but disappoint and 'betray' its interests. A key issue, therefore—if not *the* key issue—was how to win the workers away from such reformists. The numerous twists and turns in the communist answer to this question will not be traced here, but for our purposes they form a text (sometimes 'sub-', and sometimes 'supra-') in many of the documents in this collection.

Document 34

RGASPI 495–94–15. no date [early 1924], ECCI: letter: to EC of CPA. Typescript.

This letter is a complaint from ECCI that the CPA is not engaged properly in building the party. It rejects, in particular, the view that the CPA should be focused chiefly on work in the trade unions; it advocates reaching beyond trade union leaderships to the workshop. Attempts to replace or bypass trade union leaderships led to the departure from the Party of Jock Garden and his supporters in 1926.

To the Executive Committee of the CP of Australia

Dear comrades,

After reading thru your statutes and especially your last report, we ask you kindly to take up your statutes and party rules for consideration and revision. We do not wish to criticize them from here; we only ask you yourself to find out in which way they could be improved.

It is one of the most important problems for your party to find the forms for the best application of the communist organization in Australia. The experience of the last year has shown that you have not been on the right path, as your membership has sunk down to 250, according to your last report, dated November 1923.

One of the most important questions, when discussing the statutes for a party, is: where is the centre of gravity to be placed?

We think that the "centre of gravity" should not be in the Trade Unions—although this is one of the most important fields—but in the workshop. The shop nucleus must be the heart of the communist party. The workers are scattered over the places where they live, but in the shops the party finds them concentrated, and the shop is the place where the party must organize the workers.

The party is a political body, the trade unions have their activity on the economic field. That is one reason why the party also not should be based upon the trade unions. But also in the trade unions there is a very great task for the party, and this is the reason why it is very necessary for every good communist party to have active and well organized groups of communists in every trade union. But these communist trade union factions should not be the base for the party organization. They should be suborganisations of the party, like factions in the parliaments, in municipal bodies, in cooperatives, in military units etc.

In your statutes you have abandoned the local branches. This is a fault, then still there always is a need of local meetings of the workers; around the places where the party members live there still are many important tasks, which must be attended to by the party.

To dissolve every kind of territorial organization is as bad as to organize only industrial branches, as some American comrades have proposed.

The main local tasks can in the best way be attended to by small local groups with clearly defined tasks. We refer to the enclosed document about the organisation of nuclei and working groups, from which you may see, how these groups are to be organized and what kind of work they are supposed to do.

When entering a Communist party a worker certainly should hand in recommendations from at least one or two earlier party members, but the time of probation can be different in different countries. In a country like Russia, where the Communist Party is in power, the probation must be much harder and taken for a longer time than in the capitalist countries. We ask you to consider the question, if your probation time, three months, is not a too long time for a worker in Australia. We do not claim that this time is too long for a non-proletarian intellectual. With the temporary removal would it not assist you in the development of your party to a real mass party?

A small party like yours is very likely to get infected with sectarian tendencies, if the natural growth of it is hampered by too many difficulties put in the way of true revolutionary workers, wishing to become members of the party. Your first task now in Australia is to build a real good and fighting Communist Mass Party.

We advise you to go very thoroughly into this matter. A careful study of the Thesis on the Organisation of the Communist parties (3. world-congress)[2] will give you much valuable advice and assistance.

The Organisation Department of the Executive Committee of the CI is working on a general plan about party-organisation—putting especial stress upon the structure of shop-nuclei. In the next future a copy of this plan will be sent to you.

We are sure that you yourself will find which dangers there are in your present form of organisation, which will develop the party—based as it is only upon the basis of the trade unions—to a general opposition movement in the trade unions, but not *to* a real fighting Communist Mass Party

With the best wishes for a successful work we are
Yours for communism

Document 35

RGASPI 495–94–24. 18 August 1924, Secretary ECCI: letter: To CC of CPA. Typescript.

In this letter the ECCI puts its view that communication between the CPA and Moscow is poor, a view supported by the lack of an Australian representative at the Fifth Comintern Congress, and by the paucity of information about the CPA arriving in Moscow. What little of the Party's press that has been seen is uninspiring. The ECCI states that the Australian section is one of the weakest in the Comintern, and requests information immediately on a range of organizational and background matters.

To the Communist Party of Australia
Central Committee

Dear Comrades,

The Fifth Congress of the Comintern has now concluded, and I expect you will receive a report covering the main decisions from Dora Montefiore. She fell ill, and had to return to Germany before the Congress actually concluded, but I gathered from her that she intended procuring all the available material in order to compile a complete report for you.

During the last two years, the contacts and communication between the Australian Party and the Secretariat have been very bad indeed. The supply of information regarding the whole situation in Australia has been totally inadequate to enable us to form any real impression of what is happening. This is also true regarding party information itself. We have no up-to date knowledge of the condition of the Party, or whether its membership and influence is increasing

---

[2] This seems to be a reference to the 'Theses on the Structure of Communist Parties and on the Methods and Content of their Work' adopted by the Third Comintern Congress in July 1921. Lenin, following this conference, complained of this resolution that it was 'too Russian' (Degras 1956, 257–71).

or decreasing. We receive no indication as to whether the policy being operated by the Party is correct, and whether it produced results. So long as this silence on your part is maintained, we can never hope to build an effective section of the Communist Party in Australia. We would very strongly urge that the Central Committee take immediate steps to remedy this deplorable condition of affairs, and to see to it that we are regularly informed of the whole of the Party's work, and of the changing situation in Australia.

Occasionally, we receive copies of the *Workers' Weekly*, and in the paper we notice a flatness and lack of animation. Our paper does not seem to be alive. Instead of being a living part of the actual every-day struggles of the masses, it tends rather to be merely an abstract pseudo journalistic "write-up" upon any subject. We would strongly recommend more concentration by you on the character of our paper. Strenuous efforts should be made to secure a regular supply of information from the workshops, factories, etc. regarding the everyday struggles. In this way, by a systematic treatment of the class struggle news supplied, our paper would, from time to time, become the means of expressing these struggles. This would attract the workers to our paper, and encourage them to begin looking upon it as their own. We do hope a strenuous effort will be made by you in this direction.

The Congress which has just terminated has sent out the slogan:

"A World Party and the bolshevisation of all its sections!" This means that our most important task for the next year must be concentrated on our weakest sections, and ensuring their development into real live sections of an effective International Communist Party.

Australia is one of the weakest sections of the Communist International. Consequently our task is heavy here.

We earnestly urge that more intensive party work be put in by our members in Australia. Workshop groups and nuclei should be formed immediately, as these form the basis for the building of our party, and without them it is utterly impossible to maintain any contact with the masses and ever to become a mass party. More intensive campaigns should be initiated amongst the workers, giving very special consideration to the trade union movement. We are sure that these things are appreciated by you, but in our opinion, they do not receive adequate attention.

We would especially urge that you immediately prepare a report for us covering the following points:

1. The Party. Its membership, where they are situated, and how their activities are organized.
2. The Paper. How it is edited and controlled, and its circulation.
3. The character of the organized trade union and labour movement:

a. Total number of organized workers
b. How they are organized
c. General influence and effectiveness.

4. A survey of the general situation and progress of the class struggle.

If you could appoint some comrades immediately to compile this material, it would help us considerably, and we on our part will endeavour from time to time to assist you in every possible way by making suggestions, offering criticisms, and encouraging where the direction and the policy of the party is correct.

The Fifth World Congress made it clear that our tasks are greater than ever, and we must therefore set to with greater and greater energy.

With Communist greetings,
The Secretary of the EC of the CI.

Document 36

RGASPI 495–94–28. no date [but presumably soon after 30 March 1926], Simonov: report: On Kushnarev. Present in German only, no Russian version located; typescript. Trans. by KW.

In this document responding to an obituary in *Pravda*, Simonov attempts to put on record some of the complicated history of the formation of the CPA from various radical currents in the Australian socialist movement, and (his somewhat heroic view of) his own role in the development of the CPA.

In the obituary devoted to Comrade I. G. Kushnarev (A. Rogov, *Pravda*, 30.3.26, No. 72), the writer, who clearly has little knowledge of Australia, commits a regrettable error. Comrade A. G. Rogov writes that Comrade Kushnarev was a member of the 'Australian International Socialist (now Communist) Party'. This party was called the Australian Socialist Party. It was sometimes called 'The International' after the name of its official organ, *The International Socialist*, to distinguish it from the official organ of the other socialist party, *The Socialist*. Both groups were factions of the same Australian Socialist Federation, which was headed by Tom Mann, while he was in Australia. After Mann's departure, the Federation declined and soon folded. One of the factions, under the name 'The Australian Socialist Party', more or less adhered to the propagation of the ideas of internationalism. On this basis it chose the name 'The International Socialist' for its newspaper. The other faction became a purely local organization of the state of Victoria (more precisely, of Melbourne, the capital city of Victoria) and an appendage of the reactionary Labor Party. Both factions, however, came to a swift dissolution. The first, the ASP, existed mainly in Sydney, but a number of provincial groups belonged to it, and Comrade Kushnarev was a member of one of these groups. Until Comrade Kushnarev's departure (before 1917) this faction was fairly active as a purely propagandist faction. It could not, however, be considered a revolutionary organization, as it was completely divorced from the masses. It regarded participation in the activity of trade unions, to which over 65% of Australian workers belong, as 'fundamentally' harmful or 'unsocialist'.

In 1917 and 1918, this 'party' finally shrank to an insignificant family group, centred round the printing press, and in reality owed its existence solely to the fact that for this group the printing press represented a certain source of income.

The rise of the Communist Party in Australia began in 1918 with small clandestine groups in Brisbane, Sydney, Melbourne and other centres. In 1920 it became (still in secret) a party with a programme and a constitution. By this time, however, it exerted significant influence over the trade unions and bore the entire weight of the propaganda campaign against the intervention in the RSFSR. Under its influence, sharply worded resolutions of protest were formulated at all trade union congresses and conferences against that intervention. These resolutions were known to have enormous influence on the Australian troops on the Archangel front, and in England, and on the Canadian and American troops in the Russian Far East.

When the ASP became aware of the great influence of the CP, it was seized with anxiety, as it had until now regarded itself as 'the organization furthest to the left' in Australia. It therefore convened a conference of 'active rebels' with the aim of establishing a legal communist party.[3] Naturally, those who attended were mainly members of the existing CP. The latter were quite sincerely prepared to take part in this conference, as they were already strong enough to show themselves openly as a party, and the ASP proposal concerning their premises, printery and newspaper suited them very well. A 'United Communist Party' was formed, and feverish activity commenced. The ASP clearly needed this as publicity for itself (weekly meetings in their hall on Sundays, with collections of funds). On what turned out to be a thoroughly unlucky day for them, their leaders proclaimed their party the Communist Party, and expelled all members of the first Communist Party from the premises and the printery, hoping in this way to strengthen their own position and destroy the first Communist Party. But the first Communist Party was already so strong that within a week it possessed a better editorial board and a better newspaper, *The Communist*, which exists to this day. As the author of these lines has been regarded as the instigator and organizer of this first Communist Party, the People's Commissariat for External Affairs and the Communist International have received numerous reports from the ASP leadership alleging that he is in the pay of Australian military intelligence and has recruited the dregs of the population of Australia

---

[3] 'Active rebels': this phrase given in English.

under the banner of a 'Communist Party' in order to discredit the very idea of communism. The usual membership of the ASP (about thirty), who until now had had blind faith in their leaders, now questioned the behaviour of these leaders and set up a special commission to investigate the whole business and to review Party affairs. The result of this investigation was the dismissal of these 'leaders' and the handover of the printing shop to the Communist Party. Thus the ASP ceased to exist. The former general secretary became a factory foreman and participated eagerly in the exploitation of the workers. His wife opened a stationery shop with the former editor of the defunct *International Socialist*.[4] From 1921 to this day the CP is the Australian section of the Comintern. Early this year it was declared illegal under a law passed by the reactionary federal government, and it is entirely possible that it will temporarily collapse, as the Australian workers still have insufficient experience to operate illegally. But the founders of the Party probably still remember their brief experience of 1918–19, and we may assume that after some time the Party will rise again as an illegal organization.

This Communist Party is therefore not the former ASP or the Australian International Socialist Party. The founders of the CP were mostly members of the IWW.

P. Simonov,

Former Secretary General and Editor of the newspaper of the Union of Russian Communist Workers in Australia until 1918, and Consul General of the RSFSR in Australia (January 1918–November 1921).[5]

13 Granatny Lane,
Moscow
Telephone: 3–41–52

---

[4] 'Former general secretary': these lines refer to Arthur Reardon and his wife Marcia. See Document 9, above: the letter from Simonov to the Comintern of 8 April 1921 (495–94–6). The former editor of the *International Socialist* is Ray Everitt.

[5] The latter date is puzzling. Simonov relinquished his office in August and left Australia on 20 September 1921. See reports in *The Communist* for these months.

Document 37

RGASPI 495–94–29. 14 April 1926. Report of the CP of Australia to the ECCI. Typescript.

This report was presented by Hector Ross to a meeting of the ECCI in April and May of 1926, a meeting requested by the ECCI after the proposed 'liquidation' of the CPA by Guido Baracchi at the end of 1925. The outcomes are presented in Documents 38, 39 and 40, below. Ross is keen to stress that the Party is a going concern, but requests financial assistance from the ECCI.

REPORT OF THE CP OF AUSTRALIA TO THE ECCI. 14.IV.26

I. ECONOMIC CONDITIONS

DEVELOPMENT OF BRITISH AND AMERICAN CAPITALISM during the last few years has been considerable in steel, textile, electric, cement, paper industries and agriculture. The present move to erect a high tariff wall, particularly in the metal industry is the result of the influx of foreign capital. This process is most clearly marked by the operations of Vickers from England and the erection of Ford's motor factories in Australia while plans are being made to transfer German nitrogen plants to New South Wales under the control of mixed company.

Inefficient Research Work.

The Australian Section has been severely handicapped through the lack of the Research Bureaux. Much of the work is voluntary, records are scarce and detailed information regarding the above growth of modern industry is not available.

The Attitude of Governments to the Workers.

All governments in Australia have developed a more ruthless policy in suppressing strikes especially in the last year when the arbitration Court has proved its uselessness as an instrument of social peace.

Labour Governments Suppress Strikers.

Queensland and West Australian Governments have during the year openly fought striking transport workers. In some cases police violence was employed and in others scabs were protected and thugs permitted to drive militants away from the fighting centre. In cases where the Labour Government assisted striking workers or remained neutral in a dispute such action resulted from direct militant pressure from the trade union movement. Such actions were invariably accompanied by considerable sabotage.

The Labour Governments have attempted to give small concessions to the workers without offending the petty bourgeoisie and in order to convince foreign capitalists of the stability of the Labour regime they have been very definite in crushing any substantial demand or any sign of militancy coming from the working class.

The open formation of a skeleton fascist organisation in Melbourne which has received the endorsement of the Prime Minister and the semi-fascist bodies in West Australia and Queensland are an indication of the struggles of the future.

General Economic Outlook.

Industry in general is in a sound position. A succession of good harvests and successful marketing have been reported. Last year's wool clip was a record, 11% above the previous year and other branches of the pastoral industry are improving their position. Industry is also fairly stable, and in some cases government bounties have been given to assist the establishment of new industries such as paper, cement and hemp.

Unemployment is not considerable and statistics are extremely unreliable, and from the official figures from the Trade Union Information unemployment generally reaches from 8–9% of the membership.

Much labour is seasonable and workers migrate to and from it, but chronic unemployment is very small and government insurance schemes and doles are able to cope with it fairly effectively.

There appeared no prospect of a crisis developing within Australia at present, the only danger appears to be from a dislocation in European economic conditions.

II. THE OUTLOOK OF THE WORKERS

Trade Unions.

These are well developed in all States and are generally under the domination of reformist leaders, but there exists a militant element in each industry centre which has put up some good fights during the year:

In Queensland, the railway men, waterside workers and seamen; in Western Australia, seamen, fire brigade and hotel employees; in New South Wales, rubber workers, stove makers and others.

The manner in which the masses rallied to the support of the British seamen demonstrated that there exists a spirit of militancy among the rank and file, but the fact that the yellow transport leaders were able to break down the fight against the proposed deportation of the Seamen's Union officials shows the power of the reformist leaders.

Left Wing Unorganised.

Numerous attempts have been made to organise the Left Wing element, but up-to-date little permanent work has been achieved. In all industrial centres, the Party has formed its groups of militants in either general or industrial groups, but these have usually weakened and disappeared. A splendid move has been commenced through the Vice-President of the New South Wales Labour Council, a splendid reliable non-Party militant. A good programme of economic demands to meet local requirements has been drafted and we regard this move as the soundest we have undertaken. But the vacillating nature of the workers as a whole has been demonstrated by the way the Bruce Government swept the poll in the Federal election with the fake anti-Communist campaign. There is plenty of fighting spirit amongst the workers of all States, but it is only visible in times of crises, otherwise the favourable economic conditions and the influence of the yellow leaders keep it in the background.

Problem of Foreign Workers.

This question applies with great importance to Queensland, where colonies of Italian workers have been driven by fascism. The Australian Workers' Union which is the dominant trade union excludes such workers from membership, and they constitute a serious menace to the local workers. The Party has launched an agitation for their inclusion in the union, which was progressing favourably when I left Sydney.

During 1925, the Party issued a series of leaflets in Italian which were printed on a small machine owned by the Party and some articles in Italian appeared in the *Workers' Weekly*. These were discontinued owing to our failure to secure a translator.

Large bodies of Slovakian workers have recently arrived and have been despatched to steel industry districts, where they are living in conditions of abject poverty, but here the language difficulty again intervenes and we have been unable to approach these workers.

The Greek and Russian Party groups in Sydney have made excellent contact with their countrymen throughout the country and supplies of literature have [been] procured for the purpose. There are no other language problems that we know of.

III. CONDITION OF THE PARTY

The process of eliminating the useless and ineffective members from the Party was completed by the end of 1925. The actual effective membership was then as follows:

NEW SOUTH WALES		QUEENSLAND	
Sydney	70	Brisbane	35
Hurstville	8	Blackall	7
Balmain	15	Cairns	17
Russian	11	Ipswich	15
Greek	11	At large	12
Lithgow	10		86
Wollongong	6	VICTORIA	
Kurri	3	Melbourne	28
Cessnock	3	At large	2
Newcastle	10		30
At large	11		
	158		
WEST AUSTRALIA	4		
TASMANIA	1		

The total membership for Australia—279

NEW ZEALAND MEMBERS:

are presently linked up as a section of the Australian Party and the estimated effective membership was 120.

Membership Scattered.

As will be seen from the figures, the Party members are scattered in small groups throughout the continent, and the long distances and slow transportation make Party organisation difficult. Practically every member is an efficient trade union worker and through this channel most of our work has been done.

Building Factory Nuclei.

Very little practical work has been done in this direction, because of the smallness of our numbers, but where more than one member is employed in any factory, they function as a nucleus. The party fully realises its obligations in this respect, and aims at recruiting new members through the workshop.

Party Press.

The Party maintains a monthly and a weekly organ. The monthly organ *The Communist* has been edited by Comrade Baracchi and was not regarded as a good journal because of the failure of the editor to deal with local conditions. The circulation has remained in the vicinity of 2,000 copies. Since Comrade Barrachi's resignation in December, Comrade Kavanagh from Canada has been appointed editor and the Executive expects the sale to increase rapidly.

The *Workers' Weekly* has a circulation of 6,000 of which 1,489 are subscribers. Both journals circulate in all States which means extremely late delivery.

Costs of Printing.

The difficulties of printing are very great. Owing to the restrictive provisions of printing laws, most printers refuse our work, while a few charge very heavily for their services. Book publishing has been entirely impossible for us, and as the only local radical publisher has abandoned this work, we are dependent on small supplies from England.

Acquiring a Printing Plant.

The Party has realised that a printing plant is essential and steps have been taken to raise funds for this purpose and a capable comrade has arrived from New Zealand to operate the machinery when it is procured. The press will not be operated in the name of the Party. It will be a great financial help to the Party as well as a much *more* efficient means of getting propaganda to the distant centres of Australia.

Party Officials.

At the present time all the official work of the Party is done on a voluntary basis which is extremely inefficient. Most of the Executive members are manual workers and the Party propagandists travel long distances at week-ends and, as almost every member is prominent in the trade unions, the bulk of our membership is overworked.

The 1926 Conference decided to strike a levy on the membership to provide a salary of £5 a week for one official, and this was in preparation when I left Sydney.

National Organiser.

In September 1925, Comrade Jeffery was despatched to Queensland in time for the sugar and meat industries [sic]. He arrived when the strike of railway servants against the Labour Government *broke out* and later on took part in the bitter struggles of the waterside workers which was in November crushed by thugs.

Comrade Jeffery did wonderful work for the Party and took a prominent part in all fights and gathered together a large number of militants who will provide many recruits for the Party when our organiser again visits there this year.

New Zealand Tour.

On returning in December, Comrade Jeffery went to New Zealand where his tour is most successful, especially as the Communist Executive is strongly represented on the Executive of the Miners' organisation. He is still engaged in this work although receiving no wages from the Party.

The affiliation of the New Zealand Communist groups to the Australian Party took place at the end of 1925 as a means of settling a very difficult unity problem. This has been successful and now experience only is needed to enable them to develop in to a useful Section of the International.

Slow Recruiting.

During 1925 the Party was subjected to the most bitter attacks in its history. The State and Federal elections and the new Zealand elections resulted in all parties attacking the Communists, and the Labour party launched a campaign of expelling all communists from the reformist party. Under such conditions, the winning of workers to the Party was extremely difficult as our small numbers and inefficient Executive machinery were powerless to deal with the monstrous campaign levelled against us.

The Crimes Bill.

The effect of the passing of the amendment of the Crimes Bill by the *Federal* Government has also made our task harder, for the provisions of the Bill threaten not only the Party but its supporters. Preparations have been made to carry on in the event of the Party being declared illegal and many splendid demonstrations have already been made by the trade union movement including the Industrial Conference held in Sydney on February 20.

The Necessity for Assistance.

In view of the great obstacles against which we struggle in Australia and the necessity for carrying the message of the Party to the distant centres, we urge the Secretariat to regard as urgent the granting of some assistance to the Australian Section without delay.

The literature available in Australia is entirely inadequate to meet the requirements. Scarcely any Marxian classics are available and then only at prohibited [sic] prices, while the essential new Leninist literature is extremely scarce.

We are confident that in the future, the Party will be faced with considerable struggles, both of the general war of the workers against the encroachments of capitalism and in our own fight for existence, and if our Party apparatus is enabled to carry out its tasks, we are confident of developing into an important factor in the impending struggles in the Pacific.

Document 38

RGASPI 495–94–29. 16 April 1926, Pepper (Chief of Agitprop, CI): letter: To CC of CPA. Typescript.

This is one of the outcomes of an ECCI meeting held during April and May of 1926 which considered political and organizational issues related to the CPA. The letter recommends increased 'Agitprop' work, and makes substantial criticisms of the *Workers' Weekly* for appearing to be more a trade union than a communist political paper.

Moscow, 16.IV.1926

To the CC of the CP of Australia.

Dear Comrades,

On the basis of the discussion with your representative we note that the CP of Australia has not as yet organised a systematic, organisationally and ideologically definite Communist Agitprop activity. In view of the numerical weakness of your Party, and of the role that it momentarily plays in the Australian labour movement, it is very clear that this work—a broad, concrete, revolutionary agitation among the working masses and a real Leninist leadership of our own membership—constitutes THE FOUNDATION OF the present existence of the CP of Australia itself, as well as the necessary premise for its further development into a mass organisation.

Let us say in advance that the present weakness of the Party must not be permitted to constitute a hindrance to the most rapid initiation and carrying out of this task. From the example of the CP of Canada, whose conditions in many respects resemble those of your Party, we have tried to show your representative how good Communist agitation and propaganda activity can be carried on even under unfavourable circumstances and with the lack of the required forces. We urge you to utilise the material sent you per the above-mentioned comrade as an INFORMATIVE pattern for the organisation of your Agitprop work. It is self-understood that you must proceed with this organisation step by step with the most exact application to your concrete conditions.

STRUCTURE OF THE AGITPROP APPARATUS

The first premise for the gradual extension of your Agitprop work is the establishment of an Agitprop apparatus, directed centrally and spread out over all provincial organisations. For this purpose we propose to you the following organisational scheme:

CENTRAL AGITPROP COMMISSION:

A Central Agitprop Commission, consisting of the Director and two or three other comrades, especially adapted for agitation and propaganda work and possessing experience in this field, is to be organised in the Central Committee.

The Chief of this Commission will be designated by the Central Committee and is responsible to the latter for the entire work. He must himself be a member of the CC in order to assure the closest connection between the Agitprop work and the general political activity of the Party. It is desirable, furthermore, that the editor of your central organ *Workers Weekly* be attached to the Central Agitprop Commission.

The tasks of this Commission consist in the organisation and direction of all agitational and propaganda work. Special emphasis must be paid to taking measures to carry out in a centralised manner the campaigns which it has planned concretely, according to a calendar schedule, with definite instructions for all provincial organisations, and that these campaigns be carried out under the most exact control and registration. The Central Agitprop Commission, in addition to its regular reports to the CC, should likewise furnish half-yearly reports on its activity as a whole to the Central Agitprop Department of the ECCI.

Agitprop Commissions of the Provincial Organisations.

In all provinces, or in the largest organisations, similar commissions will be set up consisting of two or three comrades, one of them a responsible head, nominated by the Provincial Committees. Their task is to realise the instructions issued by the Central Agitprop Commission and to carry out the whole agitation, press and cultural activity in local organisations subordinate to them.

This simple structure we consider adequate, for the present for your conditions. But so as to reckon also with the perspectives of development, we propose that insofar as in certain large cities you have good sized factory nuclei, the institution of the AGITPROP DIRECTOR be introduced.

Agitprop Directors are the organisers of the entire agitation and propaganda in the nucleus; they attend to the dissemination of our press, to the preparation of nucleus newspapers, arrange for and organise workers' correspondents from their factories to our organ, carry out the instructions of the Agitprop Commission in the initiation of campaigns, carry on individual propaganda, etc.

DECISION ON AGITPROP WORK.

In carrying out this work it is necessary that the newly created Central Agitprop Commission itself achieve complete clarity concerning the special field of Agitprop activity and its forms, as well as that the membership be informed in detail concerning same. First of all it is to be noted that our Agitprop work, although conducted through a special Party organ, is closely bound up with the entire political life of the Party. Our factory nuclei can be imbued with a real political life only on condition that all members of these nuclei carry on the necessary agitation and propaganda work among all factory workers in conformity with their actual everyday needs.

It is further desirable that the political consciousness of the membership be permeated with the essential difference between agitation and propaganda.

> Agitation is the spreading of our ideas amongst the masses in the form of a few fundamental ideas and slogans which, adapted to their concrete needs, expresses the standpoint of our Party clearly in every activity. Propaganda is a comprehensive presentation of our conception, either in a single definite field, or in our whole social philosophy of historical and dialectical materialism.

It is a matter of course that although agitation and propaganda are differentiated from one another, they nevertheless are very closely related, which in practice means for us that every agitational campaign of our Party must be propagandistically intensified and vice versa, that every propagandist activity, as for instance our Marxist-Leninist educational work, must be at the service of our agitation. To summarise it may be said: in order that the political work of the CP of Australia may more and more win access to the masses, in order that its factory and street nuclei be imbued with real political life, it is necessary to carry out agitprop work systematically within them, under a strictly centralised direction.

PROPAGANDA AND CULTURAL WORK.

If the CP of Australia is to cope with its political tasks, its entire membership must be imbued with the ELEMENTARY KNOWLEDGE of Marxism-Leninism, and its cadres of functionaries must receive SPECIAL TRAINING on this basis. For this purpose your Central Agitprop Commission must work out a definite plan for the organising of elementary schools. Next winter at least one elementary school must begin activity in each provincial organisation. As to the programme for these elementary schools we propose that you utilise the elementary programme of the CP of Canada which we have sent you. For the special training of functionaries, you must organise short-term courses on definite subjects, as for example, the trade union question, imperialism and the empire, study of the decisions of the last Enlarged Executive, etc. Special attention must be devoted to ensuring that all tasks confronting the party, for example, such as are connected with the party's political campaigns like that against the Crime Bill, the campaign against the expulsion of Communists from the Labour Party, be worked out in a propagandist-theoretical manner, by means of special functionary courses, in order by this means to gain access to the membership as a whole. As a special organisational form of these courses, we recommend the so-called week-end schools which have proved very practicable in Great Britain and Canada. A scheme for these courses was sent you.

In order to get the required literature for your general educational work, you must get into closer contact than heretofore with the Agitprop of Great Britain and of the Workers' (Communist) Party of America. The establishment of a literature fund in England to make available long-term credits on book shipments must be arranged by the Agitprop Commission of your Party with the Agitprop Commission of the CP of Great Britain. In this connection we also point out the need for a greater circulation of "Inprecorr" and the "Communist International" in Australia.

We await your reply concerning the manner in which you contemplate organising the propaganda life of your Party and what special questions and requirements you desire to address to us in this connection.

Concerning your activity on the field of agitation we have no comprehensive report. Since we have only a few issues of the *Workers Weekly* available upon which to base our judgement, we shall deal with this question in the discussion on the *Workers Weekly* since our remarks concerning your organ—mutatis mutandis—apply also to the agitation work of your Party.

THE WORKERS WEEKLY.
THE PRESENT CHARACTER
OF THE PAPER.

The organ has the character more of a trade union than of a political organ of the Communist Party. It devotes great attention to the daily demands and trade union struggles of the Australian working class and follows the practice of permitting as many workers as possible to express themselves in the form of workers' correspondence. The instructions issued in this regard, however—insofar as they are given by the paper itself—bear no systematic character, but are issued only incidentally, from time to time.

The chief shortcoming of the paper consists in that it neglects the actual policy and political tasks of the Party. It concerns itself much too little—in some issues not at all—with the inner political questions of the country, either of the governmental policies or those of the Labour party. In the appraisal of trade union struggles also the political viewpoint is left entirely out of consideration. It moves entirely upon the rails of a trade union policy rather than of a Communist policy. But also the foreign political events, even the political events of the British "motherland" are not dealt with systematically, but are only occasionally, almost incidentally, touched upon without raising the problem of British imperialism and the Empire. The trade union question, also, to which the paper devotes very much space, is dealt with from a narrow Australian viewpoint, and its connection with the INTERNATIONAL TRADE UNION MOVEMENT is given too little consideration.

All this gives the organ a provincial touch. The paper as a whole is not sufficiently Communist, which is very regrettable especially in view of the Reformist illusions of the great mass of the Australian proletariat.

There is still too little workers' correspondence and that which is available concerns itself more with general than with factory affairs, or concrete workers' questions.

The paper pays too little attention to the agrarian question.

The question of the International Labour movement in general and the Communist movement in particular receive very little notice in the paper.

The paper pays too little [attention] to the question of the relationship to Great Britain. It does not deal at all with the separatist tendencies and their effect on Australian policy, with the threatening war developments between America and Japan, between Britain and Japan, with the extension of the naval base at Singapore by Great Britain, etc. Precisely through the treatment of such and similar world political problems, the provincial horizon of the Australian workers could best be extended.

The party's campaigns are still not given adequate emphasis by the paper. True, the campaign against the Crime Act was given enough space by the paper, but it was not conducted with the necessary sharpness, nor was it sufficiently exploited agitationally. The campaign against the expulsion of the Communists from the ALP is not conducted with sufficient system and sharpness in the paper.

The organ publishes practically no theoretical matter. It prints neither extracts from the Marxist-Leninist literature, nor discussion of the decisions of the CI Congresses, nor material on the labour question in Great Britain which could well be taken from the press of the CP of Great Britain. The neglect of this task of a Communist organ of Australia where Marxist traditions are utterly lacking, is an error. It is made still worse in that the paper publishes utterly worthless un-Marxist citations, as e.g. that on revolution by a Social Revolutionary—Gardiner (!),[6] which was printed without any comment whatever. Such quotations must of course be eliminated entirely.

Our reorganisation proposals.

From the above it is apparent that the organ requires thorough reorganisation. The most important measures to be carried out and which certainly can be carried out with the limited means at your disposal, are, in our opinion, the following:

1.   It is necessary to divide the available space in the paper so that the internal and foreign political events, the politico-economic facts, the trade union movement, the Australian and the international labour movement, the Communist world movement, etc., will be assured a definite space in every issue.

---

[6] The parenthesis is Pepper's.

2.   Each issue shall contain an inner political and foreign political weekly review—a systematic presentation and comment upon the political events of the week from a Communist viewpoint.

3.   Apart from this concise weekly review various outstanding events of inner or foreign politics should be dealt with in special notices or articles.

4.   Events in Great Britain, particularly the struggles of the British proletariat and the imperialist foreign policy of the British Empire, must be consistently followed by the organ, and this from the viewpoint of Australia's role in the struggle of the imperialist powers for world hegemony, criticised from the standpoint of Australia's role in the Pacific Ocean. In this connection the events in China and India must be followed up with special attention and the whole anti-Russian incitement policy of British Imperialism must be most vigorously combated.

5.   The paper must periodically report on Soviet Russia, on its ascendancy, on the rapidly improving standard of living of the Russian worker and peasant. Material on this subject can be taken from the British and American papers of our brother Parties.

6.   The exclusion campaign of the ALP against the Communists must be followed up constantly and systematically by the paper, must be criticised and combated instead of, as has been the case until now, an occasional and incidental attack.

7.   Trade union questions should, as heretofore, be given the greatest attention, but they must be dealt with also from their political aspect.

8.   Various problems of world policy, particularly of British policy, should be dealt with more often than heretofore in theoretical articles or extracts from such articles. You will readily find whatever you need in the British and American Party newspapers and magazines.

9.   Apart from quotations from Marx, Engels, Lenin, etc., the paper should try to popularise single slogans of your campaign and international Communist campaigns, by means of headlines extending, in big letters, over several columns. All party organs appearing in the English language can serve you as examples in this.

10. The style of writing in the organ must be more Communistic than heretofore. All articles and notices must be written from the viewpoint of the living class struggle, and must be brought into connection with the big revolutionary struggle of the world proletariat and of the Comintern.

TECHNICAL MAKE-UP OF THE PAPER.

More attention than hitherto must be devoted to the make-up of the paper. Especially the first page, in content as well as technique, must have an appearance that will catch the attention of the reader and induce him to read the whole paper. The manner in which the material in a paper is distributed, and the make-up in which it presents itself to the reader, is of greatest importance to the agitational and propaganda effect, as well as to the salability of the paper

FACTORY PAPERS.

In connection with the extension of the Party on the basis of factory nuclei, the Party must encourage the establishment of factory newspapers with all energy, and this question must receive the greatest attention. It must go hand in hand with the comrades in the factories, enable the factory nuclei to issue their factory papers, and the Party must supply instructions as to the contents and technical make-up of factory papers

We urge you to send us a detailed report regularly every six months to supply us with exact information with regard to your activity on the field of propaganda, agitation and press. We also ask you to send us material such as placards, leaflets, etc, since only on the basis of concrete material can we get a correct picture of your work and help you in your activities from here.

With Communist greetings,
Pepper,
Chief of the Agitprop Dept.,
of the ECCI.

Document 39

RGASPI 495–94–27. 28 April 1926, Fried: resolution: On the question of the CPA. In German, typescript. Trans. by KW.

This is one of the outcomes of an ECCI meeting held in April and May of 1926 which considered political and organizational issues related to the CPA. It summarizes the most important organizational and political tasks, and seems to promise financial assistance.

28/4/26 On the Question of the CPA

The following must be seen as the most important organizational and political tasks of the Party:

I. the organization of the Party itself,
II. the organization of a leftist movement corresponding to the English Minority Movement.

Further to Point I:

1. a paid secretary to be appointed to the Central Committee;
2. the division of the Central Committee into organizational and political bureaux to be terminated; a single bureau to be established, and CC members to be charged with specific tasks (organizational, trade union, agitation and propaganda, or women's matters), for which they should set up committees;

3. energetic and systematic recruiting campaigns, linked with the reorganization; reorganization to be focused on Sydney, Broken Hill, Brisbane and Auckland;

4. a territorial bureau to be set up for New Zealand.

III. reorganization of the youth movement;

IV. establishment of a Red Aid section on a broad mass basis;

V. establishment of organizational and political contacts with the New Zealand Maoris and other peoples of the Pacific islands;

VI. when forming links with foreign workers, Chinese, Japanese and Indian workers, who constitute a large percentage on certain islands, should not be overlooked.

These proposals should be seen as complementary to those of Comrade Bamatter.

Fried

28 April, 1926

Document 40

RGASPI 495–94–27. 1926 [May], Presidium ECCI: Resolution of the Australian Question. Typescript.

This resolution is the most important outcome of the meeting of the ECCI in April and May 1926 with Hector Ross to discuss the 'Australian Question'. While it acknowledges the 'difficulties and peculiarities of the objective situation', it suggests that the Party—despite its expulsion from the ALP—continue to work within the Labor Party, and that it combat the 'White Australia' policy and British imperialism.

Confidential.

RESOLUTION ON THE AUSTRALIAN QUESTION

The Communist Party of Australia fights under difficult and peculiar conditions. All the forces of the nationalist reaction, the emergency legislation and the reformist labour leaders are concentrated against it. Prime Minister Bruce waged the last election under the slogan: "Save the country from the Communist peril!". The "Crimes Bill" interdicts all organisations that disturb public peace and aim at the overthrow of constitutional government. When passing this law Parliament had in mind primarily the Communist Party.[7] The labour lieutenants

---

[7] This assertion is essentially correct. Section 30A of the Crimes Act was inserted in 1926 to declare unwalful any association that advocated the overthrow of the Commonwealth Government by revolution or sabotage. Sawer (1972, 221) declares that this part of the Act was 'originally designed to deal with the Communist Party and fellow-traveller organizations, under which "seditious" associations can be dissolved after trial by a judge sitting without a jury'. (See also Sawer (1956, 268).)

of the bourgeoisie, on their part, have also outlawed the Communist Party by excluding the Communists from the Labour Party.

Our Australian brother Party must overcome, in its struggles, certain difficulties and peculiarities of the objective situation. The country is a vast one, a whole continent, and it is sparsely populated. Heavy industry is very immature and relatively undeveloped. True giant enterprises do not exist. On the other hand not less than half of the total population is concentrated in five or six towns. Small peasant strata are almost entirely lacking, since the country is covered with large scale cattle and sheep ranches. The strata of semi-agricultural and semi-industrial workers are quite large, and constitute one of the most important elements among the toilers. Partly due to conditions and partly to the conscious efforts of the bourgeoisie and reformist labour leaders, the industrial proletariat itself was almost completely shut off from the proletariat of the other continents. Certain craft traditions still dominate the trend of thought of large sections of the Australian proletariat. Certain strata of the labour aristocracy still stand upon their prerogatives, and still largely hold a leading role in the labour movement. The slogan of a "White Australia" serves as the rallying cry of all reactionary elements in the labour movement, who are steeped in nationalist ideology, and who seek to isolate themselves in aristocratic arrogance away from the coloured workers and in general from foreign proletarians. The Australian trade union movement is exceptionally powerful (having no less than 700,000 organised workers in a country with a population of 5 1/2 millions). In some places (as for instance, in the Central Trades Council of Sydney) good, militant elements have already taken leadership of this trade union movement, but in general the trade unions, as well as the Labour Party, are still dominated by petty bourgeois minded, craft narrowed elements who are integrated with the bourgeoisie. Australia was the first country to have a labour government, and even today there are five States in Australia being run by such governments. But the history of all these "labour" governments, without exception, has proven that they never represented the real interests of the proletariat, that they showed themselves the best defenders of capitalist private property and of bourgeois society.

Against this false "labour" government the CP of Australia must set the slogan of the true, the real Labour Government which will lead a relentless class struggle against the bourgeoisie and will free the proletariat from the yoke of capitalism.

Under these difficult conditions the Communist Party of Australia was founded, and from that day to this it has had to wage a desperate struggle for its very existence. The Party is still a small organisation and has been able to find connections with the broad mass in only a few localities. The emergency laws, the persecution on the part of the Government, the expulsion of the Communists from the Labour Party, and the lack of success of the Communists in the last elections have aroused an attitude in some leading comrades that endangers the continued existence of the Party. Ex-comrade Baracchi even went so far as to propose, in Sydney, the formal dissolution of the Party and the institution of a "commission of liquidators". It is to the credit of the Australian Communists that this liquidatory proposal did not receive the support of even a single comrade. The case of Baracchi and a few of his predecessors must, however, serve as a lesson to the Party. Although the Party is small and weak, and without sufficient ideological resources, its first and chief task must be the ideological and organisational assertion of the Party. Such liquidatory incidents must serve as the basis of a thorough-going Communist ideological campaign, which on the one hand indicates the necessity to the workers of the historical mission of the Communist Party, and on the other hand, the organizational anchoring of the Party by means of a recruiting campaign in the trade unions and in the most important towns.

The membership of our Australian brother Party comprises trade unionists throughout. Grim patience in the trade union detail work is one of the most important virtues of the Australian Communists. In some places the workers already see that the Communists are their best champions also in the day to day questions—the history of the great seamen's strike showed clearly the valour of the Communists and the treachery of the reformists—but the next task of the Party must consist in crystallising also organizationally the trust of the Left militant organized workers. A minority movement of the Left wing workers can and should be organized under the participation and aid of the Communist Party.

It would be wrong if the Communists were to forego their right to belong to the Labour Party merely because the reformist leaders have expelled the Communists from it. It is the duty of the Communists to be present everywhere that workers are organized. We cannot therefore agree with the conception expressed in several articles in the *Workers Weekly*, according to which the Labour Party was not really an important organ of the workers and never really represented an essential avenue between the Communists and the workers. The very fact of the exclusion itself should convince the Communists of the importance of belonging to it. The reformists want to drive us out of the Labour Party—therefore the Communists must stick with redoubled energy to the very centre of the working masses in the Labour party. The Australian comrades should not forget the advice of Comrade Lenin to the British Communists on the question of joining the Labour Party. The Australian Communists should also learn from the successes of the British Communists, which are due primarily to that correct Leninist united front tactic of affiliation and collaboration in the ranks of the trade unions and Labour party. The Communists can combat all betrayals of the so-called Labour Governments much better inside the Labour Party than when they permit themselves to be isolated from the working masses.

For these reasons alone it would be a mistake to cause a split in the Labour Party through the establishment of a "revolutionary Labour Party".

The Communist Party of Australia must combat with all its forces the ideology of the "White Australia". The slogan is not alone against the coloured workers and foreign-born proletarians, but it contradicts the true interests of the Australian working class itself. The slogan of the "White Australia" builds a bridge between the reformist leaders of the labour aristocracy and the nationalistic bourgeoisie. Under the banner of the "White Australia" Prime Minister Bruce beat down the seamen, conducted the anti-labour elections, and whipped through the "Crimes Bill" which menaces the freedom of the workers' organisations. It is one of the most important duties of the Communist Party of Australia to get a foothold not only among the masses of the native-born Australian proletarians, but also to champion the interests of the foreign-speaking element of the country. These tasks have thus far not been fulfilled with sufficient energy by the Party. In the future the Party should concentrate much more strongly on this battlefront.

The daily struggle for the economic interests of the proletariat must be in the centre of the Party's endeavours, yet it must not forget—as has happened in the past—its great historic mission: the combating of British imperialism. In its agitation and propaganda the Party should raise the question of the independence of Australia from the British Empire. Foreign capital—British and American—today dominates economically almost the whole industrial life of Australia. The foreign policy of the Australian Commonwealth is determined entirely in London by the British bourgeoisie. Membership in the British Empire signified the growing danger that Australia will be involved in all diplomatic intrigues and military undertakings of British imperialism.

The Communist Party of Australia can and will become a Communist Party in the true Leninist sense of the word, when it learns how to combine the fight for the everyday demands of the workers with the combating of the craft spirit of the Labour aristocracy, of the ideology of the "White Australia", and of British imperialism. In the interest of the future development of the Party it should be in closest possible connection with other brother Parties (especially with the Communist Parties of Great Britain, America, China, Japan and Indonesia), and with the Executive Committee of the Communist International.

Parallel with this political advice the Org. Dept., and the Agitprop Department of the CI have formulated suggestions for the organisational and the agitational-propaganda work of the Communist Party of Australia

With Communist greetings,
PRESIDIUM OF THE ECCI

Document 41

RGASPI 534–7–1. no date [late December 1926], J. Garden and J. Kavanagh: report of a debate: 'The present Central Committee has deviated from the Leninist path'. In Russian, typescript. (English version not located in CAAL, but this meeting was reported in the *Workers' Weekly* of 24 December 1926.) Trans. by KW.

At the Sixth Conference of the CPA, 25–28 December 1926, at which the previous 'Resolution on the Australian Question' was adopted, the recent expulsion of Jock Garden was confirmed. Garden had raised communists' ire by continuing his long flirtation with the Labor Council and the ALP, but matters came to a head when he was reported in the press in early December as denying he was a member of the CPA; he resigned a day later, and was formally expelled on 10 December. Shortly afterwards, Garden and Jack Kavanagh (CPA secretary) had the frank debate which is reported in the following notes. Apart from the invective, the debate reveals the confusion created by the application of the Comintern's 'united front' policy to the ALP.

Garden and Kavanagh on the Policies of the Communist Party tabSubject: 'The Present Central Committee has Deviated from the Leninist Path'

Comrade Garden voiced assertions of this kind at a packed meeting. Comrade Moxon was in the chair.

Garden began by stating that the party had departed from the true path, citing the Communist Manifesto, which sets forth the shared interests of the Communist Party and the working class, in addition to the difference between the international viewpoint of the former and the national viewpoint of the latter.

The speaker accused the Communist Party of fighting with other workers' parties and making no distinction between the leadership and the Party as a whole, which contradicts the spirit of the Communist Manifesto. The Communist Party occupies a wavering position, constantly promoting subjective conditions at the expense of objective ones.

The Central Committee had demanded that he refrain from expressing his personal opinions, as all his statements were regarded as official party statements. The speaker had complied with this instruction, and was now being criticized for staying in the background.

Contrary to the speaker's wishes, the Central Committee had declared *The Labor Daily* a scabs' paper and singled it out as a target.

After this, the decision was amended and the party evinced no reaction to the party member who spoke against it.

Two party members then criticized him in the Council over a matter about which he knew nothing at all. The Central Committee did not react. This was a deviation from Leninism.

He had drawn up the theses, upholding the idea of a new industrial (workers') party, but the theses had not been printed. Precisely because there had been no discussion of this important issue, the party had turned into a sect.

The Central Committee did not see in the new line of the Australian Labor Party the broad prospects which Loughlan and Co. understood. The Central Committee was holding on tight to the word 'communist' and did not want to hear anything else.

If the party had followed the correct line, it would by now have joined the ALP. Instead the party had taken offence at one or two words. Purely because Lang had insulted us, we had moved to the left, to the detriment of the broad workers' movement.

The speaker refused to attack Lang, as the capitalist press might then claim that he was a hireling of the Nationalists.[8]

We have done nothing to defend him against the attacks by Cohen, using a forged photograph of him. Hence the speaker concludes that the Central Committee is guided less by the interests of the movement than a wish to have Garden's head on a platter.

Comrade Kavanagh replied to all these accusations. Many of these incidents had occurred while Comrade Garden had been the party's political secretary, so he should bear some of the responsibility for them.

With regard to the forged photograph, Cohen had stated more than once that this photograph of the Eastern Bureau of the International, taken in 1922, was genuine, and the Central Committee had tried to compel Garden to demonstrate to the workers that it was genuine, and that it was a matter of pride to be in the company of politically aware workers from other countries. Garden, however, had not shown Cohen the proof that it was genuine.[9]

When the speaker arrived in Australia, the party was completely absorbed in the election campaign. At that time the hunt for votes seemed more urgent than a revolutionary programme. All those candidates who had been with Comrade Garden them had left the revolutionary movement even earlier than he.

---

[8] The Nationalist Party was Australia's major non-Labor party during this period (joining with the smaller Country Party to form coalition governments); after some name changes it became in 1944 what is currently called the Liberal Party of Australia.

[9] When the Party was challenged over this photograph (which showed Australian communists, including Garden and Earsman, in the company of Asian delegates at the Fourth Comintern Congress), it claimed—wrongly and knowingly—that it was a forgery.

Rightist tendencies had arisen in all countries following the Russian revolution, when many revolutionaries who were not sufficiently staunch became despondent because they could not understand the partial stabilization of capitalism. These elements swung to the right and, in order to justify this, invented errors of one kind or another in the party line.

The trade union movement was rife with former radicals who had gradually become bureaucrats. These, and not the rank and file workers, were the very people who had lost any understanding of the aims of the working class.

We should not refuse to criticize the ALP merely because of various palliative legislative measures. Any capitalist party in an advanced country adopts laws of this kind, for example America and Germany. They are becoming an economic necessity. The federal trade unions struck for six weeks and gave up the fight with the loss of four hours' pay. The principle of the forty-four hour week was not acknowledged.

Comrade Kavanagh then declared that the Labor Council, which had not provided guidance in the struggle against the danger of arbitration in connection with the Piddington base rates, showed an unhealthy interest in arbitration even among the leadership. In conclusion, the speaker said that, whatever the ideological errors of the members, Comrade Garden, as a prominent member of the leadership, bears equal responsibility for them.

Comrade Garden (15 minutes)

The main issue before the present session was the fact that the leaders of the movement had given directional campaign guidelines for the struggle for the forty-four-hour working week, but in many cases the masses had refused to abide by these.

He had taken the initiative in connection with the Piddington declaration. A conference of secretaries had been convened and an appropriate question addressed to the government, while his opponent was sitting in his office writing little articles...

The speaker chastised the League of Trade Union Propaganda for its revolutionary nature and for its opposition to the founding of a new workers' party, at a time when active elements were indignant at the behaviour of the Queensland Labor Party.[10] The session ended with critical comments by *The Workers' Weekly*, which had exposed a recent squabble among the waterfront workers' union leadership. We should have recommended that the seamen support the waterfront workers.

---

[10] These comments reflect a move in 1926 by the parliamentary Labor Party against its industrial wing, which led to threats of a breakaway Labor party. Garden supported this move; the executive of the CPA under the leadership of Kavanagh did not.

Comrade Kavanagh (15 minutes)

The speaker was critical of the leaders of the aforementioned struggle. Their tactics had driven the active union of seamen to the arbitration courts.

Comrade Kavanagh rejects the claim that the party's shift to the left was the cause of a fall in membership.

At present we are stronger than ever before, stronger not only because of our numbers, but because we have now shed the reformist elements which had burdened our ranks.

The speaker spoke in favour of the activities of the League of Trade Union Propaganda, which had to uphold a revolutionary standpoint if it was to fulfil its task and mobilize the active elements of the union movement.

As for Garden's charge that he had supposedly been pushed into the background, Kavanagh set forth the story of the 'Young incident', when, according to the press, Garden had denied being a member of the Communist Party.

The Central Committee had demanded that Garden retract his words and declare that he was a party member. He had been expelled from the party for refusing to do so. This proves that Garden had excluded himself by his own actions.

Concluding Remarks

Comrade Garden again repeated his charges, castigating *The Workers' Weekly* for its uncompromising line. His opponent had stated that the workers had allegedly lost the ability to fight; this was untrue, as the workers had always been prepared to fight. The speaker protested that the Central Committee had held a knife to his throat and some CC members had 'picked on him'. The Council would now move forward because he, Garden, could freely uphold a genuine fighting policy.

Comrade Kavanagh concluded the debate by pointing out that it was incorrect to claim that the Communist Party had 'undermined' Garden, who had received no instructions from the Central Committee in all the time that the speaker had been in Australia.

The speaker was certainly not saying that the workers had lost the ability to fight. He was saying that they had lost the ability to wage an open and direct struggle against the employers. Instead their leaders had forced them to squander their resources on useless court cases. The active elements should exploit the Piddington decision to campaign against arbitration.

The majority of union officials had encouraged the legal struggle. The secretary of the stonemasons' union had been the only notable exception. This nightmare must be dispelled, in order that the workers can be filled with the genuine fighting spirit which will help them achieve their final objective—liberation.

Document 42

RGASPI 495–94–33. 8 Feb 1927, Wright: letter: To Secretariat ECCI. Typescript.

This brief covering letter confirms the sequence of events already suggested by the documents above, but it adds a little more to our understanding of the difficulties of communication between Australia and Moscow. The CPA is reporting to the Comintern for the first time in a year; Moscow seems to have promised to support financially one organizer for the Party (see Document 38, above), but no money has arrived; it seems to have taken seven months for a particular letter on agitation and propaganda matters to reach Sydney from Moscow.

395 Sussex Street
Sydney
8th. Feb. 1927

To the Secretariat
ECCI

Comrades,

We are enclosing herewith our first Report since the departure for Moscow of our Delegate Comrade Ross in February 1926.

Comrade Ross reported to you regarding the organisational difficulties of our Party. We welcomed your decision on the matter of our inability to maintain even one paid official but we regret to report that to date we have received no further information on the matter.

In September 1926 we received a copy of the resolution on the Australian Question carried at the Plenum of the ECCI during Comrade Ross's visit.

The letter of instruction from the Agit-prop Dept dated 16th. April 1926, we received in November. Both were discussed together with the report of Comrade Ross given at our sixth Annual Conference held December 25th–28th 1926.

With Communist Greetings
Wright
General Secretary

Document 43

RGASPI 495–94–43. no date [1927?], J. Howie, Secretary CPA: letter: to Murphy, Secretary ECCI. Typescript.

This letter indicates, and is to some extent a cry of protest against, the isolation from Comintern activities and opportunities felt by the CPA.

J.T. Murphy,
Secretary, ECCI

Dear Comrade,

We have been privileged to receive a copy of your circular of June 14, re the enrolment of new students in the International Lenin Courses.

This circular we have read with great interest. We are glad to be able to state that there are several members of our Party whom we would consider eminently suitable for selection as students and we realise that our Party could receive no better assistance than by the attendance of one or two of our members at such courses.

This would do much to remedy our isolation and our lack of trained leaders and to help us play correctly our very difficult part in a colony of the British Empire on the Pacific Ocean.

We would have preferred to have learned of these courses before, but this is our first intimation that they are to be held.

It appears that this copy, which is addressed to the South African Party, was not intended to reach us and came only in error. Further, our Party is not shown as having any quota of new student enrolments. It seems to be unique in this respect; two students, we note, are allotted each to Canada and South Africa.

We would welcome a straight answer to the question, Do you consider our Party to be a part of the International? We quite realise that the revolutionary development of Australia will follow that of Europe and the East, and that the main attention of the Comintern must be directed to the Imperialist and the strictly colonial countries. But are our efforts never to meet with anything but complete indifference?

When, last year, our delegate visited you, he went to great trouble to provide you with all possible information on the situation in Australia. He was assured that now, at least, assistance would be given us. But nothing has come from you; even theses which he was assured would follow immediately have not yet turned up.

And now we find that we are to have no share in the *facilities* for training Communist leaders!

Can we be expected to show results worthy of a Communist Party?

In this connection we would also ask you: Are you in communication with J.S. Garden, who was expelled from the Party a year ago? He asserts that he *is* still in receipt of letters from you, and that you recognise him and *not* our Party as your representative. As you were notified of his expulsion and of the reasons, we would dismiss these assertions as palpably absurd did we not know for a fact that bodies subordinate to the Comintern are regularly in communication with him, failing to even supply our Party *with* copies of the correspondence. If his assertions are true, you are helping to consolidate an individual who is bitterly anti-Party and who is attempting to build up an allegedly militant organisation owing allegiance to himself alone and trailing at the heels of *reformist* politicians.

We are hoping that the present visit of our representative may cause you to look on the needs of our Party in a new light and to treat us with some such consideration as might be expected by a section of the Communist International.

With Communist greetings,
J. Howie
Secretary, CPA

Document 44

RGASPI 495–94–33. 29 August 1927, Organisation Department of the ECCI: letter: To CC of CPA. Typescript.

This letter registers that Tom Wright, secretary of the CPA, was in Moscow at the time to report on the progress of the Party to the ECCI. It is further evidence of the difficulties of communication between Moscow and Australia; there seems to have been little information from Australia—and no personal contact—since the visit of Ross in April 1926. Wright's visit would culminate in the ECCI's resolution, in Document 45, below, sometimes described as the 'October Resolution'.

Moscow, August 29, 1927
To the CC of the CP of Australia

Dear Comrades,

We have learned from your secretary that the letter we sent you in May 1926 concerning the organisational tasks of the CP of Australia unfortunately has not reached you. We on our part, have likewise received nothing from you during the 14 months which have passed since your representative made his report here. Please do your utmost to improve the connection with the ECCI so that we may have a more lively exchange of opinion on the fundamental questions of the movement, which is so necessary at this time. We are pleased to be able to say that according to the report of your secretary, the CPA has achieved considerable results in its organisational work during the past year. But at the same time it is certainly clear that the organisational work of the CPA remains very weak and this of course is one of the greatest obstacles in the way of the further development of the Party.

The basic defect in the organisational work of the CPA is that it does not concentrate its work on the factories, but on the territorial organisations like the Labour Party and like all such socialist parties. It has not yet commenced the work to reorganise itself on a factory nucleus basis. Therefore the Org. Department of the ECCI thinks that it is the most important organisational task of the CPA in the immediate future to entirely break with those old methods of work and to commence energetically the building up of the party on the factory group basis.

One cannot, of course, expect to build up a perfect Party apparatus as long as the CPA is so weak numerically. Therefore the numerical growth of the CPA is the most important question of its organisation work in the immediate future. However, it will be impossible to carry on effective recruiting work if the members of the Party continue to be scattered singly in enterprises and settlements.

The report placed before us on the condition of local organisations shows that in a number of states the local provincial organisations of the CPA are not yet fully organised and that the CC has to keep up direct connections with individual comrades scattered in various parts of these states. This deflects the CC from control over general Party work, scatters its forces and makes it impossible in such states to undertake any organised political campaigns. The CC should first of all set itself the task of coordinating the action of all Party members (even if there be only 3–5) in towns and other populated centres. Where there are ten or more *members* a local organisation should be set up with organiser, Sec. and Committee with departments, in relation to *size of* membership.

Another essential organisational premise for the successful reorganisation of the Party on a factory nucleus basis is the formation of capable district Party committees, thereby releasing the CC from the direct charge over individual comrades and the lower Party organisations. Considerable work in this direction will also have to be done by the CPA. As such district organisation develops the *higher* Party organisations should also be developed and consolidated—they should place the whole of the state and all its members under control of an elective state Party Committee. We enclose herewith model statutes of a Communist Party as elaborated by the 2nd International Org. Conference, which can serve you as a guide in the building up of the Party structure. Please note that in connection with the formation of a Party organisation, one should follow the rule that the structure of the Party should correspond with the existing administrative-political boundaries of the country, i.e., that every administrative-political unit should correspond with the Party organisation working within its precincts.

The Org. Department of the ECCI suggests that the work for the consolidation and development of factory nuclei should be carried on *through the* local organisations. In order with their help to concentrate all availing [sic] forces in the big enterprises of the most important branches of industry.

Work for the reorganisation of the CPA on a factory nucleus basis should consist above all in energetic work for the recruitment of new members. This recruitment should not be in the nature of a casual campaign but should be carried on continuously and systematically. The Party should concentrate all available forces on the capture of big enterprises in the most important branches of industry. *For a very large and important factory the question of party members leaving a place employing a few hands to work in them should be considered.* It should carry on this work with maximum energy and steadfastness, verifying after every non-success the methods of work in order to return to the attack with renewed strength. In order to ensure the success of recruiting work it should be directed first of all towards those branches of industry and those enterprises where it has been noticed that the workers are best prepared to struggle against the existing state of affairs. The party should take upon itself the initiative to formulate demands, to organise for struggle, gaining a leading role in the movement by able and consistent guidance and by criticism of the reformists. In such cases workers learn their lesson by the concrete experience of everyday life and realise why it is essential for them to follow the lead of the Community party. Party organisations, in their turn, should watch very attentively the conduct of every worker during the campaign. All those who show signs of revolutionary class spirit should be immediately approached for the purpose of eventually drawing them into the Party. Those in sympathy with the Communist Party should not be organised separately. They should be drawn into the Left trade union movement, and it is also of the utmost importance to draw them cautiously but systematically into everyday Party work, inviting them to district Party meetings, entrusting them with definite work, etc. In regard to sympathisers one should see to it that they should not be expected to do as much as Party members. Sympathisers should not be required to agree completely with the Communist programme and tactics: they can differ from the Party on one point or another. For such differences of opinion sympathisers should certainly not be repulsed as an alien element—on the contrary the Party should do its utmost to reeducate them in a comradely way into useful Party members. Factory newspapers are a great help to the Party in regard to its growth and consolidation. We enclose a special letter on the importance of factory newspapers and we suggest that you should begin to publish them without delay. You should also make the fullest possible use of the directions of the 2nd Org. Conference re the organisation of so-called concentration groups, i.e.

temporary nuclei formed of scattered Party workers employed in adjoining enterprises. The task of these groups or temporary nuclei consists in concentrating the efforts of such scattered Party workers in one enterprise in order to organise there an effective factory nucleus.

When the factory nucleus has been formed the local Party committee should guarantee it a correct organisation of its entire work, should continuously watch its further development, helping and instructing it, BUT AT THE SAME TIME IT SHOULD ENSURE MAXIMUM INITIATIVE AND SELF-ACTIVITY TO THE FACTORY NUCLEUS.

Side by side with the factory nuclei the Party should also form street nuclei, in accordance with the decisions of the 2nd Org. Conference, for the benefit of Party members who cannot be organised into factory nuclei work.

The CPA cannot develop into a mass political Party unless it strengthens its work in the mass organisations, first and foremost in the Labour Party and in the trade unions. The CPA should energetically oppose the idea that it should disassociate itself from the Labour Party, as advocated, to judge by the report of your secretary, by some comrades. In view of the trade unions' collective membership in the Labour Party, leaving the latter would be tantamount to leaving the trade unions; this would mean the complete isolation of the party from the masses. For our organisational consolidation in the Labour Party and in the Trade Unions, some of the most essential tasks of the CPA are: 1) Formation of fractions in accordance with the decisions of the 2nd Org. Conference and the 7th Plenum of the ECCI, [and] guarantee of correct and regular control over these fractions by the competent Party committees; 2) Help in the matter of better organisation and consolidation of the Left wing in the Labour Party and trade unions, efforts to secure a leading role for the Party in this Left movement through our practical work; 3) Intensive practical work in the trade unions and the Labour Party on all questions affecting the everyday interests of the working class, setting a personal example of utmost devotion to this task.

In conclusion, the Org. Department of the ECCI deems it necessary to deal with the question of the structure of the CC. The Org. Department thinks that in view of the numerical weakness of the CPA it is sufficient to have in the CC a presidium or secretariat as a working organ functioning in the intervals between the Plenums of the CC. You should also proceed to form the basic departments—organisational, agitational-propagandist, trade union, and for work among women. At first you should build up these departments in the form of commissions headed by a member of the CC and consisting of 3 to 5 comrades selected among the best workers in the local Party organisations, these comrades to be given certain tasks to fill. Local Party committees should be constructed in the same manner.

The party already has commenced the organisation of Party members inside the trade union. The mistake made on the field is that you have aimed to reorganise the party on this basis. The present industrial groupings, as basic units should be eradicated in place of the forementioned factory basis. The organisation of trade union fractions is essential not only as the best form of working inside the trade union but also as a necessary accompaniment for the successful development of factory activity. (In the decision of the 2nd Org. Conference will be found much detail on the question.)

The tendency to organisation of the foreign speaking members into language groups should be combatted. All party members must belong to their street or factory nuclei. This does not preclude the special work that should be conducted among foreign speaking workers.

For work among Party members and among non-Party elements who do not know the English language, commissions should be formed as necessity arises in the local organisations for work among the respective nationalities. *Through these commissions, the party should control the work among the foreign element,* playing the role of auxiliary organs of an agitational-propagandist character. If possible, one of the committee members should be at the head of the commission and 3 to 5 of the Party members of the respective nationality, appointed by the Party committee, should form part of the commission.

In addition to such committees of the Party we propose basing ourselves upon the experience of the Workers' Communist Party of America, that non-Party language clubs should be organised. In these clubs, the main task of which should be work among the proletarian masses, Communist fractions should be formed under the guidance of the local Party Committee. It would be well to organise in these clubs courses and circles for the study of the English language. Teaching English to comrades who have no command over it should be one of the duties of all Party members.

The *Workers Life* should be used as an instrument for the better organisation of the party: workers' factory letters; reports of our factory activity showing successes etc.; letters demonstrating how certain difficulties have been overcome, etc. etc.

The CPA should take up as a separate question of Org. work, the establishment of connections with the ECCI and also with English speaking Communist Parties and the Pacific countries.

Please send us regularly all material descriptive of the internal life of the CPA.

With Communist greetings

Document 45

RGASPI 495–94–31. 12 October 1927, ECCI: resolution: Resolution on the tasks of the Communist Party of Australia (manuscript marking 'Urgent'). In English, Russian, French and German copies; typescript.

This document is the political culmination of Tom Wright's 1927 visit to the Soviet Union, the so-called 'October Resolution'. It claims that the CPA has significant political influence, but must recruit more members. It sees opportunities in Australia turning away from economic isolation and into foreign markets, which will inevitably lead to a worsening of workers' conditions. The CPA must strengthen its work in the trade unions, assert its independence, work for the separation of Australia from British imperialism and oppose the 'White Australia' policy. As for the recommendations on the CPA's work in the trade unions and the ALP, matters of detail are avoided.

RESOLUTION ON THE TASKS OF THE COMMUNIST PARTY OF AUSTRALIA

The tasks of the CP of Australia in the present stage of development in the class struggle are determined on the one hand by the changes in the economics of Australia and on the other hand by the policy of British imperialism which is preparing to utilise Australia as one of the main bases in the coming war for supremacy in the basin of the Pacific.

As a result of an abnormally rapid industrialisation process, Australia has reached today a stage in its economic development when it can no longer remain isolated and reap the fruits of such isolation, but is compelled to find outside markets for its goods. The growth of Australian export is first and foremost the result of the economic expansion of Australia. An impetus is also given to it by the policy of the ruling classes of Australia who are doing their utmost to overcome the disproportion between import and export by increasing the export of raw material as well as of manufactured goods.

Struggle on and for foreign markets radically changes the whole policy of the Australian bourgeoisie.

With the help of the natural wealth of the country on the one hand and of protective tariffs which saved it from foreign competition on the other hand, the Australian bourgeoisie was a long time able to keep the existence minimum of the Australian workers at a comparatively high level. This high existence minimum was the foundation of the development of Australian reformism which came into being and assumed a definite form a considerable time before the world war. The so-called Australian Labour Party began to carry out the functions of the bourgeois Government considerably sooner than the "Socialist" Parties of continental Europe and the Labour Party of Great Britain. At the same time, there was formed in Australia a special apparatus of "industrial peace" in the shape of arbitration chambers, which functioned satisfactorily for a comparatively long period.[11]

The result of the struggle for foreign markets is determination on the part of the Australian bourgeoisie to lower the cost of production at the expense of workers' interests. The offensive against labour conditions, announced by the Australian Government at the end of last year, has practically begun.

Apart from this offensive directed against wages of *the* Australian workers, the ever growing cost of living, which is to a great extent the result of big payments for foreign loans, and first and foremost in connection with the debt to Great Britain as well as the 15% additions to prices of British goods, which benefit by so-called preferential tariffs in regard to Australia, all this combined affects adversely the real wage of all Australian proletarians. The result of the gradual worsening of the conditions of Australian workers and of the policy of the ruling classes directed towards the reduction of their existence minimum is: intensification and growing acuteness of the class struggle.

For a long time, the Australian bourgeoisie showed tolerance to the "Labour Party"[12] in the role of bourgeois government. But this attitude to the question of forms of government in Australia has undergone a change owing to the programme of offensive decided upon by the ruling classes. On the one hand, the bourgeoisie is endeavouring to weaken the autonomy of the individual States, and on the other hand, it is carrying on at present a struggle for the establishment of a strong and avowedly bourgeois government capable of carrying out energetically the programme of offensive against the conditions of labour of Australian workers. At the same time, the *frankly reactionary part of the* Australian bourgeoisie is endeavouring to get rid of the Arbitration Chambers regardless of the fact that as a rule these chambers support the capitalists in conflicts between labour and capital. The Australian bourgeoisie is endeavouring to bring the whole government apparatus into harmony with its new aspirations.

The offensive of the Australian bourgeoisie against the workers' existence minimum is in keeping with its more precise orientation in the sphere of foreign politics. At the last imperial conference, the representatives of Australia declared: "that Australia is vitally interested in keeping the territory in New Guinea in its hand and in not allowing it on any account whatever to be transferred to some foreign power."

Australian is *now* taking an active part in the fortification of Singapore, which is to enable Great Britain to rapidly move Australian troops to India in the event of a revolutionary movement breaking out there, and which at the same time means a gradual increase of the Australian war budget. According to the *Times*

---

[11] The double quotation marks in this paragraph were inserted by hand.
[12] The double quotation marks were inserted by hand.

of July 6, 1927, "expenditure for the defence of Australia amounts now to £3,000,000 and the Premier Bruce is pleased to be able to say that Australian public opinion is in favour of increased expenditure in this direction." Thus, the ruling classes of Australia are participating openly and consciously in the carrying out of the plans of British imperialism in the basin of the Pacific.

This capitalist offensive in Australia is accompanied by definite *changes of mood in the* workers' ranks. This unification takes the form of strikes, of a negative attitude to the Arbitration Chambers, of an endeavour to coordinate the hitherto disunited trade unions and finally, of conflicts between trade unions and the Labour Party which express and reflect the discontent of the masses in regard to the open defence of the interest of the bourgeoisie on the part of so-called labour governments.

In view of this growing acuteness of the class struggle, the Communist Party must make struggle against the capitalist offensive the point of departure of the campaign for the mobilisation and welding together of big sections of the proletariat.

For this purpose, the CP of Australia must first of all strengthen its work in the trade unions. The latter are controlled either by avowed reactionary reformists or by so-called Left leaders who do lip *service* to the moods of the working masses and in reality pursue the policy of agreement with employers.

The trade unions of Australia are confronted now with new tasks. For a long time their functions were those of insurance companies and of "defence" of the interests of their members before the Arbitration Chambers. Class struggle in Australia is entering upon a new stage. Trade unions will be compelled to carry out functions of organs of class struggle.[13] The Communist Party can and must play an active role in regard to the complete reorganisation of the trade unions by continually and systematically exposing the reactionary reformist leaders and by explaining to the masses the new tasks *imposed* on trade unions in connection with the capitalist offensive.

Up to quite recently, trade unions played on the one hand the role of rate and tax payers for the Labour Party and on the other hand of permanently functioning election apparatuses. The leaders of the Labour Party, most of them ministers and ex-ministers of various Australian governments have succeeded in reducing to a minimum *the* influence *of the trade unions* on the policy of the "Labour"[14] Party and the so-called Labour governments. The Communist Party is in duty bound to carry out a big campaign with the trade unions for a decisive struggle against the leaders of the Labour Party.

---

[13] This sentence appears to have been struck out by a faint manuscript line.
[14] The double quotation marks were inserted by hand.

The basic nucleus of the Labour Party bureaucracy has become indissolubly connected with the Australian bourgeoisie. The so-called Australian Labour Party cannot become a genuine Labour party unless big sections of workers and first and foremost members of trade unions do their utmost to purge the Labour Party of ministers, ex-ministers and all other officials who while sailing under the colours of the Labour Party have learned to defend more or less skillfully the interests of the Australian bourgeoisie. It is precisely for these reasons that the Australian CP must give full support to the timid attempts of individual trade unions to increase their influence on the Labour Party, exposing at the same time *those* trade union bureaucrats who profiting by the dissatisfaction of Australian workers with the Labour Party would like to occupy cushy posts in the apparatus of that Party. Neutrality in the struggle of trade unions versus Labour Party *adds* grist to the mill of the avowed social-imperialists at the head of the Labour Party who carry out the policy of the bourgeoisie within the working class.

It goes without saying that struggle against the capitalist offensive can [not] rest content with work in trade unions. Acting as an independent political Party, the CP must do its utmost to increase and extend its influence on the masses and to consolidate and give a definite form to the influence it already possesses by welding together and coordinating the workers for struggle against the avowedly bourgeois federal government as well as against the so-called Labour governments in the individual states.

Preparations for the forthcoming election campaign are carried on by the Australian bourgeoisie on the basis of the establishment of a strong bourgeois power. Regardless of the results of the campaign a majority in the Australian Senate is guaranteed to the bourgeois national party. It has also a splendid chance of retaining its power in the federal Australian Parliament and to gain power in those states where the so-called Labour Party has managed to bring disorganisation and demoralisation into the ranks of the proletariat. The Communist Party must carry on its preparatory work for the forthcoming election campaign under the slogan of welding together workers not only against the national party, but also against its agents in the person of the so-called Labour party which, by remaining under the control of social-imperialists, is paving the way to the establishment of a government of capitalist offensive.

Struggle against the capitalist attack on the workers' existence minimum must be coupled with struggle against British imperialism as well as against the imperialist policy of the Australian bourgeoisie.

In regard to British imperialism, the Australian Communist Party must explain to the workers what price they pay for being part of the "Commonwealth of the British Empire". The Australian bourgeoisie in conjunction with the British bourgeoisie, compels Australian workers to add 15% to their cost of living for the benefit of British merchants, plus 27–28 million pounds sterling yearly interest to British and other *foreign* usurers. At the same time, Australian workers have their part of expenditure for defence which, according to the competent testimony of the Premier Bruce, will continue to increase. This defence expenditure is part of the preparation of *new* imperialist wars *against the USSR as well as against the Pacific Ocean basin for* which Australian workers will pay with their blood.

However, the CP of Australia cannot limit itself *to* exposing the role of British imperialism in Australia. It must carry on a decisive and energetic struggle for the ultimate separation of Australia from the British Empire. In this struggle the Communist Party must show up the half-hearted and insincere attitude of the Australian bourgeoisie and of its lieutenants in the person of the Australian reformists in regard to this question.

In the interests of successful struggle against British imperialism, the CP must get into as close contact as possible with New Zealand and other British colonies in the Pacific, and must do its utmost towards the establishment of close relations between the Australian Labour movement and first and foremost the trade unions of Australia and the labour organisations in other countries in the Pacific.

Struggle against British imperialism must on no account interfere with struggle against the imperialism of the Australian bourgeoisie. The CP must put up as energetic a fight against Australia's direct participation in the oppression of New Guinea and also against Australia's collaboration with British imperialism in its brutal policy in regard to China, India and all colonies and semi-colonies.

In the struggle against Australian imperialism, the Australian CP must pay special attention to the methods by which Australian reformists in the person of leaders of the so-called Labour Party and of the reformist bureaucrats in the trade unions are trying to disguise the imperialist policy of the Australian bourgeoisie. Social reformists pander to the petty bourgeois patriotism and prejudices of backward sections of workers and bring forward slogans against immigration in general and against the immigration of coloured workers in particular. Instead of endeavouring to draw the new arrivals into the trade unions for joint struggle against the capitalist offensive, reformists are practically helping the ruling classes to erect barriers between the various groups of exploited proletarians. The Australian Communist Party must put up an energetic and decisive fight for free immigration not only for white, but also for coloured workers and must initiate a campaign among the trade unions in favour of new arrivals being immediately admitted to the unions and drawn in to the common struggle against capitalist exploitation. Clear and definite struggle for freedom of immigration must in no way interfere with the struggle against immigration on the strength of mass contracts organised by the British and Australian governments and directed against the European as well as the Australian proletariat.

The CP is the only Party in Australia which can take the lead in the struggle of the working class against the capitalist offensive, against British imperialism and the militarist policy of the Australian bourgeoisie.

The proportional weight of the working class in Australia is very high: one and a half million out of a 6 million population, 814,000 being industrial workers. Trade unions exist in Australia already several decades and embrace up to 800,000 workers. Separatist and guild tendencies which exist in the Australian trade union movement and are fomented by reactionary reformist leaders can only be liquidated in the process of the class struggle which is now entering upon a new stage.

The CP of Australia has a series of very genuine achievements to its credit in regard to trade union work. It has been able to effect and utilise a veering to the Left among the masses, and to consolidate it in the decision of trade union congresses re despatch of delegation to the trade union congress in the Pacific, and re despatch of delegation to the USSR. It is also an incontestable fact that the establishment of an all-Australian trade union council is *considerably* due to Communist agitation for the establishment of one united trade union centre. The success already achieved is a guarantee of the further development of Communist work and of the increase of Communist influence, in the process of the mobilisation of the masses for struggle against the Australian bourgeoisie.

The Communist Party has also been able to have a successful campaign directed against British imperialism in connection with the brutal war against the Chinese Revolution. Further struggle against British imperialism which is becoming more and more openly bellicose and which is at present preparing not only for war for supremacy in the basin of the Pacific but also for a counter-revolutionary war against the first socialist state cannot be successful unless it be closely and indissolubly linked up with the struggle against the militarist policy of the Australian bourgeoisie and against its present offensive against the existence minimum of Australian workers.

The fundamental weakness of the Australian Communist Party is its numerical weakness. The organisation strength of the Australian CP lags far behind its political influence. To do justice to the complicated and urgent tasks which the development of the class struggle has placed before the Australian Communist Party, the latter must extend and strengthen its recruiting work not only in trade unions, but also directly in factories and other enterprises. Communists must recruit new members for the Party among their fellow workers at the bench. First and foremost the Party should see to it that workers genuinely in sympathy with it should not remain outside the Party, but be drawn into its ranks as the Party cannot do justice to the fundamental tasks with which it is now confronted without successful recruiting work. Success in this direction will be the criterion of the consolidation of the Party.

The Communist Party of Australia is in its composition a purely workers' party, and this is its main strength. Recruiting work must go hand in hand with the establishment of factory nuclei. Communist nuclei in factories and works will contribute to the establishment of factory and workshop committees, the need of which will be felt more and more as the capitalist offensive develops.

The recruiting campaign is one of the urgent and most important tasks of the Communist Party. At the same time the Party Congress will have to deal very seriously with the question of forms and methods for the coordination of all honest revolutionary elements in the trade union movement and in the working class who are fighting in their own fashion against the social-imperialists in the Labour Party and against the bureaucrats in the trade unions, but who do not join the ranks of the Communist Party. The CP of Australia must study very carefully the experience of brother parties in regard to the formation of mass proletarian organisations and particularly the work of the Communist Party of Great Britain in the minority trade union movement and in the Left wing of the Labour Party.

The Communist Party of Australia works preeminently among industrial workers. The Party press and the Party as a whole do not pay sufficient attention to rural workers and agricultural labourers particularly who, even prior to the capitalist offensive, were subjected to brutal exploitation. The Communist Party must take up in all seriousness work among agricultural labourers and must go thoroughly into the question of a clear programme in regard to all problems of class struggle in the agricultural sphere.

Difficult and complicated tasks are confronting the Australian CP and the ECCI is convinced that the forthcoming Party congress will do its utmost to point the way to the transformation of the young but active and energetic Party into a genuine mass Party.

Document 46

RGASPI 495–94–41. 30 January 1928, R.W. Robson: letter to Bob Stewart, a member of the ECCI (with covering letter of April 1928). Original: Robson letter, English, typescript; covering letter, Russian, typescript, trans. by KW.

This letter from the Comintern's agent to Australia, Robson, gives a rather dismissive view of the organisation and proceedings of the CPA's Seventh Annual Conference held from December 22 to 27, 1927. The Conference adopted the 'October Resolution' (Document 45, above), but was divided over questions of application of the line to the ALP. It would be remembered, however, as one of the last CPA conferences where opinions were expressed without fear of retribution. Robson would later report directly to the ECCI along with a delegation of Australians in April 1928.

Petrovsky to Heimo
7 April, 1928

Comrade Heimo,[15]

Herewith a letter from Robson, addressed to Stewart, containing a brief account of his work in Australia. I presume the contents of this letter should be communicated to the members of the PS.[16]

D. Petrovsky

Jan. 30/28

Dear Bob,

I am booked to return on Feb. 18th and expect to arrive in London March 29th.

There has been much difficulty in booking a cheap return as the cheaper berths are booked some time in advance. However, although I would have preferred to get back sooner, I have not overstayed my limit.

It is not possible for me to give anything like a comprehensive report of my work in a letter such as this, particularly as I will be less than three weeks behind your receipt of it.

I met at first some difficulties owing to there being no full time official in the Australian Party, not even a General Secretary.

The EC was divided into two groups and had prepared nothing for the Congress which was due two or three days after my arrival. I was even doubtful whether the CC would meet before the Congress. This it did. I scoured round looking up members and insisting on this, on the night before the Congress, but with an ordinary routine agenda. Only then did I find that no statement of any kind had been considered by the CEC for the Congress, excepting one by the PB[17] which was not submitted to the CC and which was stated to be "uncontroversial".

I had to insist that the Congress must not tie our hands with resolutions about work in the unions or LP[18]—as there was strong probability of "leftist" decisions being reached—as the CEC was bitterly divided on this, as was the Party, and yet no analysis had been prepared. The CC sectarian majority obviously wished the Congress to register decisions about non-party work.

---

[15] Mauno Heimo (1896–1937) was a Finnish communist; he and his wife were arrested and executed in Russia in 1937.
[16] The reference is not immediately apparent; it may mean 'Political Secretariat'.
[17] Political Bureau
[18] Labor Party

The Congress lasted a week and was almost entirely taken up with trivial organisational matters. I was unable to stay right through as on the first day I was publicly announced by the chairman but I got almost verbatim reports. I judged it advisable to address the Congress for two reasons:

1. The extreme "isolation" manifested.
2. The seriousness of the need for mass-work and lack of full understanding of it.

Since the Congress I have worked closely with the new CEC and am of opinion that the contact will be one of very great benefit in the future. The first essential in my view was to have an analysis of the Australian situation drafted and thoroughly discussed. This has been done; from this basis it was easier to argue tasks and methods and this latter is being considered now.

It is a pity someone could not be here for a longer period as my brief visit has evidently proved very useful, but twelve months work would have consolidated a better condition of things.

Frat.

R.W.R.

Document 47

RGASPI 495–94–41. April 1928, Robson: report. Typescript.

This is one of the three reports on Australia considered by the Political Secretariat of the ECCI in April 1928. Robson, who had been in Australia briefly toward the end of 1927, concentrates in this report on the organizational weaknesses of the CPA.

[...]

The ALP is a federal body representing TUs and individual *members* organise*d* on an elect*oral* basis. Its policy is thoroughly nationalist and "white Australian". In many respects the ALP has served the interests of the growing manufacturing bourgeoisie directly, as on the question of high tariffs, State provision of services, such as railways, industrial arbitration, coercion of strikers, etc. etc.

In Queensland there has been a continuity of Labour Government for more than 12 years and in that period it has conducted itself exactly as an orthodox bourgeois party would have done. The most recent example of its attitude to the workers being that of the South Johnston sugar strike, when following the "blacking" of scab sugar by the Railway Union the Labour Government threatened a lockout of the union membership and assisted actively to break the sugar workers' strike.

This experience has left behind among the Queensland workers a strong feeling of bitterness and disillusionment—but mainly against the Labour government politicians—not particularly the ALP. Communist Party activity has not been great, but the efforts of the Party to help the workers, and the Party campaign after the strike met with an excellent response.

The Party has good prospects in Queensland and the CEC should pay considerably more attention to the situation in that State.

In New South Wales the ALP is split. On the one hand is a faction led by Lang, Willis and Garden and on the other are AWU officials. Last year the former faction secured control of the State LP machinery altering the rules so as to kill the previous dominance of the AWU. The Lang-Garden crew have been called "Reds" by the other faction with the intention of weakening their support among the workers, but actually, although the alteration of the rules allows for better representation of the TUs [and] destroys the dominance of the Electoral Leagues (Indir. members and petty-bourgeoisie), the change of rules was made as the only way to oust the clique in control. Differences of policy have played practically no part in the struggle, and the new rules specifically lay down that Communists may not be members of the LP or delegates from their union to ALP bodies.

Since the split two LP conferences have been held in NSW under the leadership of Lang & Co. The first was representative of the rural areas in NSW and was held at Young early in February. This conference was so reactionary that there was no evidence of working-class politics to be found in its proceedings and the Party was unable to make its voice heard.

A week or two later a conference of the urban section of the State LP was held in Sydney.

At this conference there were present as delegates two Communists. Under the new rules, however, no communist could act as a delegate. The Party issued a statement above the names of the two comrades to the other delegates, and the capitalist press gave publicity to same, but although non-Party militants put up a good fight on the issue, they were defeated on the vote which went 30% in favour of the Party.

The Party's weakness in this connection has resulted from the complete lack of activity in connection with the Labour Party. Nothing whatever had been done to secure as many Party members as delegates to the conferences as possible. Although the Party organs campaign against the anti-Communist attitude of the ALP leaders, no activity existed in the Party to mobilise support against these leaders except in Lithgow.

The Party centre has been divided on the question of the Party's attitude and policy towards the ALP for a considerable time and has therefore done nothing at all.

[…]

THE CP OF AUSTRALIA.

The Party has about 450–500 members. These are mainly placed in Sydney (110), Melbourne (32), N. Queensland groups (200) Brisbane (30) and Lithgow NSW (32).

It will thus be understood that the Party is scattered throughout only the three eastern States in the form of concentrated groups. Nearly half of this entire membership is newly joined. There exists a branch form of local organisation with practically no activity outside paper selling and agitation. Even these are poor. The *WW* circulation is 4,500 and agitational work is weak.

The Central Committee is drawn from the Sydney membership and appears to have largely been interested in NSW and Sydney matters, the questions affecting other states being neglected.

This has acted detrimentally to the growth of the Party in other States.

Central organisation was practically non-existent when I arrived in Sydney, about the middle of December [1927], and although steps were being taken to improve matters, this question will continue to need attention.

The annual Party Congress opened on Dec. 24 and lasted for 5–6 days. No material had been issued to the Party groups on the Congress, but CEC report was distributed among the delegates. The resolutions, of which there were a large number, sent in from local groups, dealt almost entirely with petty organisational matters.

There was no full time Party official in existence when I reached Sydney, three or four days before the Congress opened. Comrade Wright (General Secretary) had not returned from Moscow and arrived on the eve of the Congress, attending the Central Committee held on the 23rd of December.

Here I found that very little had been done to prepare the Congress. There had been no attempt to consider giving the Congress a lead from the CEC on even the most urgent questions facing the Party, but it was insisted that the Congress would decide definitely what policy the Party would pursue in the ALP.

This without any lead whatever from the CE or any section of it.

It was with difficulty that I got the CE to consent to allow Congress to discuss the question fully and refer the matter for immediate and definite decision to the new CE.

I pointed out that we (the CEC) had no time to go exhaustively into such an important and vital issue in the midst of the Congress itself and that the CI draft resolution just to hand would have to be carefully considered in connection with the whole question of Party policy.

As the CE itself could only listen to a part of the Comintern resolution being read to the meeting, and could not seriously discuss its contents, I suggested (owing to the bitter feeling existing among leading members) that it would be wisest for Com. Wright to read the second half of the CI draft to the Congress during his report on his visit to Moscow, explaining the decision of the CEC, i.e., that the whole question of policy for the ALP be considered immediately by the new CEC. To this recommendation the Congress agreed, after a lengthy discussion on the ALP.[19]

At the close of the first session the Chairman introduced a fraternal delegate from New Zealand and then surprised me by introducing me also. As I had decided to address the Congress, I was of opinion that my presence would attract police enquiries, I did so in the second session and thereafter kept away from the Congress. I arranged meetings with the various delegations however, and met the North Queensland comrades, the Lithgow (coalfield) and Melbourne delegates.

My impression from conversations with all these delegations was that there was considerable dissatisfaction with the Party's lack of programs, great anxiety to work better. No real Party training had ever been instituted or developed, and no real Party leadership existed at the centre.

Politically and organisationally the Party was and remains extremely weak and inexperienced. The Congress proceedings were of trivial character according to the verbatim report. This was very bulky and I was compelled to get rid of the copy I was bringing to England when the police held me up at Southampton.

My address to the Congress dealt briefly with the work of the CI and the chief Parties, and more fully with the mass work of the CPGB, drawing analogies and making suggestions wherever possible.

After the Congress I met the new CE and it was decided to place the centre organisation on a better basis. Subsequently a presidium of five was appointed in place of a Polit and Org-bureau. Following this, an Agitprop, Industrial and Org Department was set up and given certain preliminary organisational tasks.

I was of opinion, and remain so, that the only way to liquidate the division of opinion on the CE (there are no faction feelings within the Party membership) was for the CE to examine and discuss exhaustively the whole question of the situation in Australia.

This was agreed to and a draft statement drawn up as a basis for a thorough discussion. This draft was discussed at several meetings and was slightly

---

[19] The last sentence of this paragraph has a few pen strokes obliquely through it, suggesting that it should be deleted.

extended and amended. Finally, it was unanimously accepted by the CEC (copies attached).

Before I left Australia the question of Party organisation was discussed, and faults I have mentioned previously as applying to this CE in Sydney were admitted. It was agreed that efforts should be made to begin to build up State Party organisations under CE direction and control and that the work of the Sydney group and NSW Party must be guided by separate organs instead of by the CE.

The questions of developing activity in Queensland, in the coalfields, and among the "cocky" (small) farmers and in the more important States (particularly paying attention to the group of sympathisers in West Australia) were all fully considered and decisions registered.

The TU work was being developed, and the Agitprop Department was already showing results, bringing out a training syllabus based on that of the CPGB and instituting the formation of training groups amongst the membership throughout the country. It was agreed that it was essential to begin to prepare campaigns for recruiting new members and increasing the circulation of the Party organ, and the departments concerned were instructed to prepare plans for same. Finally, I am of opinion that the possibilities are good for the Party, and that its membership and influence can be extended considerably if the CEC will turn its attention to the development of an accepted policy, and liquidate past differences, instead of constantly tripping over them.

Document 48

RGASPI 495–94–42. April 1928, H. Moxon: Report of the Representative of the CC of the CPA on 'Party Factions'. Typescript.

This is one of the three reports on Australia considered by the Political Secretariat of the ECCI in April 1928. Moxon's factional history of the CPA in this document ends by insisting that the ALP—with which the Australian party had had a tortuous relationship because of the 'united front' policy—is no longer a working class party. The CPA, he argues, should have nothing more to do with it. He wants the ECCI to rule on the divisions within the Party. This confirms the general point that the relationship with the ALP was an abiding and divisive concern of the CPA. Moxon seems unimpressed by the actions of the Comintern's representative, Robson, during his brief stay in Australia.

7.4.1928

REPORT OF THE REPRESENTATIVE OF THE CENTRAL COMMITTEE OF THE COMMUNIST PARTY OF AUSTRALIA ON "PARTY FACTIONS".

The Australian Socialist Party adopted the Communist Manifesto and Dictatorship of the Proletariat as its policy in 1919. Early in 1920 [it] called a unity conference to form CP of A. Disputes arose over property owned by the ASP (Press, furniture, etc.) and ASP section left unity conference, and adopted CP of A as new name for ASP. Balance of Unity conference formed new CP of A and issued *Australian Communist* as official organ. The ex-ASP section (which for convenience we will call ASP) changed the name of the official organ from International Socialist to International Communist.

<u>Unity.</u>

Despite calls for unity by the CI (then the III International) the fight between the two Parties was relentless—the CPA (Garden, Baker, Earsman section) was repeatedly split—re-united and split again, whereas the ASP showed a united front (internally) until the end of 1921 or beginning of 1922 when the united front re the Labour Party and unity of two parties caused a split in the ASP. The "holy trinity" (A. Reardon, Mrs Reardon and Everitt) refused to carry out the wishes of the majority of Sydney Branch re unity and towards the middle of 1922, 20 members of ASP seceded with the furniture, library fittings and plans to the other party—thus killing the ASP including the outside branches in NSW and Queensland.

<u>1922 Split.</u>

In the CP of A we found a struggle being waged in the Sydney Branch between the Communist elements and the extremely opportunist bureaucracy (Garden, Baker, Messrs Smith, Denford & Co). This fight came to a head in connection with the election of Conference delegates to 1922 annual conference. After declining nomination as delegates the CE members learned to their dismay that Sydney Branch had a voting strength of 16 (1–10) to the CE none. At the following meeting the CE ordered a new election of delegates. Sydney branch re-endorsed previous election and passed vote of confidence in comrades elected. Several members of Sydney Branch were then expelled by the CE on frivolous charges, e.g. Mrs. Griffon was charged by Jeffery with accumulated pin-pricks and as being the most unsocial woman in the Party. Comrade Griffon [was criticised] for having made the statement that C.A. Baker was more concerned with a "meal ticket" than the Party (which was proved when Baker misappropriated "Communist" money for personal use, yet exonerated and defended by the balance of CE). Sydney Branch would not uphold the expulsions and two weeks later was expelled en-masse—leaving the Party in the hands of the bureaucracy and a few outside and insignificant branches. Sydney Branch continued to function as a separate Party until the middle of 1923 when "unity" was achieved by a complete capitulation of Sydney Branch ("No vote for six months" was one of the conditions). The proletarian element still fought the corrupt bureaucracy, which at this time passed the infamous resolution that CP members must go into the ALP and when challenged, <u>deny CP identity</u>. Many members, potentially good Communists, were lost to the ALP by this decision.

The Weaver-Thomas conspiracy case did not reflect credit on the Party. Following this came the demand for a general strike in the mining industry (on front page of *Communist*), and, just as the call was being taken up by the miners, a new order "No general strike—but go slow" was adopted, and as a direct result, the whole of the Party influence in the coalfields which had been considerable was lost and has not yet been rebuilt.

In 1924 (after Garden's and Howie's expulsion from the ALP executive), the Party conference (still dominated by the bureaucrats) reversed the decision re "ALP concealment" and instructed Party members to get expelled from the ALP; some remained in the ALP and left the Party; others are still in the ALP despite the 1924 resolution, but the best members of the Party carried out the decision and were accordingly expelled. Dozens of ALP branches in New South Wales declined, for quite a time to expel Communists, but eventually all (?) adopted the ALP Executive decision which by this time was "no CP members in ALP branches". In Queensland some ALP branches were expelled for refusing to operate the Anti-Communist Pledge (although in the majority of cases no CP members were members—just left-wingers). A Minority Movement was commenced in Q. by us, but eventually fizzled out without achieving anything (we neither made nor kept proper contact with expelled militants).

The running of candidates in NSW Elections in 1925 was a total disgrace to the Party—no proper programmes were drawn up, nor was the campaign really worth while—less than 1,000 votes for 5 candidates out of a probable 250,000 (?).

During the Seamen's Strike on the Coastal Service in 1925, the following "scab" agreement was entered into by the Marine Transport Group of the Sydney Labour Council, upon which Garden is seated, and the Shipping Companies. It is known as the Clarkson Agreement.

> And we further agree not to countenance any action of the members of the said union that would be calculated to either delay or hold up the sailing of any ship during the currency of the ship's articles.
>
> Should the Seamen's Union flout the agreement under which they sign on any vessel, and persist in preventing the sailing of ships or exercise job control this group will bring all possible pressure to bear on the union to observe the conditions aforesaid, and if the union continues in its attitude, it will be isolated from the group.
>
> In the event of these measures not being successful, the transport group will not oppose any measures affecting the manning of the ships to permit of their continued running.—Signed on Behalf of the Federation Unions.

Higgins was at that time editor of the *WW*. Kavanagh approached Higgins and suggested that the agreement be attacked. He was requested by Higgins to analyse the agreement and submit a criticism of same. When the *WW* for that week appeared instead of the criticism appearing, an article endorsing the agreement from the pen of Garden appeared instead. This endorsation of the agreement was attacked by Judd in the *Revolutionary Socialist*. The following week the editor of the *WW* replied to Judd <u>again upholding the agreement</u>.

<u>Beginning of New Era 1925.</u>

At the Annual Conference in 1925, a new note was struck. "Into the Unions and on the Offensive" was the slogan. For the first time the Party was beginning to feel itself and its mission. A new policy was drafted and adopted, less time was to be wasted on the Parliamentary side of the ALP and more time [devoted] to the masses. The UF from below was endorsed and preparations made for its fulfilment. The policy on immigration and factory and union groups was drawn up and adopted. A real Left wing (in contradistinction to the fake bodies previously fostered) was to be formed. (See 1925 Draft Programme and Policy attached).

Immediately following the Conference (in 1926) the TUEL[20] was formed—*WW* sub-drive campaigns were indulged in and the Party outlook was bright. Garden continually sabotaged the Party decisions. Denford (ex General Secretary) followed Baracchi as a liquidator. Garden was expelled for refusing to publicly associate himself with the Party, after repeated repudiations by him of Party. (Note: on November 26th, Garden as Pol-Sec of CP instructed Lithgow comrades to sign anti-CP pledge at special conference of ALP). During 1926, the anti-TU official job-by-intrigues resolution was carried. Its object was to "stop the rot" in the Party, it having been a common thing for Party members to get TU paid official jobs by intrigue and corrupt practices. (Before expulsion Garden comes out as endorsing new Labour Party.)

1926 Christmas Conference endorsed most of the Central Committee's work of previous 12 months. It was evident that a faction comprised of the remaining members or associates of the old bureaucracy was steadily working against the new policy of the Party and in the election of the Central Committee the members were 6 (old policy) 4 (new policy). The policy of the 1925 conference had been re-endorsed and more discipline was to be enforced. The CI resolution re agitprop and organisational bureaux was adopted, also the general resolution (See R.Com. Rept. Attached).

[…]

Although completely defeated by two successive conferences the Right wing oppositionists still carry on factional work and are consistently lobbying and generally disrupting the Party, e.g. the org. dept. of which Wright is Secretary

---

[20] Trade Union Educational League.

was instructed to prepare draft reorganisation scheme. Instead of calling Dept. together (4 comrades) Wright prepares draft unaided and takes same to the Presidium for endorsement—the weaknesses of scheme, etc., had to be pointed out at the Presidium which could easily have been done in the Dept. (a deliberate waste of time preventing the Presidium from getting on with Party work proper). (Further quotations from CC Minute book re RW [Right Wing] Actions to hand). Despite this, we have great opportunities to develop into a big Communist Party in Australia. In N.Q. [North Queensland] the only place in which an organiser has operated, we have ten new groups with an approximate membership of 200. The total Party membership is approximately 500–600. The ideological level is extremely low and is but now being raised by compulsory Party training.

[…]

The CC statement which is being brought to Moscow this week does not touch upon the majority of these questions. It is a general political-economic review with suggestions. Your representative (Robson) when in Australia would not hear our case, whilst continually lobbying with the Right wingers who pose as the best Party elements. Your rep. did not attend the Party Conference, excepting at the first session when nothing was done and the second session where he delivered a fine fraternal address. (Wright also reported this session). Other accounts of conference he received per medium of Right wing "runners" and of course the official report which he carried.

At the moment the CC is split, seven being of the Kavanagh-Ross faction and 3 of the Right wing Oppositionists (Wright, Higgins faction) but, unfortunately for the Party, such strategic positions as the general secretaryship and the editorship of the weekly organ are in the hands of Right wingers (Wright secretary and Higgins editor), besides them being chiefs of the agitprop and organisation departments.

Excepting the Melbourne and Lithgow groups there is little or no support for the oppositionists, therefore the split is not in the Party proper, but mainly confined to the CC.

Practically every achievement of the Party from the "into the TU policy" to the Sacco-Vanzetti demonstration and from the anti-TU session policy (anti-Shumakerism) to Party training has been initiated by the now majority section of the CC.

The majority of the Australian Party is looking to the ECCI to give a decisive ruling in connection with the faction fight for, as previously pointed out, the majority decisions of conferences are ignored and the same old fight is waged over every question by this disruptive and retarding element (See CC Minute Book extracts). The oppositionists are Right wingers, but we are far from being "Left"—we have, where the RWs would sanction it, applied the UF from below.

The Rights always consider it as from above (Note CE Report to VII Congress re Melbourne). <u>We are Leninists</u>, we do effective work in the TU movement—the <u>basis</u> of the ALP (note BWC, HOCC, LVA, Anti-Shumakerism), forming new groups (see Organisers' Report to 7th Congress and compare with Jeffery's report to V Congress).

Upon your decision rests the fate of the Australian section—Forward to a mass Bolshevik Party or back to a Garden bureaucratic controlled bastard reformist Party.

H.J. Moxon.

Document 49

RGASPI 495–94–40. 19 April 1928, Moxon and Robson: report: 'The Australian Party'. Typescript.

Given the apparent hostility between Moxon and Robson that became evident at the April 1928 ECCI meeting, it is not surprising that this brief document which appears under their names is merely a statement of facts.

19.4.28. (Moxon and Robson)

THE AUSTRALIAN PARTY

The membership of the CP of A in June 1927[21] was 296. Party groups were confined to NSW 2, Queensland 2, Victoria 1, with a total membership at large of 41 scattered throughout Australia.

The national organiser appointed in May 1927 enrolled 200 new members into 10 new groups in Queensland in six months making the total membership to date about 500. The chief weaknesses of the Party organisationally are the lack of contact with factory workers (especially in Sydney where the Party is strongest), the lack of permanent working committees in CC and the weakness or non-existence of fractions controlled by the Party. For a country where 800,000 out of a total population of 6,000,000 are organised in the unions, the Party's contact with the masses is very weak.

In Sydney where Party organisation is strongest (125 members) the membership was divided into a territorial group: 8 industrial groups and 2 language groups. Only two of the industrial groups (Building Trades and AWU) ever functioned efficiently—the balance exist on paper only.

The CC has decided to work upon area (concentration) groups and the organising of a few factory nuclei as the basis for the reorganisation of the Party to factory and street nuclei generally.

---

[21] This appears to be a typographical error in the original; the date should read June 1926.

The CC has now (Jan. 1928) been departmentalised with Agitprop, Org. and Trade Union Departments and a presidium (Polbureau) of 5 members.

The Party has conducted campaigns against exclusion of Communists from Labour Party when 26 unions and electoral branches supported the Party in NSW and considerably more in Queensland. Recently it has conducted campaigns re Hands off China, formation of Labour's Volunteer Army, a Workers' Defence Corps, Sacco Vanzetti Demonstration (one day strike with march of 11,000 workers in Sydney), International Defence Committee (engaged now on aid for Colorado miners), Anti-TU bill (amendments to Arbitration and conciliation Acts by Federal Government), Organising Italian Immigrants into Anti-Fascist League, etc.

The Party's publications are *Workers Weekly*, (4,500–5,000 circulation) and *Communist* (monthly theoretical organ—1,500 circulation). Since January the *Workers Weekly* has considerably improved, dealing more concretely with issues confronting the Australian Workers.

A series of leaflets and pamphlets dealing with China, USSR, Lenin Anniversary, May Day, Anti-Shumakerism, 10th Anniversary, etc., have been issued. A syllabus for Party training has been worked out and published by the Agitprop Dept.

Document 50

RGASPI 495–94–38. April 1928, ECCI: letter: To CEC of CPA. Typescript.

Having considered the reports above (Documents 46, 47 and 48), the ECCI handed down the decisions communicated in this letter. It had been impressed by Moxon's account of possibilities for work outside the ALP in Queensland, and this would eventually provide the CPA with a let-off, but without a real solution to its continuing ALP dilemma. It allowed the CPA to stand its own candidates in the Queensland state election in May 1929 (a performance that attracted around 3,000 votes between the two candidates).

TO THE CEC OF THE COMMUNIST PARTY OF AUSTRALIA.

Dear Comrades,

1. We have made a careful study of the reports presented to us by our representative to your Congress, as well as the reports submitted by your representative to the Comintern, and by the delegates to the Profintern Congress.

The reports show that the recent developments in the Labour movement in Australia afford tremendous possibilities for the Party. We have in mind in particular the success of the recruiting campaign in Queensland last year, and the growth of Left Wing activities in Western Australia. These facts coupled with the inner struggle in the Labour movement in Queensland, are indications that the conditions in Australia today are much more favourable for the growth and development of our Party.

In order to exploit to the greatest extent the new possibilities provided by the present stage of the class struggle in Australia, the Party is called upon, first and foremost, to strengthen and to improve its organisational apparatus, linking up this organisational work with a special campaign directed towards raising the ideological level of the working class of Australia as a whole, and of the Party itself in particular. *Special attention should be paid to the creation of local organisations based upon <u>factory and pit groups</u>.*

We wish to make here some concrete suggestions concerning the organisational tasks with which the Party is now confronted. The proposals contained in this letter should be taken together with our special resolution on the tasks of the Party in Queensland. Both of these documents are based upon the October resolution of the CI, which, according to the reports that have reached us, was <u>unanimously</u> accepted by your last Congress.

The first task of the Party is to improve the work and organisation of all organs of the Party—at the centre, as well as in the districts and in the localities.

For this purpose, the CEC should set up a commission to review the whole situation of the Party organisationally, and report back in detail regarding steps to be taken. In this connection, the decisions of the 3rd. Congress of the CI, the resolutions of the 2nd. Organisation Conference, and the CPGB Handbook on Organisation will serve as a useful basis.

2. The present organisational basis at the Centre (Presidium, with full time Trade Union, Agit-prop, and Org. Depts.) forms a good beginning for the creation of a well-adapted *central* Party apparatus. *The immediate task of the Party is to work out a concrete basis for the local organisation.*

3. The present statutes of the CP of A should be reviewed, and the clauses which allow of plural voting by delegates to Party Congresses, and the Referendum, struck out. The question of the appointment of proxy delegates should be clarified by a provision being inserted in the rules whereby such proxies must first be sanctioned by the CEC.

4. The question of State Party organisation, particularly in Queensland, NSW and Victoria should be settled on the basis of the model Statutes adopted at the *first* Organisation Conference, and made operative. It is imperative that the CEC take immediate steps to appoint capable comrades for organising and instructional work in selected districts, on a full time basis. In this connection it must be borne in mind that new members in hitherto unorganised districts can be immediately organised on the basis of the factory group. Recruiting work should not be of a casual nature, but should be carried on continuously and systematically. In the large centres, such as Sydney, the Party should concentrate all available forces

on the establishment of factory groups in the larger enterprises in the most important industries.

The Party must pay special attention to the task of establishing factory groups wherever possibilities exist, and to the building up of sound local Party organisations. Fraction work must be thoroughly organised in non-party working-class organisations where there are Party members. The CEC must see that the entire Party membership thoroughly understands and actively participates in carrying through these tasks. The Party must also be prepared to defend the principle of communist fractions in non-party bodies.

[…]

7. <u>Trade Union Department</u>—The decisions of the 2nd. Organisational Conference, which explain in detail the functions and methods of work of the Trade Union Dept., should be thoroughly studied and adapted to suit the conditions in Australia.

The winning over of the Trade Unions to the RILU and to the policy of the Party demands from the Party constant attention to the ideological development of the masses within the unions. As an essential part of this task, the Party must take advantage of every opportunity to contest official positions with Party members well suited for this work. All such contests should be under the direction of the CEC, without whose sanction no Party member can stand for an official position in the unions. Further, *as a rule* Party members contesting these positions should not conceal their identity as members of the Communist Party. They should base their claims for support upon a sound Trade Union record, as well as upon a militant class struggle platform.

[…]

10. <u>The Agit-Prop Department</u>. This Department has a particularly important task before it in developing Party training along systematic lines, as has already been commenced. Party training should not merely take the form of lectures. The primary task is to organise training for all members of the Party. Special groups should be formed for the training of active Party workers, functionaries, and so on.

[…]

14. <u>Organisation Department</u>—The primary duty of the Organisation Department is to undertake all measures necessary for the implications [sic] of the CI resolution referred to above, as well as the suggestions contained in this letter, to be carried out effectively and intelligently, and not applied in a mechanical manner. With this object in view, the Dept. must popularise, through articles and a special handbook, the decisions of the Third Congress and *both* Organisation Conferences.

[…]

26. <u>Immigration</u>—The importance of the immigration question in Australia, particularly insofar as it is linked up with the bar against coloured immigrants, calls for special attention. The CP of A must conduct careful and well thought out propaganda based upon international solidarity in opposition to the chauvinistic and anti-proletarian so-called "White Australian" policy of the ALP. The prejudices of the backward sections of the workers must not be allowed to cause the Party to weaken its propaganda in this connection. The Party must put forward the policy of unequivocal opposition to all racial barriers in the immigration laws, "championing an internationalist policy, and insisting upon equality in treatment, wages, rights, and free admittance for the workers of all countries." (See October CI resolution.) This campaign must be a permanent feature not only in the agitation and propaganda work of the Party, but also in its organisational work. The organisation and defence of immigrants, irrespective of colour, must be carried out in the most systematic way possible.

[…]

29. <u>The Differences Within the CEC of the CP of Australia</u>—We have considered very carefully and fully the various accusations and counter-accusations made by the Australian comrades against each other, and we came to the conclusion that there are no serious political differences to justify the existence of different conflicting groups within the Party.

The cause of the conflict is due to the cleavage between the Central Committee and those comrades who concentrate [mainly] upon the work in the trade unions. This cleavage led to [lack] of mutual confidence and to mutual misunderstandings. [The fact] that comrades representing the different groups were able [to] unite with us on the suggestions contained in this letter [is] a convincing proof that in Australia also the two groups [could] and should unite for common and joint work.

With a view to facilitating this joint work, we recommend that Comrades Ryan and Jeffries [sic], *who* were not elected to the CEC by the last Congress (partly as a result of the application of the method of plural voting), should be *drawn into the work of the CEC.*

Mistakes made by active comrades should be overcome through collective work and mutual comradely criticism rather than by devastating accusations. The building up of a strong and <u>united</u> Party leadership is now more essential than ever.

30. In conclusion, we wish to call your attention to the necessity for taking the most effective steps to achieve permanent contact with us, as well as with the Communist Parties of Great Britain and of New Zealand.

Document 51

RGASPI 495–94–38. 18 September 1928, Agitprop Dept of ECCI: letter: To CEC of CPA re *Workers' Weekly*. Typescript.

Having recommended greater attention to the Party's Agitprop activity since at least April 1926 (see Document 38, above), Moscow conducted a review of the *Workers' Weekly*, and in this letter roundly criticizes the CPA's newspaper.

Moscow, September 18, 1928.
To the CEC of the CP of Australia.
Re—*Workers' Weekly*.

Dear Comrades,

We herewith submit to you the findings of a review of your official organ, the *Workers' Weekly*, which are based on a general examination of the issues dating back some years and a closer examination of the issues of the first half of 1928.

At the outset it must be stated that as far as the basic policy of the paper, its contents and its make-up are concerned, there is no fundamental difference whatsoever between the issues of any given period.

In our review we have paid consideration to the many objective difficulties the Party is faced with (such as its youth, its small size, as well as the great distance separating it from other Parties etc.). We have striven to discern the major and basic lines of shortcomings, in order to set their correction as a task to be accomplished, before the Party.

The press is, or should be a reflection of the Party's mass activity. As such it will carry news of all struggles of the workers in every sphere of their life and give it a Communist interpretation. It is, if correctly developed, the voice of the masses, their coordinator, because the Communist Party "has no interest opposed to those of the working class". It must be the unfailing weapon in the struggle of the workers, and the masses must be brought to recognise it as such.

To establish such a press is a process in the course of which the Party itself has to strike roots in the masses. The growth of the press and that of the Party are [...][22] linked to the one and the same process. With the growth of the Party, and its increased activity in the everyday struggles of the masses, with the intensification of its political life, the press in reflecting this will become a factor of the greatest significance. With this understanding it can be said that the press clearly reflects the state of development the Party in question finds itself in. This is true with particular regard in the case of the *Workers' Weekly*.

---

[22] A word here is indecipherable.

Therefore in a number of major instances it was necessary to reflect on this without, however, making concrete suggestions, since this is not within the scope of the review.

By pointing out the most outstanding and fundamental shortcomings, and by making suggestions for their correction, we attempted to on the one hand give a rough outline for an editorial policy and on the other to supply areas as to the contents of the press and its organisation. We are, however, certain that even a thorough rehauling of the *Workers' Weekly* will show its lasting beneficial effects in the long run only then, when it will mark a step in the general process of the Party's growth, as well as the clarification of its policies and its Bolshevisation.

1. The two basic shortcomings of the *Workers' Weekly* are that it is not written for the masses and that it is not a political organ. Glancing through its pages we find that it tends to speak for "pure and simple" left wing trade unionism with some rather abstract political *articles* strewn in between. Perhaps it is wrong to separate the two shortcomings, for taken fundamentally they are part of one problem. There is a degree of resemblance between the *Workers' Weekly* and the organs of some syndicalists or of those of some isolated socialist groups. The basic problem as indicated by this fact seems to be that of a tendency towards sectarianism. This is the decided impression we gained by examining your paper.

Page after page is filled with material reflecting the inner life of the trade union movement. This lends the paper a predominantly trade union character. The items published are presented in a programmatic form with dogmatic declarations of policy. This is the case with most of the political items too.

[...]

As far as the news section is concerned the *Workers' Weekly* has its given limitations. Within these (the fact of its being a weekly, the lack of telegraphic news etc.), however, it must develop a high degree of efficiency. The review has convinced us that the paper lacks the proper news material. This must be corrected at once.

[...]

With the weekly being written for the masses, filled with material of interest to them and easily digested by them the increase of its circulation will naturally follow. Ever and ever wider masses will come to recognise it as an indispensable weapon in their struggle. The Party's policy, its campaigns and its activity will on the one hand be made know to the masses through the *Workers' Weekly* and on the other receive the inspired support of the workers in an increasing degree. If what has been said is correctly understood and lived up to, the *Workers' Weekly* will become the collective agitator, the collective propagandist and the collective organiser of the Australian toiling masses in the truest sense of Lenin's words.

Fraternally yours,
Agitprop Dept ECCI

Document 52

RGASPI 495–94–43. 24 December 1928, Marushchak:[23] letter to Piatnitsky, ECCI. In Russian, manuscript. Trans. by KW.

In response to Marushchak's question in this letter about Australian representation at the Sixth Congress, it can be said that Esmonde Higgins arrived from Australia in August, in the midst of the Congress, and subsequently prepared the report which forms Document 53, below.

Krasnoe Sormovo
24/12/28

To Comrade Piatnitsky,
ECCI,
Moscow.

Dear Comrade,

So far I have heard nothing from the Anglo-American Secretariat. I am appending herewith all that I have received from one of the best members of the Australian Communist Party. I am also sending his letter (the original), from which you will see that not all appears to be well in the Australian CP and that the ECCI should pay attention to this, as serious work is now beginning for the Party there in view of the sharpened class struggle, and the Party and the CC and the Sydney group in particular are beginning to veer to the right.

By the way, could you kindly let me know if anybody from Australia attended the VI Congress, as Comrade Lominadze[24] told me there was nobody, but judging from *The Workers' Weekly* there was a representative. If there was one, I wonder who it was. I am sending you the letter without translating it into Russian, since you have people there who can read and translate it, but if you can't understand it, send it to me and I will translate it and send you the translation. Under separate cover I am sending some newspapers. Perhaps you will receive them, but if not, there are some interesting things there. Please return the letter when you have finished with it. If possible, provide answers to the questions placed at the end

---

[23] Ivan Marushchak (John Maruschak) lived for some years in Melbourne. He returned to Russia after the revolution.
[24] Handwriting not clear.

of Comrade Shelley's letter. Comrade Shelley[25] fully deserves our trust. He is a good party worker in every respect.

With communist greetings,
I. E. Marushchak
Address: Locomotive Assembly Shop,
Krasnoe Sormovo, Nizhnii Novgorod province

Document 53

RGASPI 495–94–44. December 1928, Higgins: report to CPA 8th Conference: Report on the 6th world Congress of CI. Typescript.

Esmonde Higgins was the CPA's delegate to the Sixth Comintern Congress, which saw the turn away from the previous (and generally unsuccessful) 'united front' policy towards a policy of 'united front from below'. This change was an attempt to bypass and expose the traditional leaders of the working class; it led ultimately to the doctrine of 'social fascism' which declared the supposed friends of the working class (i.e., the reformist leaderships of social democratic parties and trade unions) to be worse than the fascists. The implications of this policy development would take some time to be revealed in the CPA, as in other communist parties, but they were underpinned by the notion that capitalism had entered its 'Third Period' since the First World War, a time that would be characterized by heightened capitalist crisis, inter-imperialist wars, and threats to the Soviet Union. Higgins' report lays out the development of this new line from Moscow, but is particularly interesting for its direct approach to (and rejection of) the charges that communists were simply following 'orders from Moscow'. Indeed, Higgins resisted—and would continue to resist—the strategic implications of the Third Period line.

3rd Session. 24th. December, 7.30 to 10p.m.

Chairman—Comrade Miles.

1. Message of greetings received from CPNZ
2. Greetings to be sent to ECCI, CPNZ, CPGB, CP of China, CP of Japan, and CP of Indonesia.
3. International Delegates' Report—Comrade E.M. Higgins

Report by Comrade Higgins on the 6th. World Congress of CI

My report will deal primarily with the 6th. World Congress of the Communist International whose discussions sum up and clarify the main international developments of the past four and a half years.

It is necessary first to touch briefly on the work of the previous congresses and on the situation with which the 6th Congress was faced.

Earlier Congresses. It is nearly 10 years now since the Comintern was founded. At the beginning of 1919, at the end of the imperialist war, when there was no

---

[25] Here in Latin script and spelt 'Shelly'.

Workers' International—for the leaders of the old international had linked themselves with the capitalists of their "own" countries—the Russian Communists sent out a call throughout the world to all revolutionary workers' organisations to unite. The First Congress, held in March, 1919, drew up the famous Manifesto of the Communist International and was noteworthy, in particular, for Comrade Lenin's thesis on "Bourgeois Democracy and Proletarian Dictatorship", which still stands as the clearest possible exposition of the differences between revolutionary and reformist theory.

The Second Congress (July, 1920) met when the spirit of the workers throughout Europe was still rising high. As there were many nondescript groups and parties prepared to flock into the International, it was necessary to face the task of checking the entry of elements which were so soaked in reformist ideas that they would obstruct a clear revolutionary line; hence the famous "Twenty One Points", the new conditions of entry. This congress also adopted resolutions on the national, colonial and agrarian questions. At the same time, although not actually decisions of the Congress, appeared Lenin's "Left Wing Communism" and the reply of the Communist International to the queries of the British Independent Labor Party, defining clearly the tasks of revolutionary workers in Anglo-Saxon countries.

By the time of the Third Congress (June, 1921), the capitalist offensive was beginning to be seen quite clearly, and at the same time inside the Soviet Union the end of the period of War Communism had come. The Congress was concerned especially with Trotsky's and Varga's report on the world economic situation, and with the strategy of the Russian Party in connection with the New Economic Policy.

The Fourth Congress (November, 1922) met at a time when the capitalist offensive had spread considerable confusion in the ranks of the world's workers. This Congress defined the principles of the "united front" and discussed the "Workers' Government" slogan. It also dealt for the first time with the Comintern's World Programme.

The 5th. Congress (June, 1924), meeting after the defeat of the workers in Bulgaria and Germany and the coming into office of the MacDonald Government in England and the Herriot Government in France, analysed the "democratic-Pacifist" phase of capitalism and carried further the discussions on the Workers' Government slogan.

There has been no congress since then until this year, but several enlarged executives (Plenums), which really have taken the place of Congresses, have discussed important questions which we must remember when considering the present Congress.

The 5th. Plenum (1925) was particularly concerned with estimating the degree of stabilisation which capitalism had reached at that time, and with formulating the principles of "bolshevisation" for the guidance of the Communist parties in capitalist countries.

The next year saw the rise of the Chinese Nationalist struggle, the revolt in Morocco against Spanish and French imperialism, and in Europe, a marked swing to the left. The 6th Plenum (early 1926) carried further the analysis of capitalist stabilisation, in the light especially of developments in the colonies and semi-colonies, and dealt with the mistakes of the ultra-left opposition in the German and other Western European parties.

The 7th. Plenum (Nov. 1926) met after the General Strike and the miners' struggle in Britain, and after the new opposition in the Communist Party of the Soviet Union had begun to take an actual anti-Soviet form. It laid down a very clear line with regard to the [Left] Opposition in Russia and Germany, and for the first time defined the policy of the CI towards the Chinese Revolution.

The 8th. Plenum, in May 1927, had to review the policy in China in the light of the Kuomintang counter-revolution. The British Government had broken with the Soviet Union, and the Plenum was particularly concerned with elaborating the Communist policy towards the war danger.

Finally, the 9th. Plenum (Feb. 1928) discussed the lessons of the Vienna and Indonesian insurrections and of the collapse of the Chinese Party's leadership.

It carried still further the discussion on the [Left] Opposition in the Communist Party of the Soviet Union, and in particular laid down a new tactical line for the French and British sections towards Social Democracy.

The 6th. Congress, meeting in the tenth year of the Comintern's history, had thus a rich experience behind it in dealing with the problems of our world party. The main questions discussed were, firstly, the international situation and the tasks of the Comintern, secondly, the World Programme of the Communist International, thirdly, the war danger, fourthly, the colonial revolutionary movement, and, finally, the position inside the Soviet Union and the Communist Party of the Soviet Union.

The International Situation. On the first question a report and a thesis were presented by the CPSU delegation, through Comrade Bucharin. Great care was taken to define capitalist development since the war. Three periods were distinguished:

1. In the years immediately after the war—the period of acute revolutionary crises, especially in Europe—capitalism feared for its existence and executed a series of sham retreats. This period was marked, not only by the revolutions in Russia and the Baltic States and the overthrow of the

monarchy in Germany and Austria, but by rice riots in Japan, the Bavarian Soviet, the Hungarian Soviet, and the upheaval in Italy. The climax of those revolutionary movements was reached in 1921, in the famous March rising in Germany, which, although ill-conceived, was an expression of the direct revolutionary urge amongst the German workers. This period came to a close in 1923, with the defeat of the Bulgarian and German workers.

2.   The second period was marked by the capitalist offensive and by defensive strikes and resistance of workers, particularly in Gt Britain and other European countries.

This period shows a gradual and partial stabilisation of capitalism, with the restoration of productive forces that had been upset and disorganised during the war. In this period the direct revolutionary movement passed to the colonies—China, India, Morocco, Syria.

3.   Now we are in the third period—the period of indisputable stabilisation of capitalism, where production exceeds pre-war in nearly all forms of economy.

It is marked by great improvements in the technique of production (electrification, applied chemistry, light metals, conveyor system, standardisation, mass production, etc.) and by the development of capitalist monopolies, trustification and state capitalism. As a result there is to be observed a great consolidation of capitalism. These changes are clearly set out in Varga's *The Decline of Capitalism*, which was prepared as a handbook for delegates to the 6th Congress.

On the other hand this third period is marked by the continuance and the development of the crisis of the capitalist system. In the USA there has been an absolute decline in the number of workers while output is increasing, a phenomenon that has never happened before. There has never before been such mass unemployment—there are ten million unemployed through the capitalist world.

In spite of the stabilisation of capitalism, all its contradictions are developing under the surface and are increasing in intensity. As a result of changes during the critical period following the war, there has been a fundamental structural change in the whole world economy. While, on the one hand, productive capacity has immensely increased, markets have been greatly contracted, intensifying the disproportion between productive and consumptive possibilities.

The existence of the USSR has meant that the world-wide capitalism has ceased to exist. The development of the colonial revolutionary movement has brought to the forefront tendencies which prevent any real stability of the capitalist system. Imperialist tendencies and imperialist contradictions have been greatly strengthened, and <u>War</u> can be the only possible outcome. (Hence all the signs of preparations for imperialist war—the changing alliances, "Industrial Peace" stunts, etc, —with, as the fundamental tendency, the grouping of imperialist forces against the Soviet Union.)

Thus the thesis regards the present situation as one of extreme [in]tensity, in which even small strikes [can] easily become political struggles.

The Social Democrats take comfort from the apparent stabilisation and pretend that this has disproved the Communists' revolutionary contentions. But Communists see that this very stabilisation is only aggravating the contradictions which will bring about capitalism's decay and downfall. We have in no way changed our aim of world revolution and we have not lost faith in the necessity of revolution. The Communist estimation of the position has been summed up as follows by Comrade Bucharin:-

> Capitalism is doomed to perish, not because it is rapidly degenerating into a parasitical organism, not because it is sinking into decrepitude and impotence—but because moribund capitalism has entered into its last stage, in which the inherent contradictions of the capitalist system become extraordinarily intensified and give rise to conflicts which bring about its destruction. The parasitical aspect of capitalism continues to increase, but this is not degeneration proper; it is degeneration which comes as a result of the intensification of the contractions of capitalism—contradictions arising from the law of unevenness of capitalist development—contradictions between cartelised and non-cartelised spheres of production, antagonisms arising out of the fixing of quotas, the struggle between various imperialist States.

The New Line Towards Social Democracy. The second part of the thesis on the International situation is devoted to the consideration of the role of Social Democracy and of reformism. While the Communist movement is growing on the basis of the contradictions of capitalism, Social Democracy is now growing on the basis of its stabilisation. Social Democracy is now becoming part of the capitalist State, as Hilferding said at the last congress of the Germany Social Democratic Party. The reformists are turning the unions into schools of capitalism. Social Democracy is becoming more and more imperialistic and anti-Soviet, more and more interested in industrial "peace" and in social reaction, and more ready to split the workers' movement by imposing a rigid social democratic discipline.

In view of these developments, the CI has adopted a new line towards Social Democracy, a new line of intensified struggle against it. Our aim is to capture the leadership of the working class from the reformists; to this end we must lose no opportunity of exposing the leaders as traitors. This does not mean any weakening of the united front, but a more resolute attempt to build a united front from below on the basis of struggle.

As applied to Australia, this means that it is time we abandoned altogether the idea that we can transform the Labor Party into a Workers' Party. We must recognise that the ALP is now simply part of the capitalist machinery. Our line is a struggle against the Social Democratic leadership, and an endeavour as an independent revolutionary force to win away from the existing leadership the masses who are not yet clear as to the part which is being played by reformist leaders.

The thesis went on to deal with our tasks. Great stress was laid on the need for more internationalism. Most sections were severely criticised for not paying more practical attention to such great international issues as the Chinese Revolution and the British strikes of 1926, and also for failing to link up questions of daily life and revolutionary activity in their own countries with questions of international politics.

Within the International the main danger was found to be in "right" danger since the removal of the "left" (Trotsky) opposition. The thesis insists that we must be careful above all not to give ground to Social Democracy.

On this thesis there was a long and animated discussion, in which 90 speakers from practically every country in the world took part. There was not much actual conflict in the discussion except with regard to the tasks of the different sections. Disagreement was expressed to the contention that the "third" post-war period was radically different from the "second", but finally it was agreed that the distinction must be made, as it is necessary to emphasise that the stabilisation of capitalism is now very real and cannot disappear at once.

The Comintern Programme. The next item on the agenda was the Comintern programme. This was the first attempt to formulate concretely the tasks of the Communist movement in connection with the establishment of the dictatorship of the proletariat on a world scale. It was an immense job to get into one document a comprehensive statement of what are the tasks of the Communists, of "our world plans for the future".

This was the fourth draft of this programme; the first draft had been discussed by the Fourth Congress in 1922, and ever since eager and keen discussion had been carried on throughout the International. At the 6th. Congress 900 amendments were presented opening up a hundred important problems. A section of the Programme Commission had to withdraw from Moscow for a week to digest all these amendments.

The Programme opens with a concrete analysis of imperialism and the main varieties of countries existing to-day. After dealing at length with the proletarian dictatorship (making use of the experiences of the USSR) it considers the strategy and tactics of Communist Parties in capitalist countries and examines the main reformist theories.

On economic questions, discussion centres particularly on the meaning attached to the term "finance capital", (a Persian comrade insisting that it was a dangerous term because it over-emphasised the role of the banks) and on the theory of crises (Comrade Thalheimer urges that they should be attributed to "disproportion" and not to "over-production"). There was a big fight on the question whether what has come to be known in Russia as the "New Economic Policy" is an inevitable stage of the workers' dictatorship. There were differences of opinion on the relations between Social Democracy and Fascism and on the division of countries into historical types. In the commission and in the general sessions of the Congress, these questions were thrashed out with great care and frankness.

The final draft was agreed to be the best possible statement of the principles of Communism. It is a very long document. It could not be anything else, because it has to deal concretely with problems which, when—as in 1847—the revolutionary movement was a propagandist society, could be treated abstractly. It is not merely a statement of principle, but outlines the fighting conditions and the aims of the struggles of the workers in countries of different types.

The programme is completely opposed to the assumption of the reformists that capitalism is playing a progressive role, and all the time emphasises that the overthrow of capitalism is the only hope of the workers. It is an essentially international document, the ultimate goal and the immediate demands being treated from the point of view of the world dictatorship.

The adoption of the programme was a solemn moment. Every delegate was conscious that after weeks of discussion at the Congress and years of preliminary discussion amongst the Parties, there had been worked out a magnificent statement of the aims and tasks of the world Communist movement.

Reporting to the Leningrad Party officials, Comrade Molotov said: "The Programme lays down the general and most urgent tasks of the CI for the whole epoch of the revolutionary struggle for the world dictatorship of the proletariat. Its adoption signifies the establishment of our most important perspectives of the whole epoch of international socialist revolution. In the whole history of mankind it has never yet happened that a class has possessed a uniform international programme. There has never been before a class capable of it."

This programme will be the basis of our training and of our own special programme. As soon as it comes to hand it will be printed, educational courses will be drawn up so that it can be used as textbook, and the whole of the membership of our Party will have the job of digesting it and applying it.

The War Danger. This question of the danger of imperialist war had been discussed in connection with all previous questions, but it was so big and urgent that special attention had to be given to it. The war danger is the central question of the present period, because the whole international development is proceeding in the direction of war.

The thesis drafted by Comrade Bell brought together in a single document all the important Communist ideas with regard to war and the methods of fighting the war danger. Bell's report and the reports of other comrades, and also the speeches of those who spoke in the discussion, gave a real wealth of information about the colonial wars which are already going on, about the capitalist antagonisms and the grouping of capitalist forces against the Soviet Union, about the armaments and the organisation of capitalist resources, and about the pacifist illusions which are being spread by the League of Nations and the Social Democrats.

Most Parties were criticised for failing to appreciate the war danger sufficiently. Bucharin insisted that "questions concerning the daily policy of sections of the CI must be subordinated to the question of the struggle against war, just as imperialism takes every fresh step from the standpoint of preparation for war." Such things as the Industrial "Peace" Conference and the Arbitration Amendment Act are essentially war measures. "Industrial Peace", said Bucharin, "is the most sharply expressed form of class truce—the best form of preparation for war."

The thesis on the war danger lays down very clearly the great tasks of Communists in the fight against the war danger, stressing the need for an energetic campaign against every form of warlike activity of our own capitalist class and against every form of pacifism. Questions of work amongst the armed forces, and amongst metal and transport workers, women and the youth are discussed in the light of the experience of the international.

This war thesis has already excited the rage of the capitalist press, which says that the CI and the CI alone is seriously fighting imperialism and its aims.

The Colonies. After five weeks, the Congress settled down to discuss the revolutionary movement in the colonies in the light of the experience of the Chinese, Indian and Indonesian struggles since 1920, when the Second Congress for the first time drew up a Colonial Thesis.

Bucharin put the position clearly when he declared that "hitherto the colonies have been the objects of history; now they have become its subjects." The colonial revolutionary movement is now one of the most decisive facts in the world struggle against capitalism.

After noting for a few days the conditions in Hong Kong and Shanghai, I have not yet got over the shock of the tremendous reserve power of the masses in colonial and ...[26] If they can be marshalled against capitalism, a tremendous

---

[26] Some words are obscured in the manuscript.

dynamic force is available. The Communist International is the only force trying to organise this wasted strength against capitalism. As one of the reporters on the colonial question declared, "one of the most important characteristic features of the general political orientation of the CI consists in the connection that we have succeeded in establishing between the development of the struggle of the proletariat in big capitalist countries against class oppression and class rule and the development of the struggle for the liberation of people in colonial and semi-colonial countries which are oppressed and exploited by imperialism."

The thesis provoked a very keen discussion on imperialist policy (with special reference to the question of industrialisation) and on the role of the colonial bourgeoisie in the fight against imperialism. Further elaboration and investigation is necessary before agreement is possible on these extraordinarily complex questions. The work of the 6th. Congress provides an invaluable basis for future discussion.

The Soviet Union. The other main question—the situation in the USSR and in the CPSU—I am not going to deal with here, because time will not permit me to enter into a report on Soviet Russia. The Congress resolutions took particular notice of the facts that industry in the USSR has already passed the pre-war level and is advancing far more rapidly than in the capitalist world; that the socialist sector (and, particularly, heavy industry) is growing more rapidly than private enterprise; that the conditions of the workers and of the poor peasants have greatly improved; and that by effective methods of self-criticism bureaucratic dangers have been decisively checked.

I shall never forget after two months in Russia the inspiring sight of the successful struggle for the construction of Socialism in the USSR. Since 1920, when I was last in Russia, the progress is astonishing.

The Reformists' Conference. The Brussels Conference of the Second International, which met in August at the same time as the VI World Congress of the CI, provides the best possible contrast with our Congress. It showed that the socialists of every country are lined up behind their own capitalist class. The bitterest discussions at this conference were between French and German Socialists regarding the German evacuation of the Rhine.

We find too at this Conference an utter indifference to the war danger—not a single reference to the whole thing, except a demand for "security and disarmament". The chairman did not mention the Soviet disarmament proposals, but he gave a blessing to the Kellogg Pact and the Geneva Protocol. The Russian Menshevik, Dan, declared: "We must fight Russian militarism." Even the foreign trade monopoly of the Soviet Government was denounced. On the colonial question the Conference showed its color by appointing as Chairman of the Colonial Commission an ex-Governor of Jamaica, Lord Olivier. Even the reformist delegates from India, Ceylon and Trinidad, who had been the Conference's guests, denounced the colonial resolution as an openly imperialist decision and withdrew in disgust. The Conference welcomed capitalist concentration and rationalisation, suggesting that Socialism will come through capitalist prosperity and the formation of international trusts. The whole Conference was a complete capitulation to imperialism.

On the other hand our Congress, the Communist World Congress, was concerned all through with fighting capitalism through to victory. The Congress Manifesto called on workers, farmers, colonial peoples, soldiers and sailors to struggle against capitalism and to meet the bosses' attack with a counter-attack. A telegram from the German Red Front Fighters' League to the VI World Congress described the Congress as "the most vivid expression of the revolutionary will of the growing international class front of the toilers of the whole world."

On all matters on which the Brussels Conference squibbed it, our Congress adopted a bold fighting anti-capitalist stand. It is significant that colonial parties were flocking to the Communist Congress while delegates from colonial countries were running away from the Brussels Conference.

Our Congress, further, was brutally frank with itself. When I showed a copy of Bucharin's report on the Tasks of the CI to a fellow passenger, he said: "You know, this is a queer report, it must drive people out of your Party to read all this criticism." The CI, however, welcomes vigorous self-criticism, because it is only through such criticism that real clarity on our tasks and organisation can be reached.

Facts about the 6th. Congress. A few facts about the Congress. It lasted six weeks, but you must not think that for six weeks delegates were having a joy ride in the capital of the Workers' Republic. There was very hard work all the time. Several delegates had to give in and go for a rest. Comrade Stalin, who had not had a holiday for four years, had to leave and go to the Caucasus after the Congress had been sitting for about a fortnight. With commission after commission, delegation meetings in between, and plenum after plenum, delegates were tired out, but, satisfied with work they had done, were intensely enthusiastic at the finish.

Soviet workers showed a very keen interest in the Congress. At workers' clubs in Moscow I was asked the most detailed questions on various minor points raised during the Congress discussion. One British comrade, who [was] sent into Central Siberia to report, found that Party members in remote districts had been following the Congress so closely that he was unable to answer all their queries.

There were at the Congress 515 delegates, from 55 countries; 100 came from outside of Europe; 74 from actual colonial countries. Any of you who know the history of the 2nd. International will see the extraordinary change that these figures represent. The 2nd. International even at its best period was a European organisation. The Comintern is a world party, and to the Comintern the affairs of the colonial countries, of the non-European countries generally, are as important as European affairs. From three affiliated Parties—Korea, Portugal, Cuba—which are forced to work illegally, no delegates were present. Seven new sections were admitted to affiliation at this Congress, including New Zealand, Paraguay, Colombia, Ecuador—parties from the once despised colonial countries which are still treated with contempt by the 2nd. International.

The reformists and the other agents of capitalism are fond of insinuating that the Comintern is simply a "toy of the Russians." It is interesting to observe that, of the 55 members of the Congress Presidium, only 7 were Russians. Of the 30 candidates for the new Executive, 2 are Russians; one is Australian, Comrade Kavanagh. These figures are enough to show that in contrast with any party that has appeared before the Comintern is a real world party, and to dispose of the silly talk about "Moscow putting it across other parties."

<u>"Orders from Moscow."</u> It is just as well to consider what this talk about "orders from Moscow" means. Our International has never paraded as a loose federation of national bodies but has endeavoured to become a world communist party. There is no sense in creating an international organisation if it is not to intervene in the conduct of its national sections, or to use international experiences for the purpose of straightening out the problems of the Labor movement in the various countries. We glory in the fact that we are an international party.

Decisions are come to with regard to the affairs of particular parties, generally at the instance of representatives of those parties and always with their advice. Those decisions are arrived at as the result of the freest possible international discussion; as a result of the collective Marxian analysis and the collective work of the individual delegates. Every national section is a party to the International's decisions, which once made, are loyally carried out by the sections. There can thus be no sense in the talk of one section "giving orders" to another. The Comintern is an international of workers, all bound together by the common tie of revolutionary struggle against world capitalism.

It is quite true and we glory in the fact that special attention is paid to the opinions of the leaders of the Russian Party, which has made its own revolution. We must not forget what the Russian workers have taught us. Not only do they provide an asylum to the headquarters and the persecuted members of the International, but they have given us the rich revolutionary experience of the victorious workers of the Soviet Union, who fought under the leadership of Comrade Lenin.

Take for instance the habit, which we are beginning to learn here, of prefacing our discussions on strategy and tactics with a careful analysis of economic and political conditions. This was one of the methods of the Russian Bolsheviks, for which they were looked on as cranks by most socialists in Western Europe. It has been proved that this practice is one of the surest guarantees against the development of opportunism and sectarianism, which are both due to short-sightedness and a lack of faith in the workers and revolutionary process.

The Bolsheviks, too, have taught us to see our own struggles as part of the world process, and so to turn for guidance to the international experience of the working class. The Second International's principle of autonomy for the different sections means only that the leaders of each section must be "free" to sell "their" workers to "their" capitalists as suits them best "in harmony with the national traditions."

They have pointed out, further, the necessity of a powerful Communist Party—a working party, not a talking outfit—which endeavours to win the leadership of the masses by disciplined work in the class struggle. In opposition to the idea of the Social Democrats that a party consists of a number of bureaucratic leaders, with a passive "rank and file" bound blindly to the machine, the Bolsheviks insisted that in a workers' party the "leaders" are only guides and co-ordinators of the work of the entire membership.

Finally, we cannot overestimate our debt to the Bolsheviks for their precepts with regard to parliamentary action (that our purpose is simply to rally the masses to destroy capitalism), to work in the trade unions, co-operatives, etc. (that our business is to develop the political consciousness of the workers by taking part in the daily struggles and showing the need to extend the fight against capitalism along the whole front) and the need for systematic fraction work inside non-party organisations for the purpose of organising our efforts to the best advantage. These precepts we owe to the Communist International and particularly to the Russian section.

<u>We Have a Great Responsibility</u>. The 6th World Congress has given us a clear line of policy. The Programme, in particular, enables us to proclaim where we stand. The Australian section has had the benefit also of special resolutions and letters of advice. On our principal tasks and line of policy we have no reason in the world now to disagree. It is for us now to work out our tactics.

We are faced with a grave responsibility. The allied Australian and British capitalists are carrying on a savage offensive against the workers. The Pacific area is bound to be the main storm centre of the approaching world war. Ours is the only party which can organise and direct the workers of Australia against the capitalist offensive and the danger of imperialist war, and towards the satisfaction of their class needs.

We must therefore act quickly, without delay, to fit ourselves for our tasks. The Government will not hesitate, in a crisis, to mop up the leaders of our Party; we must see to it that our Party is made strong enough to feel no ill effects from such interference. This can be done only by increasing our membership, strengthening our organisation, tightening our connections with the mass of the workers, and raising our ideological level.

Section 3

Moscow takes command: 1929–1937

The documents in this section cover the period from February 1929 until early 1937, with most of them being concentrated in the earlier years of this period in line with the general distribution of documents in the CAAL. This period marks an important shift in the history of relations between the CPA and the Comintern for two main reasons. First, because the Comintern became a direct player in the leadership struggles within the Party in 1929 (the main catalyst for which, not surprisingly, was the CPA's long-troubled approach to the issue of the ALP). And second, because it sent an organizer to Australia to 'Bolshevize' the Party in 1930–31. A new generation of leaders took over from the old, owing their positions to Moscow's patronage, and thus—until the Party was declared an illegal organization in 1940—fully compliant with the policies and wishes of Moscow. The shift in relations just outlined was part of a broader pattern in the Comintern's dealings with its sections that began after the Sixth Congress in 1928. If the 'Third Period' thesis was correct, and the world class struggle was about to intensify, and the Soviet Union to come under military attack (and, indeed, the thesis was partly correct, but partly self-fulfilling), then the Comintern needed sections that could reliably implement its policies. The Sixth Congress had been quite open about it: it now required from its national sections a 'strict party discipline and prompt and precise execution of the decisions of the Communist International, of its agencies and of the leading Party committees' (Degras 1960, 466).

In Comintern parlance, the period covered here encompasses two historical phases: the 'Third Period' of heightened capitalist crises and imperialist wars (and military threats against the USSR); and, after the political victory of the Nazis in Germany in 1933, the period of the cross-class 'Popular Front', with communists desperate to support alliances, front organizations, and governments that would prevent the rise of fascism in their own countries and protect the Soviet Union against the now looming military threat from Germany. With economic depression and talk of war, there was a growing sense of crisis in the West. This was a period when the CPA could have been expected to make major gains in membership numbers and influence. There were, of course, some gains particularly in the industrial trade unions, but the most striking fact is the continuing marginalization of the CPA in Australian life. For this, the CPA had largely itself and its Comintern connections to blame. The policies of the Third Period, dictated by Moscow and ultimately embraced by the CPA, meant a level of extremism and confrontation by communists that quickly isolated them in every campaign. The Popular Front—somewhat confused by the Australians with the 'united front', but endorsed nevertheless at the CPA's 1935 Congress—meant persistence and persuasion rather than confrontation but, however many 'progressive' people it influenced, the CPA continued to be rebuffed by the Labor Party.

Although the Comintern declared in the 'Theses' of its Sixth Congress that the Third Period would inevitably give rise to a 'fresh series of imperialist wars ... and to gigantic class battles' (Degras 1960, 456), the main battles in developed countries turned out to be within the communist, socialist and working class movements themselves. Communist parties became absorbed by internal struggles, looking for class enemies within their ranks, engaging in 'self-criticism', and changing their leaders. Whenever they looked outside, they attacked not the capitalists but what they saw as their proxies, the reformist leaders of social-democratic parties and trade unions, who were dubbed 'social fascists'. The 'main danger' to the communist parties, so the Comintern's argument went, was the danger of 'Right opportunism' within their ranks, that is, compromising with labour's established political and industrial leaders. In the United States this was said to be the crime of Jay Lovestone (a founder of the CPUSA, who was based in the Comintern's headquarters in Moscow for part of the 1920s), who advocated a theory of American 'exceptionalism' to the Third Period. The economic depression that followed the Great Crash on the Wall Street stock exchange seemed to knock a hole in that theory, and the Lovestone group was expelled. 'Right opportunism' was found even within the Comintern's leadership, when Bukharin was removed from his post as President at the Tenth ECCI Plenum in June 1929, having presided at the Congress in the previous year over the introduction of the new line. In Australia, too, Bert Moxon led a Comintern-backed challenge against the CPA leadership of Jack Kavanagh at the Party's Ninth Conference. The consequent change in leadership in 1929 was a turning point in the CPA's brief history (Curthoys 1993a, 65), though Moxon would not stay leader long enough to appreciate its significance.

The background to the 1929 leadership challenge was prepared more than a year earlier. At its April 1928 meetings on Australian issues, the ECCI had adopted at the instigation of Moxon a document on 'The Queensland Labour Party', declaring that it was 'essential that the CP should formulate a definite and clear policy upon which to take the lead in its opposition to the McCormack Government at the forthcoming State elections', held in May 1929 (CAML 495–3–64). It had proposed a mix of support for left-wing ALP candidates, withdrawal of communist support for Labor in other constituencies, and fielding communist candidates in selected constituencies. The resolution was endorsed by the Australian CEC on 12 July 1928. It was not seen as 'interference' in Australian affairs; indeed Wright regarded the discussions that produced the 'Queensland resolution' as the ECCI's first serious consideration of the Australian situation (Curthoys 1993a, 59). But whatever the merits of the strategy, it began to crystallize opposition to Jack Kavanagh's leadership, for Kavanagh could be fitted into the pattern of 'Right deviationism' then being cut in Moscow.

Having placated Moxon's Queenslanders by allowing them to stand candidates at the 1929 state election, which was lost by Labor, the general issue of the ALP returned very quickly to disturb the whole CPA. A federal election was called for 12 October 1929. The CEC decided not to take the Queensland option, but to support Labor at the federal level. The decision was made on 15 September 1929, and Lance Sharkey and Moxon sent a cable protesting it to the Anglo-American Secretariat of the Comintern three days later. The ECCI sent cables on 26 September, and then again on 29 September, insisting that the Queensland option be applied nationally. Moxon and Sharkey sent a further telegram to the ECCI on 8 October: 'Our motion that Comintern instructions be operated on received no support Central Committee'. The ECCI continued to insist that the CPA field independent candidates. Finally, on 6 December 1929, *Workers' Weekly* printed an Open Letter from the Comintern dated 13 October. The letter insisted that the CPA had to 'conduct open warfare' against the Labor Party.

The Comintern had made its views abundantly clear by telegram, convinced—as it disingenuously put it—that the CPA's forthcoming Annual Conference would adopt the corrected policy:

> CPA CONFRONTED SERIOUS PROBLEMS PRINCIPLE AND TACTICS WHICH WILL DETERMINE FUTURE DIRECTION AUSTRALIAN REVOLUTIONARY MOVEMENT STOP ... TASK CONVENTION SUBJECT SEVEREST CRITICISM DENOUNCING OPPORTUNIST ATTITUDE TOWRADS [sic] LABGOVERNMENT EXPRESSD PARTYS MANIFESTO FEDERAL ELECTIONS STOP CONSIDER CRITICISM MINORITY CEC AND CERTAIN LOCAL ORGANISATIONS THIS OPPORTUNIST ATTITUDE PERFECTLY SOUND AND NECESSARY STOP TASK CPA COME FORWARD AS ONLY WORKING CLASS PARTY STOP ... CEC ARGUMENTS DEFENCE ITS OPPORTUNIST POLICY COMPLETELY REFUTED BY EVENTS ONLY PROVES CORRECTNESS POLICY INTERNATIONAL STOP ... CONVINCED CONVENTION WILL ADOPT CORRECTED POLICY WHICH WILL ENABLE PARTY FULFIL GREAT TASKS (CAML 495–3–181)

The Comintern followed this up with another telegram on 11 October 1929:

> PARTYS DUTY AS SOLE PARTY WORKING CLASS CONDUCT INDEPENDENT CLASS POLICY OPPOSITION LABOUR PARTY TU BUREAUCRACY STOP FIRST CONDITION SUCCESSFUL CONDUCT THIS POLICY RUTHLESS COMBATING RIGIIT DEVIATIONS OWN RANKS BY INTRODUCING STRONGER WIDER SELFCRITICISM STOP ... ECCI SENT OPEN LETTER OUTLINING FUTURE POLICY COMPARTY STOP DEMAND WIDEST CIRCULATION LETTER AMONG MEMBERSHIP THOROUGH DISCUSSION PRIOR PARTY CONFERENCE STOP

EXPECT PARTY CONFERENCE BY MEANS SELFCRITICISM STRAIGHTEN
PARTY LINE ACCORDING DECISIONS SIXTH CONGRESS TENTH PLENUM
... (CAML 495–4–3)

This episode suggests that the bulk of the CPA leadership had not understood
the profound changes happening in the Comintern, as Stalin consolidated his
hold on the levers of the organization. They were perplexed by the advice they
were given. There was, in fact, nothing 'straight' about the Comintern's line.
The upshot of the Ninth Conference was that the minority—Moxon, Sharkey
and J.B. Miles—overthrew the majority of the previous CEC; in all of this, as
Curthoys (1993a, 66) argued, 'the Comintern had been the deciding factor'. It
was an assessment with which Jack Blake, with the benefit of considerable
hindsight, agreed (Blake 1972, 44). At its conclusion the new leadership sent to
the ECCI on 30 December 1929 a telegram in which the conference 'DECLARES
UNSWERVING LOYALTY NEW LINE' (Document 59).

The general position of the Comintern during the Third Period on large-scale
labour—i.e., social democratic—parties was that their leaderships had to be
exposed to the working class. This was a position that was designed for Europe,
could fit Australia, but did not fit the United States, which had no such party.
How the Americans contrived to 'expose' labour leaders was contentious and
changing, and was probably doomed from the start. It even included, among
other things, trying to form such a labour party. The problem was that
communists had great difficulty in convincing workers they were being betrayed,
and confronting social democrats during the Third Period as 'social fascists'
proved disastrous. It isolated communists, divided workers, and contributed to
the rise of Nazism in Germany.

The leadership change at the Ninth Conference of the Australian party also
reveals a marked change in the style of relations between the Comintern and the
CPA. Previously, the CPA had imagined that the relationship was reciprocal,
even if it had deferred to Comintern 'advice' with alacrity. But while the
Comintern may have been exasperated by the intermittent communications from
Australia (and vice versa), the tone of the relationship in 1929 reveals a major
change in the way that business was conducted. The Soviet party, and Stalin in
particular, were not simply *primus inter pares*, they were unchallengeable.
Whatever notions communists might previously have entertained about their
parties as forums for discussion (and they tended to be limited to notions of
discussion-for-action), these were now replaced by analogies with armies
following their leaders into battle. Trotsky's 'logic of substitutionism' had struck
again: Leninism was irredeemably centralizing.[1] Some who were closer to the

---

[1] This is not to excuse Trotsky who, once he had joined the Bolsheviks in 1917, was a champion of
centralization, as his organizing of the Red Army and his proposals for the 'militarization of labour'
show. Trotsky would probably have insisted that the key difference between his approach and Stalin's

centre noticed the change and made dramatic, but futile, criticisms. The esteemed elder German revolutionary, Clara Zetkin, for example, declared in March 1929 that the Comintern 'has turned from a living political body into a dead mechanism which on the one hand is capable of swallowing orders in Russian and on the other of regurgitating them in different languages' (cited McDermott and Agnew 1996, 86). Zetkin nevertheless remained a member. The new Australian leadership knew what was expected of them: Moscow was always right. And political differences and debate were henceforth reduced to simplistic labelling. Nearly 60 years later, Edna Ryan—wife of Jack Ryan, who was defeated in the ballot for the new CEC at the Ninth Conference and later hounded out of the CPA—reflected that something fundamental about the CPA in the 1920s had changed with the Ninth Conference: 'it didn't occur to us at the time that we were enjoying liberty of thought and expression, but there was no hushing and stifling, no fear of being accused if one proposed a tactic or an idea' (cited Curthoys 1993a, 67).

As a leader, Moxon in March 1930 urged tightening up in the CPA for better 'Bolshevization' (495–94–61), but his reign was short-lived. He embraced the Third Period with an enthusiasm that threatened to isolate the Party from the working class: advocating confrontations with police and, in April 1930, a general strike. His attacks on, and eventual expulsion of, Jack Kavanagh and Jack Ryan (both of whom were respected in the broader workers' movement) confirmed his recklessness. At a closed session of the Communist Party Plenum in January 1932, he himself was removed from the CC by unanimous decision (495–94–91). There was cable traffic between ECCI and the CPA over this move, with Moxon (and others) appealing for ECCI intervention against their expulsions (495–94–94), as Moxon had earlier appealed against Kavanagh, but the Anglo-American Secretariat was this time unmoved. All of this is faithfully recorded in the CAAL documents. Interestingly, Moxon's two former collaborators—Sharkey and Miles—would go on to have long careers as Party leaders. Sharkey was successful because he read the signs well, attaching himself to prevailing personalities, and detaching himself when required. Miles was not originally part of the Party's leadership (which was Sydney-based) because he worked in Brisbane, but after being brought to Sydney in 1931 to become Party secretary he proved to be a solid and reliable leader who would establish the Party's sense of solidity for the remainder of the 1930s. Deliberately groomed by the Comintern (by means of the Lenin School) to take on a Stalin-like image within the Australian party, Miles was held in high regard by Australian communists but never idolized.

'Bolshevization' of the CPA, however, was a process whose time had come. It appeared in the guise of Herbert Moore, pseudonym of Harry Wicks, American

---

lay in the character of the leadership; hence his efforts (and Stalin's) to be seen to be close to Lenin, who had become since his death a virtual communist 'saint'.

communist and Comintern agent to Australia. Moore's arrival in April 1930 was neither unexpected nor unwelcome, and it was the culmination of much urging by the Australian comrades. The ECCI had been asked, inter alia, for 'Despatch of a representative to work with the Australian Party as instructor for a period of at least a year. (The representative who came last year[2] was unable to do much more than investigate, as he remained only two months)' (CAML 495–6–16). Moore laid the organizational basis for the transition from a party which experienced relatively open debate to one where there was only one correct 'line', deviation from which could mean expulsion, and a party where the centre was in control. He stayed in Australia for just over a year. He came when the Party was in the throes of the leadership changes instituted by the Ninth Conference. Moore was particularly hostile to Jack Ryan, wanting him to return to the Party only if he recanted his deviationism and accepted Moore's direction. The lever against Ryan was his refusal to accept that the ALP was a 'social fascist' party. As the letters published in this section show, Ryan bent towards the Comintern line about 'social fascism', and eventually accepted it (in September 1931). Yet he was never readmitted to the Party, despite his wishes. Moore's next target was Jack Kavanagh, a respected former leader. Where Kavanagh had stressed education of Party members, Moore wanted only training; where Kavanagh tolerated diversity of views, Moore knew that there could only be one line. The process against Kavanagh was drawn-out and humiliating. Brought before the Party's Central Control Commission in mid-1930, charged with criticizing the CEC for indulging in self-criticism, Kavanagh confided to his diary: 'The manner in which self-criticism is being carried on is indicative of an infantile disorder. "Self-Criticism" is intended primarily for those who do not kow-tow to the CEC' (cited Curthoys 1993b, 28). He was censured, forced to capitulate, and was finally expelled at the beginning of 1931. Appeals to the ECCI (where he was a candidate member), fell on deaf ears. He was reinstated to the Party, on probation, from September 1931 for two years, but even at the end he was not permitted to function as a full member.

Moore's organizational changes meant greater centralization and less questioning of central authorities. Party branches were changed from a territorial to an industry base, and the Central Control Commission was strengthened and used to stop dissent. Moore was also instrumental in removing Moxon from the position of Party secretary at the end of 1930, and bringing Jack Miles from Queensland to Sydney to take that position. He boasted that during his stay CPA membership had more than doubled. After the Tenth Annual Congress in April 1931, Moore abolished the annual meetings, and advised that a Congress would be held if and when there was a change, and change would be signalled by the

---

[2] This is a reference to R.W. Robson, who attended the CPA's Seventh Conference in December 1927 using the pseudonym 'Murray'.

Comintern: 'We prepare congresses under the direction and advice of the CI' (CAML 495–94–67). Consequently, the next congress was not called until 1935, after the Seventh Comintern Congress.

Moore made quite an impression on the Australian party; nor did they want him to leave. In a letter of 2 June 1931, the Political Bureau asked the Comintern to permit the return of their instructor to Australia after he had reported to Moscow. They admitted that they had been 'very bad': the conference in 1929, they conceded, had been preceded by the 'infamous decision' to support the Labor Party in the federal elections. 'It is, however, essential that the ECCI have regard to our very bad past.' It noted a 'great improvement in the short space of twelve months', and declared it 'particularly necessary' that Moore be permitted to return to Australia (CAML 495–94–70).

The Comintern recognized that the Australian party still had problems, and in October 1932, adopted a 'Resolution on the situation in Australia and the Immediate tasks of the Party', in which it noted the growth of the Party and increased circulation of its press, but argued that the Party 'is still isolated from the basic masses of the Australian working class' (CAML 495–3–338). During the 1930s, Blake, Dick Dixon and a number of other younger members were sent to the Lenin School in Moscow in order to provide the basis for a new—Bolshevik, Stalinist, or merely more compliant, depending on one's prejudices—Australian party leadership. 'Bolshevization' had succeeded: there was no further need for a Comintern agent to steer the CPA.

The first real test of the CPA's reliability was provided by another change in the line from Moscow in 1935. Sharkey and Ted Docker were present at the Comintern's Seventh Congress, and committed themselves to its major new policy turn, the Popular Front, which aimed to fight fascism by creating strategic, cross-class alliances and supporting the (formerly demonized) social democratic parties. Communist rhetoric subsequently focused less on 'class' conflict than on uniting the 'progressive people' in defence of 'democracy'. The theoretical shifts were audacious: Dimitrov clearly distinguished between fascism and bourgeois democracy as different state forms, and argued for the extension of democracy. Although the CPA's Eleventh Congress later in 1935 readily adopted what it called the 'united front' policy, the Party took some time to realize what this policy actually meant. It was not just a matter of supporting 'progressives' in fronts against war, or against fascism, or in favour of international peace, or women, or Australian writers, or artists; it meant supporting the ALP in its election campaigns for government. So while the CPA made some ground among the middle class (Macintyre 1998, 323–25), the ALP did not requite the CPA's rediscovered attraction, and the CPA was soon called to Moscow to account for its failures. A special session of the Anglo-American Secretariat—what the documents revealingly call André Marty's Secretariat—was convened in July

1937 to consider 'the Australian Question', and took evidence over several days. Dixon, on behalf of the Australians, explained among other things the continuing difficulties of communicating with the Comintern (495–14–19).

During the 1930s, the Australian communists came under increasing domestic pressures from the federal government. Communists were frustrated when Customs would not allow many communist publications into the country, and disturbed to find their own publications banned from the postal delivery service. An amendment to the Crimes Act in 1932 had given power to the Commonwealth Attorney-General to obtain a declaration that an association was unlawful, and this continued to hang as a threat above the communists' heads though it was never successfully used against them. Nevertheless, communists remained hopeful—especially during their 'Third Period' analysis—that their ascent to power would be rapid. Moore, concluding an organizational conference, made the following notes: 'Elements of political crisis may begin to develop in this country within a fairly short time. The Party [would likely be] faced with the question of power within a reasonably short time ...' (CAML 495–94–70).

The defence of the Soviet Union, which had always been a priority for communists around the world, assumed even more urgency during the 1930s. Yet despite the decline in living standards among workers in the advanced capitalist states during the Great Depression (the effects of which lingered until the Second World War), communists found it very difficult to stir enthusiasm amongst their own working classes for the USSR. Information about life there was tightly controlled by the Soviet authorities, who used Western communists and sympathizers to paint flattering pictures for Western audiences. But the collectivization of agriculture and the wholesale deportation of large populations to remoter regions within the vast Soviet Union, the beginnings of industrialization allied with the internal passport system and reduced living standards, and ultimately the political purges, could not be entirely concealed. In building the communist future, human beings paradoxically turned out to be an expendable resource. Though the scale of the human tragedy in the Soviet Union may never be fully known, enough was known in the 1930s to deflate communist puff.

At the CPA's Eleventh Congress in December 1935, the Political Report—delivered by Jack Miles, now 'General Secretary'—had something to say about the Soviet example, and the history of the Party since 1930, when it had corrected itself:

> I want to say a word about the Soviet Union. I have given a lot of attention to developments over there in the past. My study of the position recently reveals astounding progress. I feel enthused, I feel amazed, I feel happy, when I read

about the reports to the XVIIth Congress.[3] It is necessary that we give a good deal of time to popularise the achievements of the Soviet Union ... We go before the workers full of confidence that the Soviet Union is a living example which can be followed by the toiling masses in Australia ... Since our Party got on to the line of the C.I. in 1930, no one can deny that there has been considerable progress. The P.B. to-day is better than ever fitted to interpret the line of the Comintern, to apply the line of the Comintern to Australia ... (CAML 495–94–123)

The Comintern had thus achieved its goal: it had created an Australian party that was fit to apply its line. The documents below chart how that happened.

Document 54

RGASPI 495–94–53. 21 Feb 1929, Higgins: letter: To Rob Robson. Typescript.

Esmonde Higgins and Robson resumed their earlier friendship (struck up during Higgins's time with the CPGB) during Robson's 1927–28 trip to Australia on behalf of the Comintern. In this letter, Higgins lets Robson know the progress of implementing the 'Queensland Resolution', which allowed the CPA to field candidates against the ALP in the 1929 Queensland state election. He also asks Robson to act 'as our friend at court', to get understanding and assistance from the Comintern.

THE COMMUNIST PARTY OF AUSTRALIA
SECTION OF THE COMMUNIST INTERNATIONAL

395 Sussex Street,
Sydney, NSW
Feb 21 1929

R.W. Robson,
London

Dear Rob,

Your very formal letter of Dec. 9 is to hand. Good. Also the parcel. Thanks.

Why revise the October Resolution, except in the sense of dealing with recent details of the capitalist offensive and the heavy tasks which these impose on the Party? An article of mine, written for the *Communist International* and adapted for the *Pan-Pacific Worker*, tries to do this, on the basis of the thoroughly satisfactory October Resolution. No one of us here has time to examine recent data on the present economic situation. Wish that I, for one, had. I agree entirely with your observations on trends.

You would be interested in the very honest and successful attempts which are being made to set up workers' electoral committees for the Queensland election campaign. There have been some misgivings, but none on the part of

---

[3] Seventeenth Congress of the CPSU, January 1934.

Moxon, who is working his guts out along lines that he would have abhorred a year ago. He has come down today to attend a CE meeting—the first visit to Sydney since he went north in July—and we will be able to review carefully the net total of achievements. It can safely be said that this is the only campaign which has brought forward a steady stream of news directly in answer to the Party's lead (this interests me particularly because of the *WW*), and that the Party has already been able to force all honest critics of McCormack[4] to swallow and stand for our programme of left-wing demands. The Party is certainly far more clearly on the map. The great trouble is the basic weakness of the Party, especially in numbers. We have won respect with hundreds, at least, as the only real alternative to the McCormack outfit.

You had better understand that I am giving personal opinions. Some comrades here and in Queensland are full of doubts and suspicions and regrets, but I am convinced they are needless. The Queensland campaign does of course mean a hell of a financial strain for the Party. Every blasted ha'penny had to be argued out.

The Party is in a good state, although it has no more members. We're well in the timber dispute, at the wish even of the Timber Workers' Union officials in Sydney and Melbourne. Kavanagh, as chairman of the NSW Disputes Committee, is in high favour. The Party has the wind well up the Miners' leaders. I hope that you will have a look at the *Weekly* these days and follow the developments.

The "Peace" Conference is on in Sydney, and Jock[5] is all for peace. There's going to be a crisis tonight at the Labor Council; relations have got to be defined. There were good interruptions at the sessions of the Conference on Tuesday and yesterday; you'll be surprised to know that, quite without premeditation, it was I who led the first disturbance, with enthusiastic backing from unemployed in the Gallery. Yesterday's riot of the women, led by the people you know, was a knocker. They owned the Town Hall for ten minutes. In Melbourne the Militant Women have been raiding timber yards and sitting on coppers. Jeffery has showed up brilliantly at the preliminaries of this session of the Conference.

I have been feeling very gloomy about the dirty way every promise made to me in Moscow and Berlin has been broken. There isn't time yet to know what has happened to London promises, although we haven't been getting ordered literature and have heard nothing from the Colonial Committee. Act, as you have promised, as our friend at court, and explain forcibly that we are very isolated and in need of all possible assistance. We have been getting a very few Political Letters, but possibly their fewness is the fault of the Post.

---

[4] Queensland leader of ALP, and Premier of Queensland until defeated at the 1929 state elections.
[5] Jock Garden.

I have been warring incessantly with the Customs to recover the junk they pinched at Fremantle, but without result. There is a better chance than ever of starting an all-in agitation against the Ban,[6] particularly thanks to the attention which the NSW Labor Council has drawn to it in connection with the Peace Conference.

By the way, the *Weekly* can claim modest credit for inducing the *Labor Daily* and several other papers to put Peace in quotes when talking of the Conference and for forcing Duggan to dilate at length on the charge that he and his friends had been "chloroformed".

For the moment Tommy[7] is working full time, but for decisive reasons he will have to be allowed to go back to the workshop, which is tragic.

Following at odd moments with keen interest the preliminary discussions of your congress. It's a great achievement to have stirred so much live argument.

Best of luck to all the lads, including Harry,[8] Andrew[9] and old Strudwick.

Hig

Document 55

RGASPI 495–94–46. no date [1929], Anglo-American Secretariat: letter: To the Political Commission of the Comintern. Typescript.

The Anglo-American Secretariat of the Comintern, which oversaw Australian matters, urges the Political Commission in this letter to send a representative to Australia and make other provisions for the better understanding of Australian issues in Moscow. This is one of the requests that would result in Herbert Moore being sent to Australia in 1930.

CONFIDENTIAL

To the Political Commission

The Anglo-American Secretariat urges the necessity for sending a representative of the Comintern to Australia for a considerable period for the purpose of helping the Australian Party to adopt and carry out the political and organisational line of the Comintern.

The Anglo-American Secretariat also considers it necessary to have a representative of the Australian Party permanently at the Comintern in order that the questions affecting the Australian Party may be more regularly brought before the ECCI and for providing a more regular channel for conveying the views of the Comintern to the Australian Party.

---

[6] Higgins refers to the ban on the importation of communist literature; see also Documents 55 and 57, below.
[7] Tom Wright.
[8] Harry Pollitt.
[9] Andrew Rothstein.

It is also necessary to consider the question of helping the Australian Party to maintain at least one full time worker at the Centre and two full time workers for the provinces.

In order to raise the political level of the Party it is essential to publish a monthly theoretical journal in Australia, which is particularly necessary in view of the literature ban and the obstacles to the penetration of communist literature into Australia. For this purpose also assistance must be given to the Party.

Anglo-American Secretariat.

Document 56

RGASPI 495–94–46. 20 Sept 1929, ECCI: telegram. Typescript.

In response to complaints received in Moscow from Moxon and Sharkey, the Comintern in this telegram insists that the CPA oppose the ALP in the forthcoming federal election, as per its Class Against Class line of the Sixth Comintern Congress.

Telegram
20.9.29.

WRIGHT 395 SUSSEX STREET SYDNEY AUSTRALIA

HAVE LEARNED THAT PARTY INSTEAD NOMINATING INDEPENDENT CANDIDATES FEDERAL ELECTIONS DECIDED FULL SUPPORT LABOUR PARTY STOP IF TRUE SUCH DECISION CONTRADICTORY INDEPENDENT POLICY COMMUNIST PARTY AND DECISIONS SIXTH CONGRESS STOP MUST COME OUT OWN PLATFORM EXPOSE ARBITRATION AND INDUSTRIAL PEACE COMMON TREACHEROUS ROLE OF BOURGEOIS LABPARTY AND REACTIONARY TRADEUNION BUREAUCRACY STOP EXERT ALL EFFORTS ORGANISE UNITED FRONT FROM BELOW NOMINATE COMMUNIST CANDIDATES AND WHERE NO COMMUNIST CANDIDATES COMMA SUPPORT CANDIDATES LEFTWING TRADEUNION WORKERS WHO FIGHT INDUSTRIAL PEACE ARBITRATION STOP IF THESE PROPOSALS TOO LATE RUN DEMONSTRATIVE CANDIDATES AS IN ENGLAND

EXECUTIVE

Document 57

RGASPI 495–20–3. 13 October 1929, Political Secretariat ECCI: letter: Open letter to the CEC of the CPA. In English, Russian, French and German versions. Typescript.

This 'Open Letter' from the ECCI to the CPA's CEC, dated October 1929, was published in the *Workers' Weekly* on 6 December, and thus became available to all Party members. It openly criticises the 'wrong policy' of the CPA towards the ALP, and indicates that the Party must reconsider its position at its forthcoming Ninth Conference.

Oct. 13, 1929.

OPEN LETTER TO THE CEC OF THE COMMUNIST PARTY OF AUSTRALIA.

Dear Comrades,

This is not the first time that the Communist International occupies itself with the Australian question. Already in 1927, it was found necessary to send a representative of the CI to your Party Convention, for the purpose of clarifying certain political and organisational issues then confronting your Party. In 1928, the ECCI, together with a representative from the CPA, formulated and adopted the so-called Queensland Resolution pertaining to the policy and tactics of the CP in the Queensland elections.

This time, the immediate cause for the serious consideration of the Australian question by the ECCI was the decision by a majority of your Central Committee to support the Labour Party in the Federal Elections in October of this year. This decision, plus your reply to our subsequent cable, makes it necessary to review as broadly as possible the situation at present confronting the Australian working class, and to analyse the central political tasks and organisational and tactical questions now before the CPA.

It is too obvious to permit of any doubt that the Australian working class and labour movement are at present living through a crisis of transition, which is only the reflection of the industrial and political fields of the new phase of development which Australian capitalism and economics have entered. Australian capitalism, like world capitalism, is passing through its third phase, which finds expression in the crumbling of capitalist stabilisation and in the intensification of class antagonisms.

The rather unique and privileged position of young Australian capitalism (with its huge territory and sparse population; its strong and almost monopolistic position as a producer and exporter of primary products; its keen shortage of labour in both industry and agriculture before the war; its strong State capitalistic and protectionist tendencies; its "White Australia" policy; the widespread Arbitration Court system which was in reality a more or less perfected system of industrial peace; and its comparative isolation from world politics due to its former position in relation to Great Britain),   all this is now undergoing very deep changes.

Australian capitalism is now passing through a new phase of development. Having participated actively in the last imperialist world war, it has definitely been drawn into the maelstrom of capitalist-imperialist contradictions, this time no longer as a passive annex to British imperialism, but as an active agent and participant.

Australia, with its vast possibilities of further development and its exclusive strategic position in the Pacific (where the conflict of imperial interests, especially between the two chief rivals—USA and Britain—is keenest), becomes the scene of ever sharper competition between American and British capital.

In this rivalry Australia strives to play off Great Britain against America in the effort to ensure an independent imperialist development. On the one hand the Australian bourgeoisie is still dependent on Great Britain as the main market for its primary products, and on the other it is anxious to utilise American finance capital for developing its industries. In order to compete successfully in the world market (as regards primary products), and on the home market—with the manufactures of the more advanced industrial countries, the Australian bourgeoisie is compelled to secure a drastic reduction in costs of production and to reduce the working and living standards of the Australian working class to the lower level of the British and European proletariat. This is glaringly revealed by the general capitalist offensive of the last two years:—The Crimes Act, the Anti-Trade Union Law, the Transport Act, the Literature Ban; the defeat of the seamen, the smashing of the watersiders, the lockout and bitter five-month struggle of the timber workers who have been robbed of the 44-hour week; the lockout of the miners; the attack on the railwaymen and metal workers; the attack on the NSW basic wage, etc., etc.

The comparatively privileged position which the Australian working class occupied for several decades, and which was the result of the specific characteristics of Australian capitalism and economics (outlined above), has thus also been shaken to its foundations. Instead of a keen shortage of labour in the gradually expanding industries and in agriculture, there is now an army of unemployed reaching nearly 250,000. The 44-hour week is almost non-existent at present. The basic wage is being reduced. The trade union movement, which in the course of two decades has been devitalised and demoralised by the Arbitration Courts, is now shackled by the new Anti-Trade Union Law whose drastic provisions surpass even the British Anti-Trade Union Law. All the forces of the State, the military, the police, the judiciary, are put into action against the working class (seamen's strike, waterfront strike and timber lockout). In this general capitalist offensive the methods and tactics used by the Australian bourgeoisie are the well known and tested methods of the older capitalist countries: lockouts, ruthless crushing of strikes "industrial peace" conferences on the Mond-Turner pattern, etc.

The illusions that existed among broad sections of the Australian working class and that were fostered by the social-reformist agents of the capitalism abroad, to the effect that Australia was a "social paradise" and an "exception" to the general rule of capitalist development, are rapidly being shattered. The Australian working class is being robbed of all its "privileges".

The question as to whether Australian capitalism will succeed in its plans to subjugate the working class or whether the working class will assume the counter-offensive and develop its revolutionary struggle against capitalism will depend on the ability and determination of the CP to organise and lead the counter-offensive.

The prospects are thus most favourable for the only revolutionary Party in Australia—the Communist Party.

With objective and subjective conditions in its favour, the CPA will be able to fulfil its functions as a Communist Party only if it proceeds consciously and without vacillation as the initiator, organiser and leader of the economic and political struggles of the working class, and only if it consistently works among the masses and unmasks ruthlessly the treacherous social-fascist role of the Labour Party and of the trade union bureaucracy. This has not been the case until now. The Party has been slow in learning from the experience of the British, German and French working class and from events in Australia proper. The important decisions of the VI World Congress and X Plenum of the CI as well as the decision of the IV RILU Congress seem to have been neglected by the CPA. Even at its conference of December 1928 the Party could not give a proper political estimate of the Labour Party, define its fundamentally social-fascist character, its aggressive counter-revolutionary role in the present situation.

The Party by its tactics during the elections still appears to cling to the idea that the Labour Party of Australia continues to represent in some way the interests of the working class when as a matter of fact its past history, when in and out of Government, proves it to have been an instrument of the Australian bourgeoisie. In the present, third period of post-war capitalism generally and in the specific conditions of present-day Australian capitalism in particular, the role of the Australian Labour Party as the agents of the bourgeoisie stands out more clearly than ever. Under these circumstances to persist in the tactics the Communist Party of Australia is now pursuing means, not to lead, but to mislead the working class. The Party must clearly understand that a labour organisation—however radical it may claim to be—which fails to carry out a definitely militant class policy must inevitably drift to the side of the bourgeoisie. In regard to the Labour Party of Australia it must be said definitely that it has already gone over to the side of the bourgeoisie and to support it in any way means to support the enemies of the working class. Consequently, the decision of the majority of your CEC to support the Labour Party in the last elections is a glaring example of grave Right deviation deserving the severest condemnation.

The whole policy of the Party finds its crowning expression in the following statement of the *Workers Weekly* (August 2, 1929):-

> In this country there will be no strike on August 1st. Not that the Australian workers have less need than our fellow workers in Europe to demonstrate against

imperialist war and the warmongers, but that in this country the lines of the class struggle have not yet become so clear that the working class is only beginning to realise that its enemy is capitalism and the capitalist State. The task of militants in this country is not yet to lead the working class in a direct challenge to capitalism, but to popularise the basic ideas of the class struggle amongst the workers, their wives and children.

To this we would add the following passage from the resolution passed at your last Party Conference in December 1928:-

> We must not lose sight of the fact that the way to the CP leads through this Left Wing—not because we want it so, not because we in any way hesitate to transfer these masses directly from the path of reformism and Labour Party illusions to our own revolutionary ideology and action, but because these masses still hesitate to do so.

> This transformation is not effected through political miracles, nor will we accomplish it through virtuous isolation of the CP from the masses, but it is a long and difficult process whose various phases we must help in speeding up.

It must be said that such statements border on liquidationism. They are a denial of the elementary principles of the role and functions of the Communist Party as laid down by the Communist International. In the light of these statements the decided Right deviation of the Communist Party of Australia becomes comprehensible. It also explains why the Party still has such poor organisational contacts with the masses and why it has made no headway on the road towards becoming a mass Party of the working class. Apparently, the Party regards itself as being merely a propagandist body and as a sort of adjunct to the Left Wing of the Labour Party, whereas our conception of the role and functions of the Communist Party is that it should be the leader of the working class and the principal driving force in its political and economic struggles. Instead of this the Communist Party of Australia is content to trail behind the working class and to preach to "the workers, their wives and children". The Party grossly underestimates the intensity of the class struggle in Australia and fails to appreciate its role in this struggle. Clearly, as long as this state of affairs continues it is hopeless to expect the Communist Party of Australia to be anything more than a relative handful of propagandists—however ardent—isolated from the masses. We earnestly urge you, and the whole of the Party membership, to submit your policy and tactics to a thorough overhauling and we are convinced that, if you really have the cause of Communism at heart, you will radically alter your course and henceforth pursue the line of the Communist International.

At the present turning point, where the class struggle in Australia is growing keener from day to day, with a general capitalist offensive actually in full swing, with the Labour Party politicians and trade union bureaucracy revealing their treacherous social-fascist role as allies and agents of the Capitalist State, with the inevitable radicalisation of the masses, it is urgently necessary for the CP to assert itself as the only true working class Party which organises and leads the workers in the struggle against capitalism, imperialism and its agents. At this point it is not only impermissible to support the ALP directly or indirectly (whether in State or Federal elections, and regardless of place), but it is the duty of the CP to conduct open warfare against the party of class collaboration and Industrial Peace, against the party of capitalist arbitration, against the party of such labour-fascists as McCormack, Hogan & Co., against the party of strike-breakers, wage reducers and police terror (seamen, watersiders, railwaymen in Queensland, etc.), against the party of race prejudice and White chauvinism ("White Australia"), against the party agency of British imperialism which is feverishly preparing a war against the only Workers' State, the USSR.

[…]

The Party must make a thorough study of the resolutions of the VI Congress of the CI and the X Plenum of the ECCI in all nuclei and reorganise its work on the basis of self-criticism, eliminating all opportunist waverings, deviations and mistakes in its practical work. In order to assure the carrying out of the new policy you must take effective measures to secure the attendance of the largest possible number of delegates straight from the factories at your next Congress. The Congress should be preceded by a wide discussion among the Party members on the basis of this letter with the object of finding the practical form of carrying that policy into effect. To this purpose you must publish this letter and secure its widest possible circulation among the Party membership.

We fully appreciate the enormity of the tasks that the present period of capitalism imposes upon the numerically small Communist Party. But we insist that the smallness of its membership is mainly due to the wrong policy it has hitherto pursued. We are convinced that if your numerically small Party resolutely sets to work on the lines set out above it will hew a path for itself to the masses and by proving to them that it is really their leader in their struggles it will open the way for itself to become a real mass party of the working class.

POLITICAL SECRETARIAT OF THE ECCI.

Document 58

RGASPI 475–94–48, 495–94–60. no date [October 1929], ECCI: report: The New Stages in the Tactics of the Comintern: Australia. In English and Russian; typescript.

This Comintern report is highly critical of the CPA, especially of its failure to implement the line of the Sixth Comintern Congress towards the ALP: 'The question of the Labour Party has never been understood by the Party.' It notes a 'rift' in the Central Committee, but does not appear to know the protagonists. It appears to pre-date the Ninth Conference by a few weeks, at which the rift would become open, and Moxon, Sharkey and Miles would oust the majority leadership of Kavanagh and Ryan.

THE NEW STAGES IN THE TACTICS OF THE COMINTERN AUSTRALIA

The Fight for Winning the Majority of the Working Class

The tactics to achieve the objective have not been put into effect by the Australian Party with the result that little or no progress has been made. Despite the growing number of industrial disputes, and the bitter fights waged by the workers against Labour governments, the Party still remains a mere handful of members. This position can be traced to the fact that the Party has failed to understand the changing conditions of Australian capitalism [and] the 'third period', with its resulting change in the tactics of the Party. As a result of the confusion existing in the question, and the statement made by the leadership that 'the third period' does not exist in Australia, none of the decisions of the VI World Congress or the X Plenum have been put into effect, resulting in the Party demonstrating glaring 'right wing' opportunist mistakes, chiefly on the question of the Party's relations with the Labour Party, and united front tactics.

The question of the Labour Party has never been understood by the Party. The decision of the Comintern that the Party should fight the Labour Party in the Queensland elections was carried out, but statements from the leaders of the Party reveal that this tactic was applied only because the Queensland workers had had 14 years' experience of a Labour government. When the Party had to face up to a federal election in November 1929, the utmost confusion was shown, resulting in glaring 'right wing' mistakes, as the following statement from the *Workers' Weekly*, of September 20th, 1929, on the federal elections will show: 'The Communist Party calls on the workers to smash the nationalist federal government (Conservative)[10] —the organiser of the employers' offensive—and welcomes the prospect of a Labour Government which would in present circumstances inconvenience the employers' plans, and may provide a short breathing space in which preparations could be made to meet fresh attacks'!

The domination of the trade unions by the arbitration courts does not present the task to the Party of unorganised workers. All the industrial workers as a result of arbitration are organised but at the same time disorganised to the extent that arbitration is consistently encouraging the formation of new unions. Organisers paid by the government are deliberately sent into militant unions to encourage members to break away from the union into a new organisation, with a different award and higher benefits. The Party's work in the trade unions is weak. The policy of the 'united front tactic from above' is practised instead of

---

[10] The parenthesis was added by hand.

'from below'. This considerably weakens the whole of the Party's campaign against arbitration and industrial peace. Recent industrial struggles have shown the will to fight on the part of the masses, but the Party's failure to consistently organise the masses for struggle has resulted in a reliance on a leadership permeated with an arbitration court ideology instead of a fighting leadership. The building of the MM has also shown the Party's failure to understand the preparatory organisation work necessary for such an organisation. The conference called in Sydney in July 1929 to launch the MM consisted mainly of Party members and leading militants, consequently it still remains a paper organisation. 'Unity from above' is preferred by the Party in its success in obtaining the affiliation of the NSW Labour Council to the Profintern, and the Australian Council of Trade Unions to the PP TUS.[11] With the result that the Sydney Labour Council is able to refute the letters from the Profintern without the Party being able to rally the support of the masses against the pseudo-lefts. Garden, secretary of the NSW Labour Council, has already launched an attack on the CP succeeding in removing Comrade Kavanagh from the position of trade union organiser, and has every prospect of removing Comrade Ryan from the research department. The ACTU has broken its affiliation with the PP TUS.

Street demonstrations have been held in Sydney in connection with the miners' strike and unemployment, but the Party is still afraid to organise street demonstrations on work days, confining its activities in this direction to Sundays. Labour Defence Corps have been formed in many of the mining districts; in Kurri, Cessnock, etc. and also in Sydney. News from *The Workers' Weekly* suggests that these Defence Corps have been formed under the influence of the Party, which has recently sent many members from Sydney into the mining districts.

The 1st August campaign once more demonstrates the Party's failure to break with 'legalism'. The Party's statement on the First of August campaign in *The Workers' Weekly* reveals once again the timidity, the lack of initiative, and failure to recognise the Party's role as the leader of the workers. The statement reads: 'In this country there will be no strikes on August 1st. Not that Australian workers have less need than our fellow workers in Europe to demonstrate against imperialist war and the war mongers, but that in this country the lines of the class struggle have not yet become so clear that the working class is only beginning to realise that its enemy is capitalism and the capitalist state.'—'The task of militants in this country is not yet to lead the working class in a direct challenge to capitalism, but to popularise the basic ideas of class struggle among the workers and their wives and children.'

---

[11] Pan-Pacific Trade Union Secretariat.

These examples show that the Party has not yet come out of the propaganda stage. By its right-wing policy and incorrect tactics, it has failed to lead the workers in the growing class conflicts, which has resulted in its membership remaining at about three hundred.

In recent weeks a rift has come about in the Central Committee. As yet we have received no information on the causes or nature of this rift.[12]

Document 59

RGASPI 495–94–53. 30 Dec 1929, Presidium CPA: Marconigram. Typescript.

The victors at the Ninth Conference greet the Comintern.

MARCONIGRAM

30 December 1929

ANNUAL CONFERENCE GREETS COMINTERN DECLARES UNSWERVING LOYALTY NEW LINE CONDEMNS CAPITULATORY OPPORTUNIST POLICY FEDERAL ELECTIONS AND RIGHT DEVIATIONS SINCERITY SELF CRITICISM PROVED FUTURE ACTIVITIES

LOUGHRAN BARRAS SHARKEY MILES MOXON
PRESIDIUM

Document 60

RGASPI 495–94–61. 21 March 1930, Pollitt (forwarding to an unknown comrade, perhaps in Moscow, a letter by Esmonde Higgins). Typescript.

Higgins, the only member of the 'right-wing' deviationists to be re-elected to the CPA's CEC at the Ninth Conference in 1929, writes to Harry Pollitt, a candidate member of the ECCI from the CPGB, seeking help against the new leadership of the Party, now led by Herbert Moxon. Higgins concedes that the old leadership did not understand the new line of the Comintern (though, being present at the Sixth Congress, he should have), and blames the problems in communication. He describes the atmosphere of the Ninth Conference as 'poisonous', is convinced that Moxon wants to expel those he opposes despite their being loyal communists, and asks for a 'guide' to be sent to Australia to 'knock our heads together'. Herbert Moore arrived soon after, and Higgins got more than he bargained for.

21st March 1930

Dear Comrade,

I have received a letter from an old comrade of mine in the Australian Party, comrade Higgins. He particularly wished me to treat the letter as confidential

---

[12] These two sentences do not appear in the English version. They have been appended at the end of the Russian version, by hand.

but I consider it gives such a revealing picture of the situation in the Party that for your personal information I am sending extracts from it so that you may have an idea what is going on.

All good wishes,
Yours fraternally,
Harry Pollitt

The old CC wasn't bad. We did far better work last year than ever before. But we slipped to blazes in not understanding the new line. One reason, of course, is lack of material. Although I'm supposed to be in charge of Agit-Prop, and the editor of the paper, I haven't yet had a glimpse of the Economic Tasks Resolution of the Tenth Plenum. There is one copy in Sydney (itself a gift from an accidental receiver in Melbourne), and it is being duplicated. This state of affairs is due partly to the literature ban, and partly to complete indifference of comrades in London and Berlin.

But we hadn't begun to work things out afresh, and when the Federal elections came on, we rushed excitedly about, happy in the prospect of at last getting an end to the 13 years' cry: "Wait until we get a Labour Government." And we were so impressed with the role of Bruce as the organiser of British imperialism's offensive, that we assumed that Scullin would have to make at least a pretence of being different for a while. No one dreamed that Scullin's self-exposure would be so prompt or so complete.

So with the timber strike. Everyone knew that the industry was knocked rotten, but no one realised how completely rotten. We thought there was a chance of knocking back the extra four hours, and we fought accordingly, and missed a wonderful chance to bring to life new rank and file organisations.

The so-called opposition in the CC and the Party was equally to blame throughout the year, but couldn't swallow the election line and then rationalised objections that hadn't existed on other questions. There developed a dog fight called a discussion. I, as editor, deliberately let it run its course, though it was destroying the *Weekly* as a popular paper, and though it really required direction. I wanted it to be on record as an experiment that had failed, so that next time we could discuss intelligently.

Then came the conference, in an atmosphere absolutely poisonous. The new CC was elected on the second day, and after that the conference became a dud, although it lasted three more days. The opposition ticket romped home, except for three—a bloke who has just gone to gaol for five months, a miner from Lithgow (150 miles away), and me. How I got on I don't know; evidently they thought the paper needed me!

Since then the situation has got still more poisonous. The deeds of the CC are all right. We are honestly trying to work out the new line in very complicated circumstances, getting unquestionably good results in the coalfields; there is no disunity on the CC, except that the non-opposition three distrust the judgement of the general Secretary. We are putting the Party on the map better than before.

But each meeting shows that Moxon won't be happy till he's expelled half the Party—particularly Kavanagh, Wright, Jack Ryan and Jeffery. (He would add Hector Ross and me, but we have certain modest triumphs to strengthen us.) Nothing definite but perpetual sneers and jibes and misrepresentations against which I and Lithgow have continually to protest. And this kind of talk is going the round of the Party. I expect any day a dramatic move for the expulsion of these four at least.

And there is no justification. Certainly they are inclined to be right-wingers in certain respects. (Even I had to break with them early in the discussion.) Kavanagh is a born sectarian who has never developed since the pre-war Socialist Party of Canada, Wright is caution at all costs, Ryan is inclined to attach a great deal of importance to the Trades Hall. Jeffery while one minute wanting to knife Garden even more than the rest of us, has an MM complex. But there is nothing in the activities of these blokes to suggest that they are anti-Party or even anti-new line. They accept it even if they might not relish it. They are absolutely loyal to the Party and we cannot afford to lose any of them. (Kavanagh and Ryan are excellent propagandists and the other two are wonderfully solid workers.)

You will see that our petty inner-Party difficulties are not taking on a very high political tone. We are not capable of such, and anyhow it is questionable if there has been any politics in our feuds at any stage, so terms like "conciliator" hardly apply.

The coal fight is likely to tail off soon. The police have pretty well won out with their terrorism. It is only the Party which has kept the lads' spirits up. We'll have rail and metal fights on us soon, complicated by severe unemployment (2,000 New South Wales railwaymen sacked last week).

It would do us the world of good to have some guide, philosopher and friend sent us. We're raw, and maybe he could knock our heads together.

Document 61

RGASPI 495–20–3. 30 March 1930, Political Secretariat ECCI: letter: to the CC of the CPA. Typescript.[13]

As part of the 'class against class' strategy of the Third Period, the CPA attempted to wean workers away from established trade union leaders by creating a 'Minority

---

[13] This letter is similar to a letter of 10 March 1930 sent to the CC CPA by the Political Secretariat of the ECCI and the Executive Bureau of the RILU, protesting about the methods used to organize the MM (495–94–58).

Movement' within the trade unions. Some of their attempts, however, met with disapproval from Moscow, particularly for their poor preparation and organization.

March 30, 1930

To the Central Committee
of the Communist Party
of Australia

Dear Comrades,

After hearing the report on the situation in Australia and after the careful study of the materials on the All-in Conference of the Militant Trade Union Minority Movement we desire to communicate to you the following views and recommendations:

[...]

3. Hence, we feel obliged to condemn the methods you employed in organising the "Minority Movement", notwithstanding the specific instructions we sent you on this matter. Almost no preparations were made for convening the conference. No efforts were made to establish functioning opposition groups in the reformist unions, in the factories, etc. In a word, the conference was convened before any efforts were made to establish your influence in the localities, in the districts and among the masses of the workers generally. All the work in connection with the conference was done "from the top". The conference was merely a gathering of a number of our leading comrades who, in session, declared themselves to be a "Militant Minority Movement". Such an organisational approach to the building of a revolutionary opposition in the trade union movement can only result in the formation of a small, sectarian body which will have no roots among the masses and will therefore be incapable of fulfilling the aims of the movement.

[...]

10. The economic struggles now taking place are being waged against the employers, against the forces of the Social Fascist Labour Government and the trade union bureaucracy. Under these circumstances, economic struggles tend more and more to assume the character of political struggles. It is the task of our Party to explain to the masses the full political significance of these struggles. It must make clear to the masses that every economic struggle and particularly those against rationalisation is related to the struggle against the war danger and above all against the danger of war against the Soviet Union, that it is related with the struggle of the oppressed colonial peoples. The Party must, by actively participating in and securing the leadership of the struggles of the working class—rely for this purpose on the revolutionary trade union opposition—develop them more and more into mass political strikes against the

danger of war, against the oppression of colonial peoples, against the Labour Fascist Government.

[...]

POLITICAL SECRETARIAT ECCI.

COMMUNIST FRACTION OF THE RILU.

Document 62

RGASPI 534–7–5. 25 May 1930, Moore: letter to CI. Typescript. Stamped in Russian: Secret.

Herbert Moore arrived in Australia in April 1930. His letters are a first-rate source of information about the condition of the CPA organization, its leaders, and about the attitude of communists towards Moscow. The major question taken up in this letter is the state of communist organization of the 'Militant Minority Movement' in the factories. The question of Jack Ryan's expulsion and continuing influence is also addressed.

May 25th, 1930.

Dear Comrades,

As soon as I arrived here about April 10, I took up with the Party the general line of our trade union fraction work in the Minority Movement and in the New South Wales Labor Council. I made recommendations to the Central Committee along the lines of the agreement on policy reached at joint sessions of the Communist fraction of the Profintern and the Anglo-American Secretariat of the Comintern on the day I left Moscow.

The Central Committee of the Party, after some discussion, unanimously accepted all my recommendations. It was quite apparent that the policy formulated by us in Moscow was different from the policy being carried out by the Party in Australia. In regards to the New South Wales Labor Council the Central Committee was pursuing a policy of practically ignoring the Council and confining its activities almost exclusively to attacks from the outside. I explained to the Comrades that such a policy was a form of "left" sectarianism, and after a considerable time convinced them that we should not only activise our Party members by organising them definitely into a functioning fraction inside the New South Wales Labor Council, but that we should proceed to the organisation of a Vigilance Committee for the RILU composed of our Party members and militant sympathisers in the Council and to proceed to organise similar committees in all the local unions where we have members or influence.

Our fraction has been meeting regularly and waging a fight on all class issues since the adoption of the new policy. Our strength in the Council is approximately twenty (20) whom we can rely upon out of a total of approximately ninety delegates. However, we have succeeded on a number of occasions in getting votes of censure against the Federal Labor Government in spite of the resistance of Garden and his supporters. (The arrest and deportation of Indonesian prisoners to the Dutch imperialists; the arrest and imprisonment of the May Day demonstrators at Darwin by the Federal Labor Government; the selection of delegates to the RILU congress.) In the fight for delegates to the RILU Congress Garden tried to defeat the proposal to send a delegation on the hypocritical excuse that the Council was without money and some of his cohorts raised the question about the necessity for using any money that could be obtained for unemployed relief instead of sending people on holiday trips to Europe. Our comrades at two sessions waged a determined and very effective fight in defense of the line of the RILU and pointed out that by sending delegates to the fifth Congress who would report back to the Australian workers the decisions arrived at as a result of deliberations of workers from all over the world would strengthen the Australian movement and enable us to fight more effectively both for employed and unemployed.

When Garden realised that the fight of our comrades was so effective that he could not hope to defeat them, even on the pretext of no finances, he then postponed selection of delegates for one week in order to give him a chance to organise his machine to send his own henchmen. He wanted to prevent any of the known militants going to the RILU Congress who would present the real facts regarding the shameful social-fascist policies, and expose to the RILU the slimy attacks made upon Comrade Lozovsky in connection with the letter of the RILU to the New South Wales Labor Council. The result was that of the three delegates being sent officially from the New South Wales Labor Council, only one of them (Cochrane, representing the Boilermakers' Union) is an honest worker, who generally follows the lead of our forces in the Labor Council. Another of the official delegates, Kilburn, is a member of the Executive Committee of the Australian Labor Party, a flunkey of Scullin, a left social-fascist, who in the Labor Council is always ready and willing and anxious to do any underhanded work or wage any filthy attack against our forces and the RILU at the behest of Garden. There is not the slightest doubt that Garden has definitely decided to wage an attack against our forces and against the RILU and that he intends to use Kilburn as one of the agencies for carrying on a slander campaign against the RILU and the Comintern when he returns to Australia. In plain words Kilburn is coming to the Soviet Union as our enemy and as an enemy of the Soviet Union. It is very essential that this person be given an unmerciful grilling when he arrives, that he be attacked and exposed by some of our leading members at the Profintern Congress and that the adherents of the Profintern in Australia be furnished with verbatim reports of his speeches as well as the speeches against him to be used in a campaign in defense of the RILU when he returns.

The third candidate, Lyons, is an utter non-entity, a mere rubber stamp for Garden, who will follow the line of Kilburn and repeat anything required of him. He should also meet with the same treatment as Kilburn.

In order that the real facts regarding the New South Wales Labor Council may be put before the Fifth Congress, the Vigilance Committee is sending a delegate of its own. This comrade will arrive with proper credentials. On the report of the credentials committee to the congress a special point should be made to the effect that there are three delegates from the New South Wales Labor Council and one from the Vigilance Committee. This could be discussed on the floor. Chances are that Kilburn may try to oppose it and that the comrade who comes for the Vigilance Committee will then have an opportunity to state why the Committee selected a delegate. This will expose Kilburn at the very start and also place him in an unenviable position throughout the rest of the Congress. Our policy in sending a delegate from the Vigilance Committee will be supported by Cochrane, one of the regular delegates from New South Wales Labor Council.

Other delegates are from the minefields [sic][14] and the railroads. Some of our comrades from the minefields, as well as the comrade from the Vigilance Committee of the Labor Council, will carry letters of introduction to Comrade Lozovsky. I suggest that the comrades of the Anglo-American Section of the Profintern discuss the situation in Australia with these comrades and aid them in every way in their work during the Congress as they are inexperienced, never having been outside of Australia before.

As to other work, the Party is carrying out the decisions regarding the Militant Minority Movement and the provisional nature of its executive committee. We are proceeding in all the various states in building up minority movements under different names. The militant forces work hand in hand with the Party in the formation of committees of action to resist the onslaught on wages, hours and conditions of labor. When struggles are developing these committees carry on agitation for our general program, and wage a fight for rank and file strike committees. When strikes are called and such committees are established these Councils of Action then become the driving force in efforts to extend the strike. (Details of such work will be given by our delegates, and in other reports covering mining, metal and railroad.)

The Party reacted very quickly to our new forms of organisation particularly in the minefields where the struggle was just reaching its final stages. When I arrived I discovered that the Central Committee, although following for the most part a correct political line, and raising slogans for rank and file committees, had no conception of the real function of strike committees and councils of action. The function of these organisations and their various divisions of work was

---

[14] Moore doubtless meant 'coalfields'.

explained to them in detail and so effective were these forms that within a few days after adopting them in the coalfields we succeeded for the second time in the history of the struggle in defeating the recommendations of the Union officials to accept the wage reductions of the employers.

We are holding a Party plenum (Plenary session of the Central Executive Committee) the last week of June at which time we will endeavour to set a date for the convening of a conference of the trade union opposition. Whether we actually set a date, will of course, depend entirely upon how far we have succeeded in establishing opposition movements throughout the various States of the Commonwealth. One of our greatest shortcomings is the lack of funds to work with. Were we in a position to wage a campaign over a period of months, we could build a powerful opposition movement in this country. There is not the slightest doubt that there will be a number of sharp conflicts within the next period, in fact, now small spontaneous strikes develop in the metal, on the railroads and even in the mining industry, in spite of the recent fall-out, much faster than we can react to them with our limited forces, and our lack of finance.

Another grave question for the Party and the RILU adherents is the situation on the *Pan Pacific Monthly*. Jack Ryan, who is the acting editor of the *Pan Pacific Monthly*, and who was one of the leaders of the old right wing Central Committee, that openly and insolently defied the Comintern in supporting the Labor Party against Comintern instructions, is a supporter of Garden, carrying on in a disguised manner agitation that objectively supports the Labor Party, defends compulsory arbitration. Ryan also denies that there is such a thing as social-fascism as far as the Australian Labor Party is concerned. The fact that he is the acting editor of the *Pan Pacific Monthly*, enables him to use the columns of that paper for the publication of articles at variance with the line of the RILU. As a result of his flagrant violation of Party discipline, he was in February, two months before I arrived here, expelled from the Party. Since that time I have had some conversations with him and he says that he is willing to work with the Party, but that he will not sign the statement to the effect that he was wrong in supporting the social-fascist Labor Party, nor will he admit his wrong line on the question of social-fascism. There is grave danger that as Garden develops his fight against us, Ryan will use the *Pan Pacific* on behalf of Garden, whose name still appears as the editor of the *Pan Pacific Monthly*. I suggest that this question of editorship be immediately taken up and that someone be sent here for the purpose of editing the magazine if it is to continue. At the present time its circulation is practically non-existent. Ryan claims a circulation of some 3,000, but this circulation is based solely upon bundle orders received from the unions dominated by the Garden machine. These unions pay in a certain amount of money, the magazines are placed at their disposal and lay [sic] in heaps around the trade union offices and meeting halls. It can truthfully be said that actually less than 500 copies ever reach the hands of workers who read them. The moment the *Pan Pacific* breaks with Garden, even his mythical circulation will disappear. There is no question that there is a field here for such a magazine, and that if properly set out, so that it reflects the class struggle in its columns and gives a revolutionary lead to the workers, a good circulation can be built up, but it can never be built up under present conditions.

Further information on this question will be furnished you by the delegates.

With Communist Greetings,
Herbert Moore.

Document 63

RGASPI 534–7–5. 25 July 1930, Moore: letter to CI. Typescript. Written by hand: 'very secret'.

In this letter Moore sets out his plans for reorganizing the CPA because of its deficiencies. Moore argues here that the CPA 'has never been organised on a correct basis'.

July 25, 1930
ORG. DEPARTMENT

Dear Comrades,

When I arrived I took up the question of Party organisation with the Central Committee. The Party has never been organised on a correct basis. The units of Party organisation were in the overwhelming majority still based upon the old social democratic forms of territorial locals. Only in the mining area was there any semblance of factory nuclei organisation, and for the most part these functioned in the same way as the local groups composed of members living in a certain neighbourhood. In spite of the organisational defects, there has been a steady growth of party membership, due entirely to the fact that the new Central Executive Committee that came into office at the Party Congress last December had been diligently striving to carry out the new line as laid down at the Sixth World Congress and the tenth Plenum. As a result of the long struggle in the Northern Coalfields where 12,000 (twelve thousand) miners were locked out for a period of thirteen months and are only now returning to work on the basis of a complete sell-out of the officials, who, throughout the entire struggle, resisted every effort to extend the strike, and fought to impose the terms of the mine-owners upon the workers. [sic] (A complete report of this struggle and the activity of the Party and the Militant Movement is being sent separately.)

[...]

In other industries I found that we had very few Party members, and there was not a single nucleus in any industry aside from the mining. At every meeting of the Central Committee the organisation question has been one of the principal points of the agenda. I proposed that we proceed to the organisation of factory nuclei through a re-shifting of the forces we have in the Party. <u>I recommended that we select certain factories or shops and concentrate upon them</u>. In cases where we had three or four Party members we immediately organised them into a factory nucleus. In cases where comrades were new and inexperienced members as was most generally the case, we assigned to their nucleus more experienced members from the street and neighbourhood groups. One of the first tasks assigned to these groups was the immediate publication of Communist factory bulletins. (The number of these bulletins will be given later in this report.)

[…]

On the basis of reports regarding the total number of Party members when I left Moscow, there were approximately two hundred members in the Communist Party of Australia. That membership has since grown until today there is a total dues-paying membership of exactly four hundred and eighty-six (486). The membership is distributed as follows:

Sydney....130
Northern Coalfields (Where the Lockout occurred) 90
Lithgow (Miners).... 8
South Coast (Miners)..... 6
Broken Hill (Metal Miners)..... 16
Victoria (Melbourne and vicinity)....140
South Australia (Dockworkers & Miscellaneous) 11
West Australia (Dock and waterside workers) 25
Queensland (Brisbane and vicinity).... 52
North Australia (Darwin) 7

Thus it can be seen that the Party membership is composed of healthy proletarian members from the basic industries of the country. There is a pronounced absence of intellectuals in the ranks of the Party, inasmuch that all such elements find ample means of disposing of their talents to the Labor Party and as workers in the official family of the trade union bureaucracy. Although it is only within the past weeks that a definite start has been made towards the reorganisation of the Party, we now have 17 factory and pit nuclei actively functioning and one YCL pit group. When we compare this to the situation existing at the time of the last Party Congress in December, we can gauge the development of the Party organisationally. At that time, the then Executive Secretary of the Party, Comrade Wright, in his report to the Convention, said there were no factory nuclei functioning anywhere in the Party, but added that, "An attempt in Sydney to make a start with a factory paper on the Harbour Bridge, is likely to succeed shortly."

[…]

INNER PARTY SITUATION.

The inner party situation has improved to a marked degree since the Party Congress of last December. The old right wing, opportunist Central Committee that supported the social fascist Labor Party in the elections in violation of specific instructions of the Comintern was overwhelmingly repudiated by the Party membership, and the opposition, under the leadership of Comrades Moxon and Sharkey, had the majority at the Congress. A Central Committee was selected consisting in the majority of supporters of the new line. There is only one member of the former right wing Central Committee now on the CEC—that is Comrade Higgins who, although he has certain reservations regarding some Party policies, nevertheless carries out the general political line of the Party.

One of the most persistent and unyielding right wingers of the old Central Committee was Jack Ryan, who is unfortunately occupying the position of acting editor of the Australian *Pan Pacific Monthly*. Ryan openly flaunted [sic; flouted] Party discipline and incited others to violate Party discipline. As a result of his unyielding opposition and publicly expressed contempt for the Central Committee he was expelled from the Party last February, some months before I arrived.

I have had two conferences with Ryan in an effort to persuade him to see the error of his ways and to work with the Party. He still contends that the policy of the old Central Committee in supporting the Labor Party at the time it did was correct, and that they were justfied in violating the decisions and instructions of ECCI, in continuing their campaign in support of the Labor Party after they had been forbidden to do so. However, he now says that there are evidences that the Third Period is beginning in Australia and that with the Scullin Government in power it would be wrong to repeat the support of the Labor Party. He also contends that it is wrong to refer to all the elements, especially the left elements of the Australian Labor Party, as social fascists. In his practical activity he in reality supports the line of Garden and only puts up a sham opposition to him. His editorship of the *Pan Pacific Monthly* raises certain problems for the Party. I have persuaded him to run articles in the paper written by our comrades and will endeavour to break him away from Garden, and if possible, bring him nearer again to the Party. In my last discussion with him he expressed a desire to be a member of the Party and said he would carry out decisions. The Central Committee drew up a statement to the effect that he could make application for re-entry into the Party provided he would admit his error in opposing the open letter of the Comintern, violating Comintern instructions, carry out the line of the Sixth Congress and the Tenth Plenum and admit that his action in refusing to appear before the Central Committee to account for certain opportunist articles written by him was wrong and that henceforth he will act as a disciplined member of the Party and defend the Party before the membership and the masses. He objects to signing such a statement. There the matter rests at present.

[…]

Thus this comrade [Kavanagh] not only flaunts [sic] the decisions of the Comintern and contemptuously refers to them as "tripe", which in the lexicon of Australia means a product of imbecility, of half-wits who do not know what they are talking about, but he boasts of the fact that in 1920 in Canada he at that time opposed Lenin's policy in relation to Labor Parties for that period.

[…]

Other members of the former leadership who were very bitter against the new line at the Party Congress, such for instance, as Comrade Jeffery, who is Secretary of the Militant Minority Movement, have been turned over and are now enthusiastic supporters of the Comintern line. Comrade Jeffery is the chairman of the Central Control Commission of the Party.

Generally, the Party organisation is healthy. The only opposition being confined to a mere handful, not more than six or eight members under the influence of Kavanagh in Sydney, and a few individuals in Melbourne. The latter, however, have no organisational connection with the Kavanagh element. In the coalfields and in metal mining, support for the Party is unanimous. It is very doubtful if out of the 486 members, there are even 25 who are not fully supporting the Party.

[…]

Further reports will be sent regularly

With Communist Greetings
Herbert Moore

Document 64

RGASPI 534–7–5. 24 September 1930, Moore: letter to CI. Typescript.

Moore writes of the CPA's successes despite organizational weakness and lack of funds; it is noteworthy that after less than six months in Australia he has adopted the Australian complaint about being neglected by Moscow.

SYDNEY
September 24, 1930

Dear Comrades,

Conditions are increasingly favourable for our work here. The arbitration courts are being utilised as the initiators of every attack on conditions in the unprecedented campaign of wage cuts, lengthening of hours, speed-up, and all the other accompaniments of an intense rationalisation drive. Our prestige increases tremendously with every struggle. We are the only section of the working class that is not aggressively aiding in the capitalist offensive; the only section that makes even a gesture toward organising resistance to the attacks on the working class.

In spite of deplorable organisational weaknesses, and a condition that can be described only as complete financial bankruptcy we have participated in every struggle against the offensive in every part of the country—from Sydney to Perth and from Tasmania to Darwin.

[…]

Please see to it that we get more of your material. We have had absolutely nothing on the 5th Congress. During its sittings we did not even receive an Inprecorr wire. In fact we never receive a damn word about anything until we get the foreign press and the Party press from other countries. We use some of the meagre funds we can sometimes scrape together for purposes of telegraphing and cabling for information, but never get any response. We know we are far away, but still we are fighting more or less effectively, and don't like to be forgotten when something important is going on.

Best wishes and revolutionary greetings,
MOORE.

Document 65

RGASPI 534–7–6. 25 Sept 1930, Moore: letter to Pan. Typescript.

In this letter to a friend in the Comintern, based in Moscow, Moore suggests that without the stiffening of the Comintern or its agent (himself), the CPA would slide back into their pre-Ninth Conference attitude towards the ALP. The identity of Moore's correspondent is not clear. 'Pan' may either have been Lozovsky, with whom Moore would have worked in the RILU before coming to Australia, or G. Sydor Stöler, a RILU official who helped to establish the *Pan-Pacific Worker*.

September 25, 1930

Dear Pan:-

Yours received yesterday. Had almost abandoned hope of hearing from you at all and thought perhaps your plans had not materialised. The enclosure will interest you. It is a copy of document recently handled here; and dispatched. When you finish with it please forward it also through your connections so, in case the first one did not arrive, this one will reach the proper destination.

As to the situation in the family, it is a vast improvement over the situation five months ago. All differences are overcome and everything is harmonious, except the periodical brain storms of JK [Kavanagh], who is now generally regarded as somewhat of a bluff, trying to exist in the present on his imaginary past glories in the wilds of Vancouver and other points east in the dominion of Canada. His alleged Marxism is of the shallowest kind and consists only of phrase-mongering. Although he made what he regards as proper statements admitting his past right errors, he utterly fails to perceive the basis of such blunders. However, he admits that they were all in error in regard to the federal elections. He is gradually approaching the line, inasmuch as his outburst are becoming less and less frequent.

Tommy[15] is impotent as I presume he has always been. What you might call a paltry fellow. His statement was better than JK's, but he is saturated with pessimism and tries to evade work of every sort.

I have handled Tommy's successor without gloves and have put him straight in regard to dealing with JK, Tommy and the others. Norman [Jeffery] is 100% for the line and is doing good work. In fact he is the best of the bunch. Hig [Higgins] is engaged in Anti-Imp work, but tries to evade every other duty, including resistance to standing as a candidate in elections here. If left to themselves I am sure the old bunch would repeat in NSW the same errors they were guilty of in the federal elections last year, because they think that Lang[16] is better than Scullin[17] and because certain elements close to them are for Lang.

However, there is to be a general review of the situation soon, through a discussion, and I am sure all of them will definitely come into line before it is over. There is no such thing as organised resistance to anything that is done, and I have utilised a degree of patience I hardly knew I possessed in dealing with them. All of them are very friendly toward me and have respect for my policies as applied to new developments.

As to Jack [Ryan], he is a problem. I have talked with him on many occasions and tried to persuade him to retrace his steps, make a statement regarding his participation in the errors of last year, repudiate his denial of social fascism and admit his error in flaunting [sic] the requests of the leading committee to explain some of his writings. He was excluded solely because of violation of discipline. However, his actions since have been reprehensible. He one time agreed to write a letter, and then wrote a short note saying that he would be pleased to resume his duties when he was reinstated. Of course that was nothing other than mere childish insolence. Then, the next outbreak [sic] from him was that he still believed that he was correct in the federal elections, but that now the line is not wrong because the ALP is now in power. The next development was his distribution of Lovestone documents—in a narrow circle, it is true, but still

---

[15] The identity of this person is not apparent; Moore may be referring to Tom Wright.
[16] Jack Lang (1876–1975), Labor premier of NSW, 1925–27 and 1930–32; he was dismissed from office in May 1932.
[17] James Henry Scullin (1876–1953), Labor Prime Minister of Australia, October 1929 to January 1932.

sufficient to show his inclinations. He told me, personally, that he believed in "reading all sides in order to get a true picture".

[...]

As to his relations with us; he has not come out openly against us, being content to spread pessimism and right opportunist propaganda among such elements as MacCauley, Macfadden, etc, people who are simple job-holders, without ability to lead any group for any purpose. His influence can be correctly estimated to embrace about six individuals, all of doubtful ability and integrity.

Personally I don't think Jack honestly wants to be with our family at all. His actions before he got out were deliberately calculated to provoke expulsion. And, of course, such a panicky, uncertain committee as existed after December, would permit itself to be provoked in just such a manner. I condemned them from the first day I heard of their expulsion, for the manner in which it was carried out, and insisted that efforts be made to rectify their own blunder in the case. If Jack had been willing to come back it would have been a simple matter, but he simply didn't want to come back, or else he thought that he would be reinstated by a higher body so that he could then have a factional argument against the leading committee here. I told him that no matter what happened he would be compelled to make a statement regarding his errors and his violation of discipline.

With the intensified activity in many fields, and with the rapid growth of influence and membership Jack is a dead issue at present. He is simply lost in the general advance and, aside from the periodical appearance of the *PPW*, with its milk and water contents, there is no evidence that he is on earth.

[...]

MOORE.

Document 66

RGASPI 495–20–3. no date [October 1930], Political Secretariat of ECCI: Resolution on the Situation in Australia and the tasks of the CPA. Typescript.

This resolution typifies the 'class against class' mentality of the Third Period Communist Party. It endorses the leadership change made at the CPA's Ninth Conference, but criticizes the leadership for the manner in which Jack Ryan was expelled in February 1930. Ryan would be a continuing problem for the CPA because of his influence as editor of the *Pan-Pacific Worker*.

RESOLUTION ON THE SITUATION IN AUSTRALIA AND THE TASKS OF THE CPA

[…]

The capitalist offensive has aroused stubborn resistance on the part of the workers, as is shown by the increase in the number of strikes, their growing militancy, and stern resistance of the workers to the police attacks, and the fact that some of them quickly develop into struggles bearing a political character (timber workers, shearers' and waterfront strike). The First of May demonstrations held this year in many parts of the country for the first time, the numerous unemployed demonstrations which frequently developed into open combat with the police, the struggle centering around the eviction of the unemployed workers, show the growth of the mass struggle of the masses against the bourgeoisie. All of the foregoing indicates that all the features of the general crisis of capitalism and of the growing class struggle of the proletariat are manifest in Australia. This completely destroys the theory of exceptionalism for Australia advanced by some former leading comrades of the CPA.

In this situation the task of the CPA is that of independently organising and leading the struggle of the proletariat against the attacks of the bourgeoisie and the Labour Government. This consists in the first place in mobilising the workers for struggle for their immediate and especially economic demands. The Party must formulate concrete demands against wage cuts, rationalisation and unemployment, such as the fight for the 7-hour day, and against the extension of the working week by the wiping out of the 44-hour week, for increased basic wages, for the abolition of the system of arbitration, for the withdrawal of the Anti-Labour Legislation (Crimes Act, Trade Union Bill and Mass Picketing Act) and for the establishment of full non-contributory unrestrictive social insurance (illness, vacation, reduction of old age limits, etc.), especially unemployment insurance, etc. The Party must give special attention to working out specific programmes of demands for the most important branches of industry (shearers, miners, waterside workers, metal and engineering, railway, etc.). These demands must be linked up with the general class demands of the proletariat and with the final aims of the Party.

The Party must understand that only by taking up and leading the economic struggles of the working class will it be able to rally the broad masses of workers to its banner and transform itself from a small chiefly propagandist organisation into a mass Communist Party.

[…]

The present situation and the interests of the struggle of the proletariat demands from the Party the consistent carrying out of the policy of class against class and the uncompromising exposure and struggle especially against Right opportunist distortions of this policy. This requires the persistent application of the tactic of independent leadership in the organisation of the economic struggles. The tactic of independent leadership means the most bitter struggle against the trade union bureaucracy and the Labour Party.

[…]

In this connection it is necessary to point out that the Party failed, in the case of the Adelaide struggle, to counter-act the manoeuvre of the trade union bureaucrats in splitting up the workers, and thus failed to rally all the workers on the docks for a common fight against the employers and their agents.

[…]

A central task of the Party *for* organising economic struggles of the workers is the transformation *of the MM* into a broad mass organisation, capable of leading the workers in the day-to-day struggles. The present situation affords every possibility for the organisation of a broad trade union opposition inside and outside the reformist unions and having strong roots in the enterprises. The Party must understand that it can become a mass Communist Party only by placing the trade union work in the centre of its activities. The Minority Movement must be the leader of the struggles of the workers in the factories, must establish groups within the enterprises, and agitate and organise for the shop committees and establish the revolutionary delegate system for the accomplishment of these tasks. It must systematically and energetically work within the reformist trade unions (including the Australian Workers' Union), build strong groups, and develop a wide revolutionary trade union opposition inside these unions. The Minority Movement must establish itself as a national organisation, must form industrial sections, district organisations and strong local groups, especially within the factories. The preparations of a national convention with which to centralise and consolidate the movement should follow the directives of the joint letter of the Comintern and Communist fraction of the Profintern of March, 1930. The MM must pursue a most intense fight against trade union bureaucracy inside the reformist unions, notwithstanding their policy of victimisation and expulsion. It must offer the most vigorous resistance to the expulsion policy, raising the slogan of democracy within the union and fighting for the re-admission of the expelled revolutionary workers, groups and locals, and rallying the masses to oust the trade union bureaucrats, and replace them with reliable revolutionary elements. The task of the MM is to broaden and strengthen its influence and position inside the reformist unions. The question of the creation of new independent revolutionary unions may be raised only if the MM will have succeeded in a sufficient degree to expose the reactionary character and strike-breaking tactics of the reformist bureaucracy, and when the wide masses of workers will have been rallied to the banner of the revolutionary trade union opposition, and when they are ready to break with the trade union bureaucrats. The Minority Movement must strictly follow the resolutions of the V Congress of the RILU in regard to the formation of new unions. "It is entirely wrong to mechanically create new unions which will only separate the most class conscious part of the working class from the rest. New unions may be called into existence only when the waves of strikes have risen to their highest, where the class struggle has become very fierce, where considerable masses of the proletariat already realise the treacherous role played by the reformist trade union bureaucracy, and where they are actively supporting the organisation of a new trade union."

[…]

The present situation is most favourable for the development of the influence and organisation of the Communist Party. The fulfilment of the above tasks, the realisation of the role of the Party as the vanguard of the proletariat, demand that the CPA increase its size, consolidate its organisation, establish strong roots in the factories, and cleanse its ideology of strong social-democratic elements and *remnants* of syndicalism. The present crisis of Australian capitalism must be utilised to the fullest extent for the building up of a large and powerful Communist Party.

The Party must take up resolutely the work of increasing its size. The recent increase in membership, in connection with mass struggles, shows that militant workers are ready to join the CPA and carry out its tasks. The Party must begin immediately a wide and energetic recruiting campaign, concentrating upon the building of pit and factory committees, especially in the most decisive sections of industry, and connecting the recruiting campaign with the work of the Party in the masses. The Party must destroy all remnants of the conception that the CPA is a narrow sect open only for a chosen few; it must welcome to its ranks all militant workers, men and women, willing to work and fight for its programme. The Party must strive to retain all new members by giving them practical Party work for which they are best fitted, by making it easy for them to acquaint themselves better with the principles and tactics of the Party and by drawing the best elements into leading Party work.

[…]

The ideological level of the Party membership must be raised; the still low ideological level creates a standing danger of deviations to the Right and Left. The Party centre must consider the question of organising a central Party training school as soon as possible, but must take measures already for the establishment of the local training courses. It must familiarise the Party membership with the programme of the Communist International, with the problems of the international Communist movement; must stimulate discussions on these problems and in this direction must give space in its weekly organ to international news, and likewise take steps to issue a monthly Communist review which will take up the theoretical problems as well as questions of practical politics of the Party.

[…]

The present situation imposes extremely heavy responsibilities on our small Australian Party, while at the same time it creates the conditions for its development and for the fulfilment of its role as the revolutionary leader of the working class. The Political Secretariat of the ECCI notes with satisfaction the progress made since the Party Congress, and the election of the new Party leadership in December 1929. The Party has recruited a considerable number of new members. Particularly in the northern coalfields, it has established new Party units; it has taken the first steps for organising the Party on pit and factory basis and has formed a number of pit and factory groups. The Party, under its new leadership, entered the miners' struggle, combated the mistakes of the old leadership and very soon won the confidence of the miners and played a leading part in the struggle. The Party is playing an active, and at times a leading, part in other important working class struggles, unemployed demonstrations, etc. A notable achievement of the CPA was the organisation of May Day demonstrations in many parts of the country, for the first time. The CPA, small as it is, has become an important factor in the political life of Australia. The present leadership is trying earnestly to apply the line of the Comintern for the class struggle in Australia. The Political Secretariat calls upon the whole membership of the CPA to support the present leadership, and to unite with it whole-heartedly in continuing the application of the Comintern line, and to repel any attempt to hamper or discredit the present leadership.

At the same time the Political Secretariat notes that former Right wing leaders still exercise influence within the Party ranks, particularly in Sydney, its main centre. This is undoubtedly due to the fact that after the last Congress the Party leadership failed to conduct a systematic and popular educational campaign in the Party to explain the new line and focus the attention of the Party on the necessity for struggle against the Right danger in the Party. The struggle that was conducted was carried on more in a formal and mechanical manner—as shown by the manner in which it expelled Comrade Ryan.

The Political Secretariat declares that Comrade Ryan advocated a pronounced Right wing policy, both before and after the Party Congress, in opposition to the line of the Comintern and contrary to the interests of the Communist movement in Australia. Instead of exposing Comrade Ryan before the Party membership, refuting his totally fallacious arguments and proving his views incompatible with membership in the Communist Party, Comrade Ryan was expelled on a formal issue which enabled him to claim that his expulsion was the result of personal vindictiveness.

The Political Secretariat believes that the question of Comrade Ryan's reinstatement may be reconsidered provided Comrade Ryan is convinced, and makes a public statement to the effect that his line was entirely wrong, that he condemns and has abandoned that line, that he has adopted the line of the Comintern, that he is prepared to work and fight for the Comintern line against the Right wingers, and that he is prepared to abide by the Party and Comintern discipline.

The Party must begin at once an ideological campaign in the ranks of the Party to explain the Right danger, in the course of which campaign it must call upon other former Right wing leading members of the Party (Kavanagh), to make their position clear and to remind them of the decisions of the ECCI that Right wing views are incompatible with membership in the Communist Party. At the same time the campaign must also explain the danger of Left sectarianism and anarcho-syndicalist tendencies that are to be observed in the Party.

The Communist Party of Australia is confronted with great possibilities for growth and for winning wider influence among the masses of Australian workers for becoming in the shortest possible time a mass Communist Party. The Political Secretariat believes that by energetically taking up and carrying through the above tasks, the Party will be able to rally the Australian workers for the revolutionary class battles ahead.

Document 67

RGASPI 534–7–6. 1 Jan 1931, Moore: letter to Pan. Typescript.

In this letter Moore is still preoccupied with the consequences of the Ninth Conference, and the positions of former leaders Garden, Kavanagh and Ryan. In this and other letters, Moore again refers to the communist movement as a 'family', in some respects a very apt expression.

Sydney, NSW, January 1, 1931

Dear Pan,

Yours of November 22nd to hand; glad to hear from you after so long a time. The decision finally and rather belatedly to break with Jock [Garden] clarified things considerably and makes our work less difficult. Jock is no longer an internal problem and has been fought openly for some time past.

Jack R[yan] is, I am absolutely convinced, working hand in hand with Jock in spite of anything to the contrary he may have written to you. His recent actions prove that conclusively.

[…]

At any rate one thing is clear now; Jack is an enemy of our family and must be regarded as such. <u>All connections with him must be instantly cancelled and</u>

everything regarding the *PPW* sent through the address you have from me. Additional addresses will soon be furnished you for various kinds of communications, literature, etc.

It has been rather difficult for us in view of the fact that Jack was receiving letters and documents on policy without the family knowing about it unless Jack saw fit to inform us. Take, for instance, the decision to hold a congress here. We knew absolutely nothing about it until an article by Hector Ross appeared. Then we took the matter up with Jack and he told us that you had agreed to such a campaign. Of course to set the date for January was ridiculous. No preparations whatsoever had been or could have been made on such short notice. So we decided that we would try to develop a campaign to hold it sometime during 1931. I am certain, however, that the Labor government will not permit it to be held, unless Jack and the rest of the fakers think that by doing so they can strike a blow against us by flooding it with delegates and placing themselves at the head of it in order to kill it. We will continue the campaign, meanwhile watching carefully the reaction to it from all quarters. Please send us some material on it at once.

Your letter to Jack resulted in a final attempt being made to induce him to change his attitude toward us, but he still insists that he and the Rights were correct in October, 1929, and that our whole family was wrong. We may as well abandon any hope of doing anything with him. The plain fact is that he is a labor faker. He was reared in an atmosphere of labor fakerism, as part of a bureaucratic machine, and when the time was rotten ripe for a break with that machine he preferred to remain in his comfortable and familiar environment rather than venture into more difficult surroundings where he would have to put up a real fight instead of "manouvering" with the bureaucracy and playing with the movement.

[...]

The worst feature of the whole situation in regard to the *PPW* up to the time we got definite information on your stand was the fact that Jack and his supporters claimed that they were working directly under your orders. We hesitated, probably wrongly, to take more decisive action because we did not want to conflict in any way with your work. This was given a semblance of reality by the fact that instructions came to Jack that we knew nothing about—such as the Congress instructions which we learned of belatedly after Hector had written one of his idiotic articles. (Incidentally Hector is about all in, having continual epileptic fits, which may account somewhat for his weird mental condition in relation to everything. He will probably kick off in a short time.) I don't know whether the fits are an expression of Rightism or whether the Right disease produces the fits. It doesn't matter much, we can only estimate the results and deal with them.

Another confusing element was introduced when the student came back and reported that a number of our family were quite perturbed that Jack was kicked out and were afraid dire calamities would befall us. Recognizing that students may not estimate the situation right, we nevertheless made special and, at times almost ridiculous efforts to pacify the three Rights—Jack [Ryan], JK [Kavanagh] and HIG [Higgins]—none of whom has any influence anywhere, with the result that they felt encouraged to continue their course. While energetically smashing their Right conceptions politically, we were very careful with them as individuals, until JK's expulsion was demanded, in fact clamoured for by the membership and many non-members. His own actions forced the issue. Before he was expelled he was completely exposed in a very effective campaign on our part. His last act was the worst I have ever seen—actually preventing masses going the police on November 7th. He became the worst sort of opportunist and defeatist.

[...]

Write oftener if possible. It is no pleasurable experience to be so far away from all former activities for such a length of time.

We both send our regards,
M.

Document 68

RGASPI 534–7–6. 14 September 1931, Ryan: letter: To Editor of the *Workers' Weekly*. Typescript.

The long-running conflict between Moore and Jack Ryan (expelled in February 1930 from the CPA, but still influential in the workers' movement) came to a head in late 1931. Ryan here objects to remarks made about him by Moore, but takes up the key theme of 'social fascism', to which he had long objected. The issue, he seems to argue here, is not whether the ALP is a 'social fascist' party, but whether the workers will understand what the communists mean by that.

---

20 Realm St.,
Arncliffe.
14th. Sept., 1931.

The Editor,
Workers' Weekly.

Dear Comrade,

In the pamphlet *Australia & the World Crisis* by Herbert Moore, recently published by the Communist Party, there are several very personal and vicious attacks made upon me.

While I welcome political criticism of any of my actions, the attacks contained in the pamphlet are so scurrilous that I am compelled to expose their untruthfulness.

At the same time I quite realise that many of the personal attacks on Jack Kavanagh and myself could not have been made seriously because Kavanagh has been readmitted to the Party despite the assertions in the pamphlet of ... "the shameful betrayal of the timber strikers in which Kavanagh participated with Garden" and ... "who aided the capitalist class defeat [of] the timber strikers". It is obvious that the Party does not believe that Kavanagh was guilty of such treachery to the workers, otherwise he could not have been readmitted to the membership under any circumstances whatever.

However, there may be a few readers of the pamphlet, who, because they are not fully acquainted with the facts, really believe that I am as disgusting as Herbert Moore says. Therefore I will answer his charges point by point.

On page 2 the following appears:-

> By clarifying the question of social fascism the Party was able to wage a more effective struggle against the right wing and against such agents of the pseudo-lefts in the camp of social fascism as the renegade, Jack Ryan, who denied the existence of social fascism, because to admit its existence would be to indict himself and his political boss, Jock Garden, who maintains him in his job at the Trades Hall, compiling lying statistics for the social fascist campaigns of the Labor Party.

I have never denied the existence of social fascism. On the contrary I have consistently stated, in articles and public speeches, that the Labor Party, assisted by the majority of the trade union officials, has been, and still is, ruthlessly attacking the workers in a futile attempt to solve the capitalist crisis. Moreover I supplied Herbert Moore with two quotations from capitalist financial journals that bear out this viewpoint and which were printed on page 23.

The reason why I usually avoid the term "social fascism" is because it is meaningless to most workers in Australia. In European countries where the social fascists are known as social democrats, it is quite probable that workers would easily grasp its significance. But in this country it is the Labor Party that is social fascist. To simplify matters I have frequently suggested that "Labor fascist" or "Labor Party fascism" could be used with better effect.

Wherever possible I use words and phrases that workers can readily understand. For this reason I eschew such terms as "bourgeoisie", "proletariat" the "materialist conception of history" and so on. That does not indicate that I deny the existence of the bourgeoisie and the proletariat or the soundness of the materialist conception of history, but I always make sure that I do not confuse the workers with unfamiliar words. It says little for Herbert Moore's honesty that I have, on several occasions, discussed this very matter with him.

[…]

Document 69

RGASPI 495–94–94. 8 January 1932, N. Jeffery: letter/report: To International [Control Commission]. Typescript.

The Party's Central Control Commission was responsible for ensuring the political integrity of the Party by investigating those suspected of heresy, or spying, or sabotage, and expelling those found guilty. A Control Commission was first established in the Party in 1927, but it was strengthened as a result of Moore's reorganization which put Norman Jeffery in charge. In this letter, Jeffery assures the Comintern that the CCC has matters in hand and that the Comintern can expect an improvement in its Australian Party. During the 1930s the CPA was indeed subjected to infiltration by police agents, as it had been in the previous decade, but the CCC's chief role was to ensure that the Comintern's political 'line' was upheld by all communists on pain of expulsion.

COMMUNIST PARTY OF AUSTRALIA.
Central Control Commission
SYDNEY.
8/1/32.

To International …[18]

Dear Comrades,

The Central Control Commission of the Communist Party of Australia has taken up the matters mentioned in your communication of the 16th October.

Many weaknesses still exist in the Party regarding the treatment of suspected traitors or provocateurs both in the flippancy with which suspicions are expressed and the laxity in rooting out spies and traitors.

However, much improvement can be noted in our work in this regard during the recent months, but considerable improvement is still needed because the Party faces severe struggles in which illegality may eventuate.

During the period 1930–1931 several police spies and provocateurs found their way into the Party, the most notorious being Constable Cook, attached to the police force in Sydney. This individual was responsible for some filthy provocative work inside the Party in Sydney and it was because of the laxity of the party apparatus, that, although he was long suspected, he was never dealt with.

---

[18] Words obliterated.

He was the chief police witness in the Clovelly eviction cases and several other cases, where it was shown clearly how he had advocated murder, torture, poisoning etc. The manner in which he was exposed left much to be desired. His companion Spry was ably dealt with and he was expelled from the party, but not till after he had been allowed a little latitude, but he did no damage like Cook.

Another police spy, and provocateur, Parsons[19], also found his way into the Party and was slowly working his way into more trusted activity when he was discovered. Here, as previously, our intelligence work in detecting these spies was very faulty. A characteristic of these provocateurs is their activity inside the Party, being most zealous in carrying out the tasks allocated to them. The Central Control Committee has not developed as yet the proper measures for the detection of these traitors and police spies. Further, our campaigns against them need improvement.

Some suspected traitors and spies have been dealt with expeditiously, although in this regard care has got to be taken that idle chatter is not taken for well grounded suspicions. In the recent seamen's strike, two suspected spies found their way onto the strike committee as representatives of the unemployed workers. They were, however, immediately dealt with and no trouble eventuated.

Considerable tightening up has taken place in the Party so that spies find it difficult to do real damage to the Party.

The communication from the International Control Commission was published in the official organ of the Party, the *Workers' Weekly*, almost as soon as it arrived.

Anyone found defending traitors is dealt with and expelled summarily, although we have had no difficulty in this regard because there had been no supporters in the Party for the police agents and provocateurs.

A fruitful ground for activity of these police pimps are the fraternal organisations such as for example, the Unemployed Workers' Movement, where Parsons first became active, etc. Much needs to be done to take the necessary precautions to deal with these people in the Unemployed Workers' Movement, etc.

The CCC has these matters in hand and a general all round improvement can be expected because it is recognised that greater vigilance, the selecting of special comrades for investigating work, intelligence activity, etc. is an important task needing attention in the combating of provocateurs and traitors, etc.

---

[19] A New South Wales policeman who joined the Party in January 1931 undercover and was expelled in June 1931 for acting as an *agent provocateur*.

Regular reports will be sent to the International Control Commission on our work and directives and information for our work will be appreciated.

(Signed) N. Jeffery,
Chairman, Central Control Commission.

Document 70

RGASPI 495–94–95. 12 January 1932, Organisation Department of the CC, CPA: letter: 'Re The Threat of Illegality'. Typescript.

This letter to all 'Committees and Units' of the CPA reveals that the Party authorities had considered their responses to the possibility that the Party would be declared illegal, and provides directions about how to organize and work under illegal conditions. Given the confrontational style adopted by the Party during the Third Period, threats to make the Party illegal would seem hardly surprising. A conservative, United Australia Party government was elected at federal level at the end of 1931, and the 1932 amendments to the Crimes Act put the CPA on the defensive, but they were also the perfect excuse to stifle any dissent within the Party.

ORGANISATION DEPT. Central Committee. SYDNEY. 12/1/32.

To All Committees and Units.

Comrades,

RE THE THREAT OF ILLEGALITY.

The CC PLENUM held recently stressed the importance of being organisationally prepared against the threat of illegality which is being persistently pursued by our class enemies. In connection with this question the following general directives must be impressed upon our membership.

Party units in the workplace provide the most stable basis for our organisation. Therefore increased activity in establishing factory groups must be our main response to threats of illegality.

The aim of illegality would be to destroy our mass influence, therefore the Party will instensify its mass work. With its roots deep in the masses the Party will be able to defeat the efforts to destroy it. Under conditions of illegality the Party membership would intensify its activity in all the legal mass organisations of the working class and would seek legal expression in every sphere of activity in addition to its illegal organisation and work.

In each district competent instructors must give training to all Party functionaries on every detail possible concerning work under illegal conditions. Particular attention must be given to training members who are active in rural centres because of the special difficulties involved.

Personal contact will be maintained throughout the organisation by means of the system of instructors from higher to lower Party organs [...].

Working under illegal conditions all individual members and committees must be doubly cautious in guarding documents, names and addresses. Documents and literature which must be kept safe from our enemies must not be left in members' rooms.

The ordinary mailing addresses must not be used for confidential correspondence. In such cases, addresses unknown to our enemies must be used. Confidential mailing addresses must not be centralised so that detection of one would perhaps cut off all contact. In the localities a system of couriers must be organised to establish personal contact between the various Party organs for delivering instructions and literature. A separate address must be used for each contact.

Party meeting places are of great importance and every precaution must be taken to see that they are not discovered by our enemies. In this connection particular care must be taken when entering and leaving meeting places, not to crowd and attract attention. Care must be taken that spies do not follow members to meeting places.

Greater care will be taken in the acceptance of new members. The unit must be certain as to the character and sincerity of the applicant. Where necessary applicants may be given tasks in legal organisations where their conduct may be observed before accepting them into the Party.

[...]

Under illegal conditions, membership would not be divulged without necessity. In the event of arrest, questions concerning membership in the Party would not be answered either at the preliminary hearings or in the courts. The Party will fight strenuously to maintain its legal existence. In this struggle the Party organiser must be carefully guided by the leading committees which will determine the best form of challenge according to the situation.

<u>The Party membership is warned against those who may seek to capitulate before the threats of illegality, causing a degree of panic and commencing a process of "burrowing". The Party fights for its legality. If defeated its work is continued despite all the risks that may be involved.</u>

With Communist greetings,
CC ORG. DEPT.
CC SECRETARIAT. CPA

Document 71

RGASPI 495–94–86. 15 August 1932, W. Orr: report: 'To overcome our isolation …'. Typescript.

Bill Orr was a miner and a strong supporter of the CPA's attempt to build the 'Minority Movement' within the trade unions. In 1934 he would be elected to the position of General Secretary of the Australian Miners' Federation, the most substantial achievement by the communists in the union movement to that date. This document sets out Orr's considered view that the CPA could end its isolation from the working class by concentrating on day-to-day issues of concern to workers rather than simply criticizing the workers' reformist leaders. It was a protest against those who embraced the 'class against class' rhetoric of the Third Period as an excuse for denouncing the 'social fascists', and who consequently reinforced the CPA's isolation.

15.8.32

TO OVERCOME OUR ISOLATION
ERADICATE ALL FORMS OF SECTARIANISM
LET US LEARN TO TRUST THE WORKERS. LET US STUDY LEADERSHIP

The question of sectarianism has been a burning issue with our Party and the most consistent of all our campaigns has been waged around this shortcoming. We have not succeeded, however, in overcoming all the manifestations of sectarianism which permeate our ranks.

In our endeavours to avoid many of the mistakes of our former right wing leadership, we have shown tendencies to veer to the opposite extreme. I shall deal only with one such issue, in which our leading committees have wrongly directed our Party and the MM, and of which I also have been guilty.

The issue to be raised here is the question of the "United Front" and "independent leadership". On the latter point especially, to take up the question of what are the organs of independent leadership, and how they are formed.

Before going into the points raised, it is necessary to emphasise the tremendous importance of real clarification of these issues so that our Party can really move into the leadership of the vast movement of unrest now sweeping the working class of the Commonwealth. Such a careful study is all the more necessary in view of the success that has attended the "left" social-fascist moves to lead this movement into harmless channels.

[…]

We, the only Party really fighting capitalism, should ask ourselves: wherein does our weakness lie? Why is it that these workers, who are anti-capitalists, should still not only vote for, but supply the election funds of the capitalist agents in the leadership of the ALP? Why is it that these workers, who are desirous of fighting the loan council proposals, should still be without the organs of struggle in the factories and mines where the main weight of the capitalist offensive falls?

[…]

Our work amongst the masses takes on too much a negative character, and we do not raise as the main issue in all our propaganda the need for the "united front" of the working class for struggle against the daily encroachments of capitalism on our living standards. This does not minimise the importance of the struggle against the social fascists who more openly come out as the agents of the bourgeoisie in assisting to transfer the burdens of the crisis onto the backs of the working class. The smashing of the influence of the social fascists must be pursued more relentlessly than ever if we are to succeed in leading the workers to the revolutionary way out of the crisis. The struggle against social fascism, just because of their identity of interests with capitalism, will succeed all the more rapidly to the extent that we are able, on the basis of our work amongst the masses in the enterprises and amongst the unemployed, to develop the struggle against wage cuts and worsened conditions and for the revolutionary way out of the crisis. In the agitation and preparation of the workers for struggle, and in the carrying through of these struggles, we shall be able, in the most concrete fashion, to expose the role of social fascism as the purveyors of defeatism, disorganisation and strike-breaking, and in such a way make our exposure real and convincing to the masses who are drawn into such activity.

[…]

We lead in the development of such "united front" work when, through our agitation, we initiate discussions amongst the workers for common action in struggle, which we help the workers to formulate. A condition for the success of our "united front" work is the overcoming of lack of faith in the workers. This lack of faith expresses itself not so much in an underestimation of the willingness of the workers to struggle, as in a lack of confidence in the ability of the workers to struggle intelligently. This is reflected in our insistent raising of such slogans as "only the militant workers on the organs of struggle". Such an attitude not only reflects our weakness in the factories and our lack of faith in our class, but is a form of sectarianism which must be combatted ruthlessly.

Another shortcoming which does not contradict the above statement is our overestimation of the revolutionary consciousness of the masses, reflected in our mechanical measures against the social-fascists when, in many cases, political discussion is discarded in favour of abuse of the reactionary leaders.

Document 72

RGASPI 495–20–6. 27 July 1932 (?), ECCI: Draft Inner Resolution of the ECCI Secretariat for the CPA Central Committee on the New Zealand question. In German, typescript. At top: 'Most Secret'. Trans. by KW.

This draft of a Comintern resolution on the New Zealand question requests that the CPA send 'one of its responsible comrades' to New Zealand for a period to sort out the factional strife in the New Zealand Communist Party. In its draft form, the resolution is inconsistent on whether the period is three months or one year.

Draft Inner Resolution of the ECCI Secretariat for the CPA Central Committee on the New Zealand Question

The ECCI Secretariat requests that the CPA Central Committee send one of its responsible comrades to New Zealand for three months with the task of preparing and holding an extended Central Committee plenum with the aim of discussing and implementing the proposed main resolutions and subsequently helping the New Zealand CP to implement these resolutions.

The draft resolutions should be discussed in advance by the Politburo and, with the amendments made by the Politburo, form the basis for the discussion in the New Zealand CP Central Committee. It is essential to invite the leading Party activists, who perform mass work at the district and local level and especially in the trade unions, to take part in the Central Committee plenum. For this reason the draft resolutions prepared by the Politburo must be sent to all leading CP comrades. The extended Central Committee plenum must be informed of the Politburo discussions and the positions of the various comrades in the discussion.

The Central Committee resolutions must be widely discussed and studied in all Party organizations. The resolution headed "For the Prosperity and Freedom of the New Zealand People" is intended for broad dissemination and popularization. The resolution headed "For the Strengthening of the CP, the Best Weapon of the Workers' Movement" is intended for internal Party use.

In order to bring good mass workers into the Party leadership it is vital to re-elect the Politburo at the Central Committee plenum. The leading committees should also be re-elected in all Party groups.

After the plenum a report on the internal situation in the New Zealand Party Central Committee must be sent here.

The ECCI Secretariat requests that the CPA Central Committee send a responsible comrade to New Zealand for one year to assist the Party in overcoming its isolation, developing a good collective leadership in the Party and finally eliminating factional strife in it.

Document 73

RGASPI 495–20–3. October 1932, Comintern: Resolution on the situation in Australia and the immediate tasks of the party. In English, Russian, French and German versions. Typescript.

This resolution is a product of the Comintern's Twelfth Plenum in October 1932. It urges the Australian comrades to build a mass revolutionary party. The ECCI acknowledges that the Party has had some successes following the reorganization by Moore in 1930–31, but it remains isolated. In particular, the Party is criticized for its incorrect positions on the ALP and 'social fascism' in general. It orders the CPA to direct 'its main fire', not against the bourgeoisie, but against the 'social fascists', who are here depicted as the main support of the bourgeoisie.

15/10/32

Confidential

RESOLUTION ON THE SITUATION IN AUSTRALIA AND THE IMMEDIATE TASKS OF THE PARTY.

Since the XI Plenum of the ECCI, the Australian CP has been able to achieve a series of successes. There has been a considerable growth of the Party membership and of the circulation of the Party press. The Party has taken the first serious steps to reorganise its work on the basis of the factories and has succeeded in building a number of factory nuclei. The Party has commenced the building of a mass Minority Movement with groups in the factories and the reformist trade unions, and has won over a number of local branches of the reformist unions. The Party has obtained these successes in the struggle against the attack of the bourgeoisie, in the struggle against the treachery and the "Left" manoeuvres of the social-fascist politicians of the Labour Party and the TU bureaucrats, and in the struggle against the Right danger in the ranks of the Party. The Party has taken part in strike struggles and has led a number of strikes, has organised considerable sections of the unemployed in the struggle for immediate relief, against evictions, etc., and has led a number of mass actions against the fascist New Guard.

However, these successes are only the first steps to transform the Party into a mass Communist party. The Party is still isolated from the basic masses of the Australian working class. The end of the relative stabilisation of capitalism, and the development of the revolutionary upsurge still further emphasise the absolute necessity of overcoming this isolation and converting the Australian CP into a mass Bolshevik Party which will be able to prepare the working class for the revolution in Australia.

I. THE END OF CAPITALIST STABILISATION AND THE GROWTH OF THE WORKING CLASS STRUGGLE IN AUSTRALIA

2. The tremendous deepening of the world economic crisis, and especially the agrarian crisis, have hit Australian capitalism with great force, due particularly to the situation of Australia as a second-class imperialist power, and due also to the rapid fall in the prices of agricultural products which play a decisive role in the exports of Australia.

While England has preserved its dominating economic and political positions with regard to the Australian Dominion, there has been increased penetration of American capital into Australia. This together with the importance of Australia as a base in the Pacific Ocean, in case of an imperialist war, makes Australia an ever more important arena in the development of the sharpening Anglo-American struggle. Although this circumstance creates certain possibilities for the Australian bourgeoisie to manoeuvre between Great Britain and the USA on the question of loans, tariffs, etc.—not without friction at times, in the ranks of the Australian bourgeoisie—in the long run it has led to a weakening of the internal positions of the Australian bourgeoisie which has been displayed with particular clearness by the world economic crisis. The development of industrial and agrarian crisis has led to a severe financial crisis and to a fall in the exchange rate of Australian currency.

[…]

In reply to these growing international and internal contradictions of Australian capitalism, the bourgeoisie of Australia is increasing its imperialist military preparations to strengthen its position in the Pacific in face of the growing aggressiveness of Japanese imperialism and the Pacific becoming the main arena of the new world imperialist war. At the same time, with the aim of fighting Soviet exports, and in order to make ideological preparations for the active participation of Australian imperialism in the counter-revolutionary war against the USSR, the bourgeoisie, with the most active—although sometimes concealed—support of the social-fascists is increasing its campaign against the Soviet Union, the campaign of "dumping" and "forced labour". (Bruce at the Ottawa Conference).

The war which has commenced in the Far East and tremendously increased imperialist aggressiveness, especially in the Pacific Basin, the concealed support of the Japanese invasion of Manchuria by British imperialism, the active support of the Australian bourgeoisie of the war of Japanese imperialism on the Chinese people by supplying war materials, is ever more drawing Australian imperialism into the coming imperialist war conflicts and making inevitable its participation in the developing imperialist war conflicts, and primarily in the intervention against the Soviet Union.

The whole situation of the end of capitalist stabilisation is forcing the bourgeoisie of Australia along the path of a violent solution of the ever-sharpening contradictions on the internal and international arena.

[...]

6. The growth of the revolutionary upsurge of the Australian working class has, from the other side, called forth a consolidation of bourgeois imperialist counter-revolution, as it is expressed in the growth of fascism and political reaction.

Utilising the growing dissatisfaction of the petty bourgeoisie in town and country, the bourgeoisie formed the "All for Australia" league which rapidly assumed huge proportions and made this the basis for the creation of the United Australian Party under the leadership of Lyons, the Ex-Treasurer in the Scullin Labour Government. The new Party is carrying on a more flexible policy on the question of tariffs; it has wide support in the ranks of the bourgeoisie; it has succeeded in carrying with it considerable sections of the petty bourgeoisie in town and country, and has taken over the leadership of the offensive against the working class from the Labour Governments in the federal arena and in the states of New South Wales and Victoria.

Parallel with this, the bourgeoisie has formed militant fascist organisations ("New Guard", "Silent Knights"), which openly proclaim their objective as the forceful suppression of the revolutionary organisations of the working class. However, these organisations are only one side of the growth of fascism, of the rapid transformation of the hidden dictatorship of the bourgeoisie into an open bourgeois dictatorship. The fierce attack of the Labour Government on the working class, the formation of the United Australian Party, and its coming to power, and the decision of this Government not to allow revolutionary literature to enter the country, the attack on the revolutionary press, *Workers' Weekly*, *Red Leader*, etc., the passing of anti-working class laws, the increased resort to open terror, and the growing centralisation of power in the hands of the federal government—all this marks a significant stage in the process of the growth of bourgeois "democracy" as a hidden form of dictatorship of the bourgeoisie into fascism, as the open dictatorship of the bourgeoisie.

7. The political and economic offensive of the bourgeoisie, and the part played by the Labour Party and the trade union bureaucracy in this offensive, have clearly shown up the role of social-fascism as the chief social support of the bourgeoisie. The Australian Labour Party, from the very start of the crisis, has carried on the most treacherous tactics, helping the bourgeoisie to deprive the working class and the toiling masses of their elementary economic and political gains of the past, attempting to disorganise and prevent any effort of the workers to resist the capitalist offensive, and fighting against the Communist Party and the advanced workers who were trying to form a united front of the workers in the struggle against the bourgeoisie. The Labour Government enforced wage reductions of over 25%, reduced the old-age pensions, maternity payments, reduced the miserable unemployed benefit, introduced the degrading permissible

income regulations, put a tax on the wages of employed workers, carried out brutal evictions, strengthened the arbitration system, increased the use of the police against strikes and demonstrations, etc.

[...]

8. The Party in this struggle against fascism and social-fascism has, in the main, carried on a correct line. It has mobilised the broad sections of the workers for the struggle against the capitalist offensive; it has organised the workers with considerable success for active struggle against the fascist "New Guard", and, at the same time, has directed its main blows against the social-fascists, and, first of all, against "left" social-fascism. However, in this struggle there were many shortcomings, and a number of serious mistakes were made. In carrying on the struggle against the fascist "New Guard", the Party did not sufficiently link up this struggle with the exposure of bourgeois democracy as a concealed form of the dictatorship of the bourgeoisie, as distinguished from fascism, which is the open form of bourgeois dictatorship, thus contrasting fascism to bourgeois democracy.

This mistake was all the more serious because in NSW where the "New Guard" is strongest, the Lang Labour Government was in office and was carrying on a sham struggle against fascism. This, in view of the incorrect position of the Party on the question of fascism, made it more difficult to expose the role which social-fascism plays in the development of fascism. "The social-fascists restrain the workers from revolutionary activity against the capitalist offensive and growing fascism, play the part of a screen behind which the fascists are able to organise their forces, and build the road for the fascist dictatorship." (Thesis of the 12th Plenum). In Australia, this was clearly shown, for example, during the struggle of the workers in NSW against the "New Guard", when the "left" social-fascists issued directives not to allow the members of the Australian Labour Party to participate in the united front against fascism established by the CP.

The Party did not see sufficiently clearly that the existing difference in the policy of fascism and social-fascism is a difference in methods. "Both fascism and social-fascism stand for the maintenance and the strengthening of capitalism and the bourgeois dictatorship, but from this position they each adopt different tactical views." (Thesis of the 12th Plenum). While the fascists chiefly use open attacks and terror to overcome the resistance of the working class, at the same time developing social and nationalist demagogy, the social-fascists make more use of phrases about socialism, democracy, etc., behind which they proceed to disorganise the struggle of the workers, using, at the same time, also open terror against the working class, at moments of special acuteness of the class struggle.

While explaining to the working class the nature of fascism and social-fascism, the Party must not fall into the opposite mistake, which it has done sometimes, when, in attempting to rectify its previous mistake, it has put fascism and social-fascism into one category. The Party must carefully explain the specific role of each of them in preserving the dictatorship of capital.

[...]

There was also an incorrect tendency to declare the Labour Party to be the chief enemy of the working class. As the decisions of the CI point out, the chief enemy of the working class is the bourgeoisie. But social-fascism is the main social support of the bourgeoisie. In order to defeat the bourgeoisie, the CP must destroy its chief social support—social-fascism. Therefore, the CP, in the period of preparation and unfoldment of revolution, must direct its main fire against social-fascism.

[...]

II. THE IMMEDIATE TASKS OF THE PARTY.

10. The growing revolutionary upsurge of the working class raises before the CPA the task of organising and leading the masses in the struggle against the bourgeois offensive for their immediate demands, on questions of wages, unemployed relief, unemployed insurance and social insurance, the defence of workers' organisations, against political reaction and fascism, against imperialist war, in defence of the USSR and the Chinese Revolution. The Party must strive to develop and enlarge this struggle, raising it to a higher stage of the MASS POLITICAL STRIKE.

[...]

12. The basic prerequisite for the fulfillment of the tasks of the Party, for combatting and defeating the chief enemy of the proletarian revolution inside the working class—social-fascism—is the concentration of the whole Party for everyday work in the factories, the firm rooting of the Party in the factories, mines etc. The experience already obtained in the penetration into the factories, and the construction of factory nuclei, must be widely discussed in the Party press, in the Party committees and nuclei. This experience must be utilised in the building of new factory nuclei and for activising the work of the weak and badly working nuclei. The leading committees must carefully check up on the work of the factory nuclei, giving them personal assistance and leadership in their work.

[...]

The Party nuclei must work illegally in order to prevent the employers driving the communists and revolutionary workers out of the factories (see directives in the Org. letter). This does not mean that the work in the factories must be narrowed down or weakened. On the contrary, it demands that the members of the Party, by forming various committees, workers circles, etc., such as factory committees, committees of action, sport clubs, dramatic clubs, etc., and by work inside the trade unions and any organisations of the workers which are under the influence of the employers or the social-fascists, must extend their activity winning ever more workers for the struggle in the factories, and thus extend and consolidate the influence of the factory nuclei, whilst at the same time protecting and maintaining the members of the Party and the revolutionary workers in the factories against the terror of the employers and police.

[…]

Recently the Party has carried on considerable work in the trade unions, but at the same time the instructions of the letters of 1929–30 to the CP of A, and also the decisions of the XI Plenum of the CI on the question of the leading role of the CP in the sphere of the construction and leadership of the Minority Movement, have up to the present only been very slightly carried out, which is expressed in the very small percentage (15%) of Party members who take part in the work of the MM. The XII Plenum emphasised this weakness with regard to all sections of the CI, and still more decisively pointed out that one of the chief tasks of the CPs is the strengthening of their work among the non-Party workers and the reformist workers.

[…]

16. The chief condition for the success of the work of the Party is the rallying of the members of the Party in the struggle on two fronts, against right opportunism as the main danger, and against left sectarianism, for the general Party line.

In the struggle against opportunism, the Party has brought about a considerable consolidation of its ranks. But, as was shown by the right opportunist mistakes in the miners' strike in Lithgow, the capitulation of Moxon to the TU bureaucrats (Melbourne), manifestations of opportunist passivity in a number of Party organisations, and sectarian mistakes in strikes (ignoring the everyday demands of the workers in Party work), this struggle against the right and "left" deviations is the main prerequisite for the development of the Party. The struggle against opportunism in the Party must be carried on in the form of a wide ideological campaign throughout the Party, exposing the roots of all deviations, and explaining the need for an energetic struggle for the correct Bolshevik line. On this basis must be carried on a Bolshevik consolidation of the Party and the raising of the ideological level *and* the political vigilance of the Party members.

The CC must take steps to develop in all the work of the Party real Bolshevik self-criticism, using this to help the Party members and the Party organisations to understand and overcome the mistakes which have been made in Party work, and to improve all the work of the Party.

[…]

21. The sharpening of the class struggle raises sharply before the Party the question of the threatening danger of the suppression of the Party and illegality. Preparations must be made for the Party to go underground in case of necessity, without losing its contacts with the masses. The Party must carry on the reorganisation of the existing clumsy Party committees. In the factories, particularly in the war factories, on the railroads, in ports, etc., the Party nuclei must carry on their work on an illegal basis, using at the same time the widest and most varied forms of mass work.

III. THE STRUGGLE AGAINST WAR AND FOR A REVOLUTIONARY WAY OUT OF THE CRISIS.

23. One of the chief shortcomings in the work of the Party has been the weakness of its campaign against the danger of imperialist war and intervention in the Soviet Union. The resolution on the war danger adopted by XII Plenum of the ECCI states:

> The XII Plenum of the ECCI considers it to be the chief task of all the CPs to organise and lead the struggle of the workers and peasants and all the toilers for the defence of China and for the defence of the USSR against the intervention which is approaching, and in defence of the toilers of capitalist countries against a new imperialist war.

The anti-Soviet policy of the Australian bourgeoisie, its role as one of the detachments of British imperialism in the struggle against the revolutionary movement in the colonies, makes it essential for the CPA to bring about a determined mobilisation of the broadest masses of workers and toilers in defence of the USSR, in defence of China.

The chief shortcoming in carrying out this task of the Australian Party has been the fact that it has reacted too slowly to the events in the Far East, and that the propaganda and the agitation of the Party have had a very abstract character. Very few attempts were made to expose concretely the war preparations of Australian imperialism. The Party has not linked up its anti-war propaganda with the everyday economic and political questions which are agitating the masses.

With this is connected the failure of the Party to organise any kind of strike on water transport to prevent the delivery of war materials to Japanese imperialism and to develop a really broad mass movement and mass activity against imperialist war in defence of China, in defence of the Soviet Union.

The rapid increase of the danger of a new imperialist war and intervention against the Soviet Union makes it obligatory for the CPA to increase its anti-war activity.

[…]

The Party must mobilise the broad masses of the employed and unemployed workers in a mass struggle against this plan of the imperialists and the social-fascists. The Party must much more widely popularise the construction of socialism and the classless society in the USSR, linking this up with the struggle against the danger of imperialist intervention in the USSR, and with the propaganda of the Party, for a revolutionary way out of the crisis. The Party must show to the workers that the dictatorship of the proletariat in Australia on the basis of an alliance of the working class with the poor and middle farmers, by the formation of planned economy, will solve the problem of unemployment, the agrarian crisis, will raise the standard of life of the workers and toiling masses, will develop the broadest proletarian democracy, and will open up the path for the construction of a classless society. All this must have the aim of bringing about the broadest mobilisation of the masses for an immediate struggle and must prepare the conditions for the inevitable decisive struggle for the victorious proletarian revolution, for the dictatorship of the proletariat in Australia.

Document 74

RGASPI 495–94–104. 22 October 1933, Freier: memo: On the situation in Australia. In Russian, French and German; typescript. Trans. from the Russian by KW.

In early 1933, Adolf Hitler came to power in Germany, and the analysis of 'social fascism' was finally and tragically revealed as bunkum. In this memo on the Australian situation, Freier argues that the ALP is collapsing, and that the CPA has perhaps the best opportunity of any communist party in the world to reach out to the working class, yet it is failing to realize those opportunities. Having analysed the Party's Central Committee minutes, Freier finds that 'the Party leadership, while committing no serious political errors, is too dogmatic in its approach to all matters, too non-specific in its decisions'; he recommends that the Comintern send an 'instructor' to Australia. This, however, does not seem to have eventuated.

Freier: Australian Situation
Dictated 22 October, 1933

Most secret

Memorandum of the Anglo-American Secretariat for the Political Commission. To Comrade Lozovsky.[20]

On the Situation in Australia

Despite another cut in wages, a reduction in unemployment benefits and the introduction of compulsory public work in exchange for these benefits (work for the dole), no strong strike movement has been seen in Australia this year. The primary reason for this is the policy of the reformist trade unions, which

---

[20] These two lines in handwriting.

have distracted the workers' attention from direct struggle against the employers and the government towards petitions and the arbitration courts. For their part, the latter support the reformist policy of the unions and manoeuvre adroitly in matters of wages, raising them in isolated cases for limited categories of workers and lowering them sharply for the largest categories. Recent Australian newspapers have provided a most striking example. This season wool prices have gone up by 45 per cent over last year (owing to increased purchases by Japan). However, the shearers' bid to have their former wage level restored was rejected by the arbitration court on the grounds that (1) nobody knows whether the increase will last, and (2) a 45 per cent price rise does not guarantee that graziers will receive their 'legitimate' profit. The reformists have lately resorted to new manoeuvres. They declare their support for the strike movement, while backing only those claims which affect broad masses of workers, i.e. in practice supporting general strikes. For example, the reformists in Melbourne launched a slogan about preparing for a general strike to make good a ten per cent pay reduction that affected 300,000 workers.[21] In this way the reformists block all partial and local workers' strikes. But at the same time, this new manoeuvre by the reformists demonstrates that a watershed has been reached in the working masses and that all illusions concerning the possibility of securing pay rises through the arbitration courts are losing ground.

Crucial to an understanding of the present situation in Australia is the process of collapse in progress in the ranks of the Labor Party. The clearest manifestation of this process can be seen in New South Wales. In this state, the Labor Party under Lang, which came to power[22] last year and has split from Federal Labor, remains the strongest political organization among the workers. But within Lang's Labor Party a trend by the name of 'socialization nuclei' has formed in recent years. These have drawn in the most revolutionary elements from the ranks of the workers who are members of that party. Up to this year, these 'socialization nuclei' were engaged mostly in self-education and discussion of the conditions necessary to implement various kinds of socializing projects that figure in the Labor Party programme, and so on. This year in the 'socialization nuclei' discontent with Lang's reformist policy has risen sharply. At a number of conferences the leaders of the socialization movement have been obliged to speak out against Lang and company. The latter, in turn, have implemented a series of disciplinary measures against the 'socialization nuclei', with the aim of restricting their autonomy and bringing them fully under control.

As a result, within the 'socialization nuclei' themselves a division is now taking shape between those who support determined revolutionary policies and those who are loath to leave the Labor Party. While the number of members in

---

[21] The figure here is not clearly legible.
[22] Russian corrected by hand to 'was in power'.

the 'socialization nuclei' is unknown, there is no doubt that these events have very great significance for the work of our party. As was absolutely correctly pointed out at a session of the CPA Politburo, 'It is very important that our party should understand that in the elements which are emerging from the "socialization nuclei" we have new cadres for our Party, workers who are the best elements of the Labour Party, energetic and active. If we succeed in drawing them into the Party, we shall acquire the best elements that we need.'

In addition to the revolutionizing of the socialization movement, there are other indications of the collapse of the Labor Party. The Australian comrades calculate that in the last two and a half years the membership of the Australian Workers' Union has fallen by at least half. This union is the central bulwark of the markedly right-wing Federal Labor Party. The number of members leaving the Labor Party is rising. At a Politburo meeting, some comrades counted roughly 1,400 departures in only three districts in the last six months.[23] The number of local Labor Party and trade union organizations that accept a united front with the communists is growing, despite their leaders' threats. In one district, for example, during parliamentary elections, the workers raised an election fund which they decided to share equally between the Labor Party and the Communist Party.

The movement against war, organized and led by the Party, has achieved particular success. According to an outdated report read to the Politburo on 27 May, 37 anti-war committees had been set up. Two local branches of the Labor Party went into voluntary liquidation and declared themselves anti-war committees. According to reports in the bourgeois press, over fifty trade unions affiliated to Lang's party have put their signatures to a demand that the municipality grant the use of the town hall for an anti-war conference. (It was supposed to be held in late September, but there is no information on it as yet.) About sixty local branches of Lang's Labor Party decided to support the movement against war and many of them selected delegates to the conference. The following note, which appeared in *The Sydney Morning Herald* on 7 September, is of particular interest.

> Fearing further revolts within their party, the leaders of the Garden-Graves faction have decided to modify their attitude towards the forthcoming conference of the anti-war movement. At a recent meeting of the Lang executive it was decided to forbid any member of the [Lang Labor] party to attend the conference under the penalty of expulsion. The conference, it was held, was a bogus movement of Communist origin. Now, however, the leaders have advised members that they cannot represent Labour leagues at the gathering, but they will be allowed to represent unions. The decision is regarded as a further

---

[23] The figure here is not clearly legible.

capitulation by the ruling faction to their extreme followers, who had made it clear that they intended to be present at the gathering.[24]

How is the Communist Party exploiting the favourable situation which has arisen? The CPA has opportunities probably unequalled by any communist party in the world to reach reformist labour organizations. In Sydney there is a labour council and a central committee of rank-and-file workers, which forms part of the reformist trade union movement. Among the membership of these bodies are communists and workers who are prepared to work under the leadership of the Party. Local workers' organizations often invite communists to give lectures etc. The Party, however, does not make sufficient use of these opportunities. At Politburo meetings complaints have often been heard that the party masses have not been mobilized for work with the 'socialization nuclei', that they do not understand the importance of what is happening in the ranks of the Labor Party. The Minority Movement is making no progress; members are quitting the Australian Workers' Union by the thousand. Our Pastoral Workers' Industrial Union[25] has only 500 members. The Friends of the USSR and the League Against Imperialism are faring miserably. Work among the unemployed has slackened, although Party agitation to raise unemployment benefits is beginning to bear fruit and the struggle of the unemployed is intensifying. The anti-war movement has become a popular movement, even the most popular movement among Australian workers. The Party, however, is not taking advantage of it to step up Party and trade union work. In the meantime, a mass of reformists and liberal pacifists are penetrating the movement. The Party leadership is aware of the danger, but has no clear idea how to combat it.

The existing materials are quite insufficient for an all-round appraisal of the Party's work. The general impression created by the Politburo minutes is that the Party leadership, while committing no serious political errors, is too dogmatic in its approach to all matters, too non-specific in its decisions and does not show the Party organs HOW they should implement those decisions, confining itself to general directives. It is typical, for example, that, while discussing the recruitment of members and matters of trade union work, the Politburo has never discussed specifics of the work of individual nuclei or minority groups.

A new resolution or letter from the Comintern will hardly set matters right. The far-reaching resolutions adopted last year and the appraisal by the Party plenum set forth in *Inprecorr*[26] will suffice as general directives. *These directives, in particular those regarding improvements to the newspaper, have mostly not been implemented as yet.*[27] For more focused directives, (a) there is insufficient material,

---

[24] *Sydney Morning Herals*, 7 September 1933, p. 12.
[25] The PWIU was formed by communists as a breakway union from the AWU in 1930.
[26] The usual acronym for the Comintern's journal, *International Press Correspondence*.
[27] Sentence inserted by hand.

and (b) it is six months old by the time it reaches Australia. The tragedy of the leading Australian comrades is that, while ardently wishing to operate in a revolutionary fashion, they lack the experience to make sense of the truly complex situation caused by the collapse of the Labor Party, although this collapse was in no small measure precipitated by the work of the Communist Party.

In order to resolve the complex questions now confronting the Australian Party, what the latter now needs most is lively leadership. For this reason, the most expedient decision would be to send an instructor. Pacific affairs, the development of events in the Far East, and the importance of Australia as a base for our work in the East in the event of war constitute an additional argument in support of such a decision.

B. Freier

Document 75

RGASPI 495–94–114. 1934?, ?Billet (Anglo-American Secretariat): report: Socialist Construction in the Soviet Union: Australian material. Typescript.

This is an analysis for the Anglo-American Secretariat of the Australian Party's propaganda on behalf of the Soviet Union, and its shortcomings. It also describes other newspapers in Australia that have been used by communists to spread positive images of socialist construction in the USSR.

22.6.34

SOCIALIST CONSTRUCTION IN THE SOVIET UNION
Australian Material.

Party Press Propaganda.

Propaganda articles dealing with various phases of socialist construction in the Soviet Union appear regularly in the Communist Party press of Australia. These articles give prominence to the success of the first Five Year Plan and marvellous strides being made in the fulfilment of the Second Five Year Plan.[28]

Considerable use has been made of the descriptive accounts of events, and the sights seen by members of the workers' delegations which toured the Soviet Union from Australia and other countries.

The lies and distortions appearing in the bourgeois and Labour party press concerning "authentic" information supplied by some enemy of the working class who is stated to have journeyed through the Soviet Union and seen things "first hand" is rebutted with a truthful account of what is really transpiring in the first Workers' Republic.

---

[28] The First Five-year Plan was 1928–33; the Second Five-year Plan was 1933–38.

<u>Party Press Propaganda Shortcomings.</u>

While a fairly good coordinated account of the planned socialist construction now being effected is published in the Party organs, there is a noticeable failure to contrast the situation of the life of the workers and poor farmers in Australia with that of the workers and peasants of the Soviet Union.

There is lacking in the Party press articles comparing the misery and poverty of the 400,000 unemployed who exist on a mere pittance of a dole or are forced to labour in camps for their food, to the position of the workers in the Soviet Union, where unemployment has been abolished, and where there is in fact a shortage of labour.

Similar comparisons are lacking concerning the life of the factory workers in Australia, who suffer wage cuts, long hours, and worsened conditions, to that of the workers in the Soviet Union whose standard of living is steadily rising.

These omissions would tend to impart an abstract appearance to the propaganda published in the Party press, instead of it being of such a character that would interest the workers and arouse them to actively participate in the struggle against the employers for improved wages and conditions, and draw them into the revolutionary movement and the struggle for Soviet power.

<u>The Attitude of the Reformist Leadership.</u>

Due to the favourable attitude shown towards the Soviet Union by tens of thousands of its members and supporters, the ALP *(Australian Labour Party)* press and politicians adopt a very guarded and at times <u>seemingly</u> sympathetic attitude towards socialist construction in the Soviet Union. The point of view expressed by some of the reformist leaders is to faintly praise the situation in the Soviet Union at the same time stressing the point that all these and other accomplishments can be obtained through parliamentary democracy. That, while the use of revolutionary methods may have been necessary to overthrow the Czarist Despotism, the more literate and cultured Australian workers can attain their goal constitutionally and peacefully by using the democratic franchise.

Lang, the "Left"[29] Reformist leader in New South Wales, who is yet very popular with tens of thousands of workers, has not over a period of years made an attack upon the Soviet Union. He has on a number of occasions strongly condemned dictatorships, *both* "Russian and fascist". Lang and other reformist leaders strive to confuse the workers by creating the impression that there is no fundamental difference between a fascist dictatorship and the dictatorship of the proletariat, which is the widest form of democracy.

On the other hand there is Garden, the secretary of the New South Wales Labour Council, a close associate of Lang and powerful figure in the trade union

---

[29] Quotation marks have been inserted by hand.

movement and Labour Party, who, in his public utterances both at meetings and in debates unstintingly praises the progress being made in the Soviet Union. At the same time while Garden speaks in this strain he speaks slightingly of the Communist Party, and has stated that "Lang is greater than Stalin", that the program of the Lang party is more constructive and more suitable for the working class than the program of the German Communist Party as enunciated by Comrade Thaelman [sic; Thälmann].

It is quite evident that Garden's intentions are directed with the object of retaining the thousands of members of the ALP who are favorably disposed towards the Soviet Union from leaving the Labour party and joining the revolutionary movement.

The *Labour Daily*, the official organ of "left"[30] reformists in New South Wales, has from time to time in its weekly supplements published articles dealing with socialist construction in the Soviet Union *showing an objective attitude towards the USSR*. Appearing on the same page are articles by the foremost "theoretician" of the ALP who writes under the name of Solomon Briggs, who distorts the writings of Marx, Lenin and Stalin in the most impudent fashion. In his praise for the Roosevelt plan, Solomon Briggs ridicules the idea that planned production is not possible under capitalism.

[…]

Commencing from about February 1934, the *West Australian* which has the largest circulation of all the papers of West Australia, published a series of articles written by Katherine Suzannah Pritchard [sic], the well known Australian novelist, who recently toured the Soviet Union. A reprint of these articles appeared in a Melbourne paper which likewise has a considerable circulation. These articles contain splendid information, giving a very vivid account of the situation in the Soviet Union, as this short extract will show.

[…]

Although the *Newcastle Morning Herald* is unfavourably disposed towards the Soviet Union, it nevertheless throws open its columns to workers' correspondents, and has published without deletion articles on socialist construction in the Soviet Union and the work of the Communist Party. The fact that Newcastle, the second largest city in New South Wales, is predominantly working class, is undoubtedly the reason which actuates this bourgeois paper in adopting this liberal attitude.

The same is also true of a number of provincial papers, especially those circulating in mining and other working class towns. The Party is certainly open

---

[30] Quotation marks have been inserted by hand.

to criticism for not making best use of the opportunity presented by supplying a regular stream of material to these papers.

[...]

Document 76

RGASPI 495–94–121. 17 July 1935, Billet (Anglo-American Secretariat): letter: Dear Friends. Typescript.

The Anglo-American Secretariat here recommends that Katharine Susannah Prichard be used to 'conduct work among the intellectuals, petty-bourgeoisie, etc., and should not be brought to the forefront as a Party member and activist', which might diminish her ability to contribute to the communist cause. Implicit in this letter is the notion that while Prichard should work within her circles as a 'friend' of the Soviet Union, she should not appear as a Communist.

July 17th, 1935.

Dear Friends

[...]

There is still another matter requiring attention. This is in reference to the work of Katherine Susanna Prichard [sic]. Being a Party member, the responsible Party Committee should decide which sphere of revolutionary activity she is to engage in. It has been decided that Comrade Prichard is to devote her energies to antiwar and anti-fascist activities, and to the Writers' League. Being one of the foremost writers in Australia, with also a world reputation, a fact even admitted by bourgeois critics, Comrade Prichard should be prominently used to conduct work among the intellectuals, petty-bourgeoisie, etc., and should not be brought to the forefront as a Party member and activist, as was the cause in the *Red Star* of May 3rd, where it is stated that Comrade Prichard made the following declaration at a public meeting on May 1st: "Comrade Throssel said that she was proud to have been a member of the Party since its inception, in Australia". Again, in the June 7th issue, there is published a front page appeal by Comrade Prichard on behalf of the *Workers' Weekly*. To utilise the services of Com Prichard in this fashion, will, under the present conditions in Australia, have a tendency to impair the important work she is best suited for.

Billet.

Document 77

RGASPI 495–94–121. 8 August 1935, L Sharkey: letter: To secretariat ECCI. Typescript.

In this letter to Moscow, Sharkey proposed that because of the Australian Customs ban on the importation of communist literature, and the desirability of Australian communists becoming acquainted with Comintern decisions, the ECCI endorse the notion (and perhaps ultimately funding) of an Australian edition of *Inprecorr*.

STRICTLY CONFIDENTIAL.

Aug. 8, 1935.
Secretariat ECCI.

Dear Comrades,

It is very essential that the members of the Party, especially the leading cadres and functionaries, be acquainted with all the experiences of the Comintern, its policy and tactics. This is particularly necessary now in view of the 7th Congress decisions and the further extension of our united front tactics, and their working out by the various Sections.

In view of the fact that not one copy of the CI Magazine has reached Australia for several years because the Federal Government has placed a ban upon the importation of "seditious" literature, it is very essential to overcome this ban by printing and publishing an Australian edition of the CI Magazine.

Were such an edition published in Australia, we feel confident that we could sell at least 1,500 copies monthly, if sold at 3d per copy, which is the price of the English edition. It is very likely, however, that the magazine could not be sold for less than 6d per copy if the cost of production is to be realised.

It is difficult from here for the Australian delegation to work out a precise estimate of the cost of producing 1,000 copies of the CI Magazine, but we consider that it would approximately cost at least 40 English pounds per month.

The difficulties of sending the material to Australia could be overcome by forwarding it to London, and then air-mailing to cover addresses in Sydney, taking, in all, about 15 days to reach its destination.

We make the request that the Secretariat endorse the principle of publishing an Australian edition of the journal, and allow us to work out later precise details as to the cost of production.

L. Sharkey

Document 78

RGASPI 495–20–828. 27 May 1936, S. Mason letter: to Dimitrov. In Russian, typescript (the script indicates 'From the English by Kup[isko]', but the English version is not located in CAAL). Trans. by KW.

This brief letter is included because it give an indication of how the Comintern directed its parties, by preparing and approving resolutions in Moscow, and then sending them to parties for adoption at Central Committee or Congress level. 'Mason' was the pseudonym of an Australian communist whose real identity remains unknown. J.B. Miles had used the pseudonym, but was not at this stage in the USSR.

27 May, 1936
Secret

Comrade Dimitrov,

I enclose the text of the proposals for the Australian party drafted by a committee comprising Com. Ribi [phon] (Australia), Com. Arnot (England)[31] and myself.

I would like to have them endorsed or amended so as to be able to dispatch them to Australia.

I recommend sending the proposals by air mail.

S. Mason
Representative of the CP of Australia.

Document 79

RGASPI 495–14–305. late 1936/early 1937, S. Mason: report to ECCI: Information to Secretariat of ECCI re Trotskyism in Australia. Typescript.

From the late 1920s, after he was expelled from the Soviet Union, Trotsky was able to publicize a relatively coherent critique—based on advocating Leninism and opposing Stalin(ism)—both of the Soviet regime and of the Comintern's policies. Its fundamental position, however, was continued support for the world's first 'workers' state', despite its 'degeneration'. This view attracted a number of dissident or disaffected communists around the world, who established oppositional communist parties and eventually joined together as the 'Fourth International' in 1938. These parties were generally very small, the strongest being in the United States. In Australia, former communists established the Workers' Party of Australia (Left Opposition) in 1933. Though never an effective challenge to the Comintern-endorsed Communist Parties, the Trotskyists were a constant thorn in their side, and Stalin himself would not rest until Trotsky himself had been murdered. Trotskyists, too, were murdered wherever Communists had a chance, particularly in the Soviet Union itself and in Spain during the Spanish Civil War (1936–39). Moscow's fear of Trotskyist influence meant that its parties were required to report on Trotskyism in their countries. This document is one such report. It gives the background and some of the activities of the Trotskyists in Australia, though the reporter, Mason, admits that he has been away from Australia for some time.

17.1.37

INFORMATION TO SECRETARIAT OF ECCI RE TROTSKYISM IN AUSTRALIA

A Trotskyist group first showed itself, as such, early in 1933. It was composed of a small group of renegades who had been expelled for carrying on a fractional

---

[31] R.P. Arnot (1890–1968) was a founding member of the CPGB in 1920. A member of the Party's Central Committee, he was arrested in 1925 in the lead up to the General Strike and charged with 'incitement to mutiny'; he served 6 months in prison. He authored a 2-volume *Short History of the Russian Revolution* (1937).

struggle against the Party in the latter half of 1932. It was led by a Professor Anderson, professor of philosophy at Sydney University. He has never been a member of the Party, although having connections with us up to the middle of 1931.

The Trotskyists only succeeded in establishing organisations in Sydney and Melbourne. At its strongest in 1934, it could only succeed in getting 22 members in Sydney.

During 1934 they issued first a roneoed and then a printed monthly paper, which collapsed and ceased publication at the beginning of 1935.

During 1934 they also attempted to organise one weekly lecture. The attendance was small, made up in the main of armchair philosophers and Party members who went there to interrupt.

During 1934 they attempted to penetrate the organised labor movement with the concealed help of the Labor Party leadership and a section of trade union officials. This took the form of attempting to establish a Relief Workers' Union in opposition to the Unemployed and Relief Workers' Councils led by the Party, with the aim of it becoming affiliated to the Sydney Trades and Labor Council. The Party mobilised the unemployed and relief workers to the Trades Hall where they repudiated the Trotskyists, forcing the Labor Party and trade union leaders to disown them.

They also attempted to penetrate into an International Labor Defence and Annual Unemployed Conference during 1934. In the first instance they never had credentials and were refused admittance. In the second instance a couple got in but were thrown out by the conference.

In 1935, one Trotskyist got credentials from a relief job and attended the annual Unemployed and Relief Workers' Conference. He was exposed there and left before the Conference finished.

Prior to 1934 they had been in the recognised unemployed movement but were driven out and in Sydney only succeeded in maintaining contact with two unemployed locals which, under their influence went out of existence whilst at the same time we built two new locals with them outside. In a couple of centres in Melbourne they had contact with unemployed locals.

In 1935 they again attempted to penetrate the organised labour movement through the Committee for Defence of Democratic Rights. Again we succeeded in having them repudiated.

During 1935 they attempted to hold Sunday meetings in the Sydney Domain in opposition to our position on sanctions re Abyssinia. In this they secured an ally in Kavanagh, ex-General Secretary of Party and leader of 1929 right wing, who had been finally expelled from the Party earlier in 1935 for Trotskyist smuggling. But whilst we were getting big meetings, theirs turned into a fiasco and were finally abandoned.

At the end of 1935 their activity was almost negligible. Their paper ceased publication, their public weekly lectures in Sydney were abandoned. The only activity we knew of was that of one individual on a relief job and steps were being taken to combat him there. This person had about six people grouped around him in the suburb where he lived.

Since being here [in Moscow] the only activity of theirs which I have been able to note through the press is as follows:

First, Professor Anderson gave a broadcast talk over the air on the recent trial of the terrorists here.[32] One of our members, recently returned from Moscow as a delegate at the invitation of the broadcasting station, also spoke on the same subject a few nights earlier.

Secondly, they issued a leaflet concerning the trial of the terrorists.

The only international contacts they had, of which we know, was contact with the Trotskyists of the USA.

Outside of Anderson's contacts, we had no information of direct contact with the bourgeoisie, nor of direct contact with the police. However, in 1933, when the Party was threatened with illegality and our general secretary was underground, these scoundrels informed the police through their paper.

At the present time the Party does not mention them in its press, i.e. the Australian Trotskyists. It has carried on a consistent and aggressive policy against them in relation to the recent trial here and at a recent meeting of the Central Committee passed a resolution calling upon the Party for vigilance against any Trotskyist or semi-Trotskyist tendencies which may express themselves in the organised labour movement.

I have been away from Australia too long to know the concrete situation relating to their present activity and organisation, therefore I cannot make any additional concrete proposals for the struggle against them.

Greetings,
S. Mason,
Australian Representative

---

[32] Mason probably refers to the second (of three) show trials held in Moscow against the Old Bolsheviks who were accused of plotting to restore capitalism in Russia. The main defendants of the first trial, held in August 1936, were Grigory Zinoviev and Lev Kamenev; Radek, with sixteen others, was tried and found guilty in January 1937 at the second trial. Most of those tried were executed.

Section 4

The price of subservience: 1938–1940

The documents in this section take the story of the relationship between the CPA and Moscow to a convenient terminus: the declaration by the Australian government on 15 June 1940 that the CPA was an illegal organization. But though it may be the end-point for these documents, it was not the end of the CPA: the Party continued many of its activities despite the government's prohibition, its legality was re-established at the end of 1942, and it emerged after the Second World War—for a short time—with an enhanced reputation and membership (Davidson 1969, 82, 93). As the Cold War set in, the Communist Party became increasingly feared and loathed, but despite its impact on the industrial trade unions it was never a major threat to Australian democracy. The declaration of illegality is nevertheless convenient for our purposes, because contact between the Party and the Comintern seems to have been cursory between 1938 and 1940 (occupying only three *dela* in the CAAL)[1] and became minimal thereafter, until the Comintern was abolished by Stalin in 1943. Furthermore, the circumstances leading to this declaration of illegality provide abundant evidence that the CPA had in policy matters become nothing more than Moscow's handmaiden.

In the period under discussion, the CPA's fundamental orientation was towards creating alliances and fronts to combat fascism and war, and defend the Soviet Union. Where the Party had, during the 'Class against Class' period (approximately 1929–34), sought confrontation with reformist labour leaders, it now sought alliances; where it had stressed its communist radicalism, it now emphasized its democratic and 'progressive' sympathies; where it had stressed proletarian internationalism, it now claimed a link with Australian radical and cultural traditions. The new strategy was developed after Dimitrov's accession to the leadership of the Comintern in April 1934; at the Seventh Congress in the following year Dimitrov was formally elevated to the post of General Secretary of the Comintern, and the shift to the policy of 'fronts' was confirmed. Indeed, it was Franz Borkenau's view that the 'Popular Front' strategy saved the Comintern and its parties, after their influence had sunk to its lowest level ever in 1934 (Borkenau 1962, 360). But the period of confrontation had one important corollary: like the Australian party, most of the communist parties of the world underwent changes of leadership and became transformed into organizations that were, in Borkenau's words, 'ready to obey anything' (375).

---

[1] 495–14–306, 495–14–308 and 495–14–309.

The question of the public image of the USSR was one that continued to preoccupy Western communists during the late 1930s. Against hostile, but generally accurate, Western press reportage, they worked hard to be positive, for their fate was inextricably linked to the USSR. Moscow continued to orchestrate a campaign to present a better public image, a campaign that in one form or another had been conducted since the beginning of the Australian communist movement. In the roneoed CPA District Committee publication *Red Star* of 3 February 1933, readers were told by one Rudolph Messel that 'The first thing that impresses the traveller to the USSR is that everyone he sees in the streets looks happy and healthy.' On 19 June 1936, to take a further example, the *Workers' Star*, the communist newspaper in Western Australia, trumpeted the new Soviet Constitution under the headlines: 'Most Democratic in World!', and 'Committee, Headed by Stalin, Completes Task'. Later that month, the Constitution was described in headlines as 'A Charter of Human Freedom' (31 July 1936).

The perceptions of the USSR by communists who had visited it were mostly positive, but their exposure to Soviet reality was carefully controlled. They often visited what under an earlier regime were called 'Potemkin villages', where people were well fed in spite of starvation in the countryside around them. Audrey Blake, after visiting the Soviet Union, returned to tell Australians: 'Comrades, the youth of Australia must know that there is a youth happy and free, a youth with a brilliant future, the youth of the Soviet Union; and if it gets to know the truth about that surprising country, it will be filled with great love and admiration for the Soviet Union and its great leader, Comrade Stalin' (cited Skorobogatykh nd, 11). Such observations must have been built on a profound willingness to believe, since not all visitors to the USSR were duped by Potemkin villages. Blake's contemporary comments must be tempered by those in her memoirs, where she reflects on the disappearance of communists from the Hotel Lux, where she and her husband, Jack, lived in 1937, and on the shortages and petty regulations that made everyday life in Moscow difficult. Yet even here she admits that 'None of us knew of the camps which were filling up with Soviet people' (Blake 1984, 24).

The difficulty of maintaining one's belief in the Soviet Union's economic and political advances in the face of the often factual expositions of 'bourgeois propaganda' was compounded by the fact that in the period 1937–38 internal repression against real and supposed enemies intensified. In September 1936 Nikolai Ezhov was elevated to the head of the NKVD, and there followed two years of what has come to be called the 'Ezhovshchina'. Levels of fear and suspicion about spies, saboteurs, and foreigners increased, and much of that suspicion was turned against veteran Party members. This was the time of the great show trials against the Old Bolsheviks, Zinoviev and Kamenev (in August 1936) and Bukharin (in March 1938), accused of conspiring against the Soviet leadership; but they were only the tip of an iceberg of mass arrests, cursory trials, and swift executions. Only Trotsky was able, from his temporary refuge in Mexico, to expose the absurdity of the charges against him—he was the chief defendant *in absentia*—and the others by way of an independent commission headed by the philosopher John Dewey (Dewey 1972). The Comintern, meanwhile, demanded that its parties exercise vigilance against wreckers secreted inside the movement, and many Comintern members within the USSR were swept away by the xenophobia that was created, and perished in the purges. In examining this period, Chase has argued that while it is highly likely there were some spies within the USSR, the frenzied response to what were in fact systemic problems of economic development in the 'command economy', rather than sabotage, was disastrous: 'No spy network could have inflicted the damage [on the USSR] that the NKVD did' (Chase 2001, 9).

The campaign against Trotskyism, orchestrated from Moscow, reached its height in the period covered in this section. The charge of 'Trotskyism' had been bandied about for some years, of course, since Trotsky had been internally exiled in the USSR in 1927, and expelled from the country in 1929. The first Trotskyist sympathizers expelled from a foreign communist party were James Cannon and Max Shachtman from the CPUSA at the end of 1928. But the first recorded charge of Trotskyism in the Australian party seems to come from September 1934, in a report from J. Billet headed 'Two Trotskyites expelled from Party' (495–94–114); they were Ted Tripp and Jack Kavanagh. Trotskyism was always a marginal feature of the Australian communist scene, but by the late 1930s 'vigilance' against enemies had become paranoia.

Communists and communist parties faced the ultimate test of their support for the Soviet Union in 1939. The Non-aggression Pact signed by the foreign ministers of Soviet Russia and Germany, Molotov and Ribbentrop, on 23 August 1939 came as a profound shock to them. It ended six years of communist vilification of Hitler, and forced many to ask how such a treaty could have been made with someone described for so long as a heinous criminal and enemy of the workers' state. Communists had difficulty in interpreting the change, and they had been given no prior warning of it. This was the case inside the USSR as well as abroad. The Comintern itself had enormous difficulties in advising its parties how to respond to the Pact and the subsequent war (Dallin and Firsov 2000, 148–88), as the swift movement of *Realpolitik* blew away any semblance of principle. How much more difficult it would have been had they known of the Secret Protocol of this Pact, which divided eastern Europe (and most notoriously Poland) into German and Soviet spheres of influence. The Germans invaded Poland from the west on 1 September 1939, triggering the response from Britain and France that started the Second World War; the Russians invaded from the east on 17 September, but not as part of that war.

The difficulties created by these events can be seen clearly in the Australian case. The Pact was described by the Australian communist newspaper, by this time entitled *The Tribune*, as Hitler being 'forced to seek terms' with the Russians (25 August 1939). A week later, Britain declared war on Germany when it did not cease its invasion of Poland, and Prime Minister Robert Menzies announced in his memorable radio broadcast that Australia was also at war. On 5 September 1939, without the authorization of Moscow, *Tribune* declared 'For the defeat of Hitler'. The CPA was very soon informed, via a Soviet cable on 'peace', that the war was an imperialist war and that genuine communists could not take sides in it. Churchill was as bad as Hitler. This change was first reported in *Tribune's* issue of 6 October, and through November 1939 the paper gave significant space to the Soviet foreign minister's outpourings: 'Molotov flays war makers', and Soviet Russia 'Remains Neutral'. In Western Australia, the local communist paper *Workers' Star* had tackled the doubters head-on in its headlines of 25 August 1939: 'Press, Public, Jump to Conclusions', and 'USSR is not Selling Out'. Whether they were believed is doubtful.

Soviet actions in making a pact with Hitler may have sent the CPA into confusion (and thus 'error'), but Moscow had only to transmit the 'correct' line for it to be adopted. Indeed, the only error in the communist movement was disagreement with Moscow. A few years later, in 1944, Lance Sharkey took the Soviet criticism on the chin. There was, he conceded, a 'brief moment' when the Party had made an 'incorrect appraisal of the character of the war'. Relief was quickly at hand, as the Comintern sent out its directives and rectifications. As Sharkey more circumspectly put it, 'the Party quickly oriented itself on a correct Leninist estimation and policy' (Sharkey 1944, 36).

The war raised a number of important issues: Moscow's control of communist parties (now proved beyond doubt); the loyalty of communists to their own countries or to the Soviet Union; Moscow's espionage network; and—once again—the question of 'Moscow gold' for communist parties. In a confidential letter of 2 October 1939 to the Secretariat of the ECCI, the CPUSA bureaucrat Pat Toohey wrote that Earl Browder, the Party's leader, had given testimony before the US Congress Dies Committee. 'The Committee sought to prove that the CP is a branch of Moscow, that it is financed by Moscow … that the CP is an agent of a "foreign principal", i.e. Moscow and the Comintern'. The Committee brought in a former member, Ben Gitlow—'stool-pigeon and provocateur' in Toohey's estimation—who testified that from 1922–29, the Comintern sent to the CPUSA $100,000 to $150,000 yearly and made claims of subsidies to the *Daily Worker* and other publications (515–1–4084). Toohey describes these claims as 'lies', but although they seem exaggerated, they are certainly not impossible.

Getting Moscow's money to the communist parties of the occupied and Allied countries became particularly difficult, however, since most of them were unsurprisingly prosecuted or banned by their governments for opposing the war after September 1939, in line with Comintern instructions. They were eventually put out of their 22-month, take-no-sides misery by Hitler himself. The USSR was invaded by the Wehrmacht on 22 June 1941, and the *Communist Review* for that month was headlined: 'All Aid to the Soviet Union', 'Everything for Victory of the Red Army'. By this stage, the CPA had been outlawed. But elsewhere in the world, some communist parties offered to disband if that would help the war effort to save the Soviet Union. Eventually in 1943, in the same cause, the Comintern itself was disbanded. Hitler's invasion of the Soviet Union, then, had the practical effect of allowing communist parties to support their governments' war efforts against Hitler.

Perhaps the main theme to emerge from the documents in this section is an increasing focus on what might—with a touch of cynicism—be called 'reliability'. The Comintern needed 'reliable' parties, that is, parties that would do its bidding. It kept a close watch on this reliability, by examining party documents and journals, by commissioning reports from trusted agents, and by compiling information on party members, particularly leaders. As the Comintern bureaucrat, André Marty, wrote in a directive to Australia in 1940:

> We must tighten control of our personnel to ensure that they are fully devoted to the USSR, the CPSU (Bolshevik), and Comrade Stalin, the leader of the working class and the working people of the entire world. There must be complete clarity about this. What the CPSU (Bolshevik) and Comrade Stalin do is exclusively in the interests of the working class of the whole world. There must be no doubt about this matter, and the personnel must be able to find their bearings on this basis. (Document 85)

What the Comintern had in fact created was a collection of parties which constantly looked to the centre for direction, which could not exercise judgement, and in which fear of being out of step with Moscow paralysed independent thought and action. The Comintern may have succeeded in controlling its organization, but at the cost of weakening its parties. The CPA's subservience to Moscow led to its disdain for the anti-Hitler cause and to its outlawing in 1940.

Document 80

RGASPI 495–14–308. no date [early 1939?], Tom Ewen: report to Comintern: The CPA since the Seventh Congress of the CI. Typescript.

Tom Ewen was the representative of the Communist Party of Canada to the Comintern in Moscow. This is a report he prepared about the CPA since 1935 for Comintern purposes, but it concentrates on the outcomes of the CPA's 12th Congress of November 1938. The report is drawn entirely from CPA press materials, and it appears that Ewen did not have first-hand knowledge of the Australian Party. Despite its considered view that the CPA has 'many serious shortcomings and weaknesses', the report ends on a positive note linking the CPA to Australia's democratic traditions.

<u>Confidential</u>

<u>THE COMMUNIST PARTY OF AUSTRALIA</u>
<u>SINCE THE SEVENTH CONGRESS OF THE CI.</u>

The Party

In the struggles of the Australian people against growing reaction, crisis, and the threat of war sharpened by the fascist war incendiaries, the Communist Party of Australia, as the leader of these struggles, has followed the line and decisions of the 7th World Congress on all major issues.

It is evident, however, from a review of the Party press, that the CP of A has many serious shortcomings and weaknesses, which hinder it from taking full advantage of the favourable objective conditions for mass recruiting into its own ranks. Its membership grows far too slowly; syndicalist and sectarian methods of work stand in the way of its rapid growth. The CPA loses much of its identity in its practical work, and is schematic and sectarian in its approach to the basic questions of building a People's Front movement in Australia. Its approach to the questions for a revised Constitution for Australia that would bring a greater measure of democratic progress, and greater assurance of peace to the Australian people needs to be improved.

These shortcomings are, first of all, reflected in the painfully slow growth of the CPA. In the Jan. issue of the *Communist Review* after the 12th Party Congress, Comrade Sharkey refers to Party recruiting as follows:-

Attention was drawn to the slowing up in the rate of recruiting, approximate figures being:—in the period of 1929–32 the Party increased its membership from 300 to 3,000; in the period 1932–38 only 2,000 new members were permanently recruited, a total of around 5,000.

Comrade Sharkey is in error when he says "permanently recruited"; it is clear from the above figures that not only is recruiting into the Communist Party of Australia at an extremely low ebb, but that fluctuation in membership recruited during 1932–38—a period of six years—is almost 90%.

Comrade Sharkey says further that "the 12th Congress of the Party generally agreed with the paragraph dealing with the slower recruiting in the CC report." This paragraph, as quoted, gives some of the reasons:—"immersion in trade union work, a relative decline in mass propaganda, distortion of the United Front concept, hiding the face of the Party and sectarian errors, inability to seize on the issues agitating the masses, more than 'prosperity' are the reasons for the slow growth."

If the 12th Congress of the CPA accepts a formulation which in essence means that the CPA is so much "immersed" in trade union work *to the extent* that it has no time to build its own ranks, then the logic of such a premise *would be* to get out of the unions if you want to build the Party, which is not only <u>incorrect, but absurd</u>. A much closer examination of the slow growth of the Party among the basic sections of the workers *would show that the Party is not making full use of the situation to increase its membership*. The CPA is well established in the Australian trade union movement in influence and numbers, but is apparently unable to utilise the situation to increase its membership in keeping with its influence.

Comrade Miles, writing in the Nov. issue of the *Communist Review* (page 59), also speaks of the too slow growth and heavy fluctuation in the Party. From his analysis it is clear that the CPA membership is well distributed in the trade unions, but are now known and do not work as Communists. Comrade Miles shows that the independent role of the Party—in the unions, in the anti-fascist and peace movements, and in the localities generally—is practically nil.

"Propaganda," writes Comrade Miles, "though improved in content and attractiveness, is relatively less than some years ago, in part because fewer workers are unemployed." The obvious conclusion to be drawn from this is that organized propaganda and agitational work of the CPA was confined mainly to the ranks of the unemployed—that the CPA found its main <u>open</u> base of work among the unemployed, and as unemployment decreased, Party propaganda and agitational work relatively decreased also. On the other hand, organized Party propaganda and agitation that would bring the Party prominently before the masses seems to have been taboo in the trade unions and other fields of activity, thus resulting in low recruiting and high fluctuation. While it would be incorrect to minimize work among the unemployed, it is also incorrect to make work among the unemployed the only sphere of open Party activity.

There are no recent figures that would give an approximate picture of the social composition of the CPA, its distribution in the various States of the Commonwealth, or its distribution by industries, in the trade unions, etc. It is clear, however, that, while the CPA is well established in the Unions of the Australian Council of Trade Unions (ACTU), our Party has been unable to take advantage of its leading and strategic position in these unions to consolidate and strengthen its ranks, or to achieve the fullest unity between the ACTU and the Australian Labor Party (ALP), thus creating a strong core for the building of a broad People's Front Movement.

Only in the *Communist Review* of Sept. were the pages of the Party's theoretical organ opened for pre-Congress discussion in preparation for the 12th Party Congress held in November of 1938. The first article in the Sept. issue is by Comrade Miles. In the October issues, the last before the Congress, there are three articles by Comrades Gould, Gibson, and Sharkey. [This amounts to] a total of four articles, covering the entire area of Australia, with *very little* differentiation upon the basic *separate* problems of six different States of the Commonwealth.

The central question before the 12th Congress was the building of a strong People's Front, uniting all bodies, trade unions, Labor Party, farmers, middle classes, etc., with the objective of ousting the reactionary Lyons government, and replacing it with a government of the people. To do this, differentiation and clarity on the problems *facing the people of* the various States are vitally necessary if these are to be won for this objective.

In none of these pre-Congress contributions on the special and particular problems facing the CPA in giving leadership to the people of Australia is any mention made of the farmers, only a bare reference in Comrade Gibson's article about the threatened action of the Wheat Growers' Association. It is clear that in a country like Australia, with a diverse farm population of approximately 400,000, almost 16% of the population—and a vitally important percentage besides—that all of the best intentions for the building of a People's Front with the farmers left out will be fruitless. There is no appeal either to the party to acquaint itself with the farmers, or for the farmers to seek a solution to their problems in the programme of the Party. It is true that in the 13-point Programme adopted by the Congress, "Debt relief to the Farmers" is included, but unless this is accompanied by active work and interest in the problems of the farmers and a determination to build the Party in the farm areas, then it simply remains a paper decision.

[…]

Trotskyism

There is little to determine the extent of influence of Trotskyism in the Australian Labor movement or in the Party. There is little doubt however that [it is] the Lang reactionary groups in the ALP, and in some of the unions where syndicalist and left ideology is strong, that Trotskyist elements have infiltrated.

In the Sept-Oct-Nov-Dec 1937 issues of the *Communist Review* Comrade Jamieson wrote a series of articles on Trotskyism, its origin, its counter-revolutionary programme, and its open orientation towards fascism. But Comrade Jamieson presents the question of Trotskyism as a Russian phenonema [sic], and in no case links it up with, or draws any conclusions for the Australian Labor movement.

In the *Communist Review* of Aug. 1938 Comrade Purdy has a brief article on the role of Trotsky as a prophet and supporter of fascism. None of these contributions even remotely relate to the trotskyist menace within the ranks of Australian Labor, how to detect it, how to expose and combat it. Trotskyism is dealt with by our Australian comrades as an abstract theoretical discussion, unrelated to its present-day role as an enemy of the people.

[…]

[Spain]

It is clear by the absence of a broad anti-fascist movement, that not all that could have been done for Spain by the Australian movement has been done, and much of the fault can still be adduced [sic] to the narrow sectarian outlook of the CPA. The task of forming a broad anti-fascist movement that will reach into the broadest masses of the Australian people still needs to be developed. Such a movement, while not excluding its present strong *base* in the trade unions, must win the support of wider sections of the ALP, the Church, middle class people, and even bourgeois elements that are breaking or have broken with their reactionary affiliations.

[…]

The Labor Party.

The influence of the CPA in the Australian Labor Party has increased considerably in the period between the 11th and 12th Congresses. *A better spirit of unity and cooperation is developing between the two parties since the defeat of Lang.*[2] The ALP itself has made progress in recent years, and although this progress is not uniform in regard to policy, nor uniform in each state, still it can be said that its influence and prestige is growing. It has been able to carry through the defeat and isolation of Lang and his reactionary group in New South Wales, as a result of the work of our Party, and the *Labour Daily*, once the organ of Lang for carrying through reactionary policies, has now been transformed to the *Daily News* under progressive editorship. The policy of slandering the CPA and the international Communist movement has ceased, and in general a better spirit of unity and tolerance exists between the ALP and the CPA. There is, however, still an ALP "inner group" dominated by the reactionary Lang elements who continue as a disruptive force between the various sections of the ALP. The final cleaning out of this group will depend upon the bringing of the Labor Party as such under the centralized leadership of the ACTU. The present leader of the ALP, Mr Curtain [sic], vacillated upon any basic questions, seeking shelter for his opportunism behind the non-agreement and lack of stronger unity in the

---

[2] Jack Lang (1876–1975) was the Labor Premier of New South Wales (from 1925–27 and 1930–32) who, in February 1931, proposed suspending the state's interest payments to the Bank of England, payments subsequently made by the Federal government. On 13 May 1932, as a consequence of a related matter—instructing state public servants not to pay money into the Federal treasury, as they were required to do under the new Financial Agreements Enforcement Act—he was dismissed from office by the NSW Governor, Sir Philip Game. Lang had already earned the ire of his federal counterparts by splitting the ALP, and continued leading the 'Lang Labor Party' through much of the 1930s; he was denounced by the CPA at the time as a 'left social fascist', for perpetuating the illusion that capitalism's effects on the working class could be ameliorated.

ranks of the ALP. *In the "Daily News" of Dec 30/38 Curtain [sic] advances a 5 point programme to unite the ALP from within and free it completely from the influence of the Lang group.*

In the building of a People's Front movement that will smash the reactionary Lyons Government, the CPA declares that the "ALP must become the centre of this People's Front", and that around it must be built the widest strata of the people. To this end the CPA will extend its approach to petty-bourgeois elements, farmers, etc., and seek to establish a strong alliance between the ALP and the farmers.

The recent convention of the West Australia ALP showed considerable progress over past years. It removed the anti-Communist pledge which its members must take from the Constitution. However, it must be noted that this pledge wasn't removed until the West Australia ALP Executive had expelled a leading Communist from the ALP because he had written to other ALP members asking them to join the Communist Party.

[...]

<u>The CPA Constitution and Australian Traditions.</u>

The 12th Congress of the CPA adopted a new Constitution. Its preamble reads:

> Upholding the achievements of democracy and standing for the right of the majority to direct the destinies of our country, the CPA fights with all its strength against any and every effort, whether it comes from abroad or within, to impose upon the Australian people the arbitrary will of any selfish minority group, or party or circle.

In this paragraph are embodied all the fighting traditions of the Australian people in their struggle for liberty and the democratic future of Australia. It is still less than 100 years ago (1840) when the convict ships of English took their cargoes of rebel workers and peasants to the penal settlements of Australia;—*when England* made of Australia one huge prison camp—because these English and Irish and Scotch workers and peasants revolted against tyranny and oppression. These "convicts" brought a tradition of independence and revolt against oppression that still vitalizes the blood of the Australian people. The CPA is the inheritor of these glorious traditions, and the decisions of its 12th Congress, in spite of all the shortcomings, is the guarantee that the flame of revolt will be kept burning in Australia.

Tom Ewen—Canada

Document 81

RGASPI 495–14–308. 25 May 1939, Tom Ewen: report/letter to Comrade Kuusinen: Australia. Typescript.

Ewen's remarks in this brief letter to his ECCI colleague Kuusinen have a more critical tone than those of his earlier evaluation of the CPA since 1935 in Document 80. What had happened to change Ewen's tone is unclear.

May 25th 1939
AUSTRALIA

Comrade Kuusinen:

Just recently there has come to hand the report of the 12th National Congress of the Communist Party of Australia, held in Sydney, NSW on November 18–19–20th. This report is printed in a 96-page pamphlet entitled *The Way Forward*.

In addition to this pamphlet there is another, the *Constitution and Bylaws of the CP of Australia* adopted at the 12th Congress. The new Constitution of the Party contains 12 rules and a section on Bylaws governing the organization and structure of the CP of A [...]

The Way Forward contains the main report of general secretary of the Party, Comrade J.B. Miles, as well as the reports of other leading comrades. The main line in all the reports is the need for greater unity in the Australian labor movement to defeat the reactionary Lyons government. (Lyons himself has since died and Menzies is the new Premier, but the policies of Lyons still prevail.) Special emphasis is laid upon the strengthening and unifying of the Australian Labor Party (ALP). The growing unity that is evident since the Congress in the victories of a number of labor candidates in State and municipal elections shows that the decisions of the Congress are being realized.

In a number of the speeches reported, greater attention is urged towards giving leadership to the struggles of the farmers. The agrarian crisis is deepening very rapidly in Australia and is creating widespread activity among the farmers. From the Congress reports it is evident that the CP of Australia was pretty well isolated from the masses of the poor farmers.

In the report of Comrade Sharkey the Party membership has grown as follows;- 1929—300; 1932—3,000; 1938—5,000.

This growth, in view of the favorable objective conditions, is considered by the Congress to be far too slow, and special measures for rapid Party building were undertaken. The CP of Australia wields a strong influence in the Australian trade unions—an influence far in excess of its membership. The Party has not utilized this influence to build its ranks and consolidate its press in the trade unions, and the Congress directed its attention to overcome this weakness.

The Congress laid down a 16-point programme for the building of a "People's Front for Australia", which would serve the labor movement, the farmers and the middle classes, and enable the growth of a great mass movement in opposition to the reactionary policies of the Canberra government. In domestic and foreign policy these points demand economic and collective security for the people of Australia.

In the Congress resolution on a "Programme for Peace" the CP of Australia raises "the danger of conscription", and somewhat negatives [sic] its policy of defence of Australia from aggression by abstract demands for the personnel of the standing army. It demands "no compulsory military training or conscription". Traditionally, the Australian labor movement has always opposed conscription, which perhaps explains in part the position of the CP of A in the present period and its failure to correctly estimate the changed conditions that make conscription essential to effective defense.

In its resolution on the study of Marxism-Leninism the Congress makes no reference to the *History of the CPSU(b)—Short Course*. It is possible however that the vital importance of this work had not reached our Australian comrades at the time of their Congress in such a form as to be fully appreciated.

Taken as a whole, *The Way Forward* indicates a healthy understanding of the tasks facing the CP of Australia on the way towards a real mass Bolshevik party. It calls for the doubling of the Party membership by the end of 1939, for the raising of the theoretical level of the Party leadership from top to bottom, and for the extension of the *Workers' Weekly* and *Workers' Voice* into daily papers. These tasks the Congress declares to be the main pre-requisites for the building of a broad anti-fascist people's movement in Australia.

Tom Ewen
Rep. CP of Canada

Document 82

RGASPI 495–14–308. 1939 [November?], author unknown: report to Comintern: Proposals for the CPA. Typescript.

In September 1939, during the first few weeks of the Second World War, the CPA advocated the defeat of Hitler by the Allies. Having become Stalin's new-found 'friend' by virtue of the Non-aggression Pact, however, Hitler had no wish to be antagonized by Stalin's communist parties around the world. The word soon went out that communist parties must not take sides in the war, and they should not assist the war against Hitler. This document—possibly written by Tom Ewen—is one of the first analyses by the Comintern of the Australian errors in responding to the outbreak of war, and what could be done to rectify them.

Confidential
Australia
PROPOSALS FOR THE CPA.

Even with the limited material available, it is obvious that up until September 16th (London *Times*), [and] August 30th (*Guardian* CPA) the CPA was following an incorrect line in relation to the war. The first pre-requisite to the effective mobilization of the Australian people against imperialist war is the speedy orientation of the CPA to a correct political position on the war.

Mobilising the Australian people in active opposition to the war should be made the central point in the CPA building "crusade" outlined in the August 19th issue of the *Guardian*.

Under the slogan of "Free Australia from the bloody chess game of British imperialism", the CPA should mobilize the Australian people for the defeat of the Menzies government as the tool of Chamberlain, and the election of a People's government pledged to fight against the war.

Raising the slogan of "not a soldier nor a gun for Chamberlain" the CPA should intensify and unify the struggle against conscription; to defeat the National Register and all forms of military and industrial conscription.

Strengthen Australian defenses independent of British imperialism and raise the boycott and opposition to Japanese imperialism to a new high level.

2. The CPA should raise the issue of Australia becoming the initiator of a great Pacific anti-imperialist bloc with the perspective of weakening British imperialism on two fronts—first in active opposition to Japanese imperialism; second—in active support of the Indian people against British imperialism.

3. For the defense and extension of civil liberties and rights; freedom of organization, press and assembly. Smashing of the "dog-collar" legislation of the "Arbitration Laws" that are used to cripple the organized activity of the workers, and the trade unions in particular.

4. Utilization of the Menzies war-budget for the economic needs of the Australian people; struggle against rising prices, living costs, and war profiteering.

5. The extension of the Marxist-Leninist understanding of the CPA by mass distribution and use of the *History of the CPSU* and the classical works of Marx-Engels-Lenin-Stalin. The transformation of the *Communist Review* into the Marxist-Leninist theoretical organ, orientation upon Australian conditions, thus strengthening the CPA and the Australian working class against reactionary British imperialism which dominated Australia.[3]

---

[3] In [the] *Guardian*, August 30th, it is reported that only about 1,000 copies of [the] *History* have been sold. The membership of the CPA is roughly 4,500–5,000, while the ACTU in which the CPA wields a

6. A sharp struggle against the reactionary Socialists and Trotskyites in the leadership of the Australian and State Labor Parties, directed towards the uniting of the rank and file of the Labor Parties against the war and the ousting of the reactionary officialdom in the Labor Party and in the ACTU.

7. For helping to correct the CP line. To send advice to England suggesting that a letter be sent to the CPA signed by Comrades Tom Mann and [William] Gallacher. This letter should be written in a personal and informative manner, outlining the changes that have taken place in the CPGB and the working-class in respect to the imperialistic war. It should indicate that, while in some of the British Dominions: Canada, Australia, New Zealand, etc., as well as in Britain, the Communist Parties and other sections of the Labor movement supported the war in its early stages, believing it to be a war against fascism, that in the process of events they have realized its imperialistic aims, and are now mobilizing in active opposition to the war. This letter should also point out the necessity of carefully examining the nature of peace, in order to avoid the imposition of a "super-Munich" by Chamberlain and his imperialist allies, directed against the USSR. Through the medium of such a letter the CPA will draw the correct conclusions on the errors of its own policy in respect to the imperialist war.

This letter would be sent to all Dominions.

Document 83

RGASPI 495–14–309. 25 November 1939, R. Naumann: report to Comintern: The CPA at the beginning of the imperialist war. Typescript.

This document was written nearly three months after the Second World War had begun. It assesses the initial errors of the CPA in relation to the war, and their rectification. The Australian communists are here characterized as having misunderstood the complex theoretical realities behind the Non-aggression Pact. Their theoretical reliability seems to have been tested and found wanting by the war. Naumann argues, against other assessments of the Australian position by Tom Ewen, that the Australians took a wrong position on the war because they did not understand the Pact.

---

25 Nov 1939
Australia
Confidential

THE COMMUNIST PARTY OF AUSTRALIA AT THE BEGINNING OF THE IMPERALIST WAR.

At the beginning of the imperialist war in Europe, the CP of Australia took a wrong position, declaring for the support of the reactionary Menzies

---

big influence has approximately one-half million membership. This is obviously far below what is easily possible. [This footnote appears in the document; the ACTU membership seems to be half a million.]

Government in its participation in the imperialist war on the side of the Chamberlain Government. J.B. Miles, General Secretary of the Party, declared:

> We will not obstruct any genuine move of the Menzies Government to assist the Polish people against the present barbarous Nazi attack. (*Tribune*, Sept 8, 1939)

This wrong attitude on the part of the CC in relation to the war in Europe was not accidental. It was a result of not fully understanding the non-aggression pact concluded on August 23rd between the Soviet Union and Germany. Therefore the Party was unable to explain correctly and convincingly the pact to the masses. The CC and the CP were ardent defenders of the pact, but it took partially a defensive attitude—tried to apologise for the pact and came to a wrong conclusion about the nature of the war and about the tasks of the Party. The Party looked upon this question too much from an Australian and not international point of view, expressing in this way some influence of British imperialism in the ranks of the CP of Australia, and was therefore unable to arrive at a correct position at the moment of the outbreak of the imperialist war in Europe.

That the leading comrades did not understand the essence of the Soviet-German Pact can be seen from a statement in the Central Organ of the Party, *Workers' Weekly* of August 25th:

> Therefore, to enter into an agreement to that effect does not alter the Soviet's policy towards Germany an iota. (My emphasis)

Because the Party leadership did not see that the Soviet policy toward Germany was altered and that it was altered as a result of the breakdown of the French-British-Soviet negotiations, being the result of the imperialist interests and anti-Soviet intentions of the Chamberlain-Daladier Governments, the Party leadership continued the old tactical line relating [to] the "democratic" governments of Britain and France. It wrote:

> The Soviet Union is not preparing to enter into an alliance of the nature of the one offered to Britain, already largely in existence with France and previously with Czechoslovakia.

> If the British Government can be compelled to sign the military alliance desired by the Soviet Union, Hitler will be compelled to renounce his aggressive intentions against Poland and the smaller States and against Britain and France also. (*WW*, 25.xiii.39)

This line was followed up to September 8th, the last paper at our disposal, almost a week after the outbreak of the war. Even then the central organ of the Party wrote in a leading article:

The Soviet-German pact is not the kind of military alliance that was offered to Britain and France. <u>Soviet Russia</u> is in the same position as the United States, <u>that of a neutral, with a difference that Marshal Voroshilov made it perfectly</u> <u>clear that Poland or Britain and France could secure all the war materials they</u> <u>wanted.</u> (My emphasis, RN)—*Tribune*, September 8, 1939

The Party leadership also drew a wrong conclusion from the pact for the situation in Australia. Instead of exposing the imperialist policy of the Chamberlain and Menzies Governments, which led to such a situation *where* as a result of the failure of the British-French-Soviet negotiations, the danger of an attack on Australia by Japanese aggression increased very much, the Party paper *emphasized the other side*, that the pact reduced the danger of a Japanese attack on Australia, and made the situation of the British and French forces easier.

The declaration of the CP, for example, states,

This pact has brought about the neutrality of Japan, which is of the utmost importance to Australia. And in the event of war can mean that <u>British and</u> <u>French forces do not have to fight in the Pacific as well as in Europe at the same</u> <u>time.</u> (My emphasis, RN)—*Tribune*, Sept 5, 1939

Comrade Dixon wrote:

The non-aggression pact between the Soviet Union and Germany ... <u>reduced</u> <u>the danger of a Japanese attack on Australia</u>, and will strengthen Britain's hand in Europe. (My emphasis, RN)—*Workers' Weekly*, August 29th

The CC in its declaration on the war, as well as the leading members of the Party, emphasize so much the advantages of the pact for Britain and France and Australia that the impression is created that the Party wants to excuse the pact before the masses, that the Party retreated before a wave of chauvinistic, imperialistic sentiments, instigated by the Government.

On the other hand it must be noted that Comrade <u>Dixon</u>, in his article published in the *Workers' Weekly* of August 28th, gave a very good estimation of the coming war—in my opinion one of the best estimations given by any of the Anglo-American parties. He wrote among other things:

If war should come, however, black reaction will settle on the capitalist world.

In England, Chamberlain has invested himself with all the powers that Hitler has. In Australia, Mr Menzies apes Mr Chamberlain. Our freedom is in the balance.

The workers, as never before, must unite to resist fascism.

<u>If war comes we will be told we are fighting for democracy against fascism.</u>

<u>But there will be no democracy if the governments have their way. Fascism will</u> <u>have been established throughout the British Empire.</u>

Capitalism breeds fascism: it makes war inevitable.

Lasting peace and democracy will be achieved only with the crushing of capitalist rule and the establishment of Socialism.

If war comes we Communists will strike at the cause of the war—capitalism. We will inscribe on our banner the struggle for Socialism. (My emphasis, RN).

Comrade Sharkey, the editor of the Party paper at the same time made a similar declaration on the pact. In this declaration he concentrated his fire against the policy of the Chamberlain Government, and concludes it in the following manner:

It is Chamberlain and Hitler, the leaders of capitalism, who are the responsible parties for the second imperialist war.

Whilst there is capitalism and fascism, war cannot be abolished from earth.

Only Socialism can guarantee peace. (*Workers' Weekly*, August 29).

But this good beginning was not further developed, neither by these Comrades nor by the CC. On the contrary, the position of the comrades became worse. Comrade Dixon, for example, two days after publishing a good statement on the Soviet-German pact, where he declared: "If war comes we Communists will strike at the cause of the war—capitalism. We will inscribe on our banner the struggle for Socialism", he made a contradictory declaration. In one place he declares:

If war breaks out the Communist Party would support any or every measure for the defeat and destruction of German fascism.

And in other places he declares the opposite task:

If we must fight fascism then the first blow must be delivered against fascism in Australia. (*Tribune*, Sept. 1st)

The consequences of the misunderstanding of the Soviet-German pact were that the Party considered the war of the Polish Government as a just war. Germany was still considered as the aggressor and Poland as the victim of fascist aggression. The declaration of the CC, published September 5th, immediately after the beginning of the war, states for example:

The savage German fascists have launched a new aggression against Poland, and the British Empire and France are at war with Germany.

This war, launched for the purpose of the conquest of Poland and its subjection to the fascist Empire of Hitler, of Krupp and Thyssen, the German monopoly capitalists, is an act of stark aggression, without justification of any kind whatever.

Therefore, lovers of justice and liberty throughout the entire world will support the struggle of the Polish people for their independence and against the enslavement of a foreign power.

What has brought the world to this dreadful pass where it is faced with a repetition of the inferno that raged from 1914 to 1918? In the first place, the responsibility lies with German fascism. (*Tribune*, September 5th)

From such an estimation of the Polish war the conclusion is drawn that the Communist Party must support the Polish war "against fascist aggression". It is therefore quite in agreement with the line of the CC when Comrade Dixon wrote that the Communists will be in the forefront of the defence of Poland against fascist aggression.

We Communists refuse to give up to anyone our place of honour at the forefront of the fight against fascist aggression.

There must be no capitulation to German fascism.

There must be no sacrificing of Poland as a condition for peace with Hitler.

If war breaks out, the Communist Party would support any or every measure for the defeat and destruction of German fascism. (*Tribune*, September 1st, 1939).

The paper of September 8th, the last issue in our hands, shows that the Party still followed this line. Comrade Miles declared for the Party paper:

The *Tribune* stands for the independence of Poland, for the defeat of the Nazi and other fascist aggressors.

Connected with this mistake is the illusion that the Chamberlain and Menzies Governments can fight a just war. The declaration of the CC on the war states:

The working class, whilst supporting the measures necessary to resist the aggressor and the war of Poland for its independence, demands, if such a war has to be fought, that its aims be just, that there be no new Versailles imposed upon the German masses who have been forced along the path of aggressive war by the Hitler dictatorship.

There must be no annexations of territory or paralyzing indemnities placed upon the German people; they must be assisted to overthrow the fascist dictatorship and to restore democracy and freedom in Germany. The Austrians, Czechs, and Slovaks must have their national rights and independence restored. It is only on the basis of justice to all that a new and lasting peace can be established among the nations and necessary confidence in each other be established.

In accordance with the old line, the Party connected the struggle against fascist aggression with its struggle for the maintenance and extension of the democratic rights of the Australian people. The declaration of the CC states:

Whilst supporting the struggle against foreign fascism, the Australian working class and the defenders of democracy must keep an alert eye on their own democratic liberties. The Emergency regulations announced by [P]M. Menzies give to the Commonwealth Government dictatorial powers that could strangle our Australian freedom.

The suppression of the legitimate rights of free speech and press, of the right of the masses to organize and voice their grievances, must not be allowed to be smuggled in under any pretext whatever.

It is not much of a gain to defeat foreign fascism only to find that a dictatorship has been established in our land. To fight fascism demands that democratic liberties be extended and broadened among the people opposed to fascist war and dictatorship. Neither must military measures against German fascist aggression be used as a pretext by the capitalists to reduce the standards of living of the Australian people. (*Tribune*, September 5th)

In as much as the line of the Communist Party, in essence, was no different from the line of the Labor Party, the Party proceeded to carry through the old line of building the united front with the Labor Party. In its declaration the CC states:

The CP, which has inscribed the sign of unity upon its banners, again declares its readiness for a united front agreement with the ALP for the defence of democracy and of the living standards of the people. The CP will strengthen its efforts to establish a great, united people's mass movement for the defence of democracy and the restoration of world peace …

We must strive for the removal of the Menzies Government from office and its replacement by government of the Labor Party, pledged to a democratic peace, to defend our living standards and liberties.

United against fascism, for a democratic peace.

Unclarity in the ranks of the leadership of the Party on this fundamental question created confusion among the rank and file of the Party. It is important to note that the General Secretary of the Party, Comrade Miles, recognizes the existence of some confusion on the line of the Party. In answering slanders of the Trotskyites, who declare that a crisis exists in the Comintern, Comrade Miles states:

There is no crisis in the ranks of our Party in this country. I know it from direct contact with several areas in recent days and reports from all other areas.

As in all acute crises, there is some confusion, but the firm clarity of the great majority becomes the conviction of all but the few weaklings. (*Tribune*, September 8, 1939).

Therefore, I think that the causes for the wrong position taken by the CC of the Australian Party on the question of the imperialist war in Europe have to be found *in Australia itself*. The mistakes made by the CP of Britain could only intensify these mistakes, but that did not make them possible. I also think that the statement made by Comrade Ewen is not correct when he declared that the CP of Australia "presented the Soviet-German pact in a correct manner, but drew the wrong conclusions on the nature of the war". On the contrary, as shown above, the wrong conclusions on the nature of the war were a result of a misunderstanding of the Soviet-German pact.

R. Naumann

Document 84

RGASPI 495–14–309. 2 February 1940, S.W. Scott: report to Comintern: The Communist Party of Australia. Typescript.

Sid Scott was a New Zealand Communist who had some direct, personal knowledge of the CPA and its personnel. This report was written for the Cadres Department of the Comintern for the purpose of filing information on leading comrades in the Comintern.

STRICLY CONFIDENTIAL
THE COMMUNIST PARTY OF AUSTRALIA.

(For Cadres Department)

The writer's knowledge of the CP of Australia and its cadres is strictly limited. It is only possible to give personal impressions. It would be impossible for me to be dogmatic in my judgments:

Comrade J.B. Miles.

This comrade I heard much of but only saw on one occasion for a brief time, as he was never in New Zealand, and when I was in Australia, he was out of Sydney on tour.

It is significant, however, that everybody I met in the Australian Party spoke of him with affection and pride. "I have met Comrade this and Comrade that," was once said. "Ah, but you haven't met J.B. yet," was the reply.

My own one meeting with him was when I passed through Adelaide, and at some considerable inconvenience he came straight to see me, after a long journey from the back-country. In no way remarkable in appearance, he impressed me as being very shrewd and confirmed the report that he was the most outstanding Australian Comrade. He spoke of the international situation, quoted Comrade Stalin's speech (quite recently delivered—a month before, roughly) at the 18th Congress, predicted the breakdown of the Anglo-Franco-Soviet negotiations and expressed the opinion that the war would take place, with the Soviet Union standing outside. In this case, he stated, the war would be an imperialist war.

This clear statement, which was not duplicated by any other comrade in Australia or England—nor, was, indeed, until I heard about the pronouncements of the ECCI in later September or thereabouts—caused me to be surprised by the wrong attitude taken by the Australian Party as early as August 25th. Comrade Miles is about 51 years old. He has five children.

Comrade R. Dixon.

I know him considerably better than J.B. Miles.

He is an excellent comrade, of mild appearance, but strong character and keen intelligence, with, I think, a very good grasp of Marxism-Leninism. Of the Australian Comrades who came over to New Zealand, he impressed me as the most outstanding. He gets to the heart of a question and did not jump at conclusions the day he landed, but went into matters carefully.

Age: about 25, recently married. One of Party's best speakers. Is reputed to be Comrade Miles' "right-hand man".

Comrade L. Sharkey.

Chairman of Central Committee. Is a comrade of long experience in the Party. Editor *Tribune*. Like other two comrades, has been in Moscow. He was here in 1930–31 and again in 1935 when he became candidate-member of the ECCI.

Is capable comrade—would not be in his present position otherwise. Personally does not impress me as being so outstanding in ability or personality as previously mentioned comrades. But this, of course, is simply my personal impression. Did quite a good job of work in NZ when he came over at Christmas, 1936. Age, about 40. Married three years ago.

Comrade R. Cram.

Member of Central Committee. Newcastle District Organizer. Executive member of Newcastle Trades Council. Member of his union—I forget which. Understand he is very successful in working with non-Communist trade union officials. Is energetic, quiet-spoken comrade with likeable personality. Quite capable, but apt to jump at conclusions. (This opinion of mine is, I believe, shared with Australian CC comrades). A good all-round comrade nevertheless. Age: about 38, married, with I think two children.

E.G. Docker.

Member of the Central Committee. Leading functionary in NSW State Committee work. Age about 40. Ex-carpenter. Has been Party functionary for some years. Believe that, like most other CC members, he is attached to a union.

Good reliable comrade—not perhaps the theoretician that some of the others are, but quite capable. When he came to NZ as a fraternal delegate in 1936 (to a Plenum) and took part in a controversy with a sectarian group, he gained a reputation in Wellington for being somewhat tactless and inclined to browbeat offenders. This charge certainly had some truth in it, but I think it was because of his strong sense of Party discipline and the fact that he did not sufficiently allow for the weaker development (particularly then) of the NZ Party compared with Australia. Personally I found him a very good comrade. Like first three mentioned comrades, is on Political Bureau.

T. Wright.

Member of CC (and Political Bureau).

Secretary of the Sheet Metal Workers' Union Sydney. Vice-President of the NSW Trades and Labor Council. Age about 40. Married, with family. Capable, quiet, well-respected comrade. Told me once that he had been once removed for a period from the CC. I think it was in 1930 or thereabouts and that he sided with the Right Wing. That, however, is evidently regarded as past history in Australia now and I should think that any such errors were the result of inexperience in a time the Party, too, was weak.

Comrade Jack Simpson.

Comrade J. Simpson is the financial expert of the Central Committee. I know him from two holiday visits to NZ, which is his birthplace, as well as from meeting him in Sydney. His age is about 50. He seems to be less politically developed than the other CC members I have met and concentrates his main attentions upon the business affairs of the party, including the paper, of which he is at present, I think, business manager (or at least business supervisor). He is an expert in raising money and has a loyal, kindly and genial personality that particularly fits him for this kind of work—as does his business ability. An old Party member.

Guido Barrachi.[sic]

I met this comrade in Sydney. He is one of the acknowledged theoreticians of the Party. Age about 45. Middle-class origin, independent means (Australian born, Italian descent). Old Party member. An editor of the *Communist Review*. My impressions confirmed his reputation as a valuable and single-minded Party worker.

Other important comrades that I met during the ten days I spent in Sydney and had not known previously, I would not care to comment on. These Comrades included Lloyd Ross, Secretary, Australian Railways Union an under-cover Party member, who was once resident in NZ and is well known by reputation and writings. Several members of the Industrial Labor Party (now merged in the

Australian Labor Party) I also met. These included J.G. Hughes, now President of the NSW Labour Council. [4]

In Melbourne for only three days, I met Comrade Ralph Gibson, then Secretary of the Victorian State Committee, whom I knew by repute, but had never previously met. This comrade, whose age, I think, would be about 37, was in Moscow for 12 months, as was his wife. Originally a Workers' Educational Association organizer, a university graduate, Comrade Gibson and his wife (who is also an "intellectual" by origin) impressed me as devoted Party workers.

Melbourne is more of an "intellectual" city, less of an industrial city than Sydney and this seems to reflect itself to some extent in the Party, which, however, is very live[ly] and boasts an excellent (relatively excellent) YCL,[5] the only one, indeed, now existing in Australia. There are, or were, about 20 party members in a cell composed of daily newspaper reporters, and the connections with university people are particularly strong.

These facts seemed to me to be significant, but, of course, my knowledge of the Party in Melbourne was and is limited.

I met no outstanding comrades in Adelaide or Freemantle [sic] (i.e., the port of Perth) being unable to make the contact. In Hobart I met the Party organizer whose name I forget (Tony *Gardner*?). This comrade was trying to build a Party organization in Tasmania. He had established fair [sic] branches in Hobart and Launceston and was concentrating his main attention then on building up a waterfront unit which was publishing its own waterfront paper and shaping fairly well.

Tony seemed a fairly capable comrade, but did not have the easiest of tasks in a Labor-governed, but farmer-dominated (and in parts, very backward) Tasmania. The proletariat in Tasmania is not very well developed. Nevertheless, some progress was being made.

The Australian Party in General.

The Australian Party in general, and particularly the biggest section, the New South Wales section, strikes me as being *a* very good Party, deeply rooted in the masses and in the industrial workers particularly. Its leadership I would describe as solid rather than brilliant; using good team work and based quite strongly on Marxist-Leninist principles. I would agree with the remark I once heard about it—that its industrial work is its strongest point and is stronger than its political work. Its propaganda work has always seemed to me to be far

---

[4] Lloyd Ross and Jack Hughes were communists who had taken advantage of the split in the NSW Labor party from 1931 to gain significant influence (Hughes as Vice-President of the NSW Branch of the Labor Party; Ross as a journalist on the *Labor Daily*). In August 1940, however, the federal Labor Party suspended the executive of the NSW Labor Party after it had passed (at Easter) a 'Hands Off Russia' resolution, thereby reversing the gains that the communists had spent many years accumulating.
[5] Young Communist League.

behind its agitational and organization work in the unions. In the Trade Union movement, it is, of course, exceptionally strong. Amongst the farmers, it has little foothold—an obvious weakness (which, of course, also applies to NZ).

In my opinion, the central Party organ falls short of what it might be and its sales and indeed that of general propaganda material are poor compared with what they should be. I believe that a more suitable editor could be found than Comrade Sharkey. However, this may be going beyond what is required from me, so I will conclude by saying that in my opinion the Australian Party is strongly based, solidly led and likely to steadily increase its already considerable influence.

S.W. Scott—2.ii.40

Note: All the Central Committee members mentioned here are, to the best of my knowledge, Australian born with the exception of J.B. Miles who came out from Scotland about 30 years ago and J. Simpson who is a New Zealander.

S.W. Scott

Document 85

RGASPI 495–20–4. 11 March 1940, A. Marty: General directives for New Zealand and Australia. Present in a German version only (although the German is a translation from English), typescript. Trans. by KW.

Before the entry of the Soviet Union into the war against Hitler, communists in the Allied countries were advised to direct their struggle against the 'imperialist war' in general. In this directive to the Australian and New Zealand communist parties, Marty urges them to develop their campaign jointly.

General Directives for New Zealand and Australia
7.5.40
'Dictated by A. Marty, 11.3.1940'

Relations Between Australia and New Zealand

In connection with the development of the imperialist war, the establishment of proper relations between New Zealand and Australia is very important for the working class of both countries. One of the principal tasks of the Communist Parties of both countries is to coordinate their common struggle. Despite different conditions, the general tasks of both countries are the same. Nevertheless the two countries are isolated from each other, but New Zealand communists are closer to Australia than to America. These tasks arise for the Australian party too. Both parties must establish connections, by means of delegations, letters, consultations etc.

The principal task must be a joint struggle and a common policy with regard to the Labour Parties of Australia and New Zealand, as well as Chamberlain's policies. Both parties must develop fraternal co-operation in matters of informing the press, exchanging articles, personal visits, mutual assistance and training of personnel. This must be the foundation of competition between the two countries: to see who works best. It seems that at present such an atmosphere does not exist in relations between the two countries. It is not enough to send one or two delegations or a student from New Zealand to Australia.

Mutual relations should be developed on the following basis: opposition to the imperialist war and British imperialism, and help for the cadres of both parties, for there exists the prospect that British imperialism may be smashed, and this general aim should be achieved in the course of the war. The working class of the British dominions must help the British working class against the common enemy, the City.[6] To this end it is essential that the Communist Parties of the two countries unite in common action.

The Labor Party

In the struggle against the war a special movement must be crystallized, particularly in the trade unions. The great masses of the workers oppose the war, the politics of reaction and the anti-Soviet campaign. They support unity and a struggle in the interests of the working masses. They look favourably upon a joint struggle side by side with the communists. But at present they stand far apart from the communists, and we must therefore help them to build a movement within the Labor Party and above all in the trade unions. At the same time we must recruit members for the party from among them.

We must never for a moment forget that the British Empire must disappear and that in this struggle the social democratic parties must naturally also disappear. The question is how can we bring honest Labor Party and trade union members to join the Communist Party, the revolutionary party, and thus provide an organizational basis for the working class. This is also the way to break the power of the reformists in the labour movement. It is the first stage.

It is necessary to pay attention to the particular psychology of the New Zealand working class. It needs organization and leadership. The broad masses are dissatisfied but as yet they see no way out. The best elements still have no faith in the Communist Party. For this reason all those who are prepared to fight the reactionary trade union leaders and the Labor Party and who are therefore increasingly coming into contact with the communists should be drawn into such an organization. They will represent a socialist trend which the Communist Party must drive forward and strengthen from outside.

This question must be examined by the Central Committee. We must train these people so that they are able to struggle against the agents of British

---

[6] The City of London, meaning the financial centre of the British Empire.

imperialism in their own ranks and channel the workers' discontent with the trade union and Labor Party leadership in the right direction. Our party must not only devote attention to the declarations of the trade union and Labor Party leaders, but also above all to their actions.

On the question of compulsory conscription, in view of the fact that some leaders oppose the introduction of this, it is necessary to point out that it is not the central issue. Our aim is to end the war. Not one man for the imperialists. Not one pound for the City. In this area our joint efforts are far too feeble.

The Communist Party

In numbers and otherwise our party is far too weak. It must be greatly strengthened, and our main effort must be focussed on what should be done to consolidate it. We must make clear to the best union members why they should join the party, legally, if possible, and illegally if not, so that they will be bound to the party and submit to party discipline.

The party's second primary task is to do all in its power to increase the circulation of its newspaper. A print-run of 9,000 is reasonably good, but not good enough. The paper is the best weapon the party has. With its help we show which policies the working class should follow. With its help we lead and educate the working class and strike at traitors and reactionaries. The paper can also give material form to the alliance between the workers and the farmers against the imperialist war. It must explain all these matters and problems, making use of many arguments. It must increasingly become a paper of the working class, for the working class, and produced by the working class. It is not enough to have a weekly newspaper, or, as in Australia, one that appears twice a week. Our main aim must be to have a daily newspaper. Our concern is now not to have small groups performing small tasks, but mass work undertaken to expose and attack the policies of the Australian and New Zealand Labour Parties, as well as those of Attlee and Greenwood.

All forces should be deployed against the capitalists. For example, women should be mobilized in meetings and delegations against sending troops overseas, while bearing in mind that this is not the central issue. The primary concern is to end the war.

The party must explain the policy of the Soviet Union in particular. We must forcefully attack all anti-Soviet campaigns that are whipped up in the country. We must demonstrate that the Soviet Union is the most important and most active factor for peace in the world today. It is essential to publish a special booklet against British imperialism. In addition, New Zealand and Australia are situated very close to China. They must establish connections with China.

The Question of Personnel

Finally, the question of personnel is one of the most important questions. We must tighten control of our personnel to ensure that they are fully devoted to the USSR, the CPSU (Bolshevik), and Comrade Stalin, the leader of the working class and the working people of the entire world. There must be complete clarity about this. What the CPSU (Bolshevik) and Comrade Stalin do is exclusively in the interests of the working class of the whole world. There must be no doubt about this matter, and the personnel must be able to find their bearings on this basis.

In France and Britain at the outbreak of war our comrades were unable to discern the correct line. As a result a certain error found its way into the party. In consequence of this our parties suffered heavy losses in Britain and France. It is therefore necessary that our parties grow stronger and stronger, and to this end we must select our personnel with great care and help them. Care must be taken to ensure that there are no Trotskyite elements or Trotskyite connections in our party, and we must work and struggle constantly to expose these.

It is vital to entrust a Central Committee comrade with the very responsible task of vetting the personnel.

In the international struggle of our parties in Australia and New Zealand, we should not forget the plight of the Spanish refugees and the International Brigades who are now in concentration camps in France. It is necessary to show to all how these outstanding comrades are being treated, and to raise the question of the possibility of bringing such people to Australia and New Zealand. It would be good for them and for the people of Australia and New Zealand if such courageous and able people as the Spanish refugees and the International Brigades went to those countries.

References

Aarons, Eric. 1993. *What's Left? Memoirs of an Australian Communist*. Ringwood: Penguin.

Alibek, Ken, with Stephen Handelman. 1999. *Biohazard*. New York: Random House.

Andrew, Christopher and Vasili Mitrokhin. 1999. *The Mitrokhin Archive: The KGB in Europe and the West*. London: Allen Lane.

Ball, Desmond and David Horner. 1998. *Breaking the Codes: Australia's KGB Network, 1944–1950*. Sydney: Allen & Unwin.

Banville, J. 1997. *The Untouchable*. London: Picador.

Beckett, Francis. 1995. *Enemy Within: The rise and fall of the British Communist Party*. London: John Murray.

Beevor, Antony. 2006. *The Battle for Spain: The Spanish Civil War, 1936–1939*. London: Phoenix.

Bernstein, Carl, and Marco Politi. 1997. *His Holiness: John Paul II and the Hidden History of Our Time*. London: Bantam Books.

Blake, Audrey. 1984. *A Proletarian Life*. Malmsbury: Kibble Books.

Blake, J.D. 1972. 'The Australian Communist Party and the Comintern in the early 1930s'. *Labour History*, 23, pp. 38–47.

Borkenau, Franz. 1962. *World Communism: A history of the Communist International*. Ann Arbor: University of Michigan Press.

Borovik, Genrikh. 1994. *The Philby Files: The Secret Life of the Master Spy—KGB Archives Revealed*. Edited Phillip Knightley. London: Little, Brown & Co.

Braddock, Jack and Bessie. 1963. *The Braddocks*. London: Macdonald.

Braun, Otto. 1982. *A Comintern Agent in China: 1932–1939*. Translated J. Moore. St Lucia: University of Queensland Press.

Broué, Pierre. 1997. *Histoire de l'Internationale Communiste 1919–1943*. Paris: Fayard.

Brown, Anthony Cave, and Charles B. MacDonald. 1981. *On a Field of Red: The Communist International and the Coming of World War II*. New York: G.P. Putnam's Sons.

Bullock, Alan. 1992. *Hitler and Stalin: Parallel Lives*. London: HarperCollins.

Burgmann, Verity. 1995. *Revolutionary Industrial Unionism: The Industrial Workers of the World in Australia*. Cambridge: Cambridge University Press.

Cain, Frank. 1983. *The Origins of Political Surveillance in Australia*. Sydney: Angus and Robertson.

Carr, E.H. 1982. *The Twilight of Comintern, 1930–1935*. London: Macmillan.

Chase, William J. 2001. *Enemies within the Gates? The Comintern and the Stalinist Repression, 1934–1939*. New Haven: Yale University Press.

Claudin, Fernando. 1975. *The Communist Movement: From Comintern to Cominform*. Translated B. Pearce. New York: Monthly Review Press.

Courtois, Stéphane et.al. 1999. *The Black Book of Communism: Crimes, Terror, Repression*. Translated J. Murphy and M. Kramer. Cambridge MA: Harvard University Press.

Crossman, Richard (ed.). 2001. *The God that Failed*. New York: Columbia University Press.

Curthoys, Barbara. 1993a. 'The Communist Party and the Communist International (1927–1929)'. *Labour History*. 64, May, pp. 54–69.

Curthoys, Barbara. 1993b. 'The Comintern, the CPA, and the Impact of Harry Wicks'. *Australian Journal of Politics and History*. 39:1, pp. 23–36.

Dallin, Alexander, and F.I. Firsov (eds). 2000. *Dimitrov and Stalin, 1934–1943. Letters from the Soviet Archives*. New Haven: Yale University Press.

Davidson, Alastair. 1969. *The Communist Party of Australia: A Short History*. Stanford CA: Hoover Institution Press.

Deery, Phillip. 1997. 'Cold War Victim or Rhodes Scholar Spy? Revisiting the Case of Ian Milner'. *Overland* 147, Winter. pp. 9–12.

Degras, Jane (ed.). 1956. *The Communist International 1919–1943: Documents. Volume 1, 1919–1922*. London: Oxford University Press.

Degras, Jane (ed.). 1960. *The Communist International 1919–1943: Documents. Volume 2, 1923–1928*. London: Oxford University Press.

Deutscher, Isaac. 1970. *The Prophet Armed: Trotsky 1879–1921*. London: Oxford University Press.

Dewey, John. 1972. *Not Guilty: Report of the Commission of Inquiry into the Charges made against Leon Trotsky in the Moscow Trials*. New York: Monad.

Draper, Theodore. 2003a. *The Roots of American Communism*. Edison NJ: Transaction Publishers.

Draper, Theodore. 2003b. *American Communism and Soviet Russia*. Edison NJ: Transaction Publishers.

Ellis, M.H. nd. *The Red Road: The Story of the Capture of the Lang Party by Communists, instructed from Moscow*. Sydney: Sydney and Melbourne Publishing.

Evans, Raymond. 1988. *The Red Flag Riots: A Study of Intolerance*. St Lucia: University of Queensland Press.

Evans, Raymond. 1989. 'Radical Departures: Paul Freeman and Political Deportation from Australia following World War One'. *Labour History*, 57, pp. 16–26.

Farrell, Frank. 1981. 'Freeman, Paul', in *Australian Dictionary of Biography*, Vol. 8 (1891–1939). Carlton: Melbourne University Press.

Farrell, Frank. 1981. *International Socialism and Australian Labour: The Left in Australia 1910–1939*. Sydney: Hale and Iremonger.

Fry, Eric C. (ed.). 1965. *Tom Barker and the I.W.W.* Canberra, Australian Society for the Study of Labour History.

Funder, Anna. 2002. *Stasiland*. Melbourne: Text Publishing.

Gaddis, John Lewis. 1997. *We Now Know: Rethinking Cold War History*. Oxford: Clarendon Press.

Gallacher, William. 1966. *The Last Memoirs*. London: Lawrence and Wisharts.

Garton Ash, Timothy. 1997. *The File: A Personal History*. London: Flamingo.

Govor, Elena. 2001. *My Dark Brother*. Kensington: UNSW Press.

Hobsbawm, Eric. 1994. *Age of Extremes: The Short Twentieth Century 1914–1991*. London: Michael Joseph.

Hoyle, Arthur. 1993. *Jock Garden: The Red Parson*. Canberra: A.R. Hoyle.

Inglis, Amirah. 1995. *The Hammer and Sickle and the Washing Up*. Melbourne: Hyland House.

Inglis, Ken, assisted by Jan Brazier. 1998. *Sacred Places: War Memorials in the Australian Landscape*. Carlton: Melbourne University Press.

Jacobson, Jon. 1994. *When the Soviet Union entered World Politics*. Berkeley CA, University of California Press.

Klehr, Harvey, John Earl Haynes, Fridrikh Igorevich Firsov. 1995. *The Secret World of American Communism*. New Haven: Yale University Press.

Klehr, Harvey, John Earl Haynes, Kyrill M. Anderson. 1998. *The Soviet World of American Communism*. New Haven: Yale University Press.

Knightley, Phillip. 1997. 'A traitor's heart'. *The Australian's Review of Books* 2(6), July, pp. 4–5.

Koehler, John O. 1999. *Stasi: The Untold Story of the East German Secret Police*. Connecticut: Westview Press.

Lazitch, Branko. 1966. 'Two Instruments of Control by the Comintern: The Emissaries of the ECCI and the Party Representatives in Moscow'. In M.M. Drachkovitch and B. Lazitch (eds), *The Comintern: Historical Highlights. Essays, Recollections, Documents*. Stanford CA: Hoover Institution Press, pp. 45–65.

Lenin, V.I. 1976 [1920]. *'Left-Wing' Communism—An infantile disorder*. In *Selected Works* vol. 3, Moscow: Progress Publishers.

Lessing, Doris. 1997. *Walking in the Shade: Volume Two of my Autobiography, 1949–1962*. London: HarperCollins.

Lovell, David. 1984. *From Marx to Lenin: An evaluation of Marx's responsibility for Soviet authoritarianism*. Cambridge: Cambridge University Press.

Lovell, David. 1994. 'Jean Jaurès: Socialism as republicanism'. In F.J. Fornasiero (ed.), *Culture and Ideology in Modern France: Essays in Honour of George Rudé 1910–1993*. Adelaide: Department of French Studies, pp. 84–102.

Lovell, David. 2001. '1989 and personal narratives: Western communists evaluate the communist experience'. In Sascha Talmor and Rachel Ben-David (eds), *Twentieth Century European Narratives: Tradition and Innovation. Proceedings of the Sixth Conference of the ISSEI, August 1998, Haifa University, Israel*, CDROM

Lovell, David. 2007. 'Strained Relations: Russia, Australia and the Comintern, 1920–40'. In A. Massov, J. McNair and T. Poole (eds), *Encounters Under the Southern Cross: Two Centuries of Russian-Australian Relations, 1807-2007*. Adelaide: Crawford House Publishing, pp. 163–184.

Lovell, David. 2008. '"Unswerving Loyalty": documenting Australian communist relations with Moscow, 1920–40'. *Quadrant*, LII:5, pp. 80–86.

Macintyre, Stuart. 1998. *The Reds: the Communist Party of Australia from origins to illegality*. Sydney: Allen & Unwin.

Manne, R. 1997. 'Battle for History's High Ground'. *The Weekend Australian*. June 7–8, 1997, p. 23.

Martin, A.W. 1999. *Robert Menzies: A Life*. vol. 2, 1944–1978. Melbourne: Melbourne University Press.

Massov, Alexander, John McNair and Thomas Poole (eds). 2007. *Encounters Under the Southern Cross: Two Centuries of Russian-Australian Relations 1807-2007*. Adelaide: Crawford House Publishing.

McDermott, Kevin, and Jeremy Agnew. 1996. *The Comintern: A history of international communism from Lenin to Stalin*. Basingstoke: Macmillan.

McIlroy, Jim. 2001. *The Red North*. Sydney: Resistance Books.

McLoughlin, Barry, and Kevin McDermott (eds). 2003. *Stalin's Terror: High Politics and Mass Repression in the Soviet Union*. Basingstoke: Palgrave Macmillan.

McKnight, David. 1994. *Australia's Spies and their Secrets*. Sydney: Allen & Unwin.

McNair, John, and Thomas Poole (eds). 1992. *Russia and the Fifth Continent: Aspects of Russian-Australian Relations*. St Lucia: University of Queensland Press.

McQueen, H. 1997. *Suspect History: Manning Clark and the Future of Australia's Past*. Sydney: Wakefield Press.

Murphy, John. 1994. 'Loyalty and the Communists: An Interview with Bill Gollan'. *Labour History*. 66, May, pp. 114–21.

Nove, Alec. 1972. *An Economic History of the U.S.S.R.* Harmondsworth: Penguin.

Pankhurst, Sylvia. 1921. *Soviet Russia as I Saw It*. London: Workers Dreadnought.

Pontsov, A. 1999. *The Bolsheviks and the Chinese Revolution 1919–27*. Curzon Press.

Rees, Tim and Andrew Thorpe (eds). 1998. *International Communism and the Communist International, 1919–1943*. Manchester: Manchester University Press.

Ross, Edgar. 1967. 'Australia and 1917', *Australian Left Review*, 4, August-September, pp. 40–44.

Sawer, Geoffrey. 1956. *Australian Federal Politics and Law 1901–1929*. Melbourne: Melbourne University Press.

Sawer, Geoffrey. 1972. *The Australian and the Law*. Revised edition. Harmondsworth: Penguin.

Schedvin, C.B. 1970. *Australia and the Great Depression: A study of economic development and policy in the 1920s and 1930s*. Sydney: Sydney University Press.

Sendy, John. 1997. 'The Octogenarian Revolution'. *Eureka Street*. November, pp. 41–43.

Serge, Victor. 1963. *Memoirs of a Revolutionary 1901–1941*, translated Peter Sedgwick. London: Oxford University Press.

Sharkey, L.L. 1944. *An Outline History of the Australian Communist Party*. Sydney: Australian Communist Party.

Short, Susannah. 1992. *Laurie Short: A Political Life*. Sydney: Allen & Unwin.

Simonoff, Peter. 1919. *What is Russia?* Sydney: The Worker Trade Union Print.

Skorobogatykh, N.S., nd. 'Australian Communists and Moscow: The 1930s'. Unpublished conference paper.

Smith, Bernard. 1985. *The Boy Adeodatus: The Portrait of a Lucky Young Bastard*. Ringwood: Penguin.

Smith, S.A. 2000. *A Road is Made: Communism in Shanghai 1920–1927*. Honolulu: University of Hawaii Press.

Stedman, Solomon. 1979. 'The Russian Revolution in Australia', *Journal of the Royal Australian Historical Society*, 65:3, December, pp. 201–7.

Symons, Beverley, with Andrew Wells and Stuart Macintyre. 1994. *Communism in Australia: A Resource Bibliography*. Canberra: National Library of Australia.

Symons, Beverley, with the assistance of Stuart Macintyre. 2002. *Communism in Australia: A supplementary resource bibliography, c. 1994–2001*. Sydney: Australian Society for the Study of Labour History, Sydney Branch.

Taft, Bernie. 1994. *Crossing the Party Line: Memoirs of Bernie Taft*. Newham: Scribe Publications.

Taylor, Kerry. 1993. 'Archive Notes: The Comintern Archives, Moscow'. *Labour History*, 64, May, pp. 139–42.

Thorpe, Andrew. 2000. *The British Communist Party and Moscow, 1920–1943*. New York: Manchester University Press.

Throssell, Ric. 1997. *My Father's Son: The Last Knot Untied*. Melbourne: em Press.

Trotsky, Leon. 1970. *The Third International after Lenin*. New York: Pathfinder.

Trotsky, Leon. 1973a [1925]. 'Where is Britain Going?'. In *Leon Trotsky on Britain*. New York: Monad Press.

Trotsky, Leon. 1973 [1940]. 'The Comintern and the GPU'. In *Writings of Leon Trotsky, 1939–40*, edited N. Allen and G. Breitman. New York: Pathfinder, pp. 348–91.

Turner, Ian. 1962. 'Socialist Political Tactics, 1900–1920'. *Labour History*, 2, May, pp. 5–25.

Turner, Ian. 1967. *Sydney's Burning*. Sydney: Alpha Books.

Victoria. 1950. *Report of Royal Commission. Inquiring into the origins, aims, objects and funds of the Communist Party in Victoria and other related matters.* Sir Charles Lowe (Royal Commisssioner). Melbourne: Government Printer.

Walker, Jamie. 1999. 'The spy who aged too much'. *The Weekend Australian,* October 2–3. p. 28.

Webb, Leicester. 1954. *Communism and Democracy in Australia: A Survey of the 1951 Referendum.* Melbourne: F.W. Cheshire.

Weber, Max. 1994 [1919]. 'The Profession and Vocation of Politics'. In Max Weber, *Political Writings,* edited P. Lassman and R. Speirs. Cambridge: Cambridge University Press, pp. 309–69.

Windle, Kevin. 2004a. 'Round the World for the Revolution: A Bolshevik agent's mission to Australia 1920–22 and his interrogation by Scotland Yard', *Revolutionary Russia,* 17:2, December, pp. 90–118.

Windle, Kevin. 2004b. '"The Achilles Heel of British Imperialism": A Comintern agent reports on his mission to Australia 1920–22. An annotated translation'. *Australian Slavonic and East European Studies,* 18:1–2, pp. 143–76.

Windle, Kevin. 2004c. 'Brisbane Prison: Artem Sergeev describes Boggo Road', *New Zealand Slavonic Journal,* 38, pp. 159–79.

Windle, Kevin. 2005a. '"Unmajestic Bombast": The Brisbane Union of Russian Workers as Shown in a 1919 Play by Herman Bykov', *Australian Slavonic and East European Studies,* 19:1–2, pp. 29–51.

Windle, Kevin. 2005b. 'Aleksandr Zuzenko i avstraliiskaia tema v sovetskoi literature', *Studia Rossica Posnaniensia,* zeszyt XXII, pp. 11–20.

Windle, Kevin. 2005c. 'Standard-Bearer of the Australian Revolution: The Interrogation of Aleksandr Zuzenko by Special Branch. An annotated transcript', *New Zealand Slavonic Journal,* 39, pp. 175–215.

Windle, Kevin. 2006a. 'A Troika of Agitators: Three Comintern Liaison Agents in Australia, 1920–22'. *Australian Journal of Politics and History,* 52:1, pp. 30–47.

Windle, Kevin. 2006b. 'Zhurnalist i revoliutsioner na trekh kontinentakh: A.M. Zuzenko'. *Tynianovskii sbornik,* 12, pp. 452–68.

Windle, Kevin. 2006c. 'Orpheus Down Under: Fragments by A. N. Tolstoi on the career of Captain Zuzenko. Translation and commentary', *Slavonica,* 12:2, pp. 91–105.

Windle, Kevin. 2007a. 'The October Revolution and Russian Involvement in the Australian Communist Movement, 1917–24: A survey of source materials'. In A. Massov, J. McNair and T. Poole (eds), *Encounters Under* the Southern Cross: Two Centuries of Russian-Australian Relations, 1807-2007. Adelaide: Crawford House Publishing, pp. 142–62.

Windle, Kevin. 2007b. 'Nabat and its Editors: the 1919 Swansong of the Brisbane Russian Socialist Press', Australian Slavonic and East European Studies, 21:1–2, pp. 143–63.

Windle, Kevin. 2008a. 'Murder at Mount Cuthbert: a Russian revolutionary describes Queensland life in 1915–1919'. Forthcoming in AUMLA.

Windle, Kevin. 2008b. 'Konstantin Paustovskii, the "Communard Captain", and William Morris Hughes. An Australian motif in an early work of Soviet literature', Slavonica, 14:2, pp. 108-18.

Index of Names

Other Works by the Authors

David W. Lovell

From Marx to Lenin: Marx's Responsibility for Soviet Authoritarianism
Trotsky's Analysis of Soviet Bureaucratization
Marx's Proletariat: The Making of a Myth
The Theory of Politics: An Australian Perspective (co-authored)
The Transition from Socialism: State and Civil Society in the USSR (co-edited)
The Sausage Makers? Parliamentarians as Legislators
Revolution, Politics, and Society: Elements in the Making of Modern France (edited)
Ideas and Ideologies: Essays in Memory of Eugene Kamenka (*Australian Journal of Politics and History*, co-edited)
The Australian Political System (co-authored)
Marxism and Australian Socialism before the Bolshevik Revolution
The Macquarie Student Writer's Friend
The Transition: Evaluating the postcommunist experience (edited)
Asia-Pacific Security: Policy Challenges (edited)
Freedom and Equality in Marx's Utopia (*European Legacy*, edited)

Kevin Windle

Sergey Zalygin, *The South American Variant* (translated and edited)
Valentin Rasputin, *'Money for Maria' and 'Borrowed Time'* (co-translated and edited)
Sergey Aksakov, *Notes of a Provincial Wildfowler* (translated and edited)
Vladimir Kabo, *The Road to Australia: Memoirs* (co-translated and edited)
Juri Apresjan, *Systematic Lexicography* (translated)
Andrzej Drawicz, *The Master and the Devil: A Study of Mikhail Bulgakov* (translated and edited)
Ireneusz Iredynski, *Selected One-Act Plays for Radio* (co-translated and edited)
Vasyl Sokil, *And Then There Was Glasnost* (translated and edited)
Laurent Danon-Boileau, *The Silent Child: Bringing Language to Children Who Cannot Speak* (translated)
Bernhard Maier, *The Celts: A History from Earliest Times to the* (translated)
Joachim Latacz, *Troy and Homer: Towards the Solution of an old Problem* (co-translated)
Reginald de Bray et al, *The Routledge Macedonian-English Dictionary* (co-edited)
Alexander Vampilov, *Four Plays* (co-translated)
Augusto Fraschetti, *The Foundation of Rome* (co-translated)
Luciano Canfora, *Julius Caesar: The People's Dictator* (co-translated)

www.ingramcontent.com/pod-product-compliance
Lightning Source LLC
Chambersburg PA
CBHW040926050426

42334CB00062B/3249